ON BORDEAUX

TO MICHAEL BROADBENT
(1927–2020)
our inspiration

ON BORDEAUX

TALES OF THE UNEXPECTED FROM THE WORLD'S GREATEST WINE REGION

EDITED BY SUSAN KEEVIL
INTRODUCTION BY JANE ANSON

ACADEMIE DU VIN LIBRARY

Published 2020 by Académie du Vin Library Ltd.
academieduvinlibrary.com

Publisher: Simon McMurtrie
Editor: Susan Keevil
Art Director: Tim Foster
Index: Hilary Bird
ISBN: 978-1-913141-05-9
Printed and bound in Italy by LEGO, Vicenza

CONTENTS

INTRODUCTION 8

PREFACE 11

CHAPTER ONE **THE POWER OF THE VINTAGE** 15

Fiona Morrison MW (2020) The Year Bordeaux Began Again 16

Stephen Browett (2020) Long Live the Vintage! 23

Joe Fattorini (2020) The Turbulent Life of 2008 26

Ian Maxwell Campbell (1948) 1871 and 1875: The Pre-Phylloxera Heroes 33

CHAPTER TWO **VIEW FROM THE VINEYARDS** 35

Margaret Rand (2010) Pruner to the Stars 36

James Lawther MW (2020) The Phoenix Grape 41

Mathieu Chadronnier (2020) On Sustainability 48

Joe Fattorini (2020) One Mad Day in the Médoc 53

CHAPTER THREE **TALES OF THE ARISTOCRACY** 61

Cyril Ray (1985) Château Lafite Rothschild 62

Hugh Johnson (2020) Château Latour 66

Nicholas Faith (1980) Château Margaux 75

Cyril Ray (1974) Château Mouton Rothschild 80

Gerald Asher (1996) Château Haut-Brion 83

Neal Martin (2012/2020) Château Petrus 91

David Peppercorn MW (1991) Château Ausone 96

Edmund Penning-Rowsell (1979) Château Cheval Blanc 99

James Seely (1998) Château d'Yquem 102

CHAPTER FOUR **THE RIVALS** 105

Steven Spurrier (1999) Claret or Burgundy – Which Is the Better Wine? 106

Edith Somerville and Martin Ross (1893) Mouton vs Lafite 111

Elin McCoy (2020) Left Bank vs Right Bank 115

Simon Gotelee (2020) Brand Bordeaux vs Appellation Burgundy 121

CHAPTER FIVE **A WINE REGION AT WAR** 125

Jane Anson (2020) Bordeaux Survives the War 126

Ian Maxwell Campbell (1948) Of Wartime Wines, Tax and Chancellors 133

Joan Littlewood (1984) Escape Across the Pyrenees 136

CHAPTER SIX **SURVIVAL OF THE FITTEST** 143

Michael Broadbent (2002) Why Bordeaux? 144

Jane Anson (2012) Survivors of the Revolution 146

Margaret Rand (2007) Sur La Place de Bordeaux 154

Count John Umberto Salvi MW (2020) First Growths Show the Way Forward 159

Bill Blatch (2020) Liquid Gold Legend 164

CHAPTER SEVEN **CADS, BOUNDERS, SCRAPES AND SCANDALS** 173

Nicholas Faith (1981) The Phylloxera Predicament 174

Cyrus Redding (1833) Bolstering with Beni Carlos 181

Joseph-François Audibert (1896) A Recipe for Fake Lafite 183

Nicholas Faith (1999) Desperate Times, Desperate Measures 184

CHAPTER EIGHT **BORDEAUX ENTERS THE MODERN WORLD** 191

Hugh Johnson (1989) Le Grand Théâtre 192

James Lawther MW (2017) A Toast to the Finest 195

Stephen Brook (2020) The Culture of Hype 202

Mathieu Chadronnier (2020) Bordeaux Goes International 208

Andrew Caillard MW (2020) Red Obsession: When Bordeaux Met China 213

Peter Vinding-Diers (2020) Bordeaux – Beware the Portuguese... 222

CHAPTER NINE **A POTTED BORDEAUX HISTORY** 229

Edmund Penning-Rowsell (1979) British for 300 Years 230

Charles Ludington (2013) The Paradoxical Rise of Claret 233

Giles MacDonogh (2020) The Wild Geese 240

Cyril Ray (1974) The Classification of 1855 253

CHAPTER TEN **DINING OUT ON BORDEAUX** 261

Michael Schuster (2014) All Pleasures Fancies Be 262

Fiona Beckett (2020) Bordeaux for Lunch 268

George Saintsbury (1920), **Baron Elie de Rothschild** (1968) **and Christian Seely** (2020) The Climate for Claret 271

Hugh Johnson (2020) The Bordeaux Club 273

APPENDIX – THE BORDEAUX CLASSIFICATIONS 280

INDEX 283

INTRODUCTION

Jane Anson

Is there another wine region that could bring together such a rich array of writings, spanning three centuries, four continents and over 40 writers? The oldest piece here dates from 1833; the youngest comes in the shape of over a dozen newly commissioned articles written in 2020.

Just a brief glance through the contents list gives a glimpse of what Bordeaux has meant to people through the years – with subjects ranging from the French Revolution and World War II, to the pleasures of food matching and choosing the perfect moment to pull the cork. They show Bordeaux to be both resilient and fallible – capable of stumbling at times but always ready to get back on its feet. I live in Bordeaux, and have spent two decades of my professional life learning about its wines, but on reading this book I found something new and arresting on every page.

We open with a front-row seat on the 1982 vintage. Fiona Morrison, Master of Wine and joint owner of the iconic Château Le Pin, talks us through what was her first harvest in Bordeaux ('the sun, the sun'), and recounts how she headed off from Pomerol into central Bordeaux to pick up the blocks of ice needed to keep temperatures down in the vats, so hot were conditions right through September and October. And as is the case time and again in this anthology, the article successfully puts its direct subject into a wider context, so you read not only about the political and technological headwinds that allowed this vintage to catapult Bordeaux back to global fame, but about how its impact is still felt today – we hear about the rise of consultant winemakers such as Michel Rolland, for example, who are now such a ubiquitous feature of the landscape of the region.

Heading further back into history, we get several fascinating looks at pre-phylloxera wines from Ian Maxwell Campbell and from Nicolas Faith, who highlight that the Médoc was the last region in Bordeaux, and pretty much France, to be impacted by the pernicious louse and so was able to take advantage of research done in other areas to deal with the consquences of its attack. It was so risk-averse, however, that it took far longer than it should have done to implement wholesale grafting of American rootstock – and that in fact the final shift only really came after World War I.

Some of the most charming moments of the collection come through the background details, like the lunch described by Maxwell Campbell in June 1945, gathering together 'Hugh Rudd, Kenneth Upjohn and I, at 3 St James's Street. After a bottle of 1917 Château Lafite, [we] enjoyed, to our surprise and delight, a bottle of 1877 Château Lafite, which I noted at the time as "no lemon, very good, still fresh, sweet and young"'. An equally casual eyewitness-to-history comment comes from Edmund Penning-Rowsell in his piece on Château Cheval Blanc, when he recounts visiting Saint-Emilion and Pomerol in June 1956, a few months after that harsh winter's devastating frosts: 'Where there should have been an expanse of green leafage, the black stumps of the vines stood bare; it looked like a battlefield.'

And one of my personal favourites, which I read for the first time here, comes from Anglo-Irish cousins Edith Somerville and Martin Ross (aka Violet Florence Martin). Together they travelled the Médoc in the 1890s with their notebooks, sketchpads and a new device they referred to as 'the Kodak'. Their comparisons of the two Rothschild properties, Lafite Rothschild and Mouton Rothschild, surely stand them among the first female wine writers. I loved their insights into the colourful flower garden outside Mouton, belying the usual story that the estate was unloved until Baron Philippe arrived in 1922, but it was Lafite that managed to overawe them, much as it does visitors today, summed up beautifully by their line describing the bottles of wine in the cellars: 'More and yet more aisles followed, catacombs of silence and black heavy air, but full of the strange life of the wine that lay, biding its time according to its tribe and family, in a "monotony of enchanted pride," as Ruskin has said about pine trees.'

Insights from insiders as varied come thick and fast – as do the indiscretions. Steven Spurrier takes on the perennial question of whether Bordeaux is better than burgundy, and recounts a lunch with harrumping Bordeaux château owners furious at having been caught out by the blind serving of a Lupe-Cholet 1934 Pommard, which they suggested came from the Right Bank. 'They were not amused at this, and the wine stayed in their glasses.' Nicholas Faith is equally revealing on the Cruse Scandal in the piece 'Desperate Times, Desperate Measures,' written in 1999, that lifts the lid on a part of Bordeaux' history that is often brushed under the carpet. This one is truly eye-popping, telling the tale of Louis Bert and his passing-off of lesser wines as classic Bordeaux. The writing is vivid and fascinating, as here on Bert: 'He was a compulsive exhibitionist, a trait that invariably led him to expose many of his schemes to discovery by the police, the Ministry of Agriculture's Fraud Squad, or the tax authorities. (He displayed this compulsion early in life: he was clever enough to be considered for the *prix d'honneur* at the Jesuit school he attended, but ruined his chances by being caught singing *The Internationale* in the street just before the prize-giving.)'

The newly commissioned pieces are equally fascinating. A definite highlight comes from Joe Fattorini on running the Médoc Marathon; it is absolutely essential reading for anyone planning to sign up to this iconic race, including tips on dress code: 'Fancy dress is compulsory at the Marathon du Médoc and everyone follows the rules…The first kilometre…is fabulous. High-fives, back-slapping, cheering, shared joy. The second kilometre involves asking yourself some quite serious questions about the life choice you made in a fancy-dress shop the previous week. Kilometres three to 42 are a series of long and distressing answers to those questions.'

Andrew Caillard MW does us all a great favour by updating his observations on the relationship between Bordeaux and China. He first recounts the process of filming and editing his brilliant *Red Obsession*, the award-winning film released in 2013 that tracked the love affair – and subsequent cooling – between the Asian powerhouse and Bordeaux wine. His article then brings us up to date with developments since the film's release, and gives us a preview of an upcoming feature documentary film called *Blind Ambition*, about four Zimbabwean sommeliers competing in the World Blind Wine Championships that will be released in late 2020.

I could go on, but I will leave you the pleasure of discovering for yourselves the full extent of this multi-layered, clear-eyed, moving and often extremely funny collection of stories that by turns celebrates, illuminates and renews our understanding of Bordeaux and its endlessly fascinating collection of characters – and the contents of their cellars.

PREFACE
Susan Keevil

Many thousands of words have been written on the subject of Bordeaux, from Samuel Pepys's first succinct reviews of 'Ho-Bryan' in 1663 and Cyrus Redding's stinging condemnations of the fraudsters (1833), to the most rhapsodic of Michael Broadbent's tasting notes. In short, the region has inspired around 300 years of wine writing. But which book, chapter or magazine appraisal is definitive? Whose voice truly encapsulates Bordeaux as a whole? Do any of them?

When Hugh Johnson, Steven Spurrier, Simon McMurtrie and Ben Howkins first discussed the idea of the Académie du Vin Library over lunch, their plan was to restore to readers the writing we rarely catch sight of, but which truly conveys the essence of the wines we drink – and *would like* to drink – along with the stories of the people surrounding them. When it came to Bordeaux, the words of favourites like Ian Maxwell Campbell and Edmund Penning-Rowsell instantly sprang to mind. How better to represent the region, thought Steven, than with an anthology of the 'best bits' from its favourite authors, spanning that 300-year history and concentrating on one of wine's favourite subjects?

And so here is *On Bordeaux*, a compilation of wine writing that explores some of the region's major themes – there are 10 in all, ranging from rivalry, plague and the primacy of the vintage, to tales of the 'first growth' aristocracy and a wary glance to the region's future – how will it tackle climate change, sustainability and marketability? Throughout each theme, in bad times and good, we see Bordeaux striving to be the best it can be, and maintaining that familiar fierce pride in the wines it shows to the world.

Not everything you read here will be in the order you'd expect it: you'll learn about the 1956 frost at Petrus before the 1870s outbreak of phylloxera. And each theme presents an array of different viewpoints – some of them opposing, many controversial. We have balanced the work of specialist commentators, many of whom live and work in the region (like Jane Anson and Mathieu Chadronnier, and Masters of Wine Fiona Morrison and James Lawther) with wine writers on the outside looking in (Joe Fattorini, Elin McCoy, Margaret Rand and Andrew Cailllard MW). We've balanced older writing (1833, 1948, 1974) with new (20 viewpoints from 2020), and Bordeaux faithfuls (Michael Broadbent, Neal Martin and Stephen Browett) with more objective all-rounders (Stephen Brook, Charles Ludington and Fiona Beckett).

Of all these, it is easy to prefer the work of today's authors, writing in the engaging style we've come to expect – these are the voices likely to trigger the most amusement. But eyebrows will be raised at the barbed comments of cousins Edith Sommerville and Martin Ross writing in 1893, and wry smiles provoked by the convoluted wit of Cyril Ray – master of the lengthy but eloquent 1950s sentence. Ian Maxwell Campbell can confound with his detailed vintage recollections, but therein lies raillery and a deep knowledge of the game. Persevere and you'll likely be captivated – we were. (To delve further, we list full details of the original titles, many of which can still be purchased online.)

Sadly, we couldn't include everything here that we would have liked; many treasured stories were left on the cutting room floor, hopefully to tell their tales another time. There could, of course, have been more from Michael Broadbent whose elegant prose and fittingly flamboyant tasting notes come closest of all to capturing the soul of Bordeaux. 'Its top wines,' he says, 'set the standards'. In doing so, they kept pace with Michael (1927–2020), who set an exceptional standard for the rest of us, and we will miss him.

While Michael has inspired, Jane Anson, Hugh Johnson, Steven Spurrier and Fiona Morrison have led the way. They have each been of invaluable help in bringing together this collection and are warmly to be thanked. With their guidance we hope to have delivered some unexpected tales, a few surprises and an entertaining insight into the life and wines of Bordeaux.

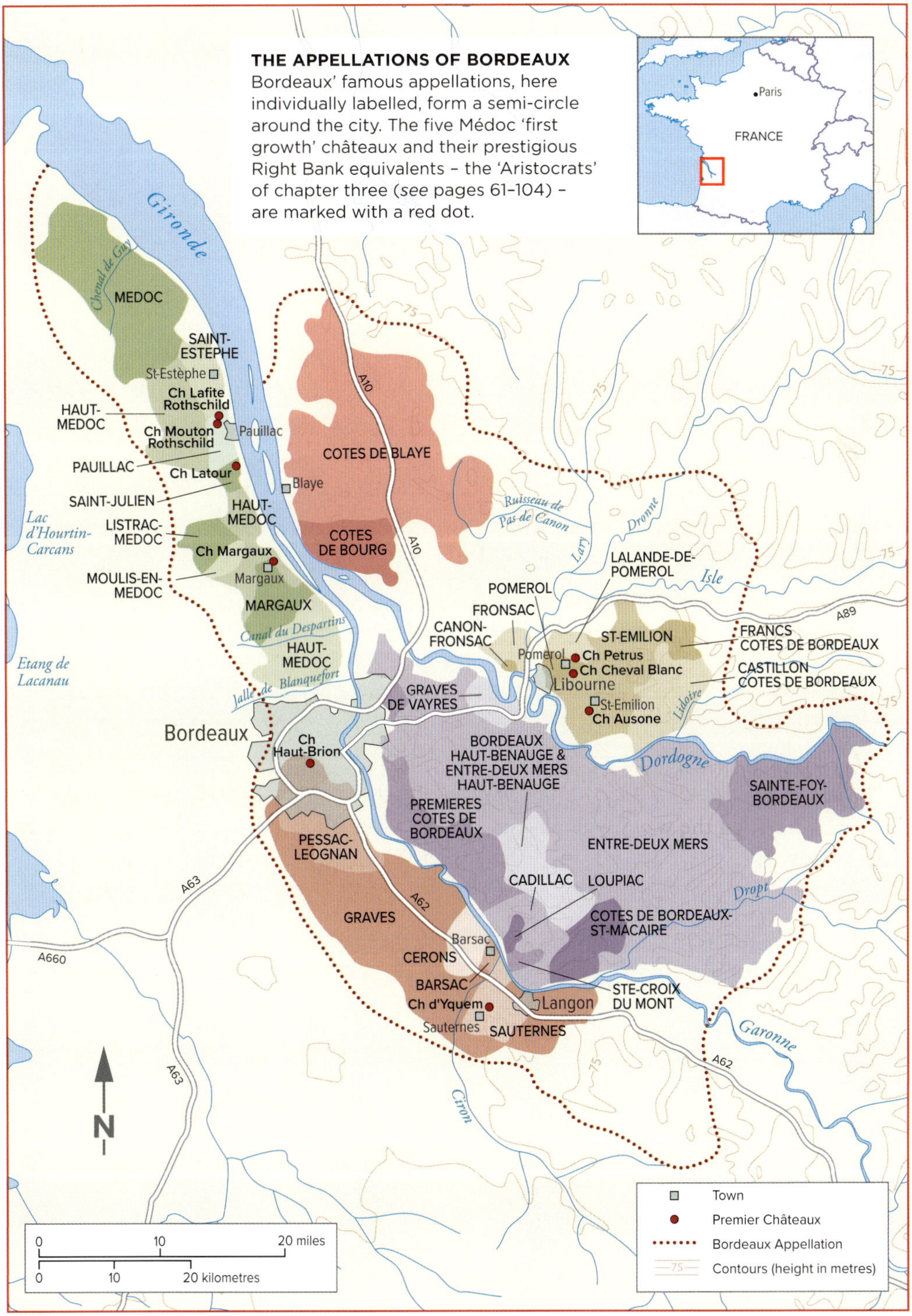

THE APPELLATIONS OF BORDEAUX
Bordeaux' famous appellations, here individually labelled, form a semi-circle around the city. The five Médoc 'first growth' châteaux and their prestigious Right Bank equivalents – the 'Aristocrats' of chapter three (*see* pages 61–104) – are marked with a red dot.

CHAPTER ONE

THE POWER OF THE VINTAGE

The nuance and variation that each year brings is what keeps us all intrigued. Every vintage in Bordeaux has its own story, its own excitement.

Fiona Morrison MW (2020)
The Year Bordeaux Began Again

Stephen Browett (2020)
Long Live the Vintage!

Joe Fattorini (2020)
The Turbulent Life of 2008

Ian Maxwell Campbell (1948)
1871 and 1875: The Pre-Phylloxera Heroes

In the 1970s no good wine was made; it was wet, damp, no one had good plant material, and the wines were miserable. The only way growers could return to the quality of the 1940s, 1950s and 1960s was by trickery and chaptalization. The vintage of 1982 changed everything. Fiona Morrison looks at Bordeaux' great bounce-back and its road to revival.

THE YEAR BORDEAUX BEGAN AGAIN

Fiona Morrison MW (2020)

It seems like yesterday and yet it is almost 40 years ago. The year that changed Bordeaux. The year that brought the region kicking and screaming back into the modern world. It was like those Doisneau photos celebrating the end of World War II, with people laughing and talking, soaking up the sunshine and the sheer pleasure of being outside. It was September 1982, my first harvest in Bordeaux.

The grapes were ripe: dusky blue-black, full and round. The sky was blue: the sky of the sea, fresh, washed, rather windswept and endless. The ground was firm: cracked and sturdy, sandy and dusty on the top, flip-flop friendly – our Wellington boots discarded by the cellar door. And the sun, the sun. Turning our bare chests and arms to burnished pink in the space of an afternoon, chapping our lips and bringing freckles to our faces and the grape skins.

In the winery, this was long before the computer-connected, temperature-controlled stainless steel tanks of today. The fermentation vats of 1982 were old wooden tuns or faded concrete cubes. As soon as the warm mush of juice, skins and pips was poured inside, the heat rose and the fermentation took off like the clappers. Day three and we were dispatched with the estate's old pick-up at five o'clock in the morning to drive down to the Quai de Paludate in Bordeaux's meat-packing district; there, we procured blocks of ice that we wrapped in hemp, carefully handling them to avoid the rubber of our gloves being peeled off by the cold. *K-schlonk*: the satisfying splash of salvaging ice that thudded to the bottom of the tank. The alcohol and temperatures dropped; the fermentations could continue.

Reading the sugar levels – rudimentary refractometers were one of the most sophisticated tools of that time – producers were delighted, but they went ahead and chaptalized anyway as usual. They should have acidified instead (a procedure unheard of at the time in Bordeaux), because a few months later reports showed that the press and trade were rather underwhelmed by the vintage, calling it 'overripe, darkling coloured, hot and flabby'. It wasn't until a year afterwards that a hero from Maryland, a Pepsi-Cola drinking, wine loving lawyer called Robert Parker, reviewed the 1982, liked what he tasted and, well, the rest is history.

As with many tumultuous events, the 1982 vintage and the shock waves that it would cause resulted from the coming together of many different factors. The personal computer had just been invented, opening up an entirely new world that would spawn a myriad of new industries. The 'special relationship' formed by Ronald Reagan and Margaret Thatcher had established a stronger-than-ever bond between the United Kingdom and United States, and Britain's success in the Falklands War had brought new confidence to British shores. The En Primeur (or 'futures') market for Bordeaux wines, which had collapsed under the weight of scandals and weak vintages in the 1970s, was ripe for renewal as wine merchants, who had dabbled less than successfully in buying wine in barrel pre-bottling, felt tempted to get back into the market. They were led by the legendary Abdallah Simon, head of the newly formed Seagram Château & Estate Wine Company, who had money to spend and could see a new generation of ambitious youngsters eager to start collecting wine. Wine was to become, for these new 'yuppies', a status symbol to rival the ski condo in Aspen or the Rolex watch.

Yet for many, the 1982 vintage had wine producers scratching their heads. After the dull wet years of the 1970s – many noted wryly that Bordeaux had not had a great vintage since 1964 – the sheer exuberance, brilliance and sexiness of the 1982s were confusing. The wine critics of the time were undecided. Many dismissed the wine for its low acidity and overripe flavours, but a handful of more heavyweight commentators began to

Even when tasted as a very young wine, straight from the barrel, the 1982 Mouton Rothschild showed a 'cassis-laden' drinkability that distinguished this vintage from its predecessors.

marvel. Michel Bettane, France's most influential wine writer, called it 'the finest vintage since 1929'. Even the great Emile Peynaud (France's revolutionary oenologist and wine researcher) placed 1982 with other legendary vintages such as 1945, 1947, 1959 and 1961.

Fairly quickly, winemakers and researchers at the Institute of Oenology realized that the 1982 vintage showed that there was more to grape maturity than sugar. It was the tannins that were so glorious. They were ripe, yes, but also velvety, round, soft and smooth, a far cry from the tannins that they'd become used to vinifying, with their green herbaceous flavours and grainy texture.

Yves Glories, a jovial professor at Bordeaux University, whose bonhomie masked a fierce intelligence and a tenacious knack of posing the right questions, began to consider

Thanks to the reviews of Robert Parker (*left*) and oenologists like Michel Rolland, Gilles Pauquet and Emile Peynaud (*mid-left to right*), Bordeaux' fortunes were turned around.

the issue of phenolic maturity. Phenols – those incredibly important elements including tannins, anthocyanins (colouring pigments) and enzymes, which we had barely heard of in the early 1980s – became the key focus. Glories and his colleagues realized that, of far more importance than sugar content, it was the phenols that would be the key to grape quality in the future.

There was just one problem: measuring phenols required equipment that was more sophisticated than most wineries could afford or comprehend. This drawback coincided with an opportunity. Increasingly large numbers of oenologists were graduating from the university and beginning to set up their own laboratories around the key regions of Bordeaux. Among them were men such as Michel Rolland, Jacques Boissenot and Gilles Pauquet, Bordeaux born and bred with an innate understanding of the region's climatology and terroirs. In the past, the oenologist's role, so exemplified by such giants as Pascal Ribéreau-Gayon (son of Jean, the founder of the Bordeaux Institute of Oenology) and Emile Peynaud, was to help châteaux with the crucial blending of their wines from a patchwork of different sites, vine ages and grape varieties. Now, these scientists had an even more important role to play.

To start with, the new-generation oenologists began to use more advanced magnetic resonance technology, encouraging the wine estates to pick later, when the ripeness of the phenols in the grapes had caught up with the sugars. They started talking a technical language with the châteaux owners and helping them understand how to improve their wines. Whereas in the past, most owners used their oenologists as they would a doctor, calling on them only if there was a problem, now they turned to these experts as technical directors. Further down the road, many of these new 'consultants' would become superstars in their own right: celebrities who fundamentally changed the style of wines in Bordeaux, often to match the type of wines that the critics and markets liked best.

Winemakers started to question whether chaptalization – the addition of sugar to increase alcohol levels, carried out almost systematically in the 1970s – was really necessary. Winemakers started to question everything. Suddenly the old way of making Bordeaux in a cool, maritime climate was questioned. Shouldn't we be using some sort of temperature control to be able to cool the fermenting must? Wasn't it better to use stainless steel tanks, which were easier to clean and quicker to temperature regulate than concrete or wood? Isn't there a method that we could use to control the amount of oxygen given to a newborn wine? Should we be encouraging the secondary, malolactic fermentation to happen quicker? For the new generation of winemakers, it was as if they were emerging into a brand-new world.

Once the press and the trade began to taste the 1982 wines, they were astounded. Here was a young wine, that was easy to taste; that was soft and fruity, bold, glistening and sweet; that would suck in a whole generation of new wine drinkers with its sensual appeal and hedonism; that would spawn a host of wine magazines, wine specialists and writers who latched onto a wine which they hadn't understood before. With the sales of the new vintage, money, for the first time in almost 20 years, started coming into the châteaux. It is hard to remember how run down and shabby most cellars, even those of the first growths, were in 1982 and how rudimentary the winemaking equipment was. Lack of investment had in many ways contributed to the dull vintages of the 1970s. Today's difficult harvests have been vastly improved by all the technical wizardry and know-how that we have accumulated since then.

Money. Today it is everywhere in Bordeaux. For the top wines, the price of the 1982s was around 50 percent higher than that of previous vintages. Châteaux limited their releases, selling their wines in a series of carefully selected 'tranches' or slices, so that no one could be fully sated by the rich pie. The coffers of their ancient châteaux filled up. As with the Doisneau photographs, the sheer exuberance of the wines suited the mood of the wine trade, who were ready for a party. The wine-starved markets of Britain and America bought and feasted on the wines.

I remember tasting the 1982 Mouton Rothschild in America a year after its birth. It was the first barrel sample I had ever tasted and I was astounded by its sheer drinkability and its gorgeous cassis-laden fruit. I have tasted it many times over the last few decades and it has never disappointed. At a memorable Fête de la Fleur party at the château in 2003, with Placido Domingo on hand to sing, magnums of the 1982 were served at the end of the dinner with such abandon that those of us who stayed on to dance afterwards vacuumed up this still-gorgeous wine with much gusto.

From the temples of success with their belfries, ballrooms, pillars and balconies, to the discrete glass-and-concrete modernist structures, Bordeaux suddenly became awash with new buildings. Cranes dotted the skyline. Cement mixers clogged the country roads. Bordeaux, which had always been a closed, rather impenetrable world, began to open its doors and accept visitors. Tourism began.

The Union des Grand Crus was founded by some of the top Bordeaux château owners and winemakers to take their wines on the road, now that they were so proud of them. Travelling throughout the world, this was one of the first times that Bordeaux proprietors met with their customers instead of allowing a négociant to be the middleman between the château and the client. As in the world of gastronomy (the celebrity chef was born at around this time) so the celebrity winemaker was created and fêted – even if you would never have found him driving a tractor or pumping-over a vat of wine.

Perhaps 1982 was the first vintage in which climate change manifested itself in Bordeaux, although at that time, people talked instead, rather vaguely, of El Niño, or a change in the path of the Gulf Stream. No one was worried about the Earth getting warmer. What they saw was a succession of warm, sunny vintages where the grapes ripened fully. When the successful 1983 vintage came along, followed by (with the two disappointing exceptions of 1984 and 1987) a string of other good to great years, Bordeaux was once again on a roll. It wasn't only the châteaux that had winning seats, but the brokers and négociants reaped the benefits too. If customers didn't buy up the wines in 'off' vintages, they had little chance of receiving good allocations when the top-quality years came back around; thus even the sales of poorer vintages boomed.

More people piled into the market; many of them young. An international following developed. Bordeaux was back in the big time again.

And so began the see-saw of great vintages followed here and there by a weak one, where prices did not follow the quality curve (going gently up and down) but continued to climb, irrespective of calibre, economic conditions or foreign exchange. Occasionally a top merchant would refuse to buy a château's new wine if the quality wasn't there (as Ab Simon famously did with Château Léoville Las Cases 1986) but there was usually someone else willing to take a punt and buy it anyway.

Thanks to Robert Parker and his 100-point scoring system, it became incredibly easy for most of the new wine collectors to decide which wines they should buy. They didn't even have to read the tasting notes. All they had to do was buy the wines that scored above 90. This race to the top, in search of that perfect 100-point score (Parker awarded lots of them during his career), meant that large areas of vineyard had to be downgraded to second wine status. And while these were probably more indicative of the character of the estate, it was the *grand vin*, or top wine, like the cream on top of an old-fashioned milk bottle, that held the special magic. Today, sadly, many of the second wines languish in the autumn sales organized by French supermarkets. Called '*les foires des vins*' (wine fairs) and loosely coinciding with the wine harvest, these have become a convenient place to sell off the 'also rans' in the ratings contest.

All this said, if ever a new set of statues was to be built around Bordeaux' Marché des Grands Hommes, one of them should be erected for Robert Parker. He almost single-handedly made Bordeaux sexy again, and through his love for ripe, juicy wines, pushed the entire region towards a more forward, rich and oaky style than that known by the traditionalists. The formula worked. All over the world, people fell in love with the new easy-to-understand wines that had shed their green coats of tannin and stemminess. And even better, they could be drunk young. As more and more young people in the 1980s piled into the big cities and into new jobs in merchant banking, derivatives or hedge funds, their newly built condos did not come equipped with wine cellars. If they purchased a top Bordeaux, it was to drink sooner rather than later.

Bordeaux had become accessible in every way but price. The phenomenal success of this vintage is manifested in the eye-watering prices it can still fetch today – the 1982 wines of Le Pin and Château Petrus, each 100-pointers made in small quantities, can bring in substantially over £5,000 a bottle. Even if critics thought that the lack of acidity in these wines meant they would not age, Bordeaux's legendary ability to climb steadily up to a plateau of drinkability for 20 years, then sit there for another 30 to 50, proved them wrong. There are countless times when the comparison between the famous 1947 Cheval Blanc, one of Bordeaux's most fabled wines, with its high alcohol and low acidity, has been rolled out in defence of the younger 1982 icon.

This may be the most controversial point of the 1982 vintage: it created a pyramid of Bordeaux wines that has led to vast inequality in the region. At the top sits the hundred or so 'blue chip' wines: château wines that are bought and sold with ease, and which on the whole will make money for everyone, delighting the sommeliers and wine critics with

At the top of the pyramid, prices can be eye-watering: 1982 vintage Le Pin and Petrus (both 100-point wines) can fetch upwards of £5,000 a bottle.

their flavours. Then there are the 'almost made its': the wines of the rest of the classified growths, Saint-Emilion *grands crus* and fairly well-known estates; when these get good scores, they sell well throughout the world, but otherwise they rely on the traditional European markets for their sales. Further down the scale are the remaining château-bottled wines that rely on either having a one-hit-wonder vintage or a charismatic winemaker who travels the wine circuit tirelessly to promote sales. At the base of the pyramid is the vast quantity of Bordeaux wine, sometimes developed into brand names or otherwise sold directly from the estate, which languishes at prices that are easily 100 times less than those at the pinnacle.

This price inflation would result in immense pressure for traditional families to sell, and following the 1982 vintage, several of Bordeaux' most famous names, including Bouteiller, Prats and Ginestet, did just that. Mentalities had changed. A decade earlier, no family member would have thought of selling their inheritance when their estate was not profitable. Now, as financial success returned to the region, heirs saw the merits in making money rather than running a wine domain. Caught in the web woven by Napoleon when he revised French inheritance rules so that all heirs inherit equally, those not involved with the wine business wanted to cash in their chips. Many of the newly arrived owners who bought them out came from other fields than the traditional ones of banking or wine. They were industrialists, supermarket owners, creators of luxury brands, real estate magnates. Their Bordeaux château was their '*danseuse*', their mistress on the side that, although expensive, came with an enviable lifestyle. Little did they know how capricious their courtesans could be.

Looking back to that sun-filled harvest, we had no idea when we were laughing and drinking at the end of the day with the other pickers, how Bordeaux would change irrevocably. Ours was a simple world, more out of a Millet painting in its sheer peasant simplicity. Our sheer amateurism, our dormitory accommodation, our riotous meals – 80 of us, all together seated at trestle tables decorated with plastic Vichy table-cloths, our drunkenness, our use of tractors, ladders, trailers and hoses that would shock any health and safety inspector today. Sadly, this crazy camaraderie disappeared as quickly as the new-found wealth arrived. Most estates now use teams from outside the region who bring their own packed lunches and stay heaven knows where.

Bordeaux has changed, as it has always changed and will continue to. Who knows which vintage, in 30 or so years, will be used as the harbinger of a different direction as planet Bordeaux continues to spin on its solid axis? But one thing is certain: 1982 transformed Bordeaux forever.

In no other wine region is the annual performance of the vineyards of such paramount importance: a vintage can make or break the reputation of a château, and escalate or destroy the hopes of an entire appellation. Stephen Browett of fine wine distributor Farr Vintners talks to the Académie du Vin Library about Bordeaux' annual evaluation.

LONG LIVE THE VINTAGE!

Stephen Browett (2020)

Why do we set so much store by the vintage? It's what sets Bordeaux apart from the other Cabernet Sauvignons of the world – why its wines are so different. If you get a Cabernet from irrigated vines – say, from Australia or Argentina – then the character will more or less be the same every year. You don't get the huge variations in character, for the bad or good. It's these that make Bordeaux interesting. Yes, there are differences in the vineyards, the blends and winemaking, but it is the annual weather that brings excitement. Vintage variation can mean anything from a £75-million turnover (2009) to £1-million (2013).

There's no doubt we are a weather-conscious nation; is obsession with vintages just a British thing? Anyone interested in Bordeaux is vintage conscious, although in Japan and China there is much more emphasis on the brand. Château Beychevelle is popular for the dragon-boat image on its label; Lynch-Bages grabs attention for being on Cathay Pacific's first class airline menu, and Lafite sells because it is easy to say (where Haut-Brion is not). The French *think* they know about wine but the British take vintages much more seriously. For us, the vintage is stronger than the château brand.

And the US? In the USA *Wine Spectator, The Wine Advocate* and James Suckling are all very vintage focused. One of these (I won't mention which) is always first at every château come En Primeur season – their taxi is always fastest, and they're always the first to post their report. Switzerland, Belgium and Denmark are constant vintage markets too.

What happens if it's not a great year? We don't talk a wine up. If you overstate a wine, then you lose customers. For 'in between' vintages, we quote Neal Martin, Jancis Robinson MW and James Suckling to give customers confidence; but the best tasting notes come from our in-house writer, Thomas Parker (no relation to Robert), who was one of the youngest ever to become an MW. Also, we only choose the good châteaux each year. This choice is the job of a good wine merchant. For burgundy, you always have to sell a domain every year if you want to keep your allocation. But with Bordeaux, it's more of a gamble. We do run the risk of losing a property if we skip a year with it, but we can only list the top wines.

Can a great score from a critic turn a vintage around? Yes. As can a new château owner. But the reality is, we can sell a property's second or even third wine from a top vintage more easily than we can a first growth from a bad year. The best thing is to have a good year.

Are the En Primeur releases a true reflection of the wine to come? En Primeur samples (at six to eight months old) are prepared to show the wine in its best light and might not necessarily be the same as the wine the château eventually sells. Some properties are honest and say they don't know what the final blend will be, or even how much longer it will stay in barrel. But the whole 'jamming-up' process, where Bordeaux made super-extracted wines to suit Robert Parker, its most influential critic, is much less aggressive now he's retired. Some still 'jam up' for the US En Primeur market, but if they want to appeal to broad-minded journos like Jancis Robinson MW or Neal Martin, then there's no need.

When is the best time to appraise a young wine? We blind taste the wines every year, just over a year after they are bottled. In spring 2020 we have just tasted the 2016s. We set up the top 250 Bordeaux in peer groups, by price and by geography. This is a good time to try them as they have had time to settle. Some really stand out, and usually it's the same wines that are outstanding when we taste them again 10 years on. 2010 has some really epic highlights but there are some wines that are over-extracted as they were still chasing Parker points at the time; 2016 is the first great vintage of the post-Parker era and there seems to be a noticeable move away from overblown wines and a general reduction in alcohol.

Which has the strongest influence, the winemaker or the vintage? Winemaking is a human process, a human art. In fact it is one of the great arts. I'm not a believer in 'natural wine'. Who wants a wine to taste like it did back in the Caucasus [the 'cradle of viticulture'], buried in a goatskin for a year and left to its own devices? No thank you! Expressing terroir is good, but there are so many decisions involved that I don't believe winemaking is a natural process. Even so, every year, the vintage takes precedence.

What's the difference between a Right Bank and a Left Bank vintage? They're different in every vintage. There are certain vintages when the Merlot (the main grape in Saint-Emilion and Pomerol on the Right Bank) gets ripe but not the Cabernet Sauvignon. And others when the Merlot gets too ripe – like 2003, when it turned to jam as it couldn't cope with the heat. Cabernet Sauvignon certainly needs more sunshine to ripen; most vineyards will pick Merlot then wait five days to start harvesting Cabernet, which makes the Médoc (Left Bank) more vulnerable. It likes a better year.

Is Bordeaux still worth investing in? People will always buy for investment. Those who buy young wine will usually sell some off at some stage for any number of reasons: they no longer like it, they divorce, etc. About half that we sell we get back again. People have to think they're getting a good deal with Bordeaux. It has to have the potential for resale.

What are your vintage 'categories'? 'Value for money vintages': these are not great years, but not 'off' years. 2012, for example, has very soft tannins and is easy and delicious as a drinking wine. There's no great potential for investment, but it has masses of charm. 2006 is the same: a drinkers' vintage, for drinking young.

'Ugly Duckling vintages': You sometimes get years that are so tannic you think they'll never come round. 2005 was like this, but then it came good. Similarly 2003 was so sweet we thought it wouldn't last, which turned out to be true, but there were some very good wines in the mix. 2001 was the classic ugly duckling: nobody wanted it to be good after the 2000s – which had been so built up as a launch to the new millennium – but if ever there were a wine that was underestimated, it was this one.

Then there's the good old 'off vintage': people say you'll never have an off vintage again because of climate change, technology and vibrating sorting tables, with higher selections even for second and third wines, but actually you do: 2013 is an example. And the 'un-identical twins': 2012 and 2014 are alike but not alike; they're both of a similar quality, ie, good but not great years, but 2012 is soft and easy-drinking now, whereas 2014 has a more tannic structure and needs a bit more time to soften.

And course there are 'great years' like 2016, 2010, 2009, 2005, 1990, 1989 and 1982.

How long will the great vintages improve? People need to do their own research to find the sweet spot; everyone's taste is different. But I'd say Bordeaux is best at 20 years. Keep it 10, then try it over the next two decades. Even the best don't keep for more than 30 – 1982 was perfect at 25. 1959 (my birth year) is one of the greatest vintages ever, it can be fabulous, but for a good one now you have to head to the Médoc first growths.

And your last word? Vintages are why Bordeaux is the best wine in the world.

Joe Fattorini began his career as a university academic, but, unable to lead a quiet life, now finds himself in demand as a radio and television presenter, wine educator and after-dinner speaker. (Among his many other wine guises, Joe has also worked as a weekly newspaper correspondent, a wine merchant and consultant.) Here, he looks at 2008, the year Bordeaux' wines became divorced from reality…

THE TURBULENT LIFE OF 2008

Joe Fattorini (2020)

What does 2008 mean to you? We all have our ways of remembering dates and years. Do you remember 2008 as Bordeaux's 'last affordable vintage', in the words of Jancis Robinson MW? Financiers remember 2008 as the year of 'the crisis'. The rest of us remember it as the year of 'their crisis'. Or me. For me, 2008 was the year my wife left. Like I said, we all have our little ways of remembering special dates.

2008 is a good vintage. But it isn't an extraordinary vintage. At a 10-year retrospective tasting in London in 2018, I asked Michael Schuster for his assessment a decade on. Michael stood thoughtfully, then declared 'a perfectly acceptable vintage of beverage wines'.

Yet the ordinary can tell an extraordinary story.

2008 was expected to emerge much like 2007. Both were conceived in an inauspicious spring, grapes reluctantly swelling pregnant through a cool summer, their birth salvaged to ripeness by a late, warm autumn. But there's something of the 'William and Harry' about the two years. 2007 turned those conditions into a dependable, eager, early-drinking vintage. 'A Sommelier's Vintage.' Early enough drinking to sell in restaurants. Cheap enough to take the markups. 2008 took the same meteorological parents and became richer. More exotic. More tannic. More international. And somehow more expensive too. Just as the product of genetic mixing is unpredictable, so is the product of weather on vines.

THE WAY SHAKESPEARE PLANNED IT

2008's life actually began a year earlier. In June 2007 Greece suffered its worst heatwave for a century. But Bordeaux's winemakers saw forecasts of much more disappointing weather on their newly released iPhones. The conditions persuaded Bordeaux's vines to produce fewer inflorescences – the microscopic embryos of 2008's bunches. Deep inside the vine, the scale of the vintage was already determined.

Celebrated by the Chinese market, the 2008 Château Lafite Rothschild flew from £2,098 a case to £14,250 – a dizzy price that wasn't to last.

By August 2007 the character of the vintage, and year to come, was developing with what looked like certainty. The cold, damp month left its mark in the following year's low vigour. On August 9th the bank BNP Paribas blocked withdrawals from three of its hedge funds in what was to be starting pistol for the financial crisis.

Winter passed with much of the wine's destiny already hidden in each vine's hibernating wood. But it was woken too soon by unusually warm weather in January, February and March. How different from the world outside. Froideur stalked the stock markets, which collapsed on January 21st. Food riots broke out in developing countries by March.

By spring, flashes of cold affected the vineyards too. On April 6th, protesters in Paris wrapped up well. It was a cold day for a march to call for the release of Ingrid Betancourt, a French-Colombian politician kidnapped six years before. By the time the chill air had reached Bordeaux on the 6th it had become a frost severe enough to drastically reduce the year's white wine harvest. The reds survived, but the frost slowed them down. By the end of May 'Believe', that year's Eurovision Song Contest winner, wasn't just a song; it was every vigneron's mantra.

Flowering carried on through June. On June 14th in Zaragoza, Spain, Expo 2008 opened with the topic 'Water and Sustainable Development'. As if to make the point, on the same day the rain stopped in Bordeaux.

Then July seemed to bring miracles. It was the driest July since 2005, allowing the vines to catch up and give winemakers something to cheer about. Meanwhile Parisian protesters of that chilly April 6th cheered as Ingrid Betancourt and 14 other hostages were rescued from FARC rebels by Colombian security forces.

August was damp and difficult. September got damper and difficulter. By this time, the vintage was turning from a drama to a tragedy. Five Shakespearean acts, and we were hurtling towards the sinking, *Gegenspiel* drama of Act Four, where the hostility of the weather-antagonist beats upon the soul of our hero, the vintage.

Then suddenly, Act Five. Denouement. On September 10th, high pressure brought cool, dry air from the north. This lasted a month. The vintage was saved. By the time pickers began harvesting reds on October 6th, smiles had broken out across the region. And our tragedy was turned into a comedy.

A remarkable story. Yet what happened next was even more extraordinary. Before 2008 had even made it into bottle, it had made, and lost, fortunes. Long-rumbling changes in the business of Bordeaux exploded as 2008 hit the market. Jancis was right. This is the last generally affordable vintage. And to see why, we must follow the money.

LET THE GOOD TIMES ROLL

In the old days, buying Bordeaux En Primeur was a bit of fun. A bit like a good day at the races. But in 2008 the gentlemanly fun ended. Buying En Primeur became more volatile, and glossy. And once the genie was out of the bottle, it proved impossible to squeeze him back in.

In 2009 I was introduced to 'David'. It's not his real name. He works in finance and likes privacy. So we'll just call him David. A mutual friend introduced us as he knew we both liked wine. He thought we'd have something in common. At the time I was moving into my parents' house because of the costs of getting divorced. Each night I was grateful my mother cooked me supper, while David had just bought 100 cases of Château Lafite Rothschild 2008. If I'm honest, beyond liking wine we didn't have a lot in common.

But I liked David. And was intrigued about what he'd bought. And why he'd bought it. What was fascinating was that David admitted he didn't like Bordeaux. Burgundy and Barolo were his thing. He would lose himself in poetic rhapsodies about domaines, *crus*, single vineyards and Piedmont villages. But with Bordeaux, he reverted to his day job. He worked in commodities. And Lafite Rothschild to him was a commodity.

In the spring of 2009, David had bought 100 cases of the 2008 vintage that had cost him around £210,000. Except it hadn't. Anyone who's tried to buy a lot of first growth claret En Primeur (I haven't, you know why) knows that (a) you have to go to a lot of different merchants as they dribble it out to their clients, and (b) you have to buy all sorts of other shrapnel to get your hands on the relatively limited number of cases of something like Lafite or Mouton, Margaux, Latour, Haut-Brion or any of the super-seconds that they're prepared to sell you. Every case of Lafite at £2,098 comes ready-wrapped with several dozen other cases of wine at lower prices (but adding up to considerably more) that will be less thrilling.

Was buying these 100 cases of Lafite just City Boy bravado? Well, no. Not in David's case. Because he wasn't buying this emotionally. (You should see his face change when he's talking about burgundy. He buys that like he's paying a ransom for a child.) He bought this financially. Logically. According to the Inland Revenue, bottles of wine are a capital gains tax 'chattel'. Money made selling chattels that are also 'wasting assets' – like wine – is generally exempt from capital gains tax. So David doesn't need to see the same return on wine as he would on stocks or bonds or property to make the same amount. And if he does make the same amount, he gets to keep more of it. And he kept quite a lot.

But there's a twist. Because with 2008 David didn't do well because of what the market wanted. With the 2008 vintage he made money because of what the market feared.

FEELING THE FEAR

In 2002 Daniel Kahneman won a Nobel Prize in for his work with Amos Tversky in behavioural economics. One of their more celebrated insights is that humans are driven more by fear of loss than anticipation of gain: two point six times more, apparently. By 2009, as the previous year's wines came onto the market, the world was waking up to the fact that American sub-prime lenders had been giving mortgages to wholly unsuitable borrowers. (I say 'borrowers' rather than people, as it emerged lenders had even given mortgages to people's pet dogs.) Ratings agencies were as inclined to look at the contents of mortgage bonds with much the same enthusiasm that Bismarck had for the contents of sausages. Whatever it was, wasn't going to be pretty. But they hoped nobody would notice. Until eventually, everybody noticed.

People in finance started to worry. They worried they were about to lose all the money they'd made over the last decade. Roughly 2.6 times more than they'd been enthused about making it. As they worked in banks, they knew the rules that operated for banks. Retail banks only guarantee the first £50,000 of your deposits. If the bank collapses – and retail banks were starting to – you lose the rest.

But what do you do if you need to find a safe home for a lot of cash? Open 10 different retail bank accounts? And then wonder what to do with the next £50,000? Or do you buy houses? But they're hard to pick up at short notice. Or buy art? But you did engineering at university to get a job in a bank. Not history of art like your brother who you don't meet up with so much anymore, what with him now being a primary school teacher and a socialist and always needing money and making sour remarks about 'the filthy rich', although fortunately you don't have to hear that very much what with him and his partner living in Burnley – why can't they just get married and make Mum happy? – and having to come on the Megabus with their noisy children wearing football shirts and mispronouncing Tatiana's name with glottal stops so they can stay in your spare room in the house in Holland Park spilling Ribena on the carpet when you were going to be in the Wiltshire pad and anyway you're not going to Burnley, not even for Christmas, and not even to make Mum happy...

I digressWhat you can do is buy wine. And that's what David did. And a few others who got in early at the original release price of £2,098 a case of Château Lafite Rothschild 2008. Or thereabouts.

David and I would meet once a year at a charity dinner. I was the compère charged with extracting cash from bankers. He was an obliging banker. A year later I asked David how his £210,000 investment in Lafite was getting on. Well, it certainly wasn't £210,000 anymore. And it was clear we were no longer in Kansas. In the previous year it had gone up 700%, making it a cool, £1,425,000. All gains tax free.

What had happened? Well, David wasn't the only financier who'd wanted to turn his liquidity into liquid. He was just one of the first. And like every good commodities trader he got in early – unlike the rest who got in late, when the roller coaster was already quite near the tipping point at the top.

IT'S A RED THING

That came from one of the other twists. A twist that happened in The People's Republic of China. The dragon had roared and was being quenched with claret. A few years ago, I was travelling in mainland China and met up with an old school friend, Ken. Ken had returned to China after school to run his family's car dealerships. 'Why do Chinese people splurge such money on wine?' I asked. 'Deals,' was Ken's answer. Wine sealed deals. Secured favours. Impressed and influenced people. And the wine of choice for all this is Bordeaux.

This hadn't passed Bordeaux's winemakers by. Château Lafite Rothschild declared that to celebrate the 2008 vintage it would put a small, red Chinese character for the number '8' on the shoulder of each bottle. Red is a lucky colour in China. And eight is a lucky number. Eight is pronounced 'Ba' in Chinese, which sounds like 'Fa', which means to 'make a fortune'. 'Fa' also contains inferences related to prosperity, success and high social status. People pay for the eighth watch in a series. A car number plate with eight in it. Red wine, celebrated for sealing deals, from 2008, with the number eight on it, painted in red... the combination was dizzying.

As was its impact on prices. They flew. All the way from £2,098 a case to £14,250.

In truth, David never saw £14,250. He told me how he'd been taught by a famous commodities trader and learned always to get out before the peak. And he had. Why walk away when there are still gains on the table? Who knows? Maybe David just figured it couldn't last. Maybe he was just happy with what he'd gained. Maybe he realized – correctly – that 2008 Château Lafite-Rothschild was no longer a bottle of wine. It had become a virtual ticket in a Chinese national mood lottery. As The Notorious BIG might have put it in American rap: 'Mao money, Mao problems.'

Not everyone in China was pleased by the way wine was being used to seal deals and grease the wheels of the economy. Because actually, wine wasn't so much grease, as graft.

THE PARTY'S OVER...

President Xi is a man partial to a bottle of red. He enjoyed Girard's 2014 Napa Valley Cabernet Sauvignon at dinner with President Trump in the US in 2017. He then enjoyed Nicolás Catena Zapata's 2014 from Argentina with Donald Trump at the G20 summit in Buenos Aires in 2018. And he enjoyed Château Petrus 2002 with President Macron in 2019. But he didn't much enjoy the idea of Communist Party officials back home passing through planning applications on the nod in return for a bottle or two of 'lucky 8' Lafite Rothschild from a market-trader-to-millionaire-property-developer in Guangdong.

And so he clamped down on using wine to grease (or graft) the space between corporate China and local government-China.

There's a certain irony. When President Xi came to the UK in 2015, there was a lot of talk about how the trip was intended to 'unlock' £30-billion worth of trade deals. The key to these deals turned out to be the one to the cellars of The Foreign and Commonwealth Office in Lancaster House. It turns out President Xi is content for some Chinese people (ie, him) to use fine wine to unlock deals (ie, his) when it's with The United Kingdom of Great Britain and Northern Ireland. But not other people.

But once again, I digress. Over the course of the next few annual meetings with David, those hundred cases of wine went from £1,425,000 to £765,000. Like a huge balloon inflated by a thousand Chinese businesspeople, it turned out the rest of the world didn't have so much puff. It's unlikely that anyone bought all a hundred cases together.

China's President Xi Jinping (*right*) and French President Emmanuel Macron (*left*) taste Bordeaux' finest as they visit France's pavilion during the China International Import Expo in Shanghai, 2019.

Much more likely there were people who'd picked up a case or two where each bottle was worth £1,187. And then found a couple of years later their solid gold 'investment' in Chinese corporate dining was worth £416. Even the most Parkerized, lush, overblown château is going to taste sour and tannic after that. Especially when your socialist, primary school teacher brother from Burnley hears about it and brings the subject up when you all get together with Mum at Christmas. And there's a sting in the tail. Or tale. In the same way capital gains are tax free, capital losses can't be set off against your tax bill. Quid pro quo, your quids in Bordeaux go. (I'll be honest, I'm not proud of that last sentence.)

I wish I could come up with something as succinct as: 'A perfectly acceptable vintage of beverage wines.' Vignerons cried. Then laughed. Then cried. Then did one of those panicky laughs you do when you realize how things turned out okay, but it could all have been so different. Fortunes were made. Then lost. And some did all the making. And some did all the losing. All with 'a perfectly acceptable vintage of beverage wines'.

TO PUT IT IN PERSPECTIVE

At the end of the first week in September 2008 the white wine harvest began in Bordeaux. About 700km away on September 10th at Esplanade des Particules in Geneva, the Large Hadron Collider – the world's largest and highest-energy particle accelerator – circulated the proton beam for the first time. The Large Hadron Collider was officially inaugurated on October 27th, just as the harvest of reds drew to a close.

Why mention this? Because at a wine conference last year someone suggested that only a quarter of a million people in the world have ever written a formal wine tasting note. The sort that were churned out at the En Primeur tastings in early 2009, that fuelled interest in 2008s, and kickstarted the spiralling prices. I looked up other things that apply to a quarter of a million people. Around a quarter of a million people have a working understanding of The Large Hadron Collider. There are as many people in the world who understand heavy subatomic particles like the $\Xi'^{-}b$ and $\Xi_{*}^{-}b$ baryons composed of one bottom, one down and one strange quark, than have ever written a phrase like 'exceptional purity and full-bodied intensity that remains light on its feet because of its fresh acids and lower pH, it represents a denser, more complete version of the 1988 and 1996'.

Context can change everything. A wine can go from underwhelming to tragic hero, all depending on the context. A commodity can go from being worth thousands to hundreds, all depending on the context. Wine might be centre of our universe. But up the road there are more people interested in studying the secrets of the universe. It all depends on the context.

The much-loved commentator on wine Ian Maxwell Campbell (1870–1954) was famed for his knowledge of wine spanning both world wars. He was one of the few writers to observe the wines of Bordeaux before and after the attack of 'that nasty pernicious little American bug', phylloxera. Here, he extols the virtues of 1871 and 1875, the last great vintages before the plague.

1871 AND 1875: THE PRE-PHYLLOXERA HEROES

Ian Maxwell Campbell (1948)

I was one of the luckiest of fellows to have been in Bordeaux in the early 'nineties before they, too, became 'naughty'. In 1892 the famous vintage of 1875 was at its best, and what a best! The fine, almost equally famous, 1874 was running strongly but most of its backers had begun to realize that it lacked something of the superlatively unsophisticated charm and sunniness of the '75.

The wines of 1878, although sweet and well-constituted, were at that time considered to be coarse and common and not in the same class as '74 and '75, while 1877s, light and elegant with just the *soupçon* of a squeeze of lemon in the final farewell, were expected to be the natural, if less captivating, successors to 1875, but fell far short. And yet, in all justice, and because 1877 is André Simon's birth year, I must record that, in June 1945, Hugh Rudd, Kenneth Upjohn and I, at 3 St James's Street, after a bottle of 1917 Château Lafite, enjoyed, to our surprise and delight, a bottle of 1877 Château Lafite which I noted at the time as 'no lemon, very good, still fresh, sweet and young'.

Those wines of 1871 that still adorned the cellars of the few were there to delight the most sensitive nose and most exacting palate. When they were first made, France was in a state of disturbance[1] and the vintage was quite neglected, a veritable Cinderella; and, like that popular heroine, it proved to be a gem of purest ray serene that did not forever blush unseen – and such a blush – for it received princely honour among connoisseurs of wine, a great many of whom declared it to be the most completely perfect and winsome claret they had ever known. I doubt if many of the proprietors, even of the classed growths, bottled their wines of 1871 at the châteaux, so little did they, or indeed anyone else at the time, appreciate the unique quality hidden beneath a rather too modest and diaphanous outward appearance. They followed too soon after the fine aristocratic 1869s

[1] The aftershocks of the Franco-Prussian War (July 1870–May 1871) were still felt.

and the pachydermatous 1870s, of which more anon. My own firm in London bought (before my time!), if not the whole crop, a good part of the 1871 Château Latour, bottled it in London and started selling it to wine merchants at 26 shillings a dozen! It was a superb wine with a perfume of summer flowers and a delicate flavour not unlike that of ripe nectarines. When my people put the price up to 36 shillings a dozen they almost felt like pioneers of a Black Market! But the wine's development and repute proved that they were fully justified and might have been a bit more greedy.

All these may be called pre-phylloxera vintages though it is possible that that nasty pernicious little American bug had already, in 1878, begun to afflict the vines. I doubt very much whether the vineyards have yet entirely recovered from the phylloxeric infection. The beetle, or bug, attacks the roots of the vines, and in the Gironde practically every one of these had to be dug up and destroyed while cuttings of the doomed plants were grafted onto clean immune young American stock: *c'était l'amende honorable.*

The vines have done their best and with age will, it is sincerely to be hoped, regain a large part of their pristine virtue.

The 1888s made a brave effort to return to type and very nearly succeeded, but alas! the reconditioned vines lacked strength to resist the second-front attacks of another aggressive and destructive enemy, mildew. As young wines the 1888s were very attractive, deliciously scented and with a pronounced flavour of hothouse grapes, but this flavour was the camouflage used by the mildew to deceive the over-trusting. The wines faded more or less rapidly away (though a very occasional bottle of the Château Margaux and one or two others may still be drinkable) and a great many keen and intelligent merchants and shippers of Bordeaux burned their fingers badly. One firm which had plunged and lost heavily on the expensive, stout-bodied, tannin-bound wines of 1870, which took over 50 years to reach maturity and become drinkable, now went to the opposite extreme and plunged heavily on the light, ephemeral, mildewed wines of 1888, most of which died in childhood. It goes to show that even the experts may err when dealing with the uncertainty of life to which the whole realm of creation is subject. But assuredly the 1888s were most deceptive when young and seemed as if they might well be the destined successors of 1875, a title which 1877 had failed to achieve.

Extract from *The Wayward Tendrils of the Vine* by Ian Maxwell Campbell, Chapman & Hall (London) 1948.

CHAPTER TWO

VIEW FROM THE VINEYARDS

There is more to terroir than earth and sky: the vines' response to the decisions of man is a vital part of its equation – a pivotal influence on the character of the wines we drink. This in mind, Bordeaux' viticulturists tread carefully as our climate changes.

Margaret Rand (2010)
Pruner to the Stars

James Lawther MW (2020)
The Phoenix Grape

Mathieu Chadronnier (2020)
On Sustainability

Joe Fattorini (2020)
One Mad Day in the Médoc

Michel Duclos is a man who can improve a château's wine simply by applying his instinctively brilliant way with a pair of secateurs. Margaret Rand spent a day with Duclos (and his dog) to try to uncover the secrets of his trade.

PRUNER TO THE STARS

Margaret Rand (2010)

'You want me to explain to you the work of 40 years in one day?' asks Michel Duclos, somewhat rhetorically. 'It's simple. It's all about simplicity. Everything should be as simple as possible.' Michel Duclos is a pruner – but not just any old pruner. Michel has been champion pruner of France and now criss-crosses Bordeaux, and indeed the world, coaxing vines into balance. That's why we are standing in a Pomerol vineyard one February morning, gazing at vines belonging to Château La Fleur-Pétrus. Michel is armed with the tools of his trade: his secateurs, his dog (a Jack Russell called Leeloo), and his hat. Does he ever remove his hat? No, he says, never. He shows me his car: the back seat has more hats, in case he feels like a change.

Vines in February, to the untutored eye, all look horribly alike. The initial post-harvest tidying-up has been done, so what we have here are bare vines that are about to be reduced to small black stumps. The next half hour will determine most of the potential quality of the 2011 vintage from this parcel. On vines that are out of balance, the maturation of the grapes will be uneven. If the crop is too heavy, there will need to be a green harvest. Michel doesn't approve of green harvesting. 'Ideally it is never necessary. At the Moueix level[1], you might remove individual grapes or bunches, but that's all.' That, to him, is logical and natural, and everything he advocates can be reduced to these principles – of logic, of nature; of commonsense, of order.

And, I should add, of instinct. Michel is dyslexic and short on technical training but long on intuition. 'I have a facility for understanding nature,' he says. 'I touch the soil, I greet the trees. It's an obligation to understand nature, to feel it. I can look at a vine and

[1] Mouiex: a highly influential merchant house, instrumental in the rise of the châteaux of the Pomerol and Saint-Emilion regions during the 1960s and 1970s. Owner of prestigious properties châteaux Petrus, Trotanoy, La Fleur-Pétrus and Magdeleine.

Michel Duclos, with a deep knowledge of vine psychology, always a hat and Leeloo the dog.

know it.' His first attempt at pruning was nevertheless not an unqualified success. His father has a property in Entre-Deux-Mers, and at the age of 12, Michel was sent out to do some pruning. 'I had 100 vines to do, and I did them faster than my father or my brother. It was the first big error of my life. My father told me never to come back.'

Forgiveness clearly followed, because he worked at the family domaine until he was 26, before moving on to other properties. And then one day he decided to enter a *concours de taille*. He came second that time, but as he says, 'I'm very competitive'. He entered more competitions, all over France, and finished as French champion. How does a *concours de taille* work? You're given 30 minutes to prune a row of vines, and you're judged on neatness and the general quality of your work. Winning the national championship got him on television, and top châteaux began to seek him out. 'It's a dream,' he says, 'meeting all these people' – and he laughs, delightedly.

But we're still in the vineyard of La Fleur-Pétrus, and the vines are waiting. What is he going to do? Basically, he's going to take the vine back to how it was last year. He's been tending these vines for a long time; major repairs are not necessary. 'The four elements that guide me are soil, air, water and sun.' And then it's observation. These vines are pruned to Single Guyot; he leaves five buds on each vine and whips the rest of the buds off with the secateurs. 'One single cut,' he says – there's no dithering, no indecision. 'You can kill a vine with secateurs. You have its life in your hands.'

The number of buds is what we all focus on, and it's certainly the way to control the crop. Five buds will give nine or 10 bunches, which will be about right here for the *rendement* (the permitted yield). 'Fifty hectolitres per hectare is good, 45 is better, but 15 is unbalanced,' he says. When we visit Château Gaby in Fronsac later in the morning, we see vines where he has left six or seven buds on vines on limestone soil, and seven to eight buds where there is more clay. For the past three years, says Damien Landouar, the manager of Gaby, they've been getting a steady 42–45hl/ha – and no more green-harvesting. 'Michel has worked here for three-and-a-half years, and we really see the change in the vineyard. We had a big problem with pruning. It's not normal to prune to 18 buds and then cut half off in July. The balance of the wine has changed now. There's more fruit, more maturity – exceptional maturity.

'In the first year, we needed the people in the vineyard to understand the work, and Michel came for one or two days a week to teach them to prune. The balance improved in the first year. Before, the *veraison* (colour ripening) would be uneven. You'd have two bunches next to each other, and one would be green and one red, and then you get different maturity on the same vine. Now the maturity is even. That means we can vinify differently. It's in the difficult years, like 2006 and 2007, that we see the difference.'

'The biggest mistake, all over the world, is to prune by habit,' says Michel. In another parcel of vines he prunes to three buds, and then he comes upon a vine where, last year, six were left. Does he cut it back to three? No, he leaves six, to calm its vigour. 'The ideal circumference of a cane is 10mm,' he says – more, and it becomes over-vigorous; less, and it's a bit feeble.

A SOCRATIC APPROACH

It can, however, be a bit of a tussle to get such direct answers out of him. He has a Socratic way of dealing with questions. Ask him how to judge the vigour of a vine, and he says: 'Come and stand next to me.' Then: 'Which of us can carry more? On the back or on the shoulders? Uphill or down? And what about sleep? It's the same with vines. If you double the buds, you will get twice this year, but next year it will be tired. It's easier to work for eight hours every day than 16 hours a day for two days. You must not tire vines.' Michel says he prunes vines to live 100 years. 'Badly pruned vines die earlier.'

After lunch (and more about lunch in a minute), we come across some vines that make him incensed. They're old, gnarled and picturesque – just the sort that you might photograph as a symbol of all that is wonderful about wine. 'They won't fruit,' he says simply. How does he know? '*C'est mon métier*' – it's my job. Well, good. 'The canes will grow from old wood. They won't fruit. They're sick, they'll die.' They can be wobbled in the ground like bad teeth; they're growing moss, and he knocks it off angrily. And sure enough, looking elsewhere in the vineyard there's a pile of dead vines. 'They died because of bad pruning, nothing else.'

How much poor pruning is there in Bordeaux? Or to put it another way, how much Bordeaux could be improved by better pruning? According to Michel, 'Ninety-nine point nine percent'. Not just Bordeaux, either – it's a worldwide problem, he says. And he works in South Africa, Chile, China, Italy and the USA, so he sees a good few vines.

But: lunch. And Leeloo. You can't really talk about Michel without Leeloo getting into the picture. (Dog haters can skip this paragraph.) Michel and I have lunch at a local restaurant, where we take a table for three – the third chair, of course, is for Leeloo. As the steak arrives, she begins to get restless, and the penny drops. 'You feed that dog at the table, don't you?' I say, all shocked Englishness. Yes, he says, and he does. And I did, too – with the result that, for the rest of the afternoon, I am Leeloo's new best friend. Every conversation is punctuated with the gentle pressure on my foot that means Leeloo has brought a stick for my attention. And if it's not Leeloo, it's passing cars hooting and waving at Michel. He knows a lot of people. 'But my dog is more famous than me,' he says.

THE FORM OF THE VINES

Back to the vines. The thing we haven't talked about yet is the form of the vines, but Michel is keen on this. He likes regularity and homogeneity in a vineyard: tidiness, with each vine having just the right space, and each vine standing up nice and straight. The sort of vines that twist in every direction before arriving at the cane are not his sort of vines at all. A vine that stands 10cm (4in) below the first wire (we're talking about Single Guyot on the Right Bank here) is his ideal, and spaced so that the buds don't have to compete for space. 'If the vine isn't straight, it's more difficult to work the soil, and the buds are less accessible. There will be less aeration and more rot… You must respect the distance between the first and second wire – it's the biggest disaster you can make.' And you want a straight trunk, because that gives a clear route for the sap, 'an *autoroute* for the sap. The sap must feed each bud efficiently. It's like us carrying a weight in different ways: you get different results.' (He comes across a slightly weak vine, for example, and cuts it back to three buds, because it's easier to carry a weight from your shoulders than at the end of your arm.) In a twisted vine, he says, the sap can't get around.

Is this anthropomorphizing nature too much? I would say not. Michel says he can feel whether a vine is well or sick. It is, he says, the physiology of each vine that interests him. And the results are there in the glass. At La Clémence in Pomerol, where he has been working for 10 years, the trunks are straight, the three to four buds evenly spaced. Oenologist Florian Fresselirat praises Michel's effect on the balance of the wine and practices cold maceration for five to 10 days and manual *pigeage* (punching down) – techniques for which you need to be certain of the quality of your tannins and, thus, the even maturation of your grapes.

The vines here are pruned to Guyot Mixte – that is, Single Guyot, but with the cane one side of the vine one year, the other side the next year. Double Guyot is more complicated, he says, more difficult to get right. 'A pruner will make more mistakes with Double Guyot than with Single Guyot.' At Château Rochebelle in Saint-Emilion the vineyards are predominantly trained with Double Guyot, and some vines have the 'Y' above the wire, some below. The results, he says, are different. It's a question of how the weight is carried.

Different proprietors want different things from Michel. At Château Jean Faure there were major repairs to be done to the vines, and the owner wants to raise the yields to optimize the quality of the grapes. So Michel has lopped off great lengths of old, twisted vine to simplify their form. He finds a bud lower down that won't fruit the first year but that will produce a cane, which will produce a bud that will fruit the following year. He's taken 20 years of growth off some vines. Ten to 12 buds had been the norm; now, for better balance, he's taking it down to five or six, which is enough for the *rendement*. It hadn't been done badly in the past here, says Michel; it's just that it could be improved.

So how does he tackle a new vineyard – and does he prefer to work with young vines or old ones? His answer to this is superbly diplomatic: Do I, he asks, prefer babies or grandmothers? He likes both – but if he's caring for a new vineyard from scratch, he will prune three times in the first year, rather than leaving it untouched from planting in about May through to the following March. Do this, he says, and then you can train it in four or five different ways.

If he's arriving at an already established vineyard, however, the first thing he does is ask the owner what he or she wants. (And what is possible.) Of course, everyone says they want better quality – but what sort of grapes? 'Then I go and look at the best vines on the property and get to know them.' And he sometimes finds that what people say and what they do are different things. Repairing a badly pruned vineyard may take 10 years or longer. Psychology, he says, can take up five or six hours of an eight-hour day; but nevertheless he's found time to prune some five million vines in his life so far. That's 150,000 a year, or 250 an hour. The work of 40 years. Simple.

First published in Issue 28 of *The World of Fine Wine* (2010) and reprinted here with kind permission of the author, Margaret Rand, and editor, Neil Beckett.

Petit Verdot has a reputation for being the least loved of Bordeaux' red grape varieties – a capricious, late-ripening blend partner, whose plantings fell to an all time low with the 2000 vintage. James Lawther saw its slump in the vineyards but now witnesses its move from Left Bank to Right as climate, and appreciation of this giddy grape, warms.

THE PHOENIX GRAPE

James Lawther MW (2020)

'Capricious,' 'demanding,' 'difficult...' these are just some of the adjectives growers in Bordeaux use to describe Petit Verdot (*pictured right*). Little wonder, then, to find this once bountiful regional grape variety with a dwindling acreage in the latter part of the 20th century. But plantings are once again on the rise, and from a low of 375 hectares in 2000, the 2018 CIVB (Conseil Interprofessionnel du Vin de Bordeaux) figures now show a total of 1,093 hectares of Petit Verdot planted in Bordeaux. Producers have clearly found something to re-enchant them with this mercurial variety.

The origins of Petit Verdot are a little hazy but it is generally thought of as a Bordeaux grape, the first references to it in the region dating from the early 18th century. Recent ampelographic and genetic research, however, takes this theory to task, giving its provenance as the Pyrénées-Atlantiques where it is known under the synonym Lambrusquet. How it gravitated to the Gironde is less clear, but its early reputation was definitively tied to Bordeaux and, in particular, the Médoc, which to this day maintains the highest percentage of plantings.

The reasons for its early cultivation have never, as far as I can surmise, been fully explained but there are one or two conjectures. Petit Verdot is naturally high-yielding, which may have suited producers at the time. It is also later budding than Cabernet Sauvignon, so planted on some of the more marginal, frost-prone zones like the *palus* (reclaimed marshland on the edge of the Gironde estuary), which it often was, it would have been less at risk. Its high anthocyanin count would also have provided plenty of much-needed colour.

A safeguard against frost, a boost in colour, alcohol and extract, Petit Verdot became a firm fixture among Médoc châteaux in the 18th and early 19th centuries, playing an important part in blends. As mentioned, though, it's an awkward variety to cultivate and late-ripening to boot, meaning it would have lacked consistency, so following the devastation of phylloxera and rise in popularity of Cabernet Sauvignon and Merlot, it diminished in the vineyards and wines.

The difficulties of cultivating Petit Verdot are the same today as they were in the 18th century; the difference is that viticultural practices have progressed. It is a vigorous variety in terms of vegetation, with shoots and stems that break easily, so needs plenty of work and attention in the vineyard (trellising, shoot positioning, de-suckering, etc). It is naturally productive with two to three bunches per shoot, so pruning needs to be decisive, as does a follow-up green harvest. 'The key to quality is the yield,' says Sabrina Pernet, technical director at Château Palmer. A yearly activity at the Margaux third growth (1855) is reducing the crop to 25–35hl/ha via a massive green harvest, a procedure introduced in the early part of the new millennium.

Bunches tend to be small and compact, but with a late ripening cycle and the need to push for optimum maturity, all the producers I spoke to mentioned the potential for split berries and ensuing rot during the harvest. Château Palmer even accepts a touch of rot as a sign of maturity and the green light for harvesting. Petit Verdot is also sensitive to powdery mildew (another conceivable reason it fell from grace as time went on) but resistant to downy mildew.

Being late-ripening, it is either the last or one of the last grape varieties to be harvested, so can fall foul of deteriorating autumnal weather. At Château Angludet in Margaux, where 13 percent of the 32-hectare vineyard is planted to Petit Verdot, it is always the last to be picked, the 2019 vintage finishing on October 20th. While at Château Haut-Bailly in Pessac-Léognan and Château Léoville-Poyferré in Saint-Julien, it is picked after the Merlot and either between the Cabernet Franc and Cabernet Sauvignon or at the same time as the Cabernet Sauvignon.

Despite its negative traits, Petit Verdot has a number of attributes that producers favour in a Bordeaux blend. It is rich in both sugar and acidity, while the high polyphenol content in the skins provides colour and tannin. It therefore has the potential to enhance colour, power, density of structure and freshness in a wine. The aromatic benefits are perhaps less emphatic but in a best-case scenario, a pinch of spicy, peppery freshness can be added. The trick, though, is not to overstep the mark and to ensure sufficient ripeness to tame the latent rusticity in the tannins. 'It's a complementary grape variety that can reduce elegance if not handled correctly,' confirms Philippe Bascaules, the general manager of Château Margaux.

Low yields are compulsory, producers today aware that 40hl/ha is an absolute maximum. This has gone a long way to assisting ripeness and improving the quality of tannins. Other factors have also helped. If the tendency in the 18th and 19th centuries was to plant on cooler, later-ripening sites, the opposite is the case today. Warmer, earlier

Château Palmer, with its abundant gravelly soils, is keen to embrace Petit Verdot, but insists on low yields from the variety to achieve top quality.

ripening sites, sometimes with sand and gravel soils but sufficient moisture to avoid stress, are the predilection, certainly in the Médoc: an aspect that has contributed to greater consistency. An exception is some of the very old plantings (70 years or more) found near the Gironde estuary at, for instance, châteaux Bolaire and Moutte Blanc in Macau, where clay soils give the Petit Verdot a more rounded, powerful style.

Other aids are the use of less vigorous rootstocks, like 10114, and climate. If the 1990s were often marked by rain during the harvest, the new millennium has generally seen warm to hot summers and clement weather during the harvesting period in September and October. 'The vegetal element in Petit Verdot is no longer a problem,' says Thierry Bos of Château de Bouillerot in the Entre-Deux-Mers. In short, it's a positive feature of global warming.

Less discussed but also of some significance is the plant material used. Vineyards in Bordeaux are either planted with unspecified old-vine Petit Verdot (from vineyards planted in the 1960s or before), a mass selection from these vines, or from clones 400 (introduced in 1975) or 1058 (introduced in 2000). A mix of mass selection and clone 400 is also typical. Two other clones, 1273 and 1274, were authorized in 2019 but it is too early to evaluate their performance.

From my unscientific research it would appear that the berries and bunches of old vine and mass-selection Petit Verdot are smaller than those of the clones, and that these vines are also less productive. This is particularly apparent when compared to clone 400, probably the clone that is most widely planted in Bordeaux. The bigger berries and looser bunches of this clone make it more productive but slightly less sensitive to rot. 'We get good results from clone 400 providing we green harvest and there's some hydric stress, whereas the mass-selection material can be problematic at flowering and is less consistent,' explains Jean-Dominique Videau, manager and technical director of Château Branaire-Ducru in Saint-Julien.

This is not, though, a universal opinion. Château Margaux replanted Petit Verdot in the 1990s using mass-selection vines produced from old vines that had been planted at the estate in the 1920s. A few rows of clone 400 were also planted for comparison. 'Both were planted on the same low-yielding rootstock and we've found clone 400 to be less concentrated, the tannins more difficult to ripen fully and, overall, qualitatively less successful,' comments Philippe Bascaules.

In terms of vinification, the general rule of thumb for Petit Verdot is to go easy on extraction due to its powerful, tannic nature. 'At Château Palmer we are obsessed with the quality of tannins so are prudent with extraction, allowing about 10 days of alcoholic fermentation and maceration in an average year, and up to 15 days in top vintages,' explains Sabrina Pernet. Alcohol levels can reach 14% but there's always balancing acidity.

The Médoc remains the prime source for Petit Verdot in Bordeaux, responsible for a good half of the surface area planted to the variety. For the majority of estates, it is a blending component, the percentage hovering between one and seven percent. But there are exceptions. Château Angludet uses 10 to 12 percent and in 2018 went to 18 percent as Petit Verdot fared better in an attack of downy mildew than the other varieties. 'It gives a depth to the wine,' says Daisy Sichel, one of the family owners.

Château Belle-Vue in the Haut-Médoc is another estate where Petit Verdot can reach 15 to 20 percent of the blend and where a single-variety wine has also been made. The true exponent of this style, though, is Patrice de Bortoli at Château Moutte Blanc in Macau. Since 1994 he has been making his single-variety Petit Verdot 'Moisin' from old vines grown on the *palus*. 'It keeps its colour and ages well, exuding aromas of cherry and kirsch as it matures,' he explains.

Amongst the classed growth châteaux, the Petit Verdot is still employed with moderation. The guiding rule is that it has to be ripe; thereafter it is used like seasoning in cuisine. 'Five percent is about right for our blend and we miss it if it doesn't make the cut,' says Isabelle Davin, oenologist at second growth Château Léoville-Poyferré. 'It's good to add as part of a blend and brings freshness and complexity but it can never be the mainstay like Cabernet Sauvignon,' confirms Vincent Bache-Gabrielsen, manager of fifth growth Château Pédesclaux in Pauillac.

Further south in Pessac-Léognan the same formula applies: top estates include a small percentage of Petit Verdot in the makeup of their vineyards. Château Haut-Bailly has some in an old-vine parcel (120-years) of mixed varieties but it is co-fermented. Another parcel was planted in 2012, and since 2015 three to four percent has been used in the blend. 'We planted it for colour and structure but not for the aromatics, which lack finesse with age,' comments technical director Gabriel Vialard.

Further east, on the Right Bank, Petit Verdot has rarely been associated with Saint-Emilion or Pomerol, but there appears to be a modicum of interest these days. In Saint-Emilion, the variety was officially listed as a *cépage accessoire* 15 years ago and is limited to 10 percent of plantings at any estate. The most high-profile examples can be found at Château Angélus, where half a hectare was planted in 2015, and at Château Simard which is owned by the Vauthier family of Château Ausone. 'It used to be planted at Château de Fonbel but the density of planting wasn't right and we were less satisfied with clone 400. So, we grubbed it up and replanted at Simard in 2015 with clone 1058 at 12,000 vines per hectare. So far, we are satisfied with the results,' explains winemaker Pauline Vauthier.

The only Petit Verdot in Pomerol can be found at Château La Fleur-Pétrus. The stimulus for planting came from California rather than Bordeaux this time; co-owner Christian Moueix is partial to the variety, which he has cultivated at his Napa estate, Dominus, for the last 40 years. There was also a gravelly parcel that seemed suitable, and wtith global warming a subject of reflection, it seemed to make sense. 'We were tempted by the experience but it's still experimental,' says Christian's son Edouard.

Across the generic region of the Entre-Deux-Mers, Petit Verdot is steadily kindling interest. The hope is that it is not just for potential yield. One fine example is that of Thierry Bos at Château de Bouillerot. His vines date from the 1960s and yield around 35hl/ha; the wine is used in an original blend with Carmenère and Malbec. A mass selection from the old vines has just been grafted onto former Merlot vines and will be in production in the next couple of years.

Petit Verdot is a trying variety for growers but it clearly has something to offer, especially in the context of climate today. When carefully managed and judiciously dosed, its features are positive. It's a blending partner in the true Bordeaux mould.

(*Overleaf*) Autumn vines at Château d'Issan. Its wines date back to 1152, when they were served at the wedding of Henry II and Eleanor of Acquitaine.

In no mood to bypass its ecological responsibilities, Bordeaux is beginning a detailed overhaul of its production methods, starting in the vineyards. Mathieu Chadronnier, president of prestigious négociant CVBG and, with his wife, a grower of organic wines himself at Château Marsau in the Côte de Francs, explains how the Bordelais are adapting their systems to meet new sustainable standards.

ON SUSTAINABILITY

Mathieu Chadronnier (2020)

When we talk of 'sustainability', the first issue that pops into most people's minds is that of organic and biodynamic versus conventional viticulture. In Bordeaux we are no different; the long-term health of our vines is of paramount importance, and organic methods would seem, as of now, to be the preferable way forward. But we are not helped by the fact that we live and work in what is among the most climatically challenged regions in which to implement organic viticulture.

The way we tackle disease in the vineyard is at the heart of what can go wrong when we tend our vines organically. The two main diseases Bordeaux' vine-growers face are mildew and oidium, and of the two, mildew is by far the greatest threat. While conventional wine growers have a range of options open to them for combating these diseases, the only permitted spray against mildew for organic producers is copper. The problem is that it only takes around 20mm of rain to wash away the copper treatment from the vines and leave them unprotected. Bordeaux, with its oceanic influence, is particularly prone to rainy springs, which puts the region at a clear disadvantage. In 2018 – the wettest spring in living memory – everything that could go wrong, did go wrong: rainfall cost some growers as much as 80 percent of their crop.

This explains why organic viticulture did not develop as fast here as in other regions. And while this situation might make our prospects for organic viticulture look remarkably bleak, it is now gaining traction so fast that it will only be a matter of a few vintages before Bordeaux is counted as one of the biggest organically farmed vine areas in France. Some of the best-known châteaux lead the trend: Pontet-Canet and Palmer were among the first – each of them certified biodynamic. Château Latour is also certified, with Lafite, close behind, currently moving towards certification. These are to name just a few.

So how has this happened? The answer is that there has been no major breakthrough, but instead a constant track of adapting, learning, researching and risk managing. As more vineyards follow the organic route, strong community experience is being accumulated and understanding becomes deeper. It takes resources, but most growers are willing to commit the required investments (when they have the financial ability). For example, being organic means we have to react very quickly to a problem when it arises. This often requires more tractors and larger, more skilled teams to operate them – and they must react on whatever day the problem occurs, weekends and bank holidays included – to spray a whole vineyard in a very short space of time. The additional costs of labour and equipment can become very substantial.

Bordeaux' Atlantic weather conditions are due to remain as much a problem moving forward as they are now. Climate change is unlikely to help. But as with everything, *how* you do things matters as much as *what* you do.

Organic viticulture should not be viewed as the only destination of sustainability. Though its benefits are significant, it is only one step (and one option) along the path – albeit an important one. Reducing sustainability to what you spray or not in your vineyards would be a misconception of the very notion of it. To me, sustainability encompasses three other vital elements: preservation and enhancement of the ecosystem, reduction of carbon footprint, and continuity of style and identity.

ECOSYSTEM PRESERVATION

Viticulture, as with any form of agriculture, should seek to protect a vineyard's ecosystem, enhancing its biodiversity both above ground and below the surface. On that front, the organic route, however meaningful, only offers a partial answer. No certification addresses soil management (to plough or not to plough?), or the protection and development of biodiversity – both areas in which huge progress is about to be made. In this respect, most of Bordeaux' organic vine growers go well beyond the requirements of the certification.

The visitor to Bordeaux will progressively see more trees and grasses bordering vines. This is happening already, on both banks, although it has not yet reached the point of being massively visible. Trees and grasses are important because they structure the soils. They enhance the biodiversity, they protect from erosion, and they offer shelter to birds and insects that contribute the balance and harmony of the entire vineyard's ecosystem. Decades ago, they were present everywhere. Then they were removed to make way for mechanization. The fact they make vineyard work more difficult remains, but because we now understand their ecological value, they are being reintroduced.

This is a truly holistic kind of viticulture, where the vineyard is part of a larger whole. It is by enhancing the harmony of the whole that we will best secure the well-being of the vine.

Over the course of the next few years, a new approach to soil management may arise with the stronger understanding of what actually happens in the soil, and of what life in the soil actually means. The way I see it is this: in large-scale biology we have a very good knowledge of the species we can see, from whales right down to ants. But our knowledge of bacteria is much more limited; if you take one gram of soil (not a kilo, a gram) from a forest floor you will find around 4,000 different species of bacteria, 2,000 of fungus; in a field dedicated to agriculture there will be less, and from intensively farmed land the activity diminishes even further. If you were to put these three samples into a bucket of water, the intensively farmed soil would collapse, and fast, but the sample from the forest floor would keep its form.

We are only just on the eve of understanding what this means for the soil beneath our feet, but it undoubtedly points the way to a revolution that will touch the whole of agriculture. Bordeaux' viticulture is likely to benefit immensely from it. The old wisdom was to plough, plough and plough, but in terms of soil erosion, hydration and biological population (not least of earth worms) this no longer seems the right thing to do.

We should admit to the mistakes of the 1960s and 1970s, where chemicals were used far too abundantly in agriculture, and take a step back. They are not the solution to every problem. But the idea that every answer to today's challenges is to be found in history is also an illusion. Downscaling our reliance on chemicals in favour of a more traditional approach is unarguably a progress, but we should listen to today's science too.

REDUCTION OF CARBON FOOTPRINT

Bordeaux is famous for its beautiful châteaux and its continually renovated cellars. The fact that so much investment goes into building state-of-the-art wineries has been a tremendous advantage for the whole region. New equipment and techniques have helped push the limits of precision and purity in wine across the whole region – stainless steel, temperature-controlled vats and elevator tanks (to avoid pumps and pipelines) are to name but two. The restoration of valuable old techniques, such as gravity-based transfer systems – our only option before the advent of mechanical pumps – has also helped progress.

While advances in winemaking techniques will continue to be made with each newly built or renovated winery, the next frontier will be energy efficiency.

Sustainability is not just about how you run your vineyard, but also about your water and energy consumption in the winery.

How can we make temperature control, especially of barrel cellars with no stainless steel, more efficient? The use of geothermal (or ground source) energy is one good area of progress here. The earth's natural heat is sourced from below the ground-level and pumped to a compression unit, where it is converted to a higher temperature ready to heat the winery buildings and equipment naturally where necessary. The reverse happens when air-conditioning or cooling is required. Heat is extracted from the building and pumped into the earth. Energy savings of between 20 and 50 percent can be made this way.

And how can we reduce water consumption? Solutions abound and are not that complex to implement; collecting rainwater from the winery's roof and using it, is just one.

More advanced are the latest 'CIP' (clean in place) tanks which, using technology already adopted by the dairy, brewing and pharmaceutical industries, have in-built cleaning systems that distribute the exact amount of cleaning agent and water needed. No waste.

Carbon dioxide is also a major by-product of the fermentation process and the moves in place to capture and re-use it represent a giant step towards carbon neutrality in the wine industry. At châteaux Montrose and Smith Haut Lafitte, systems have been implemented that collect the CO_2 from fermentation and transform it into sodium bicarbonate, which then becomes a raw material for other industries (contributing to the production of everything from animal feed to cleaning agents and fire extinguishers).

This even paves the way for vineyards in Bordeaux to have a *negative* carbon footprint – more CO_2 being absorbed through photosynthesis and captured in the winery than is required to tend the vines and produce the wine. This is potentially a major breakthrough.

CONTINUITY OF STYLE AND IDENTITY

Lastly, the path to sustainability should include the protection of the style and identity of our wines. The potential solutions arising as we respond to climate change make this of particular importance.

We do not know what our climate will be in Bordeaux in 50 years' time, but we do, unfortunately, know that it will be different. It is likely that our region will continue to get warmer, and that there will be more extreme weather episodes, be they rain, heat or drought.

Will our vineyards continue to thrive under an altered climate? The answer is probably not. So we must adapt our vineyard canopy management and planting density accordingly.

Among the first to be certified biodynamic in Bordeaux, Château Palmer leads the way in research into the region's many soil types.

In the past, growers in Bordeaux would seek maximum sun exposure for their grapes to ensure optimal fruit ripening. In the 1990s, the leaf area was increased, to boost the vines' photosynthetic capacity. But we are now in the 2020s. If temperatures were to get much warmer, we would need to protect the grapes from a potentially scorching sun, and to reduce leaf area to reduce sugar (and therefore alcohol) production.

If drought episodes became more frequent, some producers would need to consider reducing their planting density in order to limit their vines' hydric stress.

But this is the kind of adaptation there always has been, and always should be.

Some experiments take a different route: that of using different vines or grape varieties to increase temperature tolerance and resistance to disease. Personally, however interesting they are in terms of pure research, I am wary of these options because of their unknown impact on the character and quality of our wine. As we all work to ensure our vineyards adapt to climate change, sustaining our identity should be the core consideration against which all possible modifications are tested.

Bordeaux is perceived first and foremost as a fine wine region. Even if only a small fraction of its production commands the high prices, the truest part of its image will always be based on the quality it provides.

Bordeaux has always altered its methods and evolved its approach. The varieties we used before the phylloxera crisis of the 1880s were in part different from those we use today, some of the grapes now forgotten. Forty years ago the production of white wine was substantially more important than it is today. Change is the essence of life. And Bordeaux will continue to change and adapt, maybe accepting a few new varieties as a small proportion of its blend.

But it would be easy to undermine our wines by going too far. The grapes we use today – the pillars among them Cabernet Sauvignon, Cabernet Franc and Merlot – are found to thrive in so many different countries, under such a broad spectrum of weather conditions, that I have every faith that they will continue to adapt and flourish with a changed climate in our region too.

Bordeaux wine is not an industrial product. It has a special, distinct identity. This identity is forged on a cultural and historical legacy. This identity is a large part of the *raison d'être* of the wines of Bordeaux. And this identity should be protected.

We don't yet know what an accepted standard of sustainability will be – there is no sustainability score to measure by. But Bordeaux is embracing all the new knowledge it can, and developing a critical awareness of techniques that reduce its carbon footprint – a footprint that we didn't know existed 20 years ago.

Joe Fattorini takes part in the annual Médoc Marathon – a 42-kilometre race through the vineyards of Pauillac, Saint-Julien, Saint-Estèphe and the Haut-Médoc – and finds the rarefied tranquillity of this historic region overwhelmed by 50 orchestras, 23 wine-bars, refreshment stations serving chilled oysters and beakers of Château Lafite, and 8,500 runners, mostly in fancy dress.

ONE MAD DAY IN THE MEDOC

Joe Fattorini (2020)

'When people interview my husband, they normally wear a tie.' Eva Barton is uncomfortable. I am about to interview her husband, Anthony Barton.'The kindest man in the Bordeaux wine business.' *Decanter* Man of the Year. An Anglo-French-Hibernian estate owner, known throughout the world for his integrity and the fair pricing of his wine.

It's true: I'm not wearing a tie. I'm wearing vivid blue Lycra shorts and a nylon vest. I'll admit I'm a bit uncomfortable standing in a grand room at Château Léoville-Barton, laid out with formal chairs and elegant tables. Eva is also concerned that anyone wearing stiletto heels might damage the beautiful floor. She checks everyone's shoes as they enter, holding a bag of stick-on coasters to apply to any harmful heels. My running trainers pass a sort of muster.

The only person not perturbed is Anthony Barton himself. 'No, neither Jancis Robinson nor Robert Parker have interviewed me wearing Lycra. You are the first.' Anthony had a nap after lunch and is on excellent form. Like many in their late eighties, he is less interested in what he did at eight this morning than what he did when he was eight. My sports clothes inspire memories of being a schoolboy at Stowe. Running, playing team games, being outdoors. Thousands of others would discover Anthony's wines through another near-contemporary at Stowe. Peter Sichel was older than Anthony, but his Blue Nun brand introduced wine to millions. Some would then go on to discover Léoville-Barton, as Anthony restored its reputation to that of its glory days in the 1940s.

Anthony is famous for making sure that his wine, Léoville-Barton, is among the best value of the great estates in Bordeaux. I ask if he ever regrets his decision to hold his prices in 1997, when others pushed them up. And in 2000, when others profited, and he held fast to his integrity. 'Perhaps I should have charged more. Then I might live more like my neighbours!' he laughs. We've not tasted, so this isn't *in vino veritas*. But as his fellow Irishman James Joyce wrote, this could be a case of *in risu veritas*: 'In laughter, truth.'

Anthony sits with his grandson, Damian Sartorius. The next generation. I'm interviewing his grandfather in running shorts because tomorrow is the annual Marathon du Médoc. And Damian and I will be running 26.4 miles, 42 kilometres, through the vineyards of Bordeaux, wearing fancy dress. Today I'm mixing interviewing Anthony with a leg-stretch jog. Damian is a keen runner and enters the marathon each year with a team of friends. This year's theme is 'Tales and Legends'. 'I wonder what my ancestors would have thought,' says Anthony, 'if they knew one of their descendants would be running through Bordeaux... dressed as a fairy'.

'Actually, I'll be dressed as one of Cinderella's valets,' Damian assures me later, as we walk through the beautiful gardens of the château. As good wine students know, the château itself is Langoa-Barton. Léoville is the sister property over the courtyard. We walk across and descend into the chill of the cellar. Like a lady in evening dress, I'm aware of the cold on my uncovered shoulders. Damian does not offer me his jacket. 'It will be warm tomorrow,' he warns me. I'll wish I'd listened.

First I'll continue this gentle jog with my running companion for the marathon. If I'm the drinker, Jamie Ramsay is the runner. He's a full-time adventurer and only just returned from 364 days of running from Buenos Aires to Vancouver. Jamie crossed the Andes twice, ran through deserts, tropical forest and the badlands of Central America. And did the whole thing without help, pushing all his belongings in a modified pram. He hasn't drunk any alcohol in over a year. Tomorrow he breaks his fast.

We meet up and jog around the grounds of Château d'Issan. I want to show Jamie some of the history we won't see on the marathon route, which starts and ends in Pauillac, snaking through Saint-Julien and Saint-Estèphe, but not quite reaching Margaux. It misses Château d'Issan, one of Bordeaux's true castles, surrounded by fortifications and even a moat. We jog through the estate and chat to the owner, Emmanuel Cruse. He explains that wine from these vineyards was served at the marriage of Eleanor of Aquitaine and Henry II (1152), the union that started the British love affair with claret. Emmanuel tells us of how – as Château Theobon – this was the site of the last stand of the English army in 1453, at the end of the Hundred Years War. And how the English fled to a nearby port with barrels of the 1453 vintage, and set sail home, never to return. Jamie and I are seduced by the romance of the château. *Regnum Mensis Arisque Deorum* it says, carved in stone over the main entrance. 'For the table of kings and the altars of the gods.'

Emmanuel suggests we continue our leg-stretching jog down to the river, to see where the English army loaded their ships and sailed away. We do: through the rushes and trees that protect the vines from the river winds. And out... not to a historic port, but a scruffy car park. There's an overflowing bin. And scorch marks from illegal bonfires. The light is flat and fading. Two men sit looking shifty in a car. 'They look like they've come here to go dogging,' says Jamie. Too late I remember Clive Coates MW's words: 'Château d'Issan's history is long, complex and has attracted much that is apocryphal.'

The next morning the light is glaring and the temperature rising. Pauillac fills with thousands of cheery runners, yet not one dressed as a runner. There are goblins and demons, fairies and wizards, trolls and dragons. Fancy dress is compulsory and everyone follows the rules. The atmosphere is unlike any marathon in the world. Groups dressed in themes stay together. Everyone takes pictures: of themselves, of each other, of themselves with others more peculiarly dressed than they are. Someone spots Pippa Middleton, sister of the Duchess of Cambridge. She slips into the crowd before anyone can photograph her. Some costumes are risqué. Some attempt to mimick sportswear. Some are plain daft.

I'm in the last category. I am Obi Wine Kenobi, a name the actor Matthew Rhys coined during the first series of *The Wine Show*. I've dressed accurately, with the four-layer

robes and belts of the Jedi knight in *Star Wars*. I'd have been quite cosy on the Ice Planet of Hoth, battling furry Wampas and riding round a snowy course on a Tauntaun lizard like Luke Skywalker in *The Empire Strikes Back*. But in Pauillac I'm already sweaty as the sun rises and Jamie and I make our way through the crowd for a suitable position to start running. The tension mounts. There's music and laughter and anticipation and loud-hailers whooping up the crowd in excitable French. Then 'BANG!' and we're off.

The first kilometre of the Marathon du Médoc is fabulous. High-fives, back-slapping, cheering, shared joy. The second kilometre involves asking yourself some quite serious questions about the life choice you made in a fancy-dress shop the previous week. Kilometres three to 42 are a series of long and distressing answers to those questions.

If I'd bothered to look at the map before setting off, I'd see that the route starts in the streets of Pauillac. We head immediately south to Bages, Saint-Lambert, Dauprat and on to Saint-Julien-Beychevelle. At about seven kilometres we pass the gates of Léoville- and Langoa-Barton before turning inland for another seven to Château Belgrave. There, the marathon heads north, running through the vineyards and courtyards of ever-grander names until it climbs to Marbuzet, Layssac and into Saint-Estèphe. Then through châteaux Phélan-Ségur and Meyney, it turns south, to a long, tedious, flat, dull road without interest or charm along the coast until, almost without warning, you're back in Pauillac.

To be honest, it's not a marathon you can train for. As my friend Brett explained in an email, there are 'three key aspects unique to the Médoc Marathon irresponsibly overlooked by modern marathon training programmes:

1 You run on a mixture of hard asphalt roads and rough gravelly vineyard terrain.

2 You are offered wine to quench your thirst while running for extended periods.

3 The dry salted crackers, breadsticks, nuts, oysters, cheese and grilled beef that will be on offer at aid stations are well established as suboptimal nutrition for distance running.'

And he's right. It's a trail run more than a road run. On 23 separate occasions you do the one thing that's universally advised against when running a marathon – you have a glass of wine. And the food on offer is generally what you'd expect at a gallery opening.

In every possible way, it's fabulously French. Nobody completes the Marathon du Médoc. Most just about survive it. Here are my notes:

Kilometre 1: Château Grand-Puy Ducasse

Attractive depth of Cabernet fruit. Much laughter at the grander wines to come. But a fifth growth worth revisiting if you haven't tried it in a while. I explain to Jamie what a 'luncheon claret' is.

Early on I realized that I was in a terrible outfit. By the second kilometre and Château Croizet-Bages (another fifth growth – no tasting) I was already dripping. Jamie looked concerned. He'd spent the last year running in deserts and knew the damage the heat could cause. But to be honest, he was loving the wine.

Kilometre 3: Château Lynch-Bages

Ahhh – an old friend. Always a big hit in the UK, and why not? Even with all that Cabernet, it's so soft and approachable. Quite thirsty already, so a decent draught.

There's a rivulet of sweat in my bottom. This doesn't bode well. We pass by Château Haut-Bages-Liberal (I explain to Jamie that this is another excellent luncheon claret) before we arrive at...

Kilometre 4: Châteaux Pichon-Lalande and Pichon-Baron

I'm out of breath at this point. Unfortunately, Jamie isn't. He wants to know (a) why the names are so similar, (b) what is a 'super-second' and (c) if they're only over the road why would they taste so different? The answers I manage are roughly (a) it's complicated, (b) I'll explain on the way to Saint-Julien and (c) Merlot. Much more Merlot in Château Pichon-Longueville Comtesse de Lalande.

By this stage the field is thinning out. We pause for a photograph in front of Château Pichon-Baron. There are larks and holding up glasses and waving light sabres. Then we spot another *Star Wars* character: a woman wearing an R2-D2 minidress. We ask if she could join our picture and she agrees. Lots more laughing. Turns out she's British and

we chat. Then panic. We've been here too long, and a group arrives pulling the cart that indicates the back of the field. Drop behind that and we risk being dropped out of the marathon. We are now last. So we drain our glasses and hare off to Saint-Julien.

Kilometre 9.5: Château Beychevelle

Extraordinary château with grand, sweeping architecture, and a glass of its rich, ripe wine.

Kilometre 12.5: Château Gruaud-Larose

A wine with firmer, tannic grip. As we jog on, I tell Jamie a story about my friend John Graves. Now a wine merchant, he was once a rock star who played Glastonbury. On his final tour he remembered a night drinking Gruaud-Larose backstage when one of the support act came in – a singer called Damon Albarn from an unknown band called Blur.

Somewhere between Château Lagrange (Kilometre 14.5) and Château Belgrave (Kilometre 15.5) I start to shed my outfit. First the weaponry. Then the cloak. Then the under-jacket. Then a complex arrangement of belts. Then the trousers. Lagrange is the largest single estate in Bordeaux. Somewhere in a bin alongside its vines is a light sabre (a far cry from the sabres of the medieval owners of Maison Noble de Lagrange Monteil). The Lagrange was attractive, weighty and structured. The Belgrave a welcome relief. Say what you like about Michel Rolland, wines influenced by his sleek and softening touch are extraordinarily pleasant when you're a third of the way round a marathon.

Kilometre 17: Château Larose-Trintaudon

A pleasant, fresh, forward claret, 14/20. Then 10, steady, dry kilometres. In the villages of Artigues, La Poulayet and Mousset we catch up some of the time we lost before. People are starting to look tired. Inhibitions are breaking down. Jamie and I need a pee. But we're in a vineyard and, well, there's not been a sign of a loo for an hour. But the vines are in full leaf, and perpendicular to the road. So we dive in. Ten metres in we stand back-to-back and... well, you know the drill. Except we're not alone. On Jamie's side are several

Norwegian Smurfs with the same idea. On my side Maid Marion is squatting discreetly two rows away. I avert my eyes.

The châteaux tick by. And potted histories make for distracting jog-chat. Château Batailley, and how it came to be a favourite of the British. Lynch-Moussas ('I don't think I've ever had it'), Grand-Puy-Lacoste ('1981, *en magnum*, at a Paulée lunch in the Yorkshire Dales'), Pibran ('a surprise birthday present in the 1990s'), Pontet-Canet ('a generous aunt bought me a case of 1981 for my 21st birthday... all gone now') and Mouton Rothschild ('a generous uncle bought me a case of the 1983 for my 21st birthday... all gone now').

Kilometre 30: Château Lafite Rothschild

We turn left into Lafite's grand drive and a bedraggled group snakes up to the château. To our right, in the ornamental lake, several runners have stripped off and are having a swim. Like the Dionysian maenads, the runners rave – this is the one day on which inhibitions in Bordeaux can relax and ecstasy is allowed a free rein. We crowd round the tables serving Duralex beakers of Lafite Rothschild. But not everyone who runs the Marathon du Médoc is a wine expert. One woman tells her friends she'll pass on this one. 'I want to pace myself... I've had enough.' As luck would have it, Jamie and I have caught up with Damian Sartorius, Anthony Barton's grandson. Indeed, he is not dressed as a fairy.

Although in pink short-shorts and snug vest he's no valet either. His friend is dressed as Cinderella in a white gown and luxuriant beard. This gives him the impression of Conchita Wurst, the Austrian transgender winner of the 2014 Eurovision Song Contest. I introduce the non-drinking lady to Damian. And ask provocatively how the wines of Château Lafite Rothschild compare in price to his own. Less than a minute later she's elbowing her way to the front of the crowd for her first taste of Château Lafite Rothschild.

We set off again, this time with Cinderella and her valets. You leave the gates of the château, trot over the small brook that divides Pauillac from Saint-Estèphe and then face the one significant climb on the course. A steady incline up to Château Cos d'Estournel. Cinderella hares off up the hill, shouting 'Chase me! Chase me!' with a coquettish skip. Saint-Estèphe doesn't seem so austere now.

The course climbs up a lumpy, bumpy track, at the top of which we have a glass of Cos Labory. Then châteaux Le Crock and Haut-Marbuzet ('the first claret I sold as a young merchant'), Pomys, La Haye, Marquis de St-Estèphe, Laffitte Carcasset, Tronquoy Lalande, Phélan-Ségur. There are more and more first-aid stations. And I start to wonder if I'll need one. My legs are cramping. Horribly cramping. I've started to adopt a sort of hobbled jog and have to ask Jamie if we can walk for a section. But he's keen to push on.

Kilometre 35.5: Château Meyney

'I had a case of this for my 21st too… another 1982. Yes, I suppose I was already a keen wine fan,' I tell Jamie confidently. Secretly, I'm feeling quite ill.

Kilometre 37: Château Montrose

We run into Ronan Sayburn MS, the head of wine at 67 Pall Mall, the private members club for wine lovers in London. I've known Ronan for years but never seen him like this. He looks both comical and dreadful. It's not only the Robin Hood hat and green tunic; the heat has got to him as much as me. We both put on a brave face. We trot (hobble) into the courtyard of the château and have one final glass of wine. Even now, it's delicious.

There are five kilometres to go. Five long, boring, tedious, flat, featureless kilometres. Well, not quite featureless. The roadside is alive. There's a stall serving oysters, then a band, another band, and yet another band, a first-aid station working full-tilt, another band, a stall serving beef (you didn't feel like oysters and you really don't feel like beef) then there's another band and corn-on-the-cob (a challenging dish for the runner) another band, some cheese – seriously, only the French would insist on a cheese course in a marathon – another band, chocolate (the biliousness rising now), ice cream, an impressive array of road-side vomits, one more band and… turn the corner… it's the finish line.

The cut-off for the Marathon du Médoc is six-and-a-half hours. This is the target time. Any longer and you didn't run enough. Any quicker and you didn't drink enough. Jamie and I cross in six hours and 27 minutes. Hardly the Kipchoge of marathon times.

Up to now I've left out one important detail from the story. All this time, Jamie and I are being filmed for television. At Léoville-Barton. Through d'Issan. At the start line and all along the route, there have been cameramen on motorbikes and positioned along the roadside. Maybe 100 million people will see this. It turns out fear of shame is a motivator. I couldn't stop. It would be forever on camera. I couldn't vomit. Not in High Definition. Or pass out, give in, start to cry. But now we've crossed the line. Jamie and I have hugged and celebrated. We've given our reactions to the imaginary, anonymous person who sits like Hal in *2001: A Space Odyssey*, just behind the polished lends of the camera. That lens is now packed away. The tripod is back in its tube. The cameramen are having a beer.

It's time for my body to go into a devastating collapse. Suddenly I'm writhing on the floor in agony. The cramps in my legs boil and throw themselves into agonizing spasms. Jamie helps me to my feet. I quickly collapse back on the floor. The pain is searing, needle-sharp, all-consuming. I try drinking furiously. Nothing makes a difference.

Jamie and the team help me to a hospital tent. Like something from the Crimea but filled with moaning elves and wizards. And Florence Nightingale is wearing a hi-vis vest. I can hardly be pinned to the table. A *pompier* called Francis comes over and starts kneading my spasming calves like a particularly challenging loaf. You can see each muscle fibre roiling under my skin as if an alien is about to give birth. Francis is joined by a GP. She looks jaded. How many idiots has she treated before me? She kneads the other leg mercilessly. A nurse gives my friend Melanie a tray of raisins and instructs her to feed them to me. It's the best way of getting minerals back in my bloodstream that have been sweated out into a woollen Jedi knight costume, now abandoned in the corner of a vineyard far away. I scream. 'I've never heard a man make a noise like that,' says Mel. And then stop screaming. 'It was when you went silent that I really became worried,' she says later. Eventually the GP and Francis manage to insert an intravenous drip into each arm, and they squeeze me back to life.

C'est magnifique, mais n'est pas un marathon. The hospital tent turns the wounded into the walking. Within minutes of their magic massage and several litres of fluid, I'm out with the other casualties, warmly shaking Francis the *pompier* and the GP by the hand.

For 364 days a year, Bordeaux is serious, erudite and historic. For one day it is bizarre, irresponsible and comic. On that day, for almost six-and-a-half hours, you'll learn the topography by heart as you struggle up it and roll down it. You'll feel the warmth of inland Médoc and the breeze of the coast road. You'll twist ankles across the gravel of one vineyard. And shake the weight of the clay from your trainers in the next. You'll see Alice leave Wonderland to wee in the vines. And spy a living centaur striking attitudes in the fountain of Lafite. And you'll smile every time you drink Bordeaux again.

CHAPTER THREE

TALES OF THE ARISTOCRACY

A glimpse into the exalted worlds of Bordeaux' premier châteaux.

Cyril Ray (1985)
Château Lafite Rothschild

Hugh Johnson (2020)
Château Latour

Nicholas Faith (1980)
Château Margaux

Cyril Ray (1980)
Château Mouton Rothschild

Gerald Asher (1996)
Château Haut-Brion

Neal Martin (2012/2020)
Château Petrus

David Peppercorn MW (1991)
Château Ausone

Edmund Penning-Rowsell (1979)
Château Cheval Blanc

James Seely (1998)
Château d'Yquem

Cyril Ray (1908–91), the whip-smart editor of wine's *Compleat Imbiber*, charts the early career of Baron Eric de Rothschild, 'The Hand at the Helm' at Château Lafite from 1974 until 2018, and one of the family's most influential curators during its 150-year history at the property.

CHATEAU LAFITE ROTHSCHILD

Cyril Ray (1985)

We saw in the previous chapter how Eric de Rothschild – if we may so refer to one as yet unborn – escaped with his mother and his baby sister, Beatrice, from Lafite to Spain, South America and eventually the United States, where he was born in 1940. By this time his father, Alain, was in an officer's prisoner-of-war camp in Germany: Eric had been conceived, it now amuses him to say, not all that long before, 'in a hit-and-run leave from the Maginot Line'. (Eric's mother was born – in 1916 – a Gentile of a noble French family: she converted to Judaism on marriage and became, says her son, 'a very good Yiddisher momma'. Eric's wife (*see* page 64) also converted.

It was Alain's first letter to his wife from the camp that caused the infant to be named Eric. Before the war, Alain had been given a fine pair of binoculars by his close friend and fellow-yachtsman, Eric Warburg of Hamburg; in the battle after which Alain was taken prisoner the glasses had deflected to his upper arm a German bullet that might very well have found heart or lung. (Eric Warburg had left Germany in 1936, and was one of the United States Air Force officers who liberated Alain and Elie[1] from the camp at Lübeck in 1945.)

The boy named, as it were, after a pair of German binoculars lived in the United States until 1948. By which time, I gather, his parents were so concerned by the way the inheritor of a great name and heir to an urbane tradition was growing into a kind of latter-day Mickey Rooney that he was packed off to an English prep school, Hawtrey's, as a sort of halfway house between American sub-teenage anarchy and French civilization. To have gone straight from the United States to France, he says now, would have been 'too

[1] Alain and his younger brother Elie de Rothschild were captured by the Germans and held prisoner (Elie at Colditz Castle) for much of World War II. Their separate escape attempts led them to be transferred to Lübeck, one of the toughest POW camps.

In the latter part of his Lafite tenure, but with the famous dress code and boyish glint still apparent, Baron Eric de Rothschild.

much of a cultural shock'. That is no doubt to tease American friends: if it is an English guest he is chaffing he says instead that to send him to an English prep school was the surest way to get him eventually to love France. In fact, he is as international in his outlook, and as unchauvinistic, as only a Rothschild or a European royal can be.

Hawtrey's sends most of its boys to Eton, and Eric might well, at first meeting, be taken for one educated at a good English school – he has the ease of manner, the unaffected accent, the turn of phrase and the taste for dry understatement. He might have been born, not in NY but in SW1, or the shires. Only the occasional fumble for the right word, as words tumble out (he speaks quickly), reminds one that French, not English, is his mother tongue. He smiles easily, makes jokes and laughs at those of others.

From Hawtrey's, though, he was sent to read mathematics and engineering in France and in Zurich (where, I have no doubt, he also learned, or perfected, his German) before entering the bank where, he says, without either conceit or false modesty, that he did well in trading and in running transport until the Rothschild bank was nationalized in February 1982, as the 'Européenne de Banque'. (There being no restriction on the establishment of new banks, Eric and his cousin David then set up a merchant bank, the Paris-Orléans Banque. It is early days, as these words are written, but there is no doubt that Eric has more time for Lafite than his uncle Elie[2] had, and may well continue to have it – or, I am sure, to make time.)

One finds it clear, in talking to him and his team at Lafite, that he finds administration and what I suppose one must call, these days, man management both fascinating and easy, even though this may sometimes seem to be belied by what would appear to be a boyish impulsiveness. In spite of the slight fleck of grey in the thick wavy hair (as to colour it is what my wife calls 'English mouse', and she ought to know), his appearance and manner, indeed, are boyish. He is usually careless about clothes, sometimes playful – commonly to be seen in a shapeless double-breasted corduroy suit, and at one time, in the evenings at Lafite, in Asquith's privy councillor's black velvet coat, heaven knows how acquired, gaping at the seams and with some of the cut-steel buttons missing, until Jo Grimond, Asquith's grandson-in-law, a weekend guest, reclaimed it for the family. And I have seen him (felt him, damn it...) bring to a juddering halt the rattly Deux Chevaux van he was driving along Pauillac's broad riverside avenue to leap out for a paper cornet of shrimps that had just caught his eye and his fancy – and then forget all about them when we got back to the château.

He remained a bachelor until December 1983, when he was almost 44, marrying Donna Maria-Beatrice Caracciolo di Forino, of a ducal Neapolitan family, who converted, as Eric's mother had done, to Judaism[3].

Save that he is similarly tall, Eric could hardly look less like the Wellington-nosed Elie, 'probably the fiercest, most imperious family member since the first Lord Rothschild', as Frederic Morton described him in 1963. If, as I have reason to suspect, he shares with his uncle a substantial measure of Rothschild impatience with fools and their folly, it is better concealed or more tightly controlled. They differ in other ways: Elie is or at any rate was, a horseman of the highest class – he lost an eye in a polo field mishap when he was already in his 50s. Eric is immensely keen on stalking and walking: he does both in Canada and in Austria, as well as in France, and has a shoot – and maintains a distinguished cellar – in Scotland. He has a cultivated taste in music and in painting.

[2] Elie de Rothschild managed Lafite Rothschild from 1946 to 1974.

[3] The Caraccioli, according to the *Encyclopedia Italiana*, are probably the oldest of the Neapolitan noble families. The family gives its name to the splendid Naples esplanade between the 18th-century Municipal Gardens and the sea, sweeping westward from the Castel dell' Oro. Its most famous member was the duke, Francesco Caracciolo, commodore in the Royal Neapolitan Navy, hanged in 1799 in a British flagship in circumstances that reflect badly on Horatio Nelson's humanity and good faith.

A characteristic highly relevant to the theme of this book is not only a strong sense of duty but a keen enjoyment in carrying it out. How did it come about, I asked, that he took over the management of Lafite? 'Uncle Elie told me to, and French Rothschilds do as they are told.' I do not know, nor did I care to ask, whether he specified French Rothschilds to distinguish them from a disobedient branch of English Rothschilds, or to indicate simply that he spoke only for his own immediate family and was not competent to judge others....

There is no questioning the enthusiasm with which he has embraced his duties at Lafite – an enthusiasm that goes far beyond the pleasure he takes in exercising his administrative skills. I became used, after a day or so in his company, to his speaking seriously – though often with a smile, and sometimes, to make a point, with a joke – about politics or the wine trade, or what he calls the philosophy behind his expansionist policy for the Domaines Barons de Rothschild, but all this was from the head. The one occasion I heard him speak feelingly, from the heart, was one evening, relaxed after dinner (at which Beatrice and he and I had drunk, but sparingly, some great vintage of Lafite, a bottle between three of us of I know not what year, though Eric would remember) about wine, and not about Lafite in particular.

He was surprised and, I think – I am sure – disappointed in me when I had to say no to his question. Had I never felt, if only once in years, *necessarily* only once in years, the same sort of excitement, the sense of awe, even, over a particular bottle of a particular wine of a particular year that, seldom enough in a lifetime, one felt before one picture by, say Cézanne, or hearing one particular singer lift one out of oneself with one particular aria that one may well have heard often enough before?

I had to say that although I enjoyed a good wine more than an indifferent one, not even a glass of what I knew to be the greatest could move me as a great painting might, a line of poetry, or a well-turned piece of prose – that I inclined more to the view expressed by Elie, which I quote in full later in this book (*see* page 272) – that the best way to treat claret is to draw the cork and lap it up. I think that Eric was sorry for me – and for Elie.

Excerpt first published as 'The Hand at the Helm', chapter VII of *Lafite, The Story of Château Lafite* by Cyril Ray, Christie's Wine Publications (London) 1985, reprinted here with kind permission from Cyril's son, Jonathan Ray.

Hugh Johnson shares memories of his time on the board at Château Latour – of irresistible vintages, fine menus, venturous gardening opportunities, and of touring New York and Japan with the proprietors of the illustrious first growths. But there were torrid times too, when money spoke more loudly than wine...

CHATEAU LATOUR

Hugh Johnson (2020)

Perhaps Lafite can claim more glamour, Margaux more romance, Haut-Brion more history, but Latour has always had a sort of solid, noble dignity. You could describe it as Saintsbury described Hermitage: 'manly'. Its wines start life rough-hewn, uncompromising, unsmiling. When a smile eventually emerges it is no chummy twinkle, more the revealing of a considered beneficence. You feel privileged that such a stern authority should bestow such warmth on you.

That was my impression of Château Latour as a claret lover who had rarely tasted it. Each encounter had confirmed the feeling that it stood apart. Comparisons didn't really work. You might say (rarely) that Lafite (or Latour) had had a more successful year, but not that it had made a better wine. Lafite has never made a better Latour, or vice versa; could Judi Dench do a better Maggie Smith?

When in 1986 I was invited to join the Latour board, the Conseil de Gérance, I was quite unprepared; delighted, of course, but apprehensive. What could I bring to the party? The de Beaumont family, inheritors from the 'Prince des Vignes', the Marquis de Ségur, in the 18th century, had sold the majority of their holding in 1963 to what was described as 'Lord Cowdray's interests'. Cowdray was chairman of the Pearson family's business (which included the *Financial Times*). The Pearsons arranged for a quarter of the shares to go to Harvey's of Bristol, then one of Britain's major wine merchants. They appointed David Pollock, a board member, as president of the Société Civile de Château Latour. It was the de Beaumonts who had coined the notion of the 'Société Civile' in 1842, as a means of protecting themselves from the obligation to divide their inheritance. The de Beaumonts still held an important share and were represented on the board by Comte Philippe de B.

David Pollock was the first British chairman, overseeing a huge investment to bring the property into the 20th century. He was succeeded by Clive Gibson, another Pearson family member, who was succeeded as president by the Hon Alan Hare, again a family

Latour's château stands sentinel at the southern edge of Pauillac, marking the border with Saint-Julien, a change in soil type and a profound difference in the character of the wines.

member and retired chairman of the *FT*. It was he who invited me, out of the blue, to lunch one day at White's, his St James's Club (and the grandest of all). Would I join the board, for a modest fee, my reasonable expenses and an annual allowance of wine? I didn't hesitate, though I was overcome with a feeling of déja vu. Alan's elder brother, John, Viscount Blakenham, had given me lunch at the next table 10 years before to pop another question: would I join the publications committee of the Royal Horticultural Society, of which he was treasurer, to advise on the society's journal?

When the de Beaumont clan sold Latour in 1963 the word on the street was that it was in a bad way and needed serious investment. On my first visit there Monsieur Brugière, then *régisseur*, had shown me round the shuttered château. I remember the peeling wallpaper with the flower prints of a maid's bedroom. Apparently Comte Hubert de Beaumont, on his rare visits, slept on a camp bed. The equipment in the *chai* looked as old; the vines, of course, were ageing, too.

When people say what improvements the British brought I smile. Latour had just produced two of the greatest vintages of the century, 1959 and 1961, with a very respectable 1960 in between and an excellent 1962. So much for decline. The shareholders in reality were hugging themselves. They had never seen such prices, the property was worth many times their previous estimation – but was desperately in need of investment. There were scores of shareholders, mainly members of the related de Beaumont and de Courtivron families. They had the most predictable reason to sell: reluctance to see dividends consumed by capital investment.

1963 was not a propitious start for the new regime. The weather was dismal. Latour struggled to keep up its reputation (generally deserved) for making a respectable wine in a poor year. 1964 was crucial. Pearson's had made a huge investment. The old oak vats had gone; stainless steel now glittered in the *cuverie*. Only Haut-Brion, of all the first growths, had braved this radical step before. But it was not just the equipment; Pearson's had already bought more land and buildings and set about restoring the vital drainage required for the whole vineyard. The summer was fine, the grapes ripening well, when weather warnings came in from the Atlantic. Latour was taking no risks and started to pick, while other châteaux were still contemplating what the government had already called The Vintage of the Century. The rain started on October 8th and didn't stop for three weeks. (I was holed up at Château Loudenne.) Of the top châteaux, only Latour and Montrose picked early enough to escape the deluge.

THE MOST MODEST OF CHATEAUX

The little château of Latour is really nothing of the kind. It's a courtesy title for a bourgeois house that would hardly be noticed in one of the smarter Paris suburbs. The de Beaumonts had largely ignored it, but to the new English owners it was their HQ, and above all their place to entertain. A London decorator was let loose, and within the awkward confines of a building with too much symmetry and not enough space, contrived a cosy salon, a study and a dining room with red walls, big enough for a party 10 or so. The front door leads into a narrow hall that goes straight through to the garden door and steps down to a potential place to eat outside – something then considered eccentric, even risky, in France. Upstairs there are four main bedrooms, of which the yellow room, facing the river, became a familiar home to the Johnsons. The most important room, the kitchen, is beside the dining room, above a surprisingly modest wine cellar. But then the *chai*, with its stock of 50-odd vintages, is only a short walk away through the vines.

Alan and Jill Hare were gracious and cheerful hosts who kept a steady procession of variegated guests flowing through the house and enjoying the admittedly limited amenities of the estate: vines, *chai*, a walk down to the River Gironde, the meadow where a few cows passed their uneventful time while the brown tide, a mile or so wide, criss-crossed to and fro twice a day. There was usually a ship in sight, but rarely a big or beautiful one. Jill Hare was an enthusiastic gardener and soon pressed me, with my gardening knowledge gleaned from 10 years of scribbling, to offer my opinion. There was a great deal that simply needed clearing away.

The little garden at the foot of the garden steps was entirely cut off from the world, the vineyards and the view of the river, by a three-metre hedge, presumably to screen privileged guests from the eyes of the vineyard toilers. Watching others toil, though, as some guests remarked, is a privilege and pleasure. The hedge went, and toilers could enjoy the sight of guests being pampered. North of the château, too many trees totally shaded a slightly larger garden whose central feature was a henhouse. Deciding which of a mixed bag of spindly trees to fell was not easy, but the end result was satisfying. Then came a plan for a little garden *à la Française* – while out in the landscape we took a saw to all sorts of unfortunate choices.

It was perhaps not surprising that someone had thought the appropriate tree to plant as a screen to the tractor sheds in the middle of the view was one with red leaves; worse, one of those maroon-dyed cherry plums of suburbia that have an early moment of pink blossom, then grow more and more funereal as the year goes on. They had to go, to be

The iconic tower, or *pigeonnier*, at Château Latour is said to be all that remains of an important fortress, built during the 'English period' to prevent pirates and marauding French from reaching the lower reaches of the Gironde. The rest of the fortress was destroyed in the battles that led to the expulsion of the English in 1453.

replaced by proper trees: mainly the indigenous ash that peoples the riverbanks. There were many more alterations and eliminations to simplify the prospect and make sure that it was the vine-rows that became the centre of attention. One idea I stole from Château Lafite, where Elie de Rothschild had planted a row of weeping willows along the main road to half-screen the chateau. I planted half a dozen weeping willows by the back gate, on the little road north of the vineyard. Today they are quite impressive trees.

CREATORS OF THE MODERN LATOUR

The Pearsons had wisely chosen two prominent Médocains to run the property, selected for their experience and practical advice: Jean-Paul Gardère and Henri Martin, mayor of Saint-Julien and creator of the outstanding new Saint-Julien cru bourgeois, Château Gloria. The old family was represented by the gracious but modest Philippe de Beaumont.

Jean-Paul became *régisseur*, the Bordeaux term for agent, steward or manager, in a long line of famous figures who had done the château's business for 300 years. His humble origins as the son of a resin-tapper in the pine forests had not stopped him becoming one of the most respected brokers in Bordeaux. With him he had brought his own business, Ulysse Cazabonne, which became a major player in the sales of Bordeaux.

The British team were Alan Hare, Harry Waugh and I. Harry could be called the creator of modern Latour. As the presiding genius of Harvey's of Bristol he made the great decisions on how to run the estate, and directed the necessary – and vast – investments. Harry was generally considered one of Britain's (and the world's) great authorities on claret, besides being universally loved for his personality. It was he who opened up the American market, obsessed as it then was with Rothschild wines, to Latour, meeting wine lovers and giving tastings all over the country. He even found time to introduce Beaujolais to Britain. Why was I recruited? It's not for me to say.

If Harry was dynamic in business he was also the epitome of the old-school wine trade: he simply would not have understood the modern obsession with adjectives, let alone scores. A Harry tasting note would be: 'Good colour; bright. Quite aromatic. Good body. Nice wine. Perhaps a bit like the '66. That would be nice.' When he was in his 80s he was in a car accident that shut down his sense of smell. His acute sense of taste and texture somehow took over. Knowing that it was Latour he was tasting, he would hand the glass to Pru, his wife, to sniff, and take her word for it that there were no surprises. He assessed the weight, ripeness, acidity and tannins on his palate. There was no fooling him.

The board met alternately in London and at the château. We heard reports on the weather, progress in the vineyard, activities in the cellar, the vital figures of yield: how many bottles of *grand vin*, how many of Les Forts de Latour, and how many were relegated to mere Pauillac de Latour, or disposed of 'in the trade'. 1986 was my first vintage. The directors tasted regularly with the *maître de chai* and the *chef de culture*. I remember tasting the wine of this unremarkable vintage that had been excluded and protesting that it was surely worth bottling. To me it had the unique Latour flavour, if not in abundance. Some of it became Pauillac de Latour, with a simple printer's label, no embossing or gold. I gave some bottles to friends in England, and never really expected to see the wine again. Thirty years later, one of them brought a bottle to an opera picnic at Garsington. I was amazed to see it, and opened it without high expectations. It was firm, forthright, even fresh, certainly losing its fruit but unmistakably a Latour. Class will out.

PERFECT CONVIVIALITY

Lunches and dinners in the château were memorable. All of them. We had the best chef in the Médoc, the quietly genial Bruno. He welcomed us into his kitchen to watch his endlessly painstaking operations. It was here that I learned the difference between cooking and cuisine. The deliberate construction of flavours and textures that might pass as simple at table, were irresistibly delicious to eat, but never existed in nature, is surely France's unique contribution to civilization. I will quote one of Bruno's menus for an 'ordinary' dinner, on October 4th 1990: *Roulade de saumon aux crevettes*, with Puligny-Montrachet Les Champs Gains 1986, *Selle d'agneau rôtie au romarin, pommes sautées*, Les Forts de Latour 1979, *Fromages*, Château Latour 1959, *Framboises à la crème*. We normally started with a glass of champagne, often Pol Roger, had either a glass of white Graves (more rarely burgundy) or a light vintage of Les Forts with the first course, then often two vintages of the *grand vin*, one a well-known one and one from a 'lesser' or neglected year – which rarely failed to be much better than we expected.

Regular guests at lunch or dinner parties often included the remarkably few proprietors of great châteaux who actually lived on their properties. Anthony and Eva Barton from Langoa, of course, Jean-Eugène and Monique Borie of Ducru-Beaucaillou, Christian Moueix, and sometimes the man we considered the prince, duke or whatever is appropriate of Saint-Emilion, Thierry Manoncourt of Château Figeac and his wife, Marie-France. Sometimes Martin Bamford would come down from Château Loudenne. We had excellent company. Indeed, the vibe of Latour was not unlike an English country house party with (much) better food and a fabulous cellar.

There were visits to neighbouring châteaux, of course, and once we went up in a helicopter to inspect the vineyards from above. We had a shock. In many famous properties (this was in the 1980s) the vine rows visible from roads, or from next door, were full of healthy vines. But parts of the hidden centre were virtually bald, with more than half the vines missing. Yield quoted as 'per hectare' would be very far off the mark.

There were Latour escapades abroad, too: tastings in New York (one in 2000 ranged back over 25 vintages to the famous pair of 1899 and 1900, each 'flight' matched by a dish cooked by Daniel Boulud); in San Francisco, and the most memorable of all, one in Tokyo when I persuaded the proprietors of 'Les Cinq', all the Bordeaux first growths, plus Château Yquem, to invade Japan together.

We had all met at the New York Wine Experience, an annual circus run by Marvin Shanken of the *Wine Spectator* in a hotel in Times Square, a gloomy block rather like (I imagine) Sing Sing. Shanken's public belong to the cohort who want the best, and want it now. So no mere cellar masters or marketing directors pouring the samples, it had to be His or Her Nibs themselves: Eric and Philippine, Corinne and La Duchesse de Mouchy (*pictured below*). David Orr as president represented Latour. I was a consultant to Jardines in Japan at the time, and suggested, over a mediocre hotel coffee, that we could have much more fun in Tokyo. To my surprise, all five of them liked the idea. The first growths had never been on tour before, but we ended up in Tokyo and (by bullet train) Osaka, flown by British Airways, hosted by Seiji Tsutsumi, the François Pinault of Japan (who

The five first growths tour Tokyo: (*right to left*) Eric de Rothschild of Château Lafite Rothschild, host Seiji Tsutsumi, David Orr of Château Latour, Philippine de Rothschild of Château Mouton Rothschild, Monsieur Petit (first husband of Corinne Mentzelopoulos, Château Margaux) and Joan Duchesse de Mouchy of Château Haut-Brion.

was also a famous author and poet), tasting the best vintages from the biggest bottles with guests who included violinists and sumo wrestlers, the cultural gratin of Japan. There was one precaution: we never tasted the same vintage of two different châteaux. Comparisons are odious (to proprietors, that is).

FACING HARD FACTS

Alan, our much-loved president, retired in 1990, ill, alas, with cancer. His successor came from the heart of the wine trade with decades of practical experience and a different approach. David Orr had spent years in Portugal and Spain running Cockburns, then been managing director of Harvey's of Bristol. I've never quite kept abreast of the various takeovers that plagued the wine trade in the 1980s and 1990s. The 'Hiram Walker Group' merged with Allied Vintners and took David to New York and California. He ran Frederick Wildman's importing business in New York and, among other wineries, Clos du Bois in California. Judy and I had known him and Susan, his wife, for years. Jean-Paul Gardère retired sometime afterwards, to be replaced by Christian Le Sommer, not the son of the soil Jean-Paul had been, but a bright and competent manager who has since seen service as a consultant with the Rothschilds' domaines in France and South America.

My memory is poor on the precise dates of staff changes, but when Christian came we were also looking for a commercial director. I had just visited the thriving co-op at Saint-Emilion, Royal Saint-Emilion, and been shown around by the manager, John Kolasa: I was so impressed by this Hiberno-Frenchman that I proposed his name for an interview. Christian and John made a harmonious team; they stayed at Latour until the great change of regime in 1993.

The part of the board meetings that interested me least was the financial. I remember being surprised to be told that a yield of 2.5 percent on capital was considered a good result. Each meeting made a decision on the dividend going to the shareholders. Even a fraction of a share (which many had) seemed to me a pretty desirable asset. Things changed radically when the major shareholder became a public company. Hiram Walker took a different view from personal investors. As I understand the situation, questions were asked (presumably) by investment managers about why the company was bothering with such a non-core little business as a French wine estate when the profits from its usual distilling businesses were on a different scale. The instruction came down from on high that we (the Conseil de Gérance) had to find a buyer for our priceless first growth. It was raining that morning. For some reason the directors were in a minibus out in the vineyard. Michael Blakenham was with us; he was Alan Hare's nephew and at this time on the board; it was he who broke the news. We, the *conseil*, immediately instructed Lazard Frères, the Paris bank that did Pearson's business, to come up with a shortlist of possible buyers within two weeks. In strictest secrecy. Next morning it was on the front page of *Le Figaro*.

The likeliest buyer turned out to be the two Wertheimer brothers, who own Chanel – and much else. Negotiations began, and dragged on. They would pay for the château, then the vines (I don't remember the precise detail), the stock, the new wine… in instalments. Did they not realize that opportunities to buy first growths come up once in a generation? While they negotiated, François Pinault made up his mind. He (or rather his company, Artemis) would pay the asking price at the end of the week. The deal was done.

As a postscript, David Orr advised the disappointed Wertheimers that if they couldn't have a first growth there was a splendid second growth also going cheap. Château Rausan-Ségla in Margaux had been in the doldrums for years. Perhaps it lacked the status of Latour, but the potential of its vineyards had been proved ever since it was founded, as close to Château Margaux as possible, in the 17th century. The Wertheimers bought it, and shrewdly took on David as *gérant*. David in turn brought John Kolasa on board, and, with a master touch, Bruno the chef. From that moment the fortunes, the wines and the amenities of Rausan-Ségla began to justify its ancient fame. Bordeaux and its wine evidently grew on the brothers. Two years later David led them to another property that was lagging behind its peers, Château Canon on the Côtes of Saint-Emilion.

There was radio silence from François Pinault. Most of the *conseil* were given their congé, but Harry Waugh and I heard nothing. After a while I wrote saying I would be in

Paris; would he have lunch with me? The answer came: come to the three-star restaurant where he apparently had his lunch every day. I found a stocky, warmly smiling man of about my own age, sitting at table with the finance director of Artemis, the formidably elegant Patricia Barbizet. I asked what may have sounded a silly question: why did he buy Latour? Because he could, easily, he said. As soon as he heard there was a chance he looked in his wallet – *et voilà*.

Harry and I remained on the board for a couple of years. Meetings were in Paris, at short notice. After I had unavoidably missed two of them I was very politely told that Monsieur Pinault expected his directors to pull their weight. That was my congé.

Meanwhile the priorities and the tone of the château changed almost out of recognition. It was no longer a matter for amateurs. The chef, the gardener and the chauffeur, those emblems of comfort, were congéd. It was clear that Artemis had two priorities: perfection and the bottom line, and they needed no bankers to help. Pinault had found (I don't remember how) a fanatical young wine lover called Frédéric Engerer. His contribution on the *conseil* made me feel very amateur indeed.

François Pinault and his wife, Marivonne, were exceptionally generous. In 1995 *Decanter* magazine made me their Man of the Year. Its managing director, Sarah Kemp, hinted that a celebration at Latour would be acceptable. The Pinaults immediately offered a lunch for as many guests as we could fit in the big reception room. I think we were 40. What were my favourite Latour vintages? Taking a deep breath I said 1959 and 1949 (two of the greatest years of the century). 'Fine,' said Pinault. They were served with a perfect Bordeaux meal; two of the best wines, in the best company, of my life. Most touching of all, Marivonne Pinault (a passionate gardener at their château at Rambouillet) came down from Paris by train with boxes and baskets of flowers to decorate the tables.

The world knows that the Pinaults have spared no trouble or expense to maintain Latour as the pinnacle of Pauillac (and in my opinion the wine world). Since my day, every facet of the property has been renewed. It wears a far more fashionable and modern air. There are three flagpoles on the way to the *chai*. They used to fly the tricolour, the Union Jack and the national flag of a current visitor. When the Pinaults arrived, up went the pirate flag of Saint Malo, where the family originated, in the timber business, according to official sources. Though Pinault once told me, smiling, as pirates.

Nicholas Faith (1933–2018) – according to *The Guardian* a 'gentleman mischief-maker', and without doubt the most rock-ribbed of wine reporters – takes a look at the public (and presidential) perception of the wines of Château Margaux, sorting through such descriptors as 'elegant', 'poetic', 'mouth-cooling' and 'cowslip bouqueted'. For many commentators it was, and is, 'the *beau Idéal* of claret'.

CHATEAU MARGAUX

Nicholas Faith (1980)

In the first decade of the 18th century, when a few named clarets emerged from the ruck, Margaux was one of the four growths labelled as outstanding. And it has never lost that position. Among its early admirers was the first English prime minister, Sir Robert Walpole, and while not the exclusive property of politicians, it undoubtedly held an attraction for this group. Thomas Jefferson sent a friend 10 dozen bottles of the 1784 vintage. 'The best vintage which has happened in nine years,' he wrote, 'and Margaux is one the four vineyards which are admitted to possess exclusively the first reputation. I may safely assure you therefore, that, according to the taste of this country and of England there cannot be a bottle of better Bordeaux produced in France'.

Jefferson went on to note that the wine – at three *livres* a bottle – was very expensive, but remarked that his friend had not set any price limits. A later president, Nixon, was also keenly aware of the problems posed by the price of a wine which provided some solace for him as he cruised, an increasingly beleaguered man, down the Potomac on the presidential yacht *Sequoia* during the troubled summer preceding his resignation. 'The president had become something of a wine buff during his New York City days,' Woodward and Bernstein tell us in *The Final Days*, 'and the *Sequoia* was stocked with his favourite, a 1966 Château Margaux which sold for about $30 a bottle. He always asked for it when beef was served. And he had issued orders to the stewards about what to do when large groups of congressmen were aboard. His guests were to be served a rather good $6 wine; his glass was to be filled from a bottle of Château Margaux wrapped in a towel.'

More crucial to Margaux's reputation than the tastes of presidents has been the judgement of the marketplace of Bordeaux. Fortunately for the château, the historically crucial test for any claret – the tasting that preceded the submission of a selection of the Gironde's wines for the Universal Exhibition to be held in Paris in 1855 – was a triumph for Margaux. There was never any real question of which wines would be adjudged 'first growths' – the order of vinous precedence had been too solidly established by market forces over a century and a half for any sudden change to be made. Nevertheless, the order of precedence within the first growths was a matter of considerable contention. Lafite, conscious of an historic primacy, was pushing its claims – to exhibit separately, to be awarded a special medal, to be, in fact, not just the '*premier des premiers*', the 'first of the firsts', but in a totally distinct category. The estate's pretensions were finally burst by M Galos, an official of the Bordeaux Chamber of Commerce, which was organizing the tastings. 'I should point out,' he noted acidly, 'that Château Margaux ought to be placed at the head of its peers because, in the tasting, it obtained 20 marks (presumably out of 20), while Lafite was awarded only 19.'

The precedence accorded in 1855 has assumed an almost mystical significance in Bordeaux since then. So successive owners of Château Margaux would have respectable reasons for asserting that their wine ought to be placed at the head of any list of distinguished clarets, and not relegated to its place in the alphabetical order now normally employed to avoid further outbreaks of civil war between the branches of the Rothschild family, which owns Lafite and Mouton.

But the ultimate test of the wine's quality is not the preference of statesmen, or even of the experts of the Bordeaux wine market, but of those who know and love wine: and for many of them, as Ian Maxwell Campbell wrote: 'Margaux is the *beau idéal* of claret.' It is normal, and sensible, to place it in the 'golden mean' between Lafite and Latour, historically its only equals in the Médoc. Latour the big, implacable, robust wine, Lafite the most delicate of the three: qualities which each carried the potential corollaries of obvious faults – Latour coarse, Lafite thin. For true Margaux-lovers then, 'their' wine represents an ideal balance between the two extremes.

The judgement is not a new one. In 1815 William Lawton, the wine broker who then dominated the whole wine market, was probably merely summing up generally received opinion when he wrote in an internal memorandum: 'Margaux strikes a nice balance between Lafite and Latour.'

During the 19th century there was an emerging consensus about the qualities to be associated with the wines produced by the whole commune of Margaux, qualities that naturally found their fullest expression in the wines of the château itself. In the mid-1830s a guidebook to Bordeaux's wines talked of Margaux as 'the most delicate and suave of the whole *département*'.

But it was Charles Cocks, an English teacher living in Bordeaux, who produced the classic definition of the wines of the château itself, which he called 'the most highly regarded of the whole *département*'. His description has been quoted, with or without acknowledgement, with such regularity over the last 135 years since it first appeared in the mid-1840s in his guide to Bordeaux and its wines, that it forms, consciously or not, the foundation for most people's idea of Margaux's qualities. As he wrote: 'These wines are possessed of much fineness, a beautiful colour, and a very sweet bouquet which perfumes the mouth; they are strong without being intoxicating; invigorate the stomach without affecting the head, and leave the breath pure and the mouth cool.' Not that his judgement was entirely novel: a similar, though less full description, can be found in the 1833 edition of Cyrus Redding's famous book *A History and Description of Modern Wines*.

Because Cocks' guidebook was published in both French and English, later writers could change the nuances of the original. H Warner Allen, for instance, talked of the wine as being 'generous without being heady, stimulating the digestion, leaving the head clear, the breath clean and the mouth fresh'. In this (freely acknowledged) adaptation Warner Allen makes the wine sound rather like a superior sort of vinous mouthwash.

Much later, towards the end of a life devoted to the appreciation of fine wines, Warner Allen came nearest to a generally accepted idea of the – never precisely describable – sensations associated with the appreciation of the finest of wines. He talked of the 1875 vintage as 'a lovely wine' possessing 'lightness, grace and balance… always the hallmarks

Through a glass lightly: Margaux's familiar neoclassical château was built in 1812 by Louis Combes, who embraced grand gesture but abhorred decoration.

of Château Margaux'. He quotes approvingly another notable wine lover, Morton Shand, who had written of Margaux as the most delicate and poetic of the three Médocs with one of the most unmistakable flavours in the world and an entrancing cowslip bouquet'. 'I am not quite sure,' Warner Allen commented, 'about the cowslip; Châteaux Margaux for me suggests rather the raspberry or the almond. Certainly no wine can equal a fine Margaux in delicate fragrance and subtlety of taste'. In the same vein, Charles Walter Berry wrote of the 'cedary taste' of Margaux; and everyone who has written about the wine (or even merely savoured it) emphasizes the delicate, flowery bouquet of Margaux, unique among the wines of the Médoc.

The associations – cedar, cowslip, almond, raspberry – are themselves embodiments of the train of thought triggered by the words 'delicacy', 'lightness' and above all 'elegance',

Château Margaux: owner Corinne Mentzelopoulos sold financial control of the property in the early 1990s but when it came up for sale again in 2003, she bought it back.

which recur throughout vinous literature whenever Margaux's name is mentioned. But there is an obverse side to the almost magical, ethereal qualities conveyed by these words: a certain fragility which leaves it at the mercy, not only of the elements, so crucial a factor in Bordeaux, but of the need for superior attention to the winemaking as well. Man and nature could always harm Margaux far more easily than they could the more solid wines to the north in Pauillac, or even some of the commune's other major wines made further away from the river (Brane-Cantenac or Lascombes are good examples).

Significantly, Cocks preceded his eulogy of Margaux's wines with the reservation 'in a year favourable to the vine'. His caution is spelled out more bluntly by modern wine writers less inclined than Warner Allen, Morton Shand or their contemporaries to cloak their feelings in purple prose and to avoid any negative analysis of their favourite wines. In his classic *The Wines of Bordeaux*, Edmund Penning-Rowsell says that Château Margaux 'is noted for its fine bouquet and the delicacy of its flavour'. But 'on the whole it is a wine particularly successful in fine years, but correspondingly disappointing in off-vintages, although the excellent 1950 is an exception to this'. Like so many other authorities, he also makes the point that many of the disappointments encountered with Margaux are due to the human failings of earlier proprietors, but there remains the incontestable fact that, even with the most conscientious of owners and winemakers, Margaux is a fragile wine.

Hugh Johnson provided an even more brutal summing up a few years ago in *The World Atlas of Wine*: 'In great vintages its wine can justify its first growth status: it achieves unique finesse and subtlety. In recent vintages, however, the third growth Palmer has often made better wines.' Palmer's vines are, of course, situated opposite Margaux's. The two are, indeed, only a few yards apart at many points. The enigmas posed by the variation in the quality of the wine Margaux produces, as well as some explanation of the unique delights it provides at its finest can, however, be – albeit partially – provided by the geographers and the geologists.

Excerpt first published as 'The Beau Idéal of Claret', chapter II of *Château Margaux* by Nicholas Faith, Christie's Wine Publications (London) 1980, reprinted here by kind permission of Nicholas' son, Daniel Faith.

'First I cannot be; second I scorn to be; I am Mouton.' Awarded *deuxième* status in the Médoc's 1855 Classification, Mouton Rothschild put up a fight, eventually winning the right (in 1973) to become a first growth. Throughout its battle, spearheaded by Baron Philippe de Rothschild, Mouton vigorously proclaimed its individuality, 'Mouton suis'. Cyril Ray outlines the distinctive taste that changed everything.

CHATEAU MOUTON ROTHSCHILD

Cyril Ray (1974)

Of the varieties of grape permitted by INAO and thus by French law to red wines aspiring to any of the Bordeaux appellations – to clarets, that is – only three are of major importance: Cabernet Sauvignon, which is quite the most important of the three; Cabernet Franc, which for official purposes is regarded as part of the Cabernet proportion as a whole of an *encépagement*, though it differs in some respects from its near relative; and Merlot.

In the Médoc, the Verdot, Gros and Petit, is of only minor importance, as are the Malbec and the Carmenère.

(Different soils and different microclimates call for different varieties of grape: the Malbec, for instance, looms larger in the vineyards of Saint-Emilion and of Pomerol, farther to the south and on the other side of the river, than in the Médoc.)

In the soil and situation of the Médoc, the Cabernet Sauvignon gives depth of colour to a wine, as well as the tannin from pips and skin that provides hardness, backbone and staying power. The Cabernet Sauvignon is also more regular in production and more resistant to disease. It is for all these reasons that it is by a long way the leading variety of the district.

Closely related to it, the Cabernet Franc gives sugar and, therefore, alcohol, to a wine, but less colour and body, and is harder to rear.

Also more difficult to rear than the Cabernet Sauvignon, particularly because it is more subject to rot in wet weather, and can cause immense difficulties if there is heavy rain just before or during a vintage, is the Merlot. Yet there are many Médocain vineyards in which it is highly regarded because of the softness, fragrance and fruitiness that it gives.

The highly distinctive character of Mouton – and it is probably the most distinctive in a region of highly subtle and distinctive wines – is determined largely by its *encépagement*, which greatly increases and intensifies those differences in style between it and its fellow first growths and other *crus classés* that arise from situation and soil.

In the vineyards of Château Mouton Rothschild, Cabernet Sauvignon accounts for no less than 90 percent of the total number of vines, Cabernet Franc for as little as five percent, and Merlot for a mere three or four. (There is a trace – one or two percent – of Petit Verdot, as there is at Lafite. Note, too, that the figures given are percentages of the vines. In any one year, the proportions of each variety will vary according to whether it has been a good or bad year for this variety or for that. They rarely flourish equally.)

Compare this with Lafite where, ignoring the trace of Petit Verdot, the proportion is only two-thirds Cabernet Sauvignon and one-sixth each of Cabernet Franc and Merlot – about five times as much of the soft and supple Merlot as at Mouton, and only two-thirds as much of the firm, full and slow-maturing Cabernet Sauvignon.

It is easy to see why Mouton, even were other conditions precisely the same, which as between one vineyard and another they never are, will always be a bigger, fuller, harder wine than Lafite, and slower to mature.

In this respect it more closely resembles its less near neighbour Latour, which has much the same proportion of Cabernet Sauvignon in its composition, and which differs from Mouton more in bouquet than in bigness – this due probably to differences in soil and to nearness to the river and the light and warmth reflected from it.

Mouton and Latour, incidentally, are both outstanding among other top clarets for making good wine in what are regarded as 'off' years: each made, for instance, a remarkable 1946. This, too, may be due to the high proportion of Cabernet Sauvignon at each property.

'Fullness and concentration of flavour' is Edmund Penning-Rowsell's summing-up of the Mouton style, going on to say that, 'it is a rich wine, and more than once I have mistaken it for one of the top Pomerols, such as Petrus. Sometimes almost burgundian in its power…'

Indeed, I have heard one of the Rothschilds of Lafite say that, 'I don't like Mouton, because I don't like burgundy'. Which is another way of putting it – but then that was one of the Rothschilds of Lafite...

Although Alexis Lichine, in his *Encyclopaedia of Wines and Spirits*, contradicts himself not once but twice about the actual proportions of the Mouton *encépagement*, he hits the nail on the head with his description, 'heavy, full and almost fleshy, with a special taste that natives of Bordeaux refer to as a *goût de capsule*, or taste of the capsule – which is of heavy lead foil – 'from its distinctive, hard and almost metallic flavour. The high percentages of Cabernet Sauvignon grapes used make it very slow to mature and very full-bodied'.

The 'natives of Bordeaux' notice the *goût de capsule* more often than the English or American amateur of Mouton because the French drink their wines younger: the metallic taste is characteristic of many clarets not yet ready to drink, and Mouton is slower to mature than most. So that when Mr Penning-Rowsell writes that he has never caught this taste, it may well be that he has been lucky enough to have drunk only the mature wines of Mouton. The 'other alleged point of individuality, an aroma of cedar-wood, or lead pencils', has, he writes, come home to him – but that is a characteristic of the wine in its maturity.

And at a dinner-party at Mouton itself, in May 1974, when the 1947, the 1911 and the 1881 wines of the house were lavished upon us, one after another, my neighbour at table, Peter Sichel of châteaux Palmer and Angludet, drew my attention to the strong scent of blackcurrants in every one of the wines – a scent that he always associated, he said, with Mouton, and that was obvious even to my attenuated sense of smell.

They were all great wines. The 1947, which had been a long time coming into its own, is now one of the château's own favourites: it was one of the two vintages of Mouton – the other was the 1959 – served at the historic dinner given by Alan Walker, chairman of Bass Charrington, in the cellars of Hedges & Butler, in July 1973, to celebrate Mouton's elevation into the first growths. The hot summer of 1947 gave high alcoholic content and great staying power, but yielded only a moderate crop – Mouton made only 7,000 cases.

At the May 1974 dinner, the 1911, of a year more distinguished for its burgundies than for its clarets, was possibly the best-balanced and most pleasingly fragrant of the three, and the 1881 a miracle, coming as it did from a mid-phylloxera vintage.

There are those who prefer Mouton, *as a rule*, because of its sturdy, forthright character, and its tremendous concentration of colour, flavour and fragrance – its very boldness. And even those who, equally *as a rule*, would opt for a more graceful, less assertive wine, must admire it and, indeed, sometimes choose to drink it, because of its consistency, its truth to its own personality, and the majesty with which it matures.

Excerpt first published as 'Mouton Suis', chapter III of *Mouton-Rothschild, the Wine, the Family, the Museum* by Cyril Ray, Christie's Wine Publications (London) 1974, reprinted here by kind permission of Cyril's son, Jonathan Ray.

The supersized Picasso label that celebrated Mouton Rothschild's elevation to first growth in 1973.

California-based wine author Gerald Asher charts the rise of the only first growth to be located outside the Médoc. Its place among the greats earned not only for growing grapes since Roman times, and finding fame in the diaries of Samuel Pepys, but for its wines of consistently high quality enjoyed by 17th-century London society, Thomas Jefferson and ranking judges of the 1855 Classification alike.

CHATEAU HAUT-BRION

Gerald Asher (1996)

'A little rise of ground, lieing open most to the west. It is noe thing but pure white sand, mixed with a little gravel. One would imagine it scarce fit to beare any thing....' John Locke's words are taken from his journal entry for May 14th 1677. At that time, a philosopher's journey to view a vineyard at first hand and to write down his impression of it was as unlikely as the visit today of an eminent intellectual to ponder the significance of a cabbage patch. Locke's curiosity confirms a singular achievement of Arnaud de Pontac, the richest and most influential man in Bordeaux, first president of its parliament (a configuration of law courts rather than a legislature), but best remembered as Château Haut-Brion's owner from 1649 until his death in 1681. During that time, Pontac raised the status of his wine estate from agricultural anonymity to one of fame and immense value.

Samuel Pepys, later to be secretary of the Admiralty in London, had first noticed 'a sort of French wine called Ho-Bryan, which hath a good and most particular taste' in a London tavern in 1663, but Locke makes clear that what had been a novelty to Pepys had become, in a very few years, a wine so esteemed in England as to be almost an object of cult. Locke's journey to Haut-Brion and his report on what he saw there underline how identification of Pepys' Ho-Bryan wine with Arnaud de Pontac's vineyard at Château Haut-Brion helped bring that about. It is a wine-to-vineyard relationship we would take for granted today, but one that required new perception when wines were still as broadly anonymous as other agricultural products.

Pontac's great-grandfather, Jean de Pontac, a general trader descended from a pewtersmith, had acquired land at Haut-Brion in the village of Pessac outside Bordeaux through his marriage to Jeanne de Billion in 1525. In the course of a long life (he was still sound of mind and limb when he died at 101), he filled all those legal and administrative offices, for king and city, most likely to enrich and advance a man in a contentious age. While acquiring two further wives, 15 children and the largest fortune in Bordeaux, he had found time to enlarge and embellish his property at Haut-Brion long before it came, through the usual chain of inheritance, into Arnaud de Pontac's hands.

Arnaud paid close attention to the family estate at Haut-Brion. He introduced there the practice of regular racking from barrel to barrel, separating young wine from its coarse and mischievous early lees, and was among the first to realize that frequent 'topping up' to compensate for evaporation allowed wine in cask to improve rather than spoil – simple usages that allowed him to reveal to the full the inherent advantages of his vineyard.

The general lack of such care in an absence of what we might consider basic cellar hygiene normally led wine to deteriorate so rapidly in the 16th century that new wine commanded a substantial premium over old. A buyer at that time concerned himself less with the fine points that preoccupy us today than with a wine's soundness and reliable drinking.

Though this preference for new wine over old continued into the 17th century, there were by then, even among new wines, some more prized than others, the most highly regarded being those associated with powerful families, including the Pontacs, but with little attention paid, by buyer or seller, to specific vineyards. René Pijassou, of the University of Bordeaux, comments that consumers seemed to see a connection between a wine's quality and the financial strength and fame of its producer, a phenomenon not unknown today and one that might be justified by the care made possible by greater resources. The seeming lack of concern about vineyard of origin might have been no more than a worldly assumption that the families of the newly powerful administrative class would have their vineyards in privileged sites. But even if that were the case, there is no doubt that Arnaud de Pontac was the first to emphasize the relevance of his vineyards' unique terroir to the style and quality of his wine. And, in attaching Haut-Brion's quality and distinction firmly to the site where its grapes were grown, Arnaud de Pontac fathered a model, widely emulated, that is still responsible for Bordeaux's luster three centuries later.

Pontac realized, of course, that his wine would sell at a price to justify the pains he took only if it were distinguished from the general mass. But the urge both to raise quality and sharpen distinction was itself a response to changed circumstances for Bordeaux wines in London. Despite having lost possession of Bordeaux two centuries before, England remained a vital, if not principal, market for its wine. With the restoration of the English monarchy in 1660, Arnaud de Pontac and other growers had probably looked for a strengthening of that market after years of puritan restraint. But even before the return of Charles II, chocolate and coffee had already made their appearance in London. Encouraged by the king's pleasure-loving court, and by those made rich from the country's mercantile success in winning leadership at sea from the Dutch, the purveyors of these novel exotic luxuries proliferated and prospered in a city rebuilding itself after the Great Fire of 1666.

London society, euphoric and, to put it bluntly, energetically opportunist, found in coffee houses not only a revival of political and literary vigour after Cromwell's 'grim constraint of compulsory godliness,' but the possibility of commercial and financial adventure; some of these meeting places evolved into the embryonic exchanges from which London's financial institutions have sprung, while others ripened into the city's great political and literary clubs. Is it any wonder that fashionable London was seduced from the simple pleasure of a pitcher of Bordeaux wine in a tavern?

To win them back, Pontac sent his son François-Auguste, together with the chef from his own Bordeaux mansion, to open London's first restaurant, The Pontac's Head. It was elegant, expensive and roaringly successful, and in that perfect setting the Pontacs presented their wine to a clientele best able to appreciate it, to pay for it, and to further its cause.

Though he could have known little of marketing theory, and even less of its jargon, Arnaud de Pontac had used his wealth, political clout and social connections to do more than position his product: he had transformed it into the very coinage of prestige.

Because Pontac's strategy was quickly adopted by others, he secured the future of the Bordeaux wine trade in providing for the success of Haut-Brion. The war that erupted between England and France in 1688 was followed by almost two centuries of unrelieved hostility when punitive levels of duty imposed on all French wines, and sometimes their

Jean de Pontac's first marriage, to the mayor of Libourne's daughter in 1525, ensured him a dowry of land on which to build a fine château.

outright ban, restricted availability. Yet so thoroughly had the new style of wine initiated by Pontac captured London's fidelity, that while country squires made do and made merry with the cheaper port urged on them by the government's new alliance with Portugal, there were always Englishmen willing to pay the high duty, and others prepared to resort to subterfuge, rather than be deprived of Bordeaux.

Americans, after 1776 no longer bound by English policies hostile to France, were free, of course, to do as they pleased with regard to Bordeaux. Thomas Jefferson, standing in 1787 where John Locke had stood a century before him, echoed the philosopher's words in his description of the vineyard at Château Haut-Brion as 'sand, in which is near as much round gravel or small stone and a very little loam'.

The terroir had not changed. But the world had turned with the success of the policies initiated by Arnaud de Pontac. Where once the price of last year's Bordeaux wine had dropped to barely a 10th as soon as wine of the new, and therefore more reliable, vintage was available, Jefferson reported a dramatic annual increase in the price of wine as it aged, and as demand responded to its quality.

Wines of the 1783 vintage of the great growths (which by then included Margaux, Lafite and Latour as well as Haut-Brion), he said: 'Sell now [in 1787] at 2,000 *livres* the *tonneau*; those of 1784, on account of the superior quality of that vintage, sell at 2,400; those of 1785, at 1,800; those of 1786, at 1,800 tho' they sold at first for only 1,500.' For comparison, wines of the 1783 vintage had first sold at 1,350 a *tonneau*, the 1784 at 1,300, and the 1785 at 1,100, while standard red wines of the region then sold for 200 to 300 *livres* a *tonneau*, a differential that has become only more marked in recent years.

On return to the United States from his tour as ambassador in Paris, Jefferson continued to order wines from Bordeaux, asking the US consul in Bordeaux in 1790, for example, to arrange a shipment of 85 cases of wine, some for himself and some for George Washington ('packed and marked GW'). But, with other priorities and, no doubt, with other tastes, the young republic was not immediately an important customer for Bordeaux. Madeira had attracted lower duties in the English colonies, like port in England, because of the Anglo-Portuguese alliance, and an attachment to Madeira, thus established, stayed with Americans for many years, even when the Crown, and its use of import duties for political ends, had gone from the United States.

The Pontacs' heirs lost Haut-Brion along with their heads at the time of the French Revolution, and although it was eventually restored to their successors, the sustaining continuum had been broken. In 1801 it was sold to Talleyrand, Napoleon's foreign minister, who knew that diplomacy was built on a well-equipped kitchen and a well-stocked cellar. But he was rarely at Haut-Brion, and in selling it to a Paris banker in 1804, Talleyrand set in motion a chain of ownership that swung from banker to merchant. If Arnaud de Pontac had turned commercial instinct to the advantage of his estate, those who then gained control of Haut-Brion too often turned the estate to the advantage of their commercial instinct. André Jullien, in his *Topographie de Tous Les Vins Connus*, complained that Haut-Brion lost its reputation for some years because the vineyards were overfertilized – if true, it was doubtless to boost profitability by raising yields. 'But the care of the new proprietor has improved it,' he said, 'and it has regained its place among the first growths with the 1825 vintage'. He was referring, presumably, to Beyerman, a Dutch wine merchant established in Bordeaux, who had taken over the property in 1824.

The estate changed hands again in 1836, acquired by Eugène Larrieu, a retired banker, whose son, Amedée, was as devoted to restoring the grandeur of Haut-Brion as Arnaud de Pontac had been in first creating it. So far did he succeed that not only did Haut-Brion retain its rank of first growth in the 1855 Classification still binding today, but by the end of the century its wine could, and did, command prices above those of the other three first growths – Margaux, Lafite and Latour. The 1899, particularly, opened at a price almost 20 percent above that of Margaux, and had a reputation that still reverberates. Charles Walter Berry tells in his book *In Search of Wine* of refusing to allow Christian Cruse to order for him a bottle of the 1899 at an impromptu lunch in Paris in 1934 simply because it was 'one of the most famous and expensive wines to be bought'. (His sense of decorum was rewarded: at a dinner party that same night he was served the 1899 Haut-Brion with a fresh, truffled *pâté de foie gras*. It was, he wrote: 'A dream, I would like to be Rip Van Winkle, and take a bottle of this to bed with me.')

A few years ago, I, too, had an opportunity to taste the 1899 Haut-Brion at the climax of three days of tasting and drinking 26 vintages of white Haut-Brion ranging from 1985 to 1916 (the château produces about a thousand cases of white wine a year from a small parcel of Sauvignon Blanc and Sémillon vines) and 49 vintages of red. Marvin Overton, a Texas surgeon, rancher and wine lover, had organized this mammoth event as his own very original contribution to the 150th anniversary of the state. He succeeded in proving that Haut-Brion Blanc can be as greatly enjoyed with catfish eaten at a bench in the shade of an open shed as with turbot in a private dining room at Taillevent; and that the red wines of Haut-Brion can be as much at ease as we were with barbecued pig and wild rice, cowboy stew and kebabs in a field full of bluebonnets and longhorn steer.

Above all, Overton succeeded in showing us, with the help of an illuminating commentary from Haut-Brion's director, Jean Delmas, how an Haut-Brion personality – precise, refined and intense, like the sound of a silver flute in the hands of a master – could be traced consistently through all those wines despite the vicissitudes of wars, changes of ownership and the annual uncertainty of vintage.

Haut-Brion faltered early in this century when ownership passed to two godchildren of the last of the Larrieu family, and ended up as the retirement settlement of André Gibert, a director of the Société des Glacières of Paris. He took control before the 1923 vintage – 'a pretty wine, one of the most beautiful of that very charming vintage', according to Maurice Healy, an Irish barrister devoted to the idea that Haut-Brion's name had somehow descended from a 17th-century compatriot. Perhaps that explains his serving a series of Haut-Brion vintages at a Saint Patrick's Day dinner in 1931, an occasion when his friend André Simon, founder of The International Wine and Food Society, commented that the 1923 was 'almost too ready', later qualifying his remark by adding, in his book *Tables of Content*, that 'the same thing was said of the 1871s and 1875s; they were ready at a very early date and did last: in fact they are still lasting'. The 1871s might indeed have lasted 60 years, but I have to report, with regret, that in 1986 the 1923 had not. The best I can say is that its strangely scented bouquet was not unpleasant.

Gibert's 1924 and 1926 were impressive, however, and have been praised over the years. André Simon, at that same Saint Patrick's Day dinner, had found the 1924 Haut-Brion preceding the 1923 'too green to drink with due respect' but said it showed great promise, and concluded that he would be 'very much surprised if it does not turn out to be a very fine wine'. (How agreeable to have lived at a time when experienced men refrained, even seven years after the vintage, from being dogmatic about a wine's future. Today, grapes are hardly picked before someone is telling us with insolent confidence how a wine will be 10, 20 and 30 years on.) Simon was right about the 1924. It was still superb when we tasted it at Overton's ranch, with the strength and richness of bouquet – vanilla and sealing wax – that I remembered from tasting it in 1979. But the 1926, though equally forceful, was marred by the dry, hard finish which Edmund Penning-Rowsell, our most distinguished contemporary chronicler of Bordeaux, has described as 'typical of that vintage'.

Penning-Rowsell could find nothing kinder than 'poor' to say about the 1928 Haut-Brion, and gave a head-shaking 'not very good' to the 1929. The years must have tempered the 1929; I found it drying out, but fairly full and still deep of hue. Its fading bouquet of plums and violets had a nostalgic charm. Time had done little to help the 1928, however. It too was still big and dark, but its astringency was aggravated by an aftertaste others have described as medicinal but which was most likely mercaptan: an ineradicable smell and taste with a sulphur component (that fact alone will help those unfamiliar to imagine its effect) most often caused by lack of care in racking a young wine from its lees – an ironic footnote to Arnaud de Pontac's endeavours in this very matter almost 300 years earlier.

The vintages that followed must have tested sorely whatever commitment André Gibert had to Haut-Brion. After visiting him at the close of 1934, Charles Walter Berry wrote that he wasn't much impressed with the 1933 and would say nothing of 1934 beyond 'it may conceivably be an improvement on the previous vintage'. Faint praise, perhaps, yet to some extent justified. Of the three vintages of the 1930s at our giant tasting, the 1934 was the best, and it had worn better than many of which more had been expected. Nevertheless, Gibert had had enough, and when his offer of the estate as a gift to the city of Bordeaux was refused, he sold Château Haut-Brion in 1935 to the American banker Clarence Dillon, whose family, still owning and controlling it today, has worked with the tenacity and intelligence of the Pontacs and Larrieus to restore and extend its reputation.

The turreted roof of Château Haut-Brion. Michael Broadbent said of the property's wines: 'I have always insisted on serving [them] first as they are so distinctive.'

The first result had to wait until the end of the war, but then the 1945 Haut-Brion was one of the most praised of a much-praised vintage. In Marvin Overton's barn it was still alive, full flavoured, and superb. Other successful vintages followed, most especially the 1952 and 1953, the latter an epitome of Haut-Brion's 'precise, refined and intense' personality. (Unusually and unfortunately, our bottle of 1953 in Texas was slightly oxidized, and the wine was overwhelmed by the 1952). Neither the 1955 nor the 1959 were as firmly structured as the 1952, but they shared both its scale and the whiff of sealing wax typical of Haut-Brion in its bigger years.

The 1960s were a decade of transition at Haut-Brion. In 1960 the château was the first to install stainless steel fermenting tanks, the better to control the fundamental process of fermentation, and in 1961 Jean Bernard Delmas succeeded his father, Georges, as *régisseur*. The modification of style that then occurred was perhaps little more than adaptation to a series of difficult vintages, each of which presented varied problems of some magnitude. On the other hand, could the new tanks have made possible a noticeably leaner, tighter style? Or was it the result of a new philosophical direction given to, and supported by, the particularly able and perceptive new *régisseur*, a man who had been raised at Haut-Brion and understood its significance and potential?

Whatever the cause, from that time a new delicacy and restraint underlined Haut-Brion's precision, refinement and intensity. Though the new style was already obvious in the

1961, it could, and can still, be seen to even greater effect in the 1964 – a disappointing year for many because of October rain on a late vintage, but a triumph for Haut-Brion.

Though weather conditions in 1972 and 1977 also proved difficult for Bordeaux, in other years of that decade – particularly 1971, 1975 and 1978 – they allowed, and even imposed, a more robust, tannic style that has tended to continue, though more as fashion than necessity. It was obvious from the wines tasted at Marvin Overton's, however, that while respecting the more forceful characteristics imposed by those years, Haut-Brion has succeeded both in preserving the personality that evolved over centuries and in retaining its new, faultless elegance of style. The unity of these various strands can be seen most perfectly in the 1971: a seamless wine of impeccable balance that is all the Pontacs, the Larrieus and the Dillons could have hoped for as justification of their efforts. The 1979, 1981 and, especially, the 1983 seem each to possess similar harmonies of quality.

To crown our last evening with the 1899, we had tasted backwards through the years, delighted that the 1921, the praises of which we had so often read, was still able to flatter with its light cherry colour and fresh bouquet and that the 1907, though fading, had retained its Haut-Brion sealing wax hallmark after almost 80 years.

Finally, we came to Charles Walter Berry's dream wine, a wine that Hugh Johnson more recently compared to the pediment of the Parthenon. (It's never difficult to tell when wine fanciers are enthusiastic.) It was faded, of course, but surprisingly fresh and smelled of thyme. The flavour, too delicate to analyse, was astonishingly long. By then, as one might have expected, we were tired and exhilarated, so perhaps I only imagined hearing the voice of Arnaud de Pontac expressing satisfaction.

First published in *Vineyard Tales, Reflections on Wine* by Gerald Asher, Chronicle Books (San Francisco) 1996.

A unique 'blue-clay' terroir, inordinately skilful winemaking and the approbation of Robert Parker have all been contributory factors to Petrus's stellar Right Bank 'Royalty' status, but, according to Neal Martin, the maverick personalities behind the wines were – and are – an equal driving force.

CHATEAU PETRUS

Neal Martin (2012/2020)

Under the blank enamel sky, a chugging Citroën 15 gambols with childlike glee around potholes and puddles. Two gentlemen occupy the front seats, both wrapped in thick, woollen herringbone overcoats and paisley scarves, their voices raised over the rambunctious engine, words vaporizing as they meet the frozen air. The driver is the taller of the two, large in frame with jowly cheeks and heavy eyelids; his waxed black hair is flecked with grey and his large hands are tucked into warm, camel-skin gloves. His two sons, muffled in matching duffel coats and navy woollen scarves, are perched on the back seat, peering out of the frosted window at the snow-draped vines, which look as if Mother Nature had decorated the landscape with icing sugar.

Pomerol is recovering from a severe cold snap. The first fortnight in February had been relatively warm, but the wind had turned on its heel and a vicious tongue of Siberian air had pushed the mercury as low as -24°C. The snow had drifted to a metre or so deep in places, rendering some lanes impassable. Yet this is not unprecedented. Local vignerons take solace in the fact that this time their vines are dormant and the talons of this pernicious freeze have sunk into the land before their sensitive buds could be burned.

'Can we stop here?' requests the passenger. His name is Maurice Malpel, an agronomist from Toulouse. 'I would like to take a quick look at the vines. I will not be too long.'

'They are the same as last year,' quips the father of the two boys at the wheel. He would rather remain inside the car and continue their discussion on a promising artist who had recently caught his eye. 'Hold on. I'll pull over here at La Fleur-Pétrus.'

The brakes squeal as the Citroën reluctantly skids to a halt and startling silence momentarily floods the car. The father leans around towards his sons and with a single raised finger, orders them to sit quietly, ignoring the wails of protest. They have a burning desire to escape the confines of the vehicle, stretch their skinny white legs and run between the rows. Just like the vines, they need to expend the pent-up energy that has accumulated through the winter. Maurice exits the car and crouches on his haunches by one of the nearest vines. He extracts a small silver scalpel from his breast pocket and makes an incision into the trunk as deftly as a surgeon cutting open a patient.

Meanwhile, the father winds down the window and lights a Gauloises; exhaling a plume of smoke he surveys the languid rise of the land. In the distance he espies the figure of Marie Robin, attired in her black apron, scattering corn for the chickens that cluck around her ankles. Above, on the skeletal branches of a dying elm, is perched a solitary crow, envious and ravenous, desperate for his own food after the long, harsh winter. The father speculates on the forthcoming season and wonders what it will bestow, since he has heard idle chatter that 1956 will be an abundant crop like 1955; perchance it will be a 'vintage of the century' like 1945. Who knows?

After a couple of minutes Maurice stands up to attention, as if a sergeant major has hollered his name. He rolls a vine cutting between his fingers and scratches his head, a vexed expression on his face. Leaning into the driver's window, he stutters as he grapples for the right words. In the end, he comes straight to the point. 'This vine is dead. I am certain.'

Maurice is taken aback by his host's incredulous guffaw, the kind reserved for jokes in bad taste, of which this is a prime example. The father takes another long drag on his cigarette before speaking in a low timbre that seems to resonate through the air around him. 'That is impossible, Maurice. I know you are an expert but…'

'It is dead,' he interjects. 'I am sure of it. And if this vine is dead, then look around you and fear the worst, my friend.'

The father's face suddenly becomes stoic and pensive, as if unexpectedly eclipsed by the moon. He looks across the land as far as the eye can see and wonders whether he surveys vineyard or graveyard. Maurice gets back into the passenger seat feeling like a harbinger of doom, culpable for the fate that has befallen everything within sight. Part of him wishes he had

The sap froze, the roots split, the vines died: so damaging was the 1956 frost in Pomerol fewer than 1,500 cases of wine were made.

kept his thoughts to himself. What if he is wrong? What a fool he feels. He places a consoling hand on his friend's shoulder. 'You'll know what to do. You always do.'

Without a single word, the father turns on the ignition and the noise of the engine banishes the silence. For the remaining journey he is laconic and distant, lost in a more sombre train of thought....

Christian Moueix recounted this anecdote during one of the interviews he gave for my book on Pomerol; we sat on the banks of the Dordogne at 'Videlot', the family house on the outskirts of Libourne. I embellished his reminisces with the imaginary exchange between the driver, Moueix's father Jean-Pierre, and his agronomist friend Maurice Malpel. The frosts of 1956 hit Pomerol hard, perhaps harder than any other Bordeaux appellation since its clay soils are acutely exposed to the cold and lack the yawning Gironde estuary to regulate temperatures. Malpel's inquisitive nature allowed Moueix to become one of the first to comprehend the severity of damage that infamous freezing winter had wrought and its long-term implications.

At this point, Petrus was under the ownership of Madame Loubat. If Jean-Pierre Moueix was the merchant with razor-sharp business acumen, the shrewdness and the charisma to sell the wines and Pomerol to the world, then Madame Loubat was the indefatigable visionary: the formidable lady who proselytized Petrus as 'the greatest' and woe betide if you thought otherwise. Her grandiloquence was legendary: unmistakably reflected in the flamboyant plumed hat that she wore to church each Sunday, incongruous in that bucolic part of Bordeaux. She even had the hubris to gift two magnums of 1938 Petrus for the pre-wedding reception of Princess Elizabeth in 1947 – how lucky for our monarch-in-waiting!

But the 1956 frosts left Madame Loubat grief-stricken. It was only after a pep talk from the local priest, her confidante, that she rolled up her sleeves and set to work pruning the surviving vines down to a stub, loath to replant new vines like many of her Pomerol neighbours. Had these vines perished, then her efforts would have been in vain, but thanks to her fortitude – and perhaps to a bit of divine intervention – shoots began appearing the following spring. Petrus kept much of its original stock and was unencumbered by immature vines in the years to come.

On Madame Loubat's passing in 1961, she bequeathed a share of Petrus to Jean-Pierre Moueix, who eventually bought out his two fellow inheritors.

Perhaps taking a lead from his benefactress, in 1964 Moueix took a gamble. Six days prior to the harvest, he appointed a 22-year old to take charge of the winemaking at all his estates, including Petrus. The young man, fresh out of his studies at the University of Bordeaux, was gifted winemaker Jean-Claude Berrouet, and Petrus was a wine he had never drunk before. Berrouet's inaugural vintage could so easily have been a disaster, with the hot Indian summer bestowing a raft of stuck fermentations that needed constant cooling down with blocks of ice. But the wines that emerged were spectacular. He went on to oversee every vintage of Petrus until his retirement 43 years later.

Five years after Berrouet's arrival, in 1969, Jean-Pierre appointed his son Christian – the younger of those two children in the back seat of the Citroën – to manage the estate. In those days Petrus did not enjoy its current iconic status, and Christian remembers occasions where he stood at the château's entrance, handing out postcards to encourage passers-by to come and try the wine. Petrus was less well known than the Left Bank grandees and it was really only in the 1980s that it began to gain global recognition. This was partly thanks to the most powerful voice in wine, Robert Parker, who eulogized post-war vintages such as 1947 and 1949 with the new lingua franca of wine communication, the 100-point scale. Parker's praise combined with Christian's burgeoning ambassadorial skills, saw Petrus' wine become widely known as the best of its kind. Yet it retained a shard of enigma, something it has never lost despite the verbiage it attracts.

Of course, everything moves on. In 2007, Jean-Claude Berrouet retired from his duties as winemaker, handing over the reins to his son Olivier. Christian Moueix – who many, including myself, mistook as the proprietor – stepped back to concentrate upon Ets J-P Moueix and its impressive portfolio of Right Bank estates. His brother, Jean-François, who was always the actual owner, though he shied away from the limelight, began the hand over to his son, Jean Moueix, though the day-to-day running would remain in the hands of Olivier Berrouet and his team.

The winery has undergone reconstruction so that its once tenebrous facade now seems to gleam. For such a famous name, it is surprisingly rudimental, almost Zen-like inside. Simplicity in winemaking has always been an underlying principle here – there is never any need to complicate.

What makes Petrus special? Well, great wine comes from great 'dirt'. Its 11.5-hectares occupies a unique location on Pomerol's so-called 'buttonhole of blue clay', the chemical composition of which efficiently regulates the water, keeping the vines on that liminal point of suffering and persuading them to invest all their efforts into making grapes. Adjacent estates may also own vines on this blue clay, yet none can claim the entirety of their vineyard is planted on the buttonhole (which is, incidentally, more like a splodge when you analyse the soil profile). Maybe because of this exclusive site, Petrus reads from a different script to its fellow Pomerols, not necessarily at an advantage every year – as its market price might imply – but gifting Petrus an unerring ability to produce exceptional wines even in the most challenging growing season. Petrus is a maverick genius.

What does it taste like? As I once wrote: you remember your first Petrus as you do your first kiss. It is rarely an intense or powerful wine. It errs towards subtlety and is often mercurial in the glass, a shape-shifter. Nearly always deceivingly approachable, it inexplicably gains depth and body in response to aeration. The aromatics tend to veer more towards red fruit with truffle and sometimes ferrous-like traits, a seductive bouquet that threatens to overwhelm the senses when at its peak. The palate is usually deceptively pliant to the point where you hardly notice the fine tannins that provide backbone through years of bottle maturation and it is often endowed with such length that you could read a short novella in the time it takes the flavours to recede.

In an ideal world, everyone could taste Petrus once in their lives. It is easy to become caught up in the history and reputation, not to mention the price, but when you strip all that away, Petrus is simply a gorgeous and often profound wine that gives so much pleasure. On the rare occasions that I drink it, my mind replays a sepia-tinged film reel of Jean-Pierre Moueix, his agronomist friend, his two sons in the back seat, driving through Pomerol at a momentous moment that closed one chapter of the appellation and opened another. It proved that Petrus was susceptible to the malevolent forces of Mother Nature just as is any other property. Yet it survived and flourished, thanks not only to the unique nature of the vineyard but to the guardians who have tended the vines and turned their berries into wine – not just any wine, but a wine called Petrus.

Excerpt (pages 91–93) first published in *Pomerol* by Neal Martin, Wine Journal Publishing (2012), London; revised and updated by the author for 2020.

Burning paraffin *Chaufferettes* (small chimney heaters) in the vineyards is enough to raise the air temperature by 2–3°C and avoid frost. At Petrus (*right*) 1,500 were successfully employed to protect the 2017 crop. Other châteaux used helicopters to disperse the freezing air.

David Peppercorn's Bordeaux tasting notes span back to the late 1950s. He has penned many books on the subject, imported its wines and watched the region develop. Few can speak with more authority on the wines of its greatest châteaux, and here he describes one of the Right Bank's finest. It is said that, were Ausone's production not so small, it would likely have been included in the 1855 Classification.

CHATEAU AUSONE

David Peppercorn MW (1991)

This is one of the oldest and most famous properties in Bordeaux, in spite of its very small production. The small steep-roofed château is only 19th-century, but according to tradition it stands on the site of the villa of the Roman poet Ausonius, governor of Gaul, who died in 395AD. A number of contemporary writers described a villa called Lucaniacus which belonged to the poet. Gallo-Roman remains have indeed been discovered on the plateau of La Madeleine, near today's Ausone. Elie Vinet of Bordeaux, writing in the 18th century, and Vidal, the parish priest of Saint-Martin in 1778, both repeat the story, which no doubt gave Jean Cantenae, cooper and wine grower, the idea of renaming his property Château Ausone.... The Latin texts talk of a site on a high place, from which the Dordogne was visible. Enjalbert has suggested that there may have been two villas on the estate: one on the edge of the plateau close to where the present château stands, the other below at Le Palat. Certainly it is likely to have been a large property. Another owned by Ausonius near Bordeaux, of some 264 hectares, was described as only modest – the average size of Gallo-Roman estates in the third and fourth centuries was about 800 hectares.

The greatness of Ausone is due to a combination of soil and exposure. The soil is a mixture of clay and sand on limestone that is unique in the district, and is planted with old vines. No replanting took place between 1950 and 1976. So the average age of the vines is now about 50 years, with very low yields, ranging from 20 hectolitres per hectare in difficult years to about 36 in abundant years like 1982. Picking can be done at the optimum moment in such a small vineyard, usually in two afternoons. The situation of the vineyard is ideal, with steep slopes arranged like an amphitheatre, facing southeast, and so providing a perfect exposure and the maximum protection from adverse winds. The vines are also protected against frost, so that even in 1956, when many vineyards in the Libournais were virtually destroyed, Ausone's escaped. Similarly, the limestone retains moisture and so protects the vineyard from the effects of drought, even in the hottest years.

The ownership of the property has rested in the same family since the Revolution, from Monsieur Cantenac to Madame Lafargue, and through her nephews to the Dubois-Challon and Vauthier families. Ausone shared its *chai* with Belair until 1976. It is a cave cut into the hillside close by the château, under a cemetery, and reminds one more of Vouvray and Touraine than Bordeaux.

Ausone moved ahead of other Saint-Emilions in general estimation only during the last decade of the 19th century, and there is a note in the sixth edition of Cocks & Féret (1898) explaining that it had for the first time been placed above Belair because of the superior prices it had been obtaining, but did not indicate any decline in the quality of Belair. This is an interesting example of a *cru* making its reputation by preserving its old vines during the phylloxera crisis, because the vintages when Ausone's prices overtook those of Belair were 1887 to 1895. This position was well consolidated by the 1920s, by which time Ausone's special position had penetrated even the British consciousness with its Médoc bias. Colonel Campbell recalls the excellence of the 1904 and 1905, the earliest Ausones he tasted – he never saw the wine during his stay in Bordeaux in the early 1890s.

I was fortunate indeed to take part in a unique tasting held at the château in November 1988, the brainchild of Bipin Desai from Los Angeles. This gave an unrivalled panorama of vintages going back over 150 years to 1831. The 1831 was remarkable; in spite of an edgy, cheesy bouquet, it had an amazing volume of flavour, and was still fruity with some richness, an extraordinary relic from the age of Louis-Philippe and the young Berlioz. Then came a sweet and charming 1844, better than the 1849 or 1893. The 1850 had great depths of colour, still with amazing structure and power, tannic and four-square; it was even now one of the giants of the century. The 1869 must have been a massive wine; it still had vinosity and power in spite of volatility. The 1877 had a bouquet of ethereal fruit and sweetness that was still fresh and delicious and quite overshadowed the small but nevertheless charming 1879. The 1892 had a lovely opulent scent and a flavour that was still rich and full; even better was the frail but beautifully elegant and long-flavoured 1893: it remained sweet and lovely after half an hour in the glass. On a par with this was the 1894, with its sweet, lingering flavour. The 1897 was still freshly scented and fruity, with lovely, gentle, faded fruit, a seamless flavour, an almost ageless beauty. The 1899 was all one could have hoped for from this legendary vintage, a classic and wonderfully ethereal old claret bouquet, all breed and finesse, with a very complete flavour, long and delicate, very dry but quite lovely; it outshone the more opulent 1900. Certainly, the old, damp, chill cellars of Ausone had preserved these 19th-century wines in a remarkable way – but more surprising still were some of the wines in what is normally regarded as a dull period, between the great vintages of 1900 and 1920.

After a powerful but untypically aggressive 1904 came three remarkable wines. The 1905 had a bouquet that was really exotic, all concentrated richness; then came a flavour of great beauty, rich and complex with a wonderful finish – a great wine. The 1906 was only just behind, a more faded beauty, but with a wonderful long flavour, with great fruit and what I can only call gentleness still at the finish. It was in this year that the first grafted vines were planted. Then, challenging the 1905, was the 1908 with its heavenly aromas of an ethereal quality – one of the most sublime bouquets I have experienced – while the flavour had so many highlights and nuances, fruit and lingering elegance. A great wine. After this celestial trio, there was a fine 1912, elegantly scented, imperceptibly echoing away. The lovely ethereal character was there again, but with less power. The 1914 just had the edge on it, exotically scented, very cedary, a wine of ageless charm and elegance, but with less fruit at the finish than the marvellous 1917, which was still deep and dark in colour, with a tactile, opulent quality in the bouquet, lovely complex chewy fruit and just so much life and joie de vivre; it was more tannic and assertive than the 1908, but less beautiful. These forgotten years seem to show that old Ausones do not die, they go to paradise – there to become transfigured into something we dream about, but seldom experience…

I hope that this gives some idea of the extraordinary character and properties of Ausone. Only Lafite among the great Bordeaux can match it for delicacy, dimension and finesse combined with power, slowly evolving over many decades to give a bouquet unsurpassed for complexity of perfume, and a flavour full of multi-layered sensations. The old wines seem to achieve a sort of ethereal quality that is not quite of this world.

First published in the second edition of *Bordeaux* by David Peppercorn MW, Faber and Faber Ltd (London) 1991, and reprinted here with kind permission of the author.

As one of the highest ranking châteaux in Saint-Emilion's own classification, Château Cheval Blanc has always produced outstanding wines. Edmund Penning-Rowsell (1913–2002) – noted authority on Bordeaux and owner, according to Michael Broadbent, of one of the finest private wine collections in England – ascribes its success to its location, a cart track away from Pomerol.

CHATEAU CHEVAL BLANC

Edmund Penning-Rowsell (1979)

The difference in style of the Graves Saint-Emilions lies in situation and soil. The growths lie on a plateau that also includes Pomerol. This is prosperous, profitable land and the prospect is entirely vinous, with the lines of vines occupying every piece of ground not lying fallow prior to replanting. The soil is much more gravelly and sandy than on the banks of the Côtes.[1]

The outstanding wine is certainly Château Cheval Blanc, which does not mean that it is always the best wine. Over the past couple of generations it has advanced in reputation probably more than any other single property in Bordeaux; the much smaller Petrus, whose wider reputation is even more recent, is its only rival [at the time of writing] in this respect.

Cheval Blanc's reputation, as Monsieur Fourcaud-Laussac, one of the two brother proprietors, confirmed to me, really began with the famous 1921 vintage. Not that this was the first outstanding Cheval Blanc year. The 1920 was a splendid wine too, and when in the mid-1950s I opened together bottles of the 1920 and 1921, the majority opinion preferred the 1920 as a more complete wine, but I was in a minority at my own table in preferring the 1921 for its extraordinary sweetness and depth of taste. The...1921 Cheval Blanc was as famous as 1921 Yquem. That the château was making excellent wine earlier on was confirmed by the 1904 and 1911...

The secret of the special appeal of Cheval Blanc lies partly in that it is almost a Pomerol. Only the width of a cart-track separates it from La Conseillante in Pomerol, and on the minor road to Montagne-Saint-Emilion, the vineyard of Blanc is on one side and L'Evangile in Pomerol on the other. The rich, full flavour of Pomerols is embedded in

[1] Saint-Emilion has two physical/geological halves: the 'Graves' (the plateau) and the 'Côtes' (the slopes facing the River Dordogne). Château Cheval Blanc is situated on the former.

1929 Cheval Blanc: '...indescribable bouquet, perfect fragrance. A gentle, soft, glorious wine. Perfection.' Awarded five stars by Michael Broadbent.

Cheval Blanc, but the rather greater distinction of the best Saint-Emilions gives Cheval Blanc a unique quality.

This individuality, showing a fruity, welcoming aroma and a big, rich, almost sweet flavour, makes Cheval Blanc of a good year, and sometimes an indifferent one also, a very easy claret to drink. A fine Médoc often retains for some years a marked austerity and even astringency, calling for a certain experience to appreciate fully, but the softer Saint-Emilions in general, and above all Cheval Blanc, come out to meet one. Rich but not so experienced wine drinkers, buying by name, often go for wines like Cheval Blanc 1921, 1934 and 1947, and this inevitably increases demand, in the same way as an international prima donna attracts to Covent Garden opera the not-so-musical as well as the regulars. As an admirer of Cheval Blanc but not at present prices, I am constrained to misquote a celebrated remark and say, let them drink burgundy! Cheval Blanc is at its best a wonderful claret, but it is no more the consistent summit of all clarets than Lafite, Haut-Brion or Petrus are. Not, it is fair to say, that it is more expensive than these are.

The Médocains would certainly enter a protest at any undue elevation of a non-Médoc wine, and more than one château proprietor would deprecate the integration of Saint-Emilions in a new classification. Yet it was at Langoa in Saint-Julien that Ronald Barton opened for me a beautifully rounded bottle of Cheval Blanc 1926. When at Mouton Rothschild and given a choice of wines, I asked for the 1929 to precede a Mouton 1900, the *maître de chai* paid the wine (and me) the compliment of saying it was one of the best wines in the cellar. Although I would not pick a Cheval Blanc as the finest claret I have ever drunk, I think I have had greater enjoyment of more vintages of this château than any other; the frequency is partly owing to the fact that it used to be inexpensive by first growth standards, but this is no longer the case.

The vineyard of 33ha is, with neighbouring Figeac and Pavie, one of the three largest in the district. It consists of 27 percent Merlot, 43 percent Bouchet and 20 percent Pressac (Malbec). In the 1960s a little Cabernet Sauvignon was introduced, possibly owing to its important part in the neighbouring Figeac, but it was not considered a success. When I was there one September loads of soil from the *palus* by the river was being spread on the vineyard as a form of fertilizer or humus. Annual production averages 120–130 *tonneaux*, but it is variable: 145 *tonneaux* in 1964, not much more than half that quantity in 1966, a record 200 in 1970, but only 70 in 1975 and 120 in 1976.

I was a witness of the devastation that affected this part of Saint-Emilion and Pomerol in February 1956, for I visited the area the following June; where there should have been an expanse of green leafage the black stumps of the vines stood bare; it looked like a battlefield. No wonder, for there had been 24 degrees of frost. Fortunately, fewer of the vines were dead than at first thought, and they sprang up again, although at Cheval Blanc as elsewhere some died throughout the following decade. The immediate result at Cheval Blanc was that its crop for 1956 was precisely three barriques. The following year it was about 120 barriques, or 30 *tonneaux*, and reached 100 *tonneaux* only in 1959. It was not until 1961 that Cheval Blanc recovered something like its pre-frost quality, but with an output of only 40 *tonneaux*. The 1961 is certainly a fine wine and will be better, but no other vintage has yet come up to the outstanding post-war run that finished with the 1952. But that also applies to other Saint-Emilions and Pomerols.

First published in the fourth edition of *The Wines of Bordeaux* by Edmund Penning-Rowsell, Penguin Books Ltd (London) 1979, and reprinted here with kind permission of the author's son, also Edmund Penning-Rowsell.

Famed producer of luxurious sweet wines Château d'Yquem was the only white wine estate to be honoured as a first growth in Bordeaux' 1855 Classification – and the only Sauternes. James Seely (1940–2015), wine writer and specialist Bordeaux merchant, describes the exacting way in which this wine is produced.

CHATEAU D'YQUEM

James Seely (1998)

Let us attempt to analyse some of the costs of producing the precious wine of Château d'Yquem. First the soil – only the very best parts of the 103 hectares of vineyard entitled to the appellation are suitable, and at any one time only about 80 are in production, and these 80 hectares of special gravelly slopes have to be maintained and drained so as to give of their best. Some parts of the vineyard are so steep and difficult to work that horses were used right up to 1984, when technology finally produced suitable machinery to replace them. Only organic fertilizer is used, and the 100 kilometres of drainage pipe installed by Alexandre de Lur Saluce's great-grandfather have to be checked regularly and kept in good repair. All this requires immense labour, as do the later stages of viticulture and vinification, and there is a permanent workforce of over 40 people employed at Château d'Yquem. Here, as at other great wine properties, quality is only obtained at the expense of quantity. The vines are pruned with swingeing severity, and this, combined with the incredibly concentrating effect of the *pourriture noble* on the juices of the grapes, results in a yield equivalent, in a good year, to one glass of wine per vine.

Now to the harvest: a team of between 100 and 150 specially trained pickers, over and above the permanent employees, is brought in when the first grapes are at exactly the right state of rot. They will go through the vines on an average six times, picking only the grapes – yes, the individual grapes – that have reached the precise stage of maturity required. Picking stops if there is rain or if it is too hot or too cold, and the army marches on its stomach. In 1964 as many as 13 *tries* were made, and in the end none of the wine was good enough to bear the d'Yquem label. This process can be extremely lengthy, and on several occasions the harvest has continued well into December.

In the *réception des vendanges*, one's first reaction is surprise at the small scale of the vinification equipment. There are three small vertical hydraulic presses, but these are more than adequate to cope with the minute quantities of grapes brought in on any one day.

The striking medieval fortress of Château Yquem, its windows enlarged to survey the ripening vines and misty foreshore, where 90 hectares yield a mere 5,500 cases of precious wine.

There are three pressings: the must of each successive pressing decreases in volume as it increases in concentration of sugar. The juice is transferred rapidly into new oak casks where the fermentation takes place over a period of between two weeks and a month, and stops naturally when the alcohol content reaches around 14%.

The wine then spends three years or more in cask, and there are three separate cask *chais*, the wine of each suceeding vintage being moved each year. During its long stay in oak, the wine is racked every three months, and vital *ouillage*, or topping-up, is carried out twice weekly, to eliminate contact with the air and the consequent damages of oxidation. These operations result in the loss of over 20 percent of each crop by evaporation.

We are not finished yet. The ultimate moment of arbitration is the *sélection*. In spite of all the care and work involved, the standard at Château d'Yquem is so high that in some years no wine is allowed to carry the famous yellow label. This was the case in 1910, 1915, 1930, 1951, 1952, 1964, 1972, 1974 and 1992. Perhaps this goes some way towards explaining the reasons for d'Yquem's price, and why it is one of the most highly prized and sought-after wines in the world.

This excerpt first published in *Great Bordeaux Wines* by James Seely, Pallas Athene (London) 1998, and reprinted here with kind permission of the author's son, Christian Seely.

'Barley sugar,' 'orange-blossom', 'ripe peaches' – even the most evocative of tasting notes struggle to summarize the sweet exhilaration of Yquem, the coming together of 80% Sémillon, 20% Sauvignon Blanc and the noble rot *Botrytis cinerea*.

CHAPTER FOUR

THE RIVALS

Where there is quality, there is rivalry. Bordeaux is a region of many contrasts, in a country where it is not alone as a fine wine producer. Which wine wins?

Steven Spurrier (1999)
Claret or Burgundy – Which Is the Better Wine?

Edith Somerville and Martin Ross (1893)
Mouton vs Lafite

Elin McCoy (2020)
Left Bank vs Right Bank

Simon Gotelee (2020)
Brand Bordeaux vs Appellation Burgundy

Two French classics, worlds apart in terms of culture, history and style, but which is better? Steven Spurrier (no stranger to vinous controversy) knew the answer and decided to pitch the two head-to-head at dinner with fellow connoisseurs.

CLARET OR BURGUNDY – WHICH IS THE BETTER WINE?

Steven Spurrier (1999)

Is burgundy better than claret? For lovers of French wine, only the very partisan would be able to give you a straight answer to this question. For the rest of us, any response would be qualified by conflicting experiences, although we probably have a good idea where our personal preferences lie. Few people disagree that claret, as the British call red Bordeaux, is more reliable than red burgundy: it is less idiosyncratic and one is rarely disappointed. Stylistically, the wines are quite different, being made by different families on different soils with different grapes. The only thing they really have in common is that they are red and they go well with meat.

It used to be accepted that claret appealed to the intellect and burgundy to the emotions. Thus, the truly Médocain Martin Bamford of Château Loudenne could agree dismissively that 'one does not need to be very clever to like burgundy'. Today some Pomerols and Saint-Emilions are so sensuously rich that they do seem to justify their old description as 'the burgundies of Bordeaux'. Writing in 1949, Maurice Healy declared in his splendid book *Stay Me With Flagons* (essential reading for anyone who loves wine) that while one can drink great claret any evening of the week, 'burgundy at its best overtops claret at *its* best'. He then cited two wines, a Volnay-Caillerets 1889 and a Richebourg 1923, to prove his point. Throughout my early years in the wine trade, I saw no reason to agree with this and it was only the loss of an expensive bet that proved me wrong. Since that date, I have thought Mr Healy to be absolutely right.

A STRANGER AT THE TABLE

For several years from the mid-1960s I used to spend a week during the vintage at Château Langoa-Barton in Saint-Julien. It is a tradition in Bordeaux that château owners exchange wine with each other in order to have something other than their own wine to drink from time to time, but also to pay visiting colleagues the compliment of serving them their own wine – and sometimes, if they are mischievous, from a vintage that the latter no longer have in their cellars. The much-travelled Ronald Barton, uncle to the current owner Anthony Barton, used to exchange wines with his friends the Hugels in Riquewihr, and the Lupe sisters in Nuits-Saint-Georges. Wonderful old Rieslings, just cool from the cellar, were often served as an apéritif on the terrace before lunch, but burgundy never appeared at dinner on my visits until one evening in 1969.

The occasion was a largish dinner, with guests including several owners of local classed growths and Edmond Penning-Rowsell, the great authority on Bordeaux. Five wines were served: a dry white Graves, three reds and a Sauternes, all decanted, as usual by Ronald himself. And, as usual, there was animated yet discreet discussion as to what they were.

The white wine, a Laville Haut-Brion, was recognized quite easily and Edmond Penning-Rowsell spotted the Cantemerle 1953 without difficulty. The second claret proved more of a problem, but was eventually recognized, and applauded, as Léoville-Barton 1948. But it was the third red wine that caused the most discussion. General opinion was that it was from the Right Bank, and discussion centred on whether it was a great château from Pomerol or Saint-Emilion. Peter Sichel said that it was so rich it might even be burgundy, but he was firmly pooh-poohed. The table was united in finding it an amazing wine, until Ronald Barton announced that it was a Pommard 1934, from Lupe-Cholet. The guests were not amused at this, and the wine stayed in their glasses. One did not drink burgundy in Bordeaux and I do not think one does even today.

VINTAGE LAFITE

The following summer I was staying with Martin Bamford at Loudenne, along with our mutual friend David Fromkin, an American wine lover who was passionate about burgundy. It was Martin's and my plan to get David to like claret. Over a few days, we had some splendid wines and David agreed that we had a point. He added that there was a wine he thought we would enjoy at the Restaurant Darroze, then a two-star Michelin with one of the most famous cellars in France, and that, if we didn't mind drinking some burgundy as well, he would be happy to invite us for dinner.

The wine that he had in mind was Château Lafite 1806. He had spotted it the year before while lunching on his own and had thought it a tremendous bargain at 750 francs for a wine that old but, only knowing about burgundy, he let it pass. Arrangements were made, the existence of the Lafite 1806 confirmed (although the price had doubled to 1,500 francs) and a party of six of us drove down for dinner.

The wines we had were Le Montrachet Marquis de Laguiche 1952, Château Lafite 1806, Le Chambertin Domaine Rousseau 1952 and La Romanée-Conti 1945.

Martin Bamford had persuaded David to have the Lafite served as the first red wine, as its age and delicacy risked being overwhelmed by the power of the burgundies. Monsieur Darroze suggested that the Lafite not be decanted, but poured into our glasses that were lined up on the decanting table. David Fromkin insisted that he take a glass for himself of this historic wine, which he took around to the other tables present. The wine had been recorked at the château in 1953, part of a batch of 24 bottles selected from the château cellars by the great Raymond Baudouin, creator of the finest wine lists in France and founder of *La Revue du Vin de France*. He allocated six bottles to the greatest restaurants of the 1950s: Le Chapon Fin in Bordeaux, Le Coq Hardi at Bougival, Taillevent in Paris and Darroze at Villeneuve-de-Marsan. I remember the wine to this day as having a fine orangey-red colour, an ethereal bouquet of dried fruits, faded of course, but still present and sweet, and a delicately textured, dry finish. It still remains the most remarkable wine drinking experience I have ever had.

Following our dinner, Monsieur Darroze was left with two bottles of Lafite 1806. One was auctioned at Christie's in September 1977 and purchased for £8,700 by Addy Bassin of MacArthur Liquors in Washington, DC. The other was broken in an accident in his cellar. One of the bottles from Le Coq Hardi found its way to Christie's in June 1980, where it was knocked down to the great collector Lloyd Flatt of New Orleans for £3,300. Here is Michael Broadbent's tasting note, taken at Lloyd Flatt's outstanding Lafite tasting in October 1988: 'Palish warm amber with orange highlights, lovely, sweet, rich, stably bouquet with a touch of varnish, which for nearly three hours surged out of the glass; dry, fairly light, good crisp acidity, firm enough, fragrant finish.'

A TEST OF THE GREATS

Back at Loudenne we discussed the wonderful wines we had been drinking, and I told David Fromkin that, however good burgundy was, claret was better. He disagreed, so we decided to put this to the test the following year and I offered the restaurant of his choice, the loser to pay for dinner. He chose the Hôtel de la Côte d'Or in Saulieu, a restaurant he had known well under the famous Alexandre Dumaine, one of the greatest chefs of all time, and which was now run by Dumaine's protégé, François Minot. On a visit to Burgundy (for by this time I had moved to Paris, where I had a wine shop) I visited the place to check out the wine list, and saw that they had the mythical Cheval Blanc 1947 not only in bottles, but in magnums. I wrote to David to say that nothing he could put up could match this most burgundian of clarets, and offered to call the bet off. He declined, and so in June 1971 five of us this time, but still including Martin Bamford, met for dinner in Saulieu.

We agreed that we would only serve two red wines, one claret and one burgundy, in order of age. After a champagne apéritif, we progressed to the Marquis de Laguiche Montrachet 1959 and then it was time for the magnum of Cheval Blanc 1947 that I had asked to be decanted two hours previously. It literally exploded out of the glass: completely sensuous, overwhelmingly rich, devastatingly complete. Martin Bamford said he had never seen it on better form. Then David's wine, a La Tâche 1934, was poured, undecanted, into those large, shallow glasses that the Burgundians use. As its fragrance filled the room and, with just the first sip, its magical texture caressed my palate, I conceded defeat.

Little is known of La Tâche 1934 – the archives from this period disappeared during World War II – except that it was made by the grandfather of Aubert de Villaine, the current co-owner of the Domaine de la Romanée-Conti, himself the great, great, great-grandson of Monsieur Duvault-Blochet who purchased the DRC estate in 1869. Neither Christie's nor Sotheby's have a record of having auctioned the wine, although Michael Broadbent did taste it ('sweet…mouthfilling, typical La Tâche fragrance') in 1985. On the other hand, a great deal is known about the Cheval Blanc 1947. It is, alongside Petrus 1961, regularly the most expensive claret sold at auction, and its price has doubled every four years or so since 1970. The most recent price was £23,000 for 12 bottles at Sotheby's in 1999. Serena Sutcliffe MW, tasting it from a magnum a little time before, notes: 'The colour is still black, the nose still port-like; the bouquet of this most recent magnum was so sweet, the palate of chocolate and port; there are also coffee flavours and a creamy, thick texture unlike any other wine, plus the extra bonus of fireworks on the finish.' The château itself still [in 1999] possesses *quelques dizaines de bouteilles* so the legend will live on.

Which is better? Cheval Blanc 1947 (*left*), one of the most revered and expensive of all clarets, or La Tâche 1945 (*right*), lauded by Michael Broadbent for its 'peacock's tail' of flavours opening up on the palate.

A GOLDEN AGE

Which brings one to the present day. Is burgundy better than claret?

There is no doubt that it is harder to buy burgundy than claret. Premier cru vineyards in the Côte d'Or are not especially large and grand cru vineyards are tiny, whereas in the Médoc and the Graves, the better-known classed growths are generally the biggest. Uniformity is not a prime consideration in a region where a grower will produce only a few barrels of his greatest wines and often bottle each barrel individually by hand. The finest wines are quite exceptional, but most wine lovers would complain about the difficulty of obtaining them, the high prices charged and the many disappointing bottles encountered along the way.

My reply would be that burgundy, more precisely the Côte d'Or, is currently producing more interesting wines than any other wine region in the world. This situation has come about through the combination of good to excellent vintages, growing attention to the health of the vineyards, planting of lower-yielding clones, a willingness to exchange new ideas and, above all, the passion to produce wines with true personality.

What claret and burgundy have in common is that the wines have never been made with more care and attention. Today's wine lover is truly living in a 'golden age' as far as quality is concerned.

First published in *In Vino Prosperitas*, Edinburgh Financial Publishing (Asia) 1999.

NOTES FROM THE CELLAR

CHEVAL BLANC 1996

'Deep red with violet highlights. The nose seems to be closed-in, but opens up if swirled in the glass, revealing hints of blackcurrant and spices such as cinnamon. The oak is subtle, but there is a refined touch of vanilla. It is very well balanced on the palate with plenty of tannin, but of the ripe, silky variety. This elegant wine is eminently attractive. It has a beautiful, long aftertaste and a great future ahead of it.'

Tasting note from the château.

LA TACHE 1996

'Fabulous colour, intense ruby to rim, nose subdued at first but opens up sensationailly with characteristic La Tâche spiciness, an almost musky, perfumed array of black and red fruits and old, old vine density. The palate is layered, rich and sumptuous, with exceptional structure and substance, but with a purity of flavour and form that offers quite perfect balance. It may well pass into legend.'

Adam Brett-Smith,
Corney & Barrow.

Anglo-Irish cousins and writing companions Edith Somerville and Martin Ross travelled the Médoc one autumn with their notebooks, sketchpads and a new device they called 'the Kodak'. Their comparisons of the two Rothschild châteaux are tinged with the unique brand of barbed Victorian wit that endeared them to their readership as they ensure not even the most superlative of properties remain un-taunted.

MOUTON vs LAFITE

Edith Somerville and Martin Ross (1893)

A couple of undulating miles brought us in sight of a comfortable-looking white stone villa, flanked by long outhouses, and surrounded by a small and phenomenally brilliant flower garden. The vineyards ran like a smoothly swelling sea round the borders of this island that had been preserved from their inroads; the blinds of the villa were drawn down, and it seemed to look with 'a stony British stare' upon the vintage operations going forward all day under its eyes. Monsieur Z told us that it had been built in imitation of an English villa by the Baroness de Rothschild, but we did not dare to ask why she should have chosen the square modern type, dear to the heart of the retired solicitor. We asked instead why it should be called Mouton Rothschild, and found that once in the dark ages the whole of this part of the wine country had been given over to sheep, and that consequently the word *mouton* had survived; but why it should be tacked on to the name of a family could not be explained. It would be neither kind or clever to call a newly built house in the neighbourhood of Limerick, Pig Robinson or Pork Murphy; but in France, Sheep Rothschild is a name held in uninquiring reverence by the *négociant en vins*.

We left the carriage, and proceeded with all dignity to the *cuviers* at the rear of the villa, while the hot and tawny *vent d'Afrique* blew suffocatingly in our faces and covered our white veils with yellow grit, and turned the most inviting shade to mockery. It was doubtless of such heat as this that the lady's maid remarked to her mistress that it 'quite reminded 'er of 'ell!' But, for all that, we had a kind of glory in it; it made us feel that we were really abroad, and that we should be able to bore our friends about the *vent d'Afrique*, when we got home, in a manner that would surprise them. At this juncture we were halted in front of a palatial building of two storeys, and following our guide into it, we found ourselves in the twilight aisles of one of the great fermenting houses of the Médoc.

Right and left stood the huge barrels on their white stone pedestals: belted monsters, spick and span in their varnished oak and shining black hoops, with a snowy background of white-washed wall to define their generous contour, and a neat little numbered plate on each to heighten their resemblance to police constables. This was an *édition de luxe* of winemaking – at least, so it seemed to us after what we had seen of dingy sheds, wine-stained barrels, and promiscuous rubbish, with magenta legs splashing about in juice, and spilt dregs as a foreground.

We were taken up a corner staircase to the upper floor, and were there received by the superhumanly well-bred and intelligent official who is invariably found in such places; we were also received and closely examined by the swarm of fat wasps that, in the *cuviers*, is fully as invariable, and rather more intelligent. No one seems to object to these wasps and their pertinacity; Monsieur Z and the manager merely gave a pitying glance in the direction of my cousin, when, in the middle of a most creditable question about the phylloxera, her voice broke into a shriek, and after a few seconds of dervish-like insanity, she brought up from the back of her neck the fragments of a wasp, and hurled them to the floor with a dramatic force that was quite unstudied. The wasps congregated most thickly about an arched opening in the wall, through which a crane poked its long, lean arm into the open air, and dangled its chain for the tubs full of grapes that were brought underneath it by the oxen. Up came each purple load, already battered and robbed of its bloom by the crushing and packing, with the bloated yellow wasps hanging on to it, and the long arm of the crane swung it round to the *pressoir*, which here was a broad truck on wheels. The method then became of the usual repulsive kind. The grapes were churned from their stalks in a machine, the juice ran in a turgid river round the *pressoir*, and, paddling in this, the bare-legged workmen shovelled the grapes into the *cuves*, whose open maws gaped through trap-doors in the floor. Other men packed the stalks into a machine like a pair of stays; when it was full, the tight-lacing began by means of a handle and cogged wheels, and when it was over, the stalks were taken out dry and attenuated, and flung from a window, with the cheerless prospect of being utilized at some future time as top-dressing for their yet-unborn brethren.

When we got into the carriage again we were crammed with information, and a silence as of indigestion settled upon us as we whirled along the hog-backed vineyard road to Château Lafite. It is not only in wine that Mouton Rothschild is beaten by its nearest neighbour. In the matter of a château, Lafite scores still more decidedly; of that no one could have any doubt who saw this old country house, with its pointed towers, its terraced gardens with their ambushing perfumes that took the hot wind by surprise, its view over the soft country to other châteaux, and its delightful wood, where grassy walks wound away into the shadows. After these things, going to see the *cuviers* and the winemaking was like beginning again on roast beef after dessert; but the appetite came in eating. It was Mouton Rothschild over again, only more so; it could not be more dazzlingly smart than its kinsman, but it was larger: more outhouses and more imposing, a greater number of *cuves*, a more ambitious manner of regulating the temperature. We

Cousins Edith Somerville (*left*) and Violet Florence Martin (aka Martin Ross), co-wrote 13 books, the most popular being their series commentary on the life of a rural Irish magistrate. *In the Vine Country* was their only venture into wine writing.

were truly and genuinely interested, but none the less were we penetrated by a sense of the gross absurdity of our pose as students of viticulture, while Monsieur Z and the manager of Château Lafite imparted fact upon fact antiphonally and seriously, without a shadow of distrust of our capabilities. Indeed, in all our vintage experiences we met with this heartfelt devotion to the subject, and this touching belief in our intelligence, and it was both a glory and a humiliation to us.

Enfiladed thus by a crossfire of what might be called grape-shot, we progressed in fullest importance round the quiet nurseries of the claret for which such an incredible future of dessert-tables is in store, and entered at last the doorway of a long, low building. A few steps led downwards to another doorway, where a grave and courteous attendant presented us each with a candle placed in a socket at the end of a long handle, and unlocked a door into profound and pitchy blackness. It was like going to see the mummies at Bordeaux; it was even more like going into the cellar at home to look for rats, and my cousin's skirts were instinctively gathered up and her candle lowered to the ground as the darkness closed its mouth upon us. It was cool and damp, it smelled of must and wine barrels, and in some way one could feel that it was immense. Our guides turned to the right without hesitation, into a gallery whose walls, from the sandy floor to the vaulted ceiling, were made of bottles of wine. We walked on, and still on, trying to take it in, while on either side the tiers of bottles looked at us out of their partitions with cold uncountable eyes, eye-browed sometimes, or bearded, with a fungus as snowy and delicate as *crêpe lisse*, on which the specks of dew glittered as the candle-light procession passed by.

'There are here 150,000 bottles of claret,' said the manager, with prosaic calm. 'Some of them are a century old. This is the private cellar of Baron de Rothschild.'

'He will not drink it all,' said Monsieur Z; and we laughed a feeble giggle, whose fatuity told that we had become exhausted receivers.

More and yet more aisles followed, catacombs of silence and black heavy air, but full of the strange life of the wine that lay, biding its time according to its tribe and family, in a 'monotony of enchanted pride', as Ruskin has said about pine trees.

We saw very little more of winemaking, when we got out again into the blustery heat, and crawled back to the carriage, feeling cheaper and more modern than we had done for some time. A new phase of sightseeing was in store for us, and one with which we were even less fitted to compete. The inner life of a French country house does not come within the scope of the ordinary tourist; and when, later in the afternoon, we were led up the curving and creeper-wreathed steps of a château, and ushered into an atmosphere of polished floors, still more polished manners, afternoon tea and a billiard table, there was only one drawback to perfect enjoyment of the situation. The ladies of the household – there were several of them – did not speak English...

Excerpt taken from *In the Vine Country*, by Edith Somerville (1858–1949) and Martin Ross (1862–1915), W H Allen & Co (London) 1893.

The rivalry isn't in question. Differing in every detail from Merlot to Cabernet grape choice, clay to gravel soils, river-facing to sun-seeking aspect, ornate château to *garagiste* cellar, its winemakers from the sublimely offbeat to steadfastly conventional, the wines of Left and Right Bank Bordeaux may represent different sides of the same region, but Elin McCoy finds neither of them wanting.

LEFT BANK vs RIGHT BANK

Elin McCoy (2020)

On my first visit to Bordeaux several decades ago, what struck me most were the very different landscapes of the Left Bank and Right. I thought of them as the two separate countries of Bordeaux, divided by water and wine style, yet only an hour apart by car.

As I drove north to the Médoc on the D2 from the city of Bordeaux, the Left Bank appeared to be all about grandeur and solidity. Its imposing, turreted stone châteaux, vistas of vines and sweeping views of the Gironde estuary seemed deeply aristocratic, almost timeless. As home to four of the five first growths of the famous 1855 Classification, it felt hierarchical and formal, a place with plenty of blue blood and snob appeal.

On the other side of the Gironde and the Garonne River, and north of the Dordogne River that feeds into the Gironde, the Right Bank was more intimate and picturesque, with small, pretty properties set in a bucolic countryside, the kind of place you could imagine living. In Saint-Emilion, patches of vineyards overlooked the medieval village and fanned out from its stone ramparts. Driving on the winding, confusing roads here and in neighbouring Pomerol, I found a friendly, human-sized region, where châteaux of even star properties such as Ausone and Petrus seemed almost humble, their proprietors more approachable.

It was the differences between these two Bordeaux' – in culture, prestige, terroir, grapes, flavour, aroma, wine style and classification – that intrigued me, and they still do today. But much has changed on both banks since my first visit in the 1980s, and I've been fascinated by how much the two regions have influenced one another.

Early on, I prized what I thought of as the more intellectual wines, the structured and tannic Cabernet Sauvignons of the Left Bank. The sensual, drink-me-soon Right Bank Merlots, with their soft, lush fruit and smooth textures, seemed somehow less serious – with a few stellar exceptions. But that was then. Tasting widely and seeing things evolve year after year has a way of converting you to new ideas.

WHAT HASN'T CHANGED

Early histories, soils and the Left Bank classification, of course, haven't changed. The best-known region in medieval times was the area south of the city of Bordeaux on the Left Bank known as the Graves. Thomas Jefferson himself visited its most famous estate, Haut-Brion. The Médoc, north of Bordeaux along the Gironde, includes eight appellations, among them Pauillac and Margaux. The region's importance came after Dutch engineers had drained its swampy marshes in the 17th century and revealed the gravel terraces we now think of as ideal terroir for the Cabernet Sauvignon grape.

The Right Bank encompasses Saint-Emilion and its famous limestone plateau, which was known in Roman times, as well as tiny Pomerol, with its clay and gravel soil, and also a host of surrounding appellations such as Fronsac and the Saint-Emilion satellites. Since the frost of 1956, this has been the land of Merlot and, to a lesser extent, Cabernet Franc. Pomerol's identity is bound up with Merlot; the appellation, consultant Dany Rolland once told me, is like a *climat* (individual vineyard plot) of Burgundy.

The terroir has always determined the grapes, which in turn dictate the wine's taste. In the blends of the cooler Left Bank, Cabernet Sauvignon dominates, fleshed out with Merlot, and recently, more Petit Verdot, so the wines are higher in tannin and acidity. On the Right Bank, wines are the opposite: primarily juicy Merlot, balanced by a smaller proportion of Cabernet Franc; they are smoother, with less tannin, drinkable much sooner.

Mulling over why the Médoc region of the Left Bank became so important in the wine trade, its wines the focus of investment, I'm convinced that part of the reason is the five-tier hierarchy of the 1855 Classification, which has remained intact for 165 years – the only movement being the elevation of Château Mouton Rothschild from second to first growth in 1973. Though the quality level of wines from some châteaux (such as Pontet-Canet) has gone up and up, along with their reputations, their official status doesn't alter.

By contrast, Saint-Emilion's more fluid classification, established in 1955 with three categories, is periodically reassessed and better reflects current reality. It provides an incentive for ambitious owners to pour in money to up their quality, but also gives rise to regular insider squabbles and lawsuits, as happened in 2006 and again in 2012.

After all, land values are at stake. Being elevated from *grand cru* to *grand cru classé* can tip per-hectare prices to as much as three million euros – so Silvio Denz, owner of Château Faugères and Péby-Faugères told me after his properties were promoted in 2012.

Pomerol has never been officially classified, possibly because the tiny estates were virtually unknown until after World War II and only started becoming super-fashionable in the United States in the 1980s and 1990s.

So how did we arrive at the character of Left and Right Bank wines we find today? Everyone credits Professor Emile Peynaud with ushering in the modern style of Bordeaux in the 1970s through viticultural and winemaking practices that influenced both quality and style. He preached reduced yields, riper fruit, fermenting individual parcels of grapes

Bordeaux' two contrasting grape varieties: Cabernet Sauvignon (*left*) thrives on the Left Bank, while Merlot's star shines bright on the Right.

separately, creating second wines and replacing old vats and barrels with new oak. But his influence was mostly on the Left Bank, coming to fruition in the ripe, luscious 1982 vintage, packed with fruit and plush tannins.

The most radical ideas came from the Right Bank, starting in the 1990s and eventually leading to its redefinition as a hotbed of experimentation and innovation. That's thanks to four men, the new importance of America as a wine drinking country, and a movement of tradition-thumbing iconoclastic winemakers.

THE RISE OF POMEROL AND THE RIGHT BANK

Until the 1980s, the Right Bank lagged behind the Left in reputation, with a couple of exceptions. Its rise since then is surely due to Michel Rolland, who pushed Peynaud's idea of ripeness, succulent fruit and long macerations even further; Christian Moueix and his father Jean-Pierre, who had the lock on elevating the worldwide reputation of Pomerol, and critic Robert Parker, who always seemed to be on the side of the plucky underdog shaking up the status quo.

You can track changes in appreciation of Right Bank wines by price. After World War II, the top wines such as Cheval Blanc cost only half the price of the Médoc first growths, according to Benjamin Lewin MW's *What Price Bordeaux* (2009). By the early 2000s, at the height of US critic Robert Parker's power to make the Bordeaux market, the top names such as Petrus, Ausone, Lafleur and Cheval Blanc cost much more than Lafite.

The innovations were both good and not so good, in my view. Many of the earliest proponents of organic and biodynamic viticulture, such as Fronsac's Paul Barre, were on the Right Bank, and bravo to them. Barre was called crazy, but Pontet-Canet technical director Jean-Michel Comme later asked him for advice, as did others on the Left Bank.

I peg the era of *Les Garagistes* as the apotheosis of controversial experiments in Saint-Emilion. Jean-Luc Thunevin, whose Château Valandraud was a blend of tiny parcels in Saint-Emilion, was the first of this group of ambitious upstarts. They were convinced they could make great wine even on indifferent terroirs if they focused on very low yields, picked super-ripe grapes, cold-soaked them (macerated the grapes before fermentation) as in Burgundy, fermented in barrels and aged the wines in lashings of new oak. These micro-*cuvées* were flamboyant, flashy, rich, dense and expensive. Parker championed them, and they sold.

I was never a fan, and neither were châteaux on the Left Bank or traditionalists on the Right. 'I look for finesse rather than power,' more than one Left Bank proprietor told me, with a pronounced sniff. Me, too. But plenty of estates on the Right Bank, like châteaux Figeac and La Conseillante, kept the faith.

In any case, fashion is fickle.

By the end of the 2000s only the best *garagistes* had survived, and their use of excessive extraction and oak had declined. Some of their techniques, though, have been adopted on both the Right and Left Banks, and are now used to shape silky-textured wines with purity, freshness and vibrancy, as well as concentration and plushness.

Cobbled and quirky: Saint-Emilion sits atop 200km of caves, perfect for wine storage. The stones of its medieval streets originally arrived as balast in English ships fetching wine.

NEVER BETTER

Today, with more knowledge about soil and viticulture, wines on both the Right and Left Bank have never been better, and top examples are at parity when it comes to quality, though styles still differ widely, and rising alcohol levels – especially on the Right Bank – are becoming a problem.

As every new vintage emerges, critics try to decide whether it favours the Left or Right Bank. For example, 2016 was better on the Left Bank, though Pomerol shone, whereas 2015 was slightly better for Saint-Emilion and Pomerol.

But the surprise is that now, in many vintages, quality on both banks is at the same level, whether good, such as 2005, 2009 and 2010, or poor, such as 2011 and 2013.

Winemakers have taken some of the sensibility of one bank to the other. Marjolaine Maurice de Coninck moved from Saint-Emilion's Château Fonplegade to Labégorce and Marquis d'Alesme in Margaux, bringing with her a dedication to organic viticulture and modern ideas of tourism.

A spirit of experimentation has spread on the Left Bank, and precision viticulture – fermenting individual parcels separately – and investments in research are de rigueur. Think of Pontet-Canet's biodynamic vineyard and its bank of amphoras in the cellar, and Château Palmer's radical transformation to holistic rural paradise. The younger generation of owners is way more open to change than its predecessors were.

At the same time, there's a new international aristocracy on the Right Bank, with multi-millionaires and billionaires from countries as far-flung as China building the kind of famous-architect-designed cellars you see on the other side of the river. Swiss entrepreneur Denz tapped Mario Botta for his Château Faugères. Historic Château Pavie, purchased by supermarket mogul Gérard Perse in 1998, has a vast new cellar with a flashy, marble-laden reception area. Château Cheval Blanc, owned by billionaire Bernard Arnault, enlisted Christian Portzamparc to create the innovative grass-and-flower covered cellar I always love to visit.

CLIMATE CHANGE AND THE FUTURE

Lately, I find myself wondering about how the Left and Right Bank and their wines will evolve in the future. In the early summer of 2019, temperatures in Bordeaux soared to 40°C and more, another indicator of how climate change is already affecting both banks with heat waves, devastating frosts, violent storms, hail and drought.

Some warming has been welcome, especially on the slightly cooler Left Bank, where Cabernet Sauvignon – and also Petit Verdot – now ripen more easily and many châteaux have cut back on the amount of earlier-ripening Merlot in their blends because of its high alcohol. But in Saint-Emilion and Pomerol, cutting back on Merlot is not really an option, and Merlot sometimes produces wines that hit 15–16% alcohol, with cooked flavours that are less and less in fashion.

Will our ideas of where the best terroirs are shift? Research by Professor Kees van Leeuwin of the Institut des Sciences de la Vigne et du Vin (ISVV) has been part of a European project tracking temperature variability in wine regions with networks of sensors. This kind of precision testing has shown the temperatures on the Right Bank are far more variable than we thought, with differences of 1.5°C between the warmest and coolest spots. In the past, warmer spots guaranteed ripeness, but in the future, with climate change, the cooler spots may produce the better wines.

Will new grape varieties be required, changing what we regard as the essential flavour and aroma differences between the two regions? Already Baptiste Guinaudeau of Château Lafleur in Pomerol is replacing some Merlot vines with later-ripening Cabernet Franc.

Even more change will be coming. Yet the basic landscapes that first defined the two Bordeaux for me will remain – at least I hope so.

Aristocractic, timeless and distinctly formal: Château Latour (*foreground*), backed by châteaux Pichon-Longueville Comtesse de Lalande and Pichon-Baron in Pauillac (*left and right*) – properties that represent all that's imposing and grand about the Médoc.

Bordeaux is a branded wine with vast acreages at its disposal; burgundy is an appellation wine drawing from tiny Napoleonic vineyard plots. Each region is capable of producing wines of great beauty and distinction, fetching many thousands of pounds a bottle. Simon Gotelee takes a look at these 'non-identical twin behemoths of fine wine', and asks where they stand on the market.

BRAND BORDEAUX vs APPELLATION BURGUNDY

Simon Gotelee (2020)

Two personal images spring to mind when thinking about the different ways that Bordeaux and burgundy meet the world. The Burgundian one is driving south parallel to the Côte d'Or in my first car, a little Citroën Visa, full of excitement since I was young and on my way to work a harvest in Provence. Every side turning to the right bore a famous name: Gevrey-Chambertin, Chambolle-Musigny and Clos Vougeot. I pulled in to Vosne-Romanée, parked the car above La Romanée-Conti and got out the wine atlas that the French call 'Le Johnson'. I couldn't tell where the well-defined boundaries on the page were from looking at the vines – where did Richebourg start and La Romanée-Conti end?

But often the demarcation is more obvious. If you drive west out of Puligny-Montrachet, you come to a crossroads. There you can turn left to Chassagne; ahead left is the tiny south-facing *grand cru* of Bienvenues-Bâtard-Montrachet; ahead right is *premier cru* Les Pucelles, and on either side are the *villages*-level *lieux dits* Les Ensegnères and Les Meix. The French rather sniffily call the latter *communal*, but 2018 En Primeur prices were still £300 for six bottles. The *grands crus* over the road cost this much and more.

My Bordeaux snapshot is rather different, but also involves a French road trip. At a rather later stage in my career, I was driving from Cognac to Bordeaux with a colleague in a somewhat better car. We took the back roads, through an endless sea of vines. At each crest of the Route Nationale, the sea extended further. After a while, my companion, Andrew, exclaimed: 'Who the bloody hell drinks all this stuff?' At the next town we stopped for fuel, and went into the local garage and shop. Here was his answer: the cheapest bottle of Bordeaux was €1.69, emblazoned with a crest and a spurious château name. You could repeat the drive today and in 10 years' time and the lowest price would still be below €2.00. But despite my initial high and low perceptions, 'place' is an important factor in each region – an individual site in Burgundy and the prized position of a château in Bordeaux are equally compelling.

IT'S ALL ABOUT THE LAND

The initial plantings in Burgundy were monastic. The brothers saw the differences between their vineyards and had the leisure to codify and rank each one of them. Matt Kramer, whose book *Making Sense of Burgundy* (1990) delivers on its promise, talks about the 'hot wire' between the vineyard and the bottle, just like that between vinyl and speaker. Place is important to the point of obsessiveness, especially when vinifying Pinot Noir.

The fine-tuning of appellations from village up to tiny *lieu dit* level leads to the impression of irreversible scarcity in Burgundy, and this, naturally leads to sky-high prices. Bordeaux' route to the same place is somewhat different. 'Terroir' is not unimportant in Bordeaux. The patches of deep gravels and clay dirt from which the great wines of the Médoc or Right Bank come are still vital, but their geographical names rarely appear on the label. Clos Sainte Anne, whose Merlot is the core of Les Tourelles de Longueville, is a rare example of a named *cru* in the Médoc. Stephen Brook's mammoth update of *The Complete Bordeaux* details individual vineyard ownership as far as is possible, but the fame or otherwise of a Bordeaux wine rests instead on the name of the château where it has been made. Some, like Haut-Brion, are constrained by geography and urban sprawl. Others have combined or expanded their territory over the years. Either way, the wines they deliver are a consistent reflection of their vineyards. The distinction of the wines delivered by the Médoc's first growths and their peers across Dordogne, year on year, have achieved the same level of desirability – and consequent stratospheric price points.

DEALING WITH SCARCITY...

How does the market deal with scarcity commercially? The phrase 'Icon Wine' is overused, but there is a cohort of such wines worldwide that are a must for every collector, including Bordeaux first growths and *garagiste* châteaux, top Burgundy domaines, top Napa bottlings and Australia's Penfolds Grange. Not only do these wines enhance the owners' prestige, but, for the most part, they increase in value. They offer security in spades.

So how to get hold of them? The answer to the conundrum that any broker's best customers want exactly the wines of which there is least availability is horse trading. Customers (usually wine merchants) have to buy large quantities of 'lesser' wine in order to get an allocation of the most desirable *cuvées*. It's the same in both Burgundy and Bordeaux.

ULTIMATELY, THEY'RE BOTH BRANDS

Cedric Nicaise has a multifaceted view of the Bordeaux and burgundy markets. He is a Belgian, and is wine director at Eleven Madison Park restaurant in Manhattan. He has also just helped to set up the wine list at Davies and Brook at Claridge's in Mayfair, and is keenly observing the differences between customers at the two fine-dining establishments. He thinks that at the top end of the market, Bordeaux has first-mover advantage in terms of brand recognition: 'First off, I think that both are brands. I, of course, understand that Clos Saint-Jacques is a place and Haut-Brion is a producer, and that the producer is what we know to be a brand. But both are names, names that have been promoted over time and given brand recognition. People who know burgundy know that Clos Saint-Jacques is good. But who really understands why? The real difference is that Bordeaux has been promoted for so much longer than burgundy. The Classification of 1855 was almost 80 years before the appellations of Burgundy were put into law. So this has given Bordeaux' châteaux substantially longer to promote themselves. Especially since most of the bottlings coming out of Burgundy until after World War II were from négociants, who collected wines from a number of different villages and sold them under their own banner. Its appellation "brands" weren't upheld till much later.'

In Nicaise's experience: 'Burgundy drinkers drink burgundy, Bordeaux drinkers drink Bordeaux.' So once the choice between the two is made by his well-heeled and international diners, for whatever reason, it remains the default.

One thing that he does want to work on is their disinclination to experiment, the implication being that decades of recognizing the great French names – whether Bordeaux or burgundy – has dulled the UK's willingness to reach beyond the familiar. 'They need to heed the advice of our sommeliers.' Talk to the somm, London!

KEEP THE MESSAGE CLEAR

Florian Migeon, marketing director of Burgundy's Louis Latour, is succinct in his analysis of the contrast between the consumer's perception of 'claret' and burgundy. 'The first thing that the consumer sees on a burgundy label is the name of the village, area or *cru*, whereas in Bordeaux it is the name of the château. Each of these represents the same thing, a 'guarantee of quality'. In effect, they are each the 'brand' that the consumer buys into.

Migeon's view is also that simplicity is key. In Burgundy, Pommard may aspire to reach *grand cru* status; Pouilly-Fuissé had its heart set on being a *premier cru* – each wants to improve its ranking. But why complicate the kaleidoscope of burgundy further for the consumer? 'Keep the pyramid stable,' he says.

Bordeaux tied itself in similar knots with the recent announcement by the Alliance des Crus Bourgeois du Médoc that three new categories have been created: Cru Bourgeois, Cru Bourgeois Supérieur and Cru Bourgeois Exceptionnel. According to the organization, the new system creates a 'clear, impartial, objective classification that will enable consumers to buy Crus Bourgeois with complete confidence'. The wish would appear to father the thought. Almost 10 years of preparation were necessary to obtain consent from the public authorities for the creation of this new classification, but why bother? Why should any consumer outside the Bordeaux bubble care about such self-referential arcana?

I am reminded of the maverick Randall Grahm's quote when challenged by the press for making his first Chardonnay: 'I have learned that if it is too hard to explain, don't start.' This should be a marketing mantra along, with 'never assume anyone is interested'.

KNOW YOUR BORDEAUX FROM YOUR CLARET

Just as important as the geographical aspects of greater brands Bordeaux and Burgundy, are the names of the négociants, individual domaines and châteaux. If a brand is a summation of the understanding of one's product, selling reassurance to the consumer, the person or estate that makes the wine is clearly relevant. Basil Fawlty may have asserted that most of his guests 'wouldn't know a Bordeaux from a claret', but the famous names of the world's two greatest wine regions are indeed understood as brands themselves.

'Brand' is a word and concept that is often denied or denigrated in the wider 'wine trade', but wine brands have serious longevity. The châteaux of the 1855 Classification still exist, barring a few mergers, and have a similar status today as that accorded under Napoleon's famous commission. Compare and contrast this achievement with the never-ending changes in the world of big corporations. In Tom Peters' 1982 analysis of corporate America, *In Search of Excellence*, he identified 43 'excellent' American companies and tried to distil the sources of their success. Before the end of the economically booming 1980s, two-thirds of them had ceased to exist and some had become bywords for strategic failure: Wang, Atari, Du Pont, Avon, IBM and General Motors.

So maybe the fact that wine is the world's sexiest agricultural product allied to human engagement means that place and terroir can be harnessed to commercial endeavour to amplify the overall power and brand longevity in the world of wine, especially in these two classic regions? On the first page of *Wine*, Hugh Johnson wrote in 1966: 'Mysterious circumstances…make wine not only the most delicious, but the most fascinating drink in the world.' This page remains almost a manifesto for wine, and merits re-reading. If this can be allied to passion and business skill, Baron Philippe de Rothschild and Louis Latour can indeed be stronger, longer-lived brands than Atari or Du Pont.

Every vintage challenges, requires action and continuous learning from experience. Vineyards can be grubbed up, but otherwise they have a permanence that requires nurture and long-term commitment. While the modern world of wine is clearly global and uses the tools of modern business communication, somebody has got their hands dirty in the vineyard, winery or bottling line to make the product. Passionate people have baked in the sun, been drenched by rain or must, elated and dispirited in turn. A brand is the culmination of a series of conscious and unconscious decisions, and these peoples' decisions matter, even if they would not call themselves marketers. This applies equally to Mouton Cadet or an 'arch-*garagiste*', supermarket Mâcon or Le Montrachet.

Que Dieu les bénisse.

CHAPTER FIVE

A WINE REGION AT WAR

World War II brought unspeakable horrors to the people of Bordeaux, with the threat of starvation, bombing and transportation ever present. During the years 1940–45 its vineyards became neglected and many of its precious wines were sent for distillation – often then used to form the basis for German explosives. But not all was lost...

Jane Anson (2020)
Bordeaux Survives the War

Ian Maxwell Campbell (1948)
Of Wartime Wines, Tax and Chancellors

Joan Littlewood (1984)
Escape Across the Pyrenees

Ideally positioned for Nazi logistics, coastal defence against the Allies and access to fine wines, Bordeaux was an obvious focal point for the Germans during World War II. Their invasion was to alter life for the locals forever. Jane Anson has privileged access to private diaries and first growth memoirs that describe day-to-day living at the hands of the Third Reich

BORDEAUX SURVIVES THE WAR

Jane Anson (2020)

'The military presence reached everywhere. The tentacles of the German administration spread throughout the occupied zone, and no doubt extended well into the free zone too. Our access to supplies dwindled extremely quickly after the soldiers arrived.'

This observation is from the diary of the late Jean-Paul Gardère, a wine broker and former director of Château Latour, who, a few years before his death in 2014, gave me a copy of its pages – loose leaves, hand-typed, with scrawled additions studded into the margins throughout. It makes for fascinating yet somber reading, recalling a time that remains little spoken of in Bordeaux. Even the fact that 2020 marks a full 80 years since Nazi troops reached the city and began an occupation that lasted from June 28th 1940 until August 28th 1944 does not incline those few who remember to talk about it.

There are still reminders to be found. Most obviously, the submarine base with its 10-metre thick reinforced concrete walls stands in downtown Bordeaux, about to become the site of the biggest digital art space in Europe. Along the coast, remnants of the Regelbau bunkers and other military defences are still visible, if increasingly half-buried in sand. You can even find wartime graffiti in the limestone cellars beneath Château Franc Mayne in Saint-Emilion – the same on the attic walls of Château Palmer in Margaux.

Don and Petie Kladstrup's brilliant *Wine and War* (2002) covers certain aspects of the war in Bordeaux – mainly concerning itself with the Weinführer Heinz Bömers and négociants like Louis Eschenauer who worked closely enough with Bömers to later be found guilty of collaboration. I have sought, instead, stories of everyday life during the war years. Some have been shared directly with me – those of Gardère, and also Jean-Michel Cazes, Jacques de Boüard, May-Eliane de Lencquaisang, Daniel Lawton and others. Added to these are things I have learned from memoirs, letters, château archives, local history books and university dissertations. Piecing all of these memories together paints a picture of a region that was both protected and exposed because of its strategic importance.

German troops march past Bordeaux' City Hall. As France's largest port, the occupation of the city at the outbreak of World War II was swift.

THE SIEGE

The same things attracted the German army to Bordeaux as have always attracted invaders to this place: its port and its location on the Gironde estuary make it an ideal conduit for transporting men and material. Within hours of its arrival, the incoming army had set up checkpoints, requisitioned homes, unfurled Nazi flags, taken control of the port and set up gun emplacements. Having fled Paris two weeks earlier on June 10th, the French government was in Bordeaux to witness its fall. The port teemed with soldiers, and the city as a whole was crammed with refugees – many of them from northern France had arrived on foot in fear of the occupying army sweeping them out of their homes. The population of the city quadrupled from 250,000 to one million people, putting further pressure on shops that were already being cleared out by German soldiers sending fabrics, jam, coffee, chocolate and cigarettes back home to their families.

This was just a week after the Armistice had been signed – which itself came a few days after 12 German bombers had killed 65 and wounded 160 in a bombing raid on the heart of Bordeaux city, a move designed to put pressure on the French government to sign a ceasefire. Five Gironde parliamentarians had been among the 80 across France who said no to the Armistice, calling it treasonous. One of these was Jean-Emmanuel Roy, mayor of Naujan-et-Postiac in Entre-Deux-Mers, and a winemaker instrumental in the founding of France's appellation laws in 1937. But like so many others, he then had no choice but to watch it all happen.

The demarcation line that divided France into two was created at midnight on the morning of June 25th, and passed through the Bordeaux region, almost exactly halfway between Castillon (Occupied) and Sainte-Foy-la-Grande (Free France, under Vichy government control) down through Sauveterre-de-Guyenne in Entre-Deux-Mers to Langon in the southern tip of the Graves. Barsac, Sauternes, Libourne, Saint-Emilion, the Médoc, most of the Graves and Bordeaux city were all occupied. You can trace the exact line on two Michelin maps, numbers 98 and 99, that were created in 1940 and 1941 (if you find the original versions, you will see they were printed without covers to save on paper). It remained in place until March 1st 1943, a few months after the Germans moved in to the supposedly Free zone and brought the rest of France under their control.

THE ROUT OF THE CHATEAUX

All over Occupied Bordeaux, châteaux were immediately requisitioned by German soldiers. In Saint-Emilion that included châteaux Soutard, Trottevieille, Clos Fourtet and Ausone – where the German general went to great lengths to ensure he had peace and quiet, stationing guards at every gateway to the château to ensure no one could enter. Over in the Médoc, the first châteaux to be occupied were those with British or Jewish links (most famously those belonging to the Sichels, the Bartons and the Rothschilds), or those with strategic locations such as Grand-Puy-Ducasse on the Pauillac waterfront.

As high-profile châteaux under Jewish ownership, both Mouton Rothschild and Lafite Rothschild were targeted, with both branches of the family stripped of their French nationality. Baron Philippe de Rothschild was imprisoned by Vichy in 1940, freed in 1941, and crossed the Pyrenees mountains to then join the Free French forces in England in 1942 (*see* pages 136–142). His autobiography recounts that he arrived back in France in one of the later waves of D-Day landings, disembarking in the Bay de Seine near Bayeux on June 21st 1944.

Baron Elie de Rothschild of Lafite served as an officer in a cavalry regiment in the early years of the war and was captured by the Nazis. Placed first in Nienberg prisoner-of-war camp, then Colditz Castle and Lübeck, he was released in May 1945. He was one of a number of Bordeaux prisoners of war that included André Cazes of Château Lynch-Bages, who spent four years first in Nuremburg, then in a camp on the Polish frontier near to Dresden, and Thierry Manoncourt of Château Figeac, who spent three years in a disciplinary camp after refusing to work as a labourer for the Germans. Closer to the city, Haut-Brion was first turned into a hospital for French soldiers by its owners, then seized by Germans and turned into a rest home for the Luftwaffe.

SUBSISTENCE LIVING

At the same time, the Germans set up a whole series of measures to limit the circulation of people, goods and the postal traffic between two zones either side of the demarcation line. Josette de Boüard, who would go on to marry Christian de Boüard of Château Angélus in 1945, remembered in a written history of Saint-Emilion that for the first year after the Armistice, it was impossible to telephone or even send a postcard from one side to the other (although her husband remembers how, aged 17 in 1941, he smuggled a pig over the line with the local baker, butchering it in the cellars of the château).

Jean-Paul Gardère wrote that 1941 'was undoubtedly the most difficult year of the war. I am sure the administration did what it could, but a lead weight lay across France'. He recounted that the population, 'lived in permanent fear, struck dumb and in daily worry of finding food'. Electricity was on only once or twice a week, and imports were cut off; fuel and food supplies dwindled to almost nothing. May-Eliane de Lencquesaing, long-time owner of Château Pichon-Longueville Comtesse de Lalande in Pauillac, wrote in her diaries that the châteaux' vegetable gardens became increasingly important – even though the Médoc's gravel soils were never much good at growing anything but vines.

'Our everyday life is marked by a total lack of basic goods, little heating, a very restricted diet with no sugar, little bread, almost no meat, butter does not exist,' she wrote. 'We live according to the rhythm of the season, we grind corn to make a rough flour which serves as the base for most of our food. We roast barley for fake coffee.'

Gardère's diaries list rations that included 250g of bread per day for women and children (about one baguette), 350g of bread for manual workers and 100g of meat per month. Milk, butter, cheese and vegetable oils were almost never available. Cigarettes came with a ration of five packets every 10 days, and wine was only available for manual labourers, who were allowed around three litres a month. Any men in the Médoc aged between 20 and 40 who had not gone off to fight were sent to build the Atlantic Wall, the defence against Allied invasion running through Soulac, Le Verdun, Montalivet and Arcachon – he remembered that they would head off in the morning with wine in cans, then spend the day trying to set in motion small acts of resistance, *petit sabotage*, such as 'putting as much sand in the bricks as possible to ensure the defences weren't strong'.

The black market flourished from 1942, where 'the clever got very rich and the rest got poorer'. Gardère recalled certain restaurants that would never ask for your ration tickets 'for a price'. He was writing this around 20 years afterwards, trying to capture the memories, and said: 'My exact figures might be off, but I clearly remember the bread rations, and how you could buy fake coupons on the black market. If your baker knew you well, sometimes he would accept them and hide them in the middle of the real coupons.'

Bicycles, he wrote, were like gold dust, and almost anything you wanted had to be swapped for something else – so a bottle of wine for a bag of potatoes, and 'bad luck for those who had nothing to swap'. Life was easier in the countryside than it was in big towns like Bordeaux, and everyone tried to find relatives with vegetable gardens. By the end of 1943 and into 1944, the Allied bombings increased in intensity, and Gardère, who lived in Soussans just outside Margaux, built a bomb shelter that was two metres long and 80 centimetres wide, dug into his garden, covered with a frame with earth piled on top. 'Plenty of people laughed at me, but when the Allies starting bombing Pauillac and Blaye on August 5th 1944, they were lining up to get inside.'

Jean-Michel Cazes remembers that on that same day, a few miles up the road, he was sat, aged nine, with his eight-year old sister at Château Lynch-Bages watching the bombs fall 'like fireworks' on Pauillac town centre. Their mother was taking shelter in Pauillac, barely one kilometre away from the château, in a trench not unlike the one that Gardère had dug, with nothing but her handbag over her head for protection. Forty-five locals died during those raids, carried out by 306 Lancaster bombers and 30 Mosquitos from the RAF and American Airforce. Cazes also remembers that a few decades after the war, when he was over in Texas, he met one of the pilots who flew the mission.

AT HOME WITH THE THIRD REICH

For much of the population, these moments of high danger were interspersed with life continuing as normal, albeit beset by deprivations. Cazes, who was four at the start of the war and nine at its end, remembers that by 1942 he and his friends had switched from playing German soldiers in the playground to playing Allied soldiers, but most of the time they were fascinated by their new neighbours. Some of his most vivid memories are of soldiers marching through the streets of Pauillac singing German military songs, or walking in formation to go swimming in a local reservoir, in uniform but with their towels slung over their shoulders. With a father held as a prisoner-of-war, Cazes was given an extra ration of biscuits at school, and was invited every few months to the town hall with other boys whose fathers were interned. Once a month he was able to send a letter – or rather to sign a standard form letter attesting to the fact that everything was fine – and every few months they could send a larger parcel containing jam, cigarettes and other small luxuries. For the final year of the war they had no news of André Cazes at all, but in August 1945 he made his way home to Pauillac, weighing just 45 kilos, having been liberated by the Russians.

Entre-Deux-Mers was the site of particularly fierce acts of resistance and retribution. In 1944, fighters from the famous Grand-Pierre Resistance group were shot close to Blasimon Abbey, while 25-year old Roger Teillet was caught and eventually hanged by the SS on the Place de Blasimon. On the night of July 10th 1944, Resistance fighters were preparing to unload two planes' worth of ammunition and parachutists from the British forces at Saint-Léger-de-Vignague near Sauveterre-de-Guyenne, but were intercepted, many of them caught and killed. Even as the Germans retreated after the Allied victory, a few Resistance fighters confronted the troops and were killed – including 18-year old

André Loiseau who, according to witnesses who told their stories to the Historical Society of Saint-Emilion, died among the vines of Pomerol. Yves Damécourt, owner of Château de Bellevue and mayor of Sauveterre, has been instrumental in keeping the memories of these men and women alive. The town's Porte Saint-Léger gate marks the spot where the German guard post was stationed, and a memorial plaque was erected there in 2016.

Acts of defiance were played out across the region from the first days of the war. Saint-Emilion, for example, played a secret but crucial role in protecting France's treasures for future generations. The town's monolithic church, which dates back to the 12th century, has long been one of France's most celebrated historic monuments, and was selected by Georges Huisman, director of arts under prime minister Edouard Daladier, for a special mission. As the fighting became increasingly inevitable, France began making quiet preparations for the conservation of its most significant works of art, and Huisman put aside a significant budget to produce protective casings for the priceless stained-glass windows that lined cathedrals and churches around the country.

Working in secrecy with Jean Verrier, inspector general of national monuments, Huisman came up with such an effective plan that within weeks of war being declared, over 50,000 square metres of glass were carefully taken down, placed in the specially prepared casings and moved to top-secret locations for storage until peace returned. One of the stores of this precious glass was in Saint-Emilion's underground church. Huisman had correctly assessed that this vast stone tomb, crafted into existence eight centuries earlier under the orders of Seigneur Pierre de Castillon, would provide perfect shelter for some of the great treasures of French medieval art, including almost certainly the windows from Chartres and Bourges cathedrals. Very few locals ever suspected what was being stored under their feet – and still less, we can imagine, did the German soldiers.

MAKING WINE, NOT WAR

And all the while, the business of making wine continued. Thierry Manoncourt at Château Figeac came home in 1943 in time to work the harvest, not just at his own estate but at those nearby too. With so many men away fighting, he now joined his cellar master in looking after the vines at Vieux Château Certan and others, trying to keep châteaux going until their workers could return.

The difficulties in actually making wine during the war are well reported. Not only had most of the working-age men been sent to fight, but equipment was increasingly difficult to get hold of. Glass bottles were scarce, corks scarcer still, and even the paper used to record harvests and yields became thinner and thinner. Throughout the occupation the locals had to distil their wine – often a full half of their harvest – into fuel and industrial alcohol which the Germans needed as solvents or as a basis for explosives. There was no copper to make the famous Bordeaux mixture used to treat powdery mildew because all the metal was being taken and melted down for the German war machine – and this was a time when the region was suffering a series of bad harvests (until the victory year of 1945, when the weather perked up). To make matters even tougher, all the cows, sheep and oxen that were often used in viticulture had also been requisitioned for the war effort.

Inevitably, the effects of the war years were felt for some time. Rationing continued until 1949, and money was so scarce that paying harvesters was almost impossible, as was buying products for treating the vines. Broker Edouard Lawton wrote in his diary in 1947: 'I have been in business since 1891 but never have I seen such a crisis in trading.' The 1947 vintage was of brilliant quality, and yet he writes: '…I wonder how and when trading will commence. Our *primeur* business is dead. Our old buyers have disappeared, the great châteaux have become storehouses for the trade.' After the war, many estates – including the first growths – would regularly declassify their wines because a simple *vin de table* found an easier and more receptive public, who simply had no money to pay for prestigious names.

THE FALLOUT CONTINUES

All of this often fades into the background next to the unease that continued over the role of Bordeaux wine merchants during the occupation – much of it with reason. Many of those sent away to fight never returned, and those who were seen to have prospered under the occupation inevitably became the focus of anger.

Exports of wine to Allied countries became illegal from 1940 onwards – as they were to pretty much anywhere but Germany – making it complicated to judge those who continued supplying wine in order to pay their workforce and keep their businesses from closing. Individual heroics, however, are easy to find: *Wine and War* recalls the Miaihles at Château Palmer, who hid two families of Italian Jews under the noses of the German troops who were occupying their château. But far more typical are stories like the one that Gardère recounts, remembering the screams of his Soussans neighbour Madame Labat at 3am one morning as she was taken away to Bordeaux, from where she was sent to Drancy internment camp near Paris. (She returned after the Liberation, unlike so many others.)

In the end, a full 43 négociants were investigated for their close relationship with the occupying forces. Those who were especially active under the Vichy government (including Salles, Cruse, Kressmann, Martin, Lur-Saluces, de Luze and Guestier) were allowed to plead their cause before the finance minister René Pleven on December 1st 1944. In the end, almost all were exonerated, with retribution limited to fines. The national armistice that was granted in 1950 and 1951 saw full pardons for the 14 merchant companies that had come under particular suspicion. And 80 years on, the memories of those who remember it all first hand are an increasingly rare and precious resource.

The much-admired merchant, cricketer and wine commentator Ian Maxwell Campbell (1870–1954) ponders whether in wartime 'the hand of untrammelled Nature' might be a superior substitute for that of man, and whether Winston Churchill had the right attitude...

OF WARTIME WINES, TAX AND CHANCELLORS

Ian Maxwell Campbell (1948)

Through the kindness of Hugh Rudd I have seen one or two samples of each of the war years, and of these, after their hazardous journey, the representatives of 1942 and 1943 appeared to be the most promising, and the 1944 the lightest, but sweetest. Such information as I have so far been able to gather direct from Bordeaux indicates that 1940 and 1943, and probably not 1942, are the best of the war years. Since news emanating from Reims and the Côte d'Or also favours 1943 as being of exceptionally fine quality it seems quite possible that that year may become celebrated among wine lovers[1].

I have already admitted that I have mentioned in the course of my sketchy survey of claret only the *premiers crus*, or higher growths, of the different vintages, but it has been due to the general success, or failure, of most of its better-classed wines that a vintage has or has not become famous. One swallow (I allude to the bird) will not make a summer, and one or two successes in a bad year will rarely do much to enhance the final verdict on that year, nor one or two failures damn a good vintage. The excellence of the 1880 Mouton Rothschild did not avert the condemnation of its vintage, nor did the quite remarkably fine quality of 1921 Cheval Blanc constitute the vintage of that otherwise poor year a success. The sorry fate of 1928 Château Lafite and poor showing of 1929 Château Haut-Brion did nothing to detract from the fame of these two vintages and, on the other hand, the admirable quality of many of the less-known Médoc and Saint-Emilion wines of 1916 and 1917 did not succeed in making these vintages popular or renowned. It is the Churchills and Roosevelts and Stalins that make a generation historically famous and not you or I, dear reader, whatever merits (or demerits) we may inwardly know we possess.

[1] 1943 was indeed praised as the best of the wartime vintages. Michael Broadbent said it had 'richness and fruit…the best still drinking well' in his *Vintage Wine* of 2002.

When one remembers the hidden wealth of sugar in the stubborn 1870s, and the neglected but exquisite beauty of the delicate 1871s that followed them, one can only hope that *les années de la guerre* may again prove the hand of untrammelled Nature to be a not unsuccessful substitute for the skilled labour of Man. If 1944 only proved to be another 1871, none of us, perhaps, would mind paying the some 10 times higher price that Bordeaux shippers are already, and without guarantee of any sort, asking for it today! What with the exorbitant and short-sighted demands of my friends, the Bordeaux shippers, and the restrictive, almost prohibitive, duty on claret and light wines generally imposed by our own equally short-sighted legislators, it looks as though Gladstone's meritorious effort[2] to encourage the consumption of low-strength beverage wines is destined to the scrap heap; and that, wine being henceforth an expensive luxury, against Gladstone's advice, our middle classes, if they cannot for one reason or another drink beer or spirits, will take, for their alcoholic refreshment, one or other of those fermented fruit juices (by no means always grape juice) which are dangled before an easily gulled public and to which I have already drawn attention.

Beware of them. Providence has ordained that Britain shall not be by nature a wine-producing country[3]; this should be borne in mind by those, of whom there seems to be an increasing number, who possess oenophilous ambitions and wish to indulge in the, at present, tantalizing pastime of a search for wine, genuine wine. It is they who should insist on a lowering of duties. The wine trade itself might appear to be too much of an interested party, even though its demands are largely on behalf of the purchasing public. I have been on several deputations to sundry chancellors of the exchequer to discuss policy and protest against the ever-increasing burden of duties. One of the most memorable, in view of the capricious circumstances of the present day, was a visit to Mr Winston Churchill when he was chancellor (1924–29). With his most winning smile and a cigar in the corner of his mouth he told us that he wanted more money out of us, and we had to point out the growing danger to the wine trade of 'British Wine', which at that time was paying an unjustifiably small excise duty as 'British Sweets'! Churchill, with a twinkle in his eye, said: 'I must remind you, gentlemen, that Great Britain is still a part of the British Empire and entitled to some preference!' In the friendly atmosphere the chancellor engendered I asked him: 'What did Mr Gladstone do in 1860–61?' He turned

[2] In the early 1860s Gladstone attempted to revolutionize British wine consumption by making substantial duty cuts – he reduced the cost of table wines by 83 percent; fortified wines by 57 percent. Retailers were also allowed, on the payment of a small licence fee, to sell wine for consumption 'off' their premises. These changes led to a rapid growth in consumption, with total wine imports rising from 32.5 million litres in 1856–60 to 78 million in 1871. (James Simpson *The Economic History Review*, 2004, 'Selling to Reluctant Drinkers: The British Wine Market, 1860–1914'.)

[3] There are now over 2,500 hectares planted to vines in the UK (2020).

An American portrait of Churchill taken while he was prime minister. Champagne and whisky were his constant wartime companions, but he wasn't averse to taxing them if he felt he needed to.

to me, took the cigar out of his mouth and replied with most engaging simplicity: 'Ah! you must remember that Mr Gladstone was a very great man dealing with comparatively small figures, whereas I am a small man dealing with gigantic figures.' Not the answer that, at that time, one would have expected from Winston Churchill. We know him better now; we have discovered the inspiration of his leadership and the grandeur of his humility. I told this story of his father to Major Randolph Churchill when I met him at lunch at Chalié Richards' office, and he had it published in the 'Londoner's Diary' of the *Evening Standard*.

I enjoyed, too, a rather more intimate conversation with the late Robert Horne (subsequently Lord Horne) when he was chancellor of the exchequer. He refused to receive a deputation but eventually agreed to see me alone. I happened to be playing my first innings as chairman of the Wine and Spirit Trade Association that year. We chatted for a good hour, and I heard every reason under the sun why a reduction in duties was an economic and national impossibility, and, when we had exhausted the topic and touched on others, he turned to me and said with a chuckle: 'As one Scot to another, Campbell, tell me where the devil I can buy some good brandy at a reasonable price.'

Extract take from *The Wayward Tendrils of the Vine* by Ian Maxwell Campbell, Chapman & Hall (London) 1948.

Baron Philippe de Rothschild (1902–88) stayed for as long as he could in Nazi-occupied France, but as a prominent Jewish figure at Château Mouton Rothschild, his time inevitably ran out. Joan Littlewood, co-writer of his autobiography, describes his escape over the Pyrenees on foot to Spain.

ESCAPE ACROSS THE PYRENEES

Joan Littlewood (1984)

I planned to cross the Pyrenees on foot. It was the only escape route left; all the other frontiers were now firmly closed to us. I needed a guide and I knew Gaston had contacts in the Resistance at Perpignan. We ate a quiet meal; Gaston brought out a bottle of his good wine and we didn't talk about the war. I left early next morning. He had asked me if I was prepared to risk the train journey. I was: time was short. He drove me to the station.

When the train drew in my heart sank – it was crammed with German soldiers. I couldn't retreat. Quickly I bought all the collabo journals, jumped in and stood in the corridor holding the disgusting *Gringoire* in front of my face. No one ever read the rag with such concentration. Next stop, Perpignan. Two minutes' wait. This is it, Georges Philippe, alias Pierre Renard, watch your step. Get through that crowd fast. The place is lousy with Germans. I tried to look happy and relaxed, but I couldn't make it; my mouth was so dry I couldn't swallow, let alone smile. I caught sight of myself in a shop window, the one bare head among a crowd of helmets. They looked ridiculous.

Gaston's number-one contact was the town clerk. I made straight for the town hall, decided it was the wrong time of day, too early, walked round the block two or three times, regained my old confident stride, marched in through the front door, located his office and caught a glimpse of him as the door swung open to release an office boy juggling with a pile of files that reached to his chin. Then I rushed downstairs and waited and waited in the street. I walked this way and that, trying to look as if I had somewhere to go, while keeping an eye on the town hall exits. Missed him. The concierge was locking up, going to his lunch. I repeated the performance in the afternoon, with even less success. My quarry wasn't in his office. He didn't appear at all. I felt sick at heart as I watched the concierge lock up for the night.

Better try the second contact right away. It was the old man who kept the newsstand at the bus terminus. He was a pale, stern old chap. I bought newspapers, went for a walk, came back and bought more, without getting a word out of him. I bought a pack of lead pencils, a tin money box and an India rubber shaped like Felix the Cat, still not a word. Had I got the wrong man? I was about to give up when he looked me straight in the eye. 'No sense in hanging about here,' he said. 'Get yourself up to Font-Romeu, pronto.'

'I'm not on a skiing holiday.'

'On holiday, did you say? Oh yes, very nice place, do you a world of good. Want some new clobber while you're there? See my friend Josef the tailor.' He scribbled a plan of the way to Josef's shop on a scrap of paper and winked solemnly as he gave it to me.

The evening was drawing in and I'd nowhere to sleep. I decided to make for Font-Romeu straight away, if possible. Maybe I'd feel safer there. I was in luck for a change, there was a train.

It was dark when I arrived, and deserted. Nevertheless I set out to check up on Monsieur Josef. The tailor's shop existed, but it was boarded up. I tried the neighbours. After a long time, an old lady answered the door, looked at me suspiciously, but gave me some idea of where the tailor was to be found. Up by the Bella Vista Hotel, she said, waving her hand vaguely towards the hills.

I found the hotel, a seedy-looking boarding house in the suburbs, and sure enough, two doors away, Monsieur Josef's new shop, which was even poorer than the one he'd left.

It was too late to call. I tried for a room at the Bella Vista. The foyer smelt of stale cabbage and rising damp and there were plenty of empty rooms.

Next morning I called on Monsieur Josef. He got the message straight away. 'Oh dear no, nothing doing here. The last lot who tried it were brought back under arrest. You get back to Perpignan sharp, on your toes.'

I thanked him and asked him to do a little job for me. He was a Jew and obviously sympathetic. When I left the shop, my precious store of banknotes had been carefully stitched into the collar of my jacket.

Back in Perpignan I had only one chance: the town clerk. This time I waited by the side door at the lunch hour.

I was lucky. He came out that way and he was alone. I went up to him, and casually asked the way to the nearest pharmacy. He looked just another fussy little bureaucrat close to, but he walked with me a few steps and I gave him Gaston's name, then told him what I wanted.

The only people who could help me were the communists, he said. He gave me an address and exact directions, excused himself and quickly jumped on a bus. After going wrong in the back streets, I eventually found the place. It was a shoemaker's shop, small and dark; there were vases of gaudy paper flowers among the rows of broken-down shoes. The shoemaker was a subtle questioner, giving me an oblique glance as he worked over his last, throwing in a philosophical remark as the bell on the shop door rang and a customer entered. When he finally closed the shop he told me to follow him.

He took me to Juanita's house. Juanita was a Spanish republican who had organized the escape of a small army of her people and brought them to France. Now she was helping French refugees to return to the country from which she was exiled. She took me in. It was a very small house and she had a husband and two children, so my bed was in the loft. By chance one day I discovered that this young mother, so gentle and kind, was busily engaged in smuggling arms to the Resistance. She fascinated me, but that was as far as it went. She was in love with her husband and her communism. The latter might have been overcome, but it is quite useless to try to seduce a woman who is happy with her husband.

It took 15 days for her to make the necessary contacts, including fixing me some false papers. Prison had taught me patience. In the evenings I lay on my bed listening to the street sounds. One day a travelling fair moved in and at dusk I could hear the hurdy-gurdy of a carousel, the shrieks of the girls as they dived with the big dipper and the roar of a motorbike, which never seemed to go anywhere; it just whirred round and round like a fly in an upturned glass.

'What is it?' I asked Juanita. 'That's the Wall of Death,' she said. I'd never seen one. I was so curious that, on the Saturday night, it was the night before I was due to leave, she risked taking me out, walking between her husband and the children, to let me see the strange death wall, a huge cylinder with a motorcyclist riding its inner surface.

A few nights before, a tall distinguished-looking character had appeared at the house. He carried himself with an air. His coat was long, of gentlemanly cut with a black velvet collar. I kept wondering who he reminded me of. Then it came to me – he was the spitting image of Louis Jouvet. He was speaking Catalan and Juanita was translating for me. There was a long discussion about routes. Juanita asked which guide I would have. 'Sebastian, one hundred percent trustworthy,' he said. He assured me that he would be watching over me from start to finish, though I wouldn't see him. The price was agreed and he left.

I asked Juanita who and what he was. 'The king of the smugglers,' she told me. 'He controls 15 miles of the border. His word is law.'

The method of payment was ingenious. I was to deposit the money with the shoemaker, who was tried and true. Then a banknote was to be cut in half. I was to take one half with me. When my half was returned to the shoemaker, 'Louis Jouvet' got the money and he paid the others.

Of course there was nothing to stop Sebastian slitting my throat and pinching my half. I didn't think he would, though, somehow. He and his boss were in a profitable line of business; their 15 miles of border territory must have been a gold mine. The price asked was 50,000 francs. I was lucky enough to have it.

I suppose Sebastian and the shoemaker got their cuts. After the war I heard how Juanita got hers. She was denounced, and died in a Nazi camp.

It was a dull afternoon when I set out on my journey into the unknown. There were banks of clouds on the distant mountains, snow clouds probably, and I was wearing my

Philippe de Rothschild with his first wife, Elisabeth Pelletier de Chambure, from whom he separated in 1939. Elisabeth was confident that her aristocratic background would ensure her safety in Paris throughout the war. She continued her busy social life there until she was eventually captured and sent to Ravensbrück, where she sadly died. Their daughter, Philippine, became a successful chatelaine of the Mouton Rothschild estate from her father's death in 1988 until 2014.

everyday clothes and shoes so as not to arouse suspicion. I had brought a cap and hidden my half banknote in the peak. My guide, Sebastian, was a sturdy Catalan, weather-beaten and taciturn; neither of us had more than two or three words of the other's language. We took the bus to Arles-sur-Tech, a village beyond the edge of the town. If all went to schedule we should there pick up the connecting country bus without too much delay. Destination Saint-Laurent-de-Cerdan at the foot of the mountains. From then on it would be Shanks's pony.

It was at Arles-sur-Tech that I made my first and only blunder. I was standing at the stop in a cold sweat waiting for the little bus to leave. It was sitting there as empty and still as a church on Monday. All of a sudden the driver appeared and unlocked the door. He had been in a small lean-to of a place which I had hardly noticed. I did now. Two gendarmes came stepping out of it. I panicked, bolted blindly, then changed direction and hid on the other side of the bus.

Sebastian, inside, waved his arms angrily. I ran round to the door and he heaved me aboard. The driver pulled the starter, the little bus coughed and left. The gendarmes began to run. The bus continued on its way. Sebastian was plainly furious. '*Si vous pas faire comme moi dire vous frappe*.' His French was obscure, but the accompanying pantomime – brilliantly clear… We sat in silence the rest of the way.

I would have liked to make a joke of it all, but I hadn't the words, and Sebastian looked too serious. At Saint-Laurent-de-Cerdan, another shock – two dozen Germans had descended on the village. For the moment they were rollicking in the one and only inn.

Sebastian, shepherd and smuggler, knew all the byways and side ways. He took me over some rocks, down into the inn yard and put me in a cupboard of a place below some stone steps. Safer, I gathered, as he locked the door.

Hours passed. The pattern of daylight in the small grille, high in the wall, was gone. It was night. At every moment I expected the sudden flash of a torch, the command in German...

At last, a soft whistle, the door was unlocked. It was Sebastian.

In no time we were over the wall and away. There was no moon and a steady climb ahead of us. Sebastian had to keep waiting for me. It was rough going. At last I got my second wind. We were obviously keeping to the heights, avoiding the paths. I was terribly out of condition; I even cursed the small rucksack I was carrying and felt like dumping it, but it contained a change of socks and underpants and my mini electric razor.

As we were breasting the first high ridge, Sebastian began whistling 'La Cucaracha'. It was a pre-arranged signal. Danger ahead. I threw myself down and crouched under a rock. Then I heard it, the sound of men thrusting their way through the scrub. They were cursing the dark night, in German. The whistling stopped. I heard my guide exchanging a few words with one of them. What was he saying? I didn't understand German. Perhaps the whole set-up had been a trap and he was going to hand me over.

No, they went their way and he came back for me. We plodded on, without speaking, my heart still beating fast. The long ascent began, scrambling, climbing, sometimes flattened against a wall of cables, sometimes pinned against a rock face, happy to find a handful of tough grass or an obtruding root which might furnish a handhold, as one heaved oneself up. Sebastian was always 50 yards ahead. I was glad when I tumbled; it gave me a couple of seconds' respite while I dragged myself to my feet again.

It was perhaps two in the morning when the moon was suddenly revealed, riding the dark clouds. As the pale light spread over us, I thought I saw a stone dwelling, or was it just a rock fantasy? I pointed: 'Look, is that a shelter?' He nodded.

'Louis Jouvet' had told me there'd be a scheduled stop somewhere en route. Could this be it? Rest?

Sebastian was obviously keen to push on and went into his 'frappe' routine. I made him understand that I was at the point of exhaustion and very hungry. Reluctantly he changed his course and we headed for the farm – for such it proved to be: one meagre stone building and an outhouse. As we approached I noticed a lighted window. They're up. There may be a bed.

No, no, too dirty, he said, doing a vivid mime of catching fleas and killing them. He indicated that I was to stay where I was, and made off to rap at the farm door. A burly shape appeared, holding a lantern. There was a bit of backslapping and ribbing as the man glanced in my direction. They went in and closed the door. I made for the window. I could see a man writing in a ledger by the light of a spirit lamp. I moved closer. There were three other men seated at the table. Sebastian moved into the picture, bent over the ledger, a mug in his hand. It was a while before he came out.

'OK,' he said, 'a little...' and he put his head on his hand as we walked along.

'Where are we going?' 'Barn. Much cleaner.' He held his nose and pointed at the farm. 'Friends.' 'Smugglers.' 'Doing their homework?' 'Accounts,' he said.

I opened the food pack Juanita had given me and offered him some. He shook his head and strolled back to join his friends.

'*Deo gratias*,' said I, when I finished my banquet of sausage, onion and bread and stretched alone among the sweet-smelling hay. As I sank into nirvana I heard a soft munching and snorting and, through half-opened eyes, saw the cows' soft bellies and their vague, gentle eyes as they came towards me. Outside it was snowing. I remembered we were somewhere near Christmas. Away in a manger, no crib for a bed, the little Yiddisher baby, JC, laid among the cattle feed. I smelled the sweet warm breath of the big beasts as they lumbered around me, and I slept.

All too soon we were on our way again, and my feet were bleeding and swollen, much worse after the rest. Shoes? Worse than useless. On and up. All I remember is the encounter with thick ice when we reached the first peak; Sebastian floated in front of me, like a will-o'-the-wisp, then he'd disappear and I'd go on, blindly, occasionally feeling a shove up as he helped me over a wall of ice. Day and night dissolved into one. Would we never begin the descent? We did, some time during the second night, but to descend was worse, and at times precipitous. I couldn't get the action right and I was exhausted. At one point I lost control of my legs and slid down 500 metres of steep scree on my backside. I came to a painful halt. That was it, I couldn't get up. Sebastian tried to tug me to my feet, and managed it, but after two or three steps I was down again. He squatted beside me, waiting. It seemed to be getting lighter. He was pointing. Far below us, the light clouds parted for a moment; I thought I saw a thin grey ribbon of road.

'You are in Spain,' he said. I couldn't speak. I made the supreme effort expected of me and he did his best to support me as we stumbled down a rocky slope, pebbles flying, birds uttering a warning cry as they rose from their nests.

I remember coming to an isolated farm. There was someone else, a man helping me along. I remember being led to an enormous bed which filled the room and that's all. Sweet oblivion.

A minute later someone was nudging my leg. My eyes wouldn't open, the nudging went on. Where was I? I looked. Four men were sleeping beside me in the enormous bed and my guide was prodding me with a broom handle. 'Up! Up!' he was saying. 'You have had four hours.' All I wanted was to stay there forever. 'Up, up and see your father hung,' said he. I clambered over the sleeping bodies as they muttered and swore at me. 'Bus,' said my guide, '*à* Figueras'.

The road was not far away, but I was nothing but a sack and Sebastian was determined to make that bus. He called to the owner of our mountain rest and between them they got me over the last lap. And, oh, the relief of standing on a smooth, rockless road. We were in a race gorge, small streams gushing from its sides, and a stone bridge pointing to the most beautiful sight in the wide world – a Spanish bus.

The driver eyed me stolidly. He knew where I had come from, so did the black-robed peasant women who were clambering aboard. They didn't stare, they didn't even look at me. I suppose they were used to exhausted Frenchmen falling from the hills. In fact 30,000 Jewish refugees crossed those mountains to Spain; many more tried and failed.

As we sat on the bus I gave Sebastian my half of the banknote. He paid the bus fares. As we rode the hairpin bends towards the valley I wondered what the hell I would do next. I didn't have long to wonder. At the first village we came to, Besalu, the Guardia Civil were at the bus stop.

All out! I looked round for Sebastian. He had disappeared into thin air.

A small crowd gathered as I stepped down, helped by one of the old women.

As the Guardia Civil arrested me, a young boy stood staring. He couldn't take his eyes off me. '*Comment t'appelles-tu*?' I asked him. '*Cómo te llamas*?'

'Jesus,' he replied. That was a good sign, I thought – Jesus and Christmastide.

Extract first published as 'Don't Get Around Much Any More', from *Milady Vine: The Autobiography of Philippe de Rothschild* by Joan Littlewood and Philippe de Rothschild, Jonathan Cape (London) 1984. Reprinted here by permission of The Random House Group Limited.

CHAPTER SIX

SURVIVAL OF THE FITTEST

Bordeaux' châteaux produce some of the best known and most revered wines in the world, but they have always had to adapt and change to stay ahead of the game.

Michael Broadbent (2002)
Why Bordeaux?

Jane Anson (2012)
Survivors of the Revolution

Margaret Rand (2007)
Sur La Place de Bordeaux

Count John Umberto Salvi MW (2020)
The First Growths Show the Way Forward

Bill Blatch (2020)
Liquid Gold Legend

Michael Broadbent spent much of his career (and 150 little red notebooks) eloquently describing the wines of Bordeaux for eager-to-learn colleagues and avid readers. At Christie's, he re-established the fine wine auction scene and in doing so was able to taste some of the greatest, rarest and oldest clarets in existence. Here he explains why he found this wine, above all others, the most fascinating.

WHY BORDEAUX?

Michael Broadbent (2002)

Why, when the whole world is awash with new wine, do I spend so much time evaluating and re-evaluating the wines of the past, especially those of Bordeaux? I am tempted to start at the beginning, historically, but to be realistic, Bordeaux still dominates the fine wine market. The names of its châteaux are the best known, the most revered and, particularly over the past few decades, the most traded in wines in the world.

A knowledge and understanding of what lies behind the label, the wine name and the vintage, is vital. The way one château differs from another and, as crucially, one vintage from another, is of more than superficial interest. Moreover, the way each wine has evolved or is likely to evolve over a period of time is of very much more than purely academic interest.

Let's dwell briefly on size: in area, Bordeaux is the largest fine wine region in the world, with nearly 40 separate districts. It has more individual producers – many thousands – than any other region in the world and more people directly involved in the wine trade.

The greatest influence on the region is Bordeaux' maritime climate. The endlessly unpredictable fluctuations of weather during the growing season are mainly responsible for the style and quality of the wine. This is why I summarize the weather conditions of each vintage. Add to this the differences of microclimates and geology, not to mention the ministrations of individuals, and one starts to become aware of the endless permutations.

That is only the beginning. Almost uniquely in France, the wines of Bordeaux are made not just from one vine variety but from several, and it is the proportions in which the *cépages* are planted and used in the final blend by each château, that create the unique complexity of this wine.

Then there is time. Most well-made wines will keep for a period, although all have a finite life. The red wines of Bordeaux not only keep but – and this is the crucial point – are capable of evolving in bottle, being transformed from fruit-dominated young wine

'Great wines of the century', and the mainstay of Michael Broadbent's famous red notebooks: Romanée-Conti 1993, Château Latour 1953, Château Petrus 1978, Mouton Rothschild 1986, Cheval Blanc 1982, Ausone 1990, Margaux 1989, d'Yquem 1900, Haut-Brion 1929 and Lafite Rothschild 1846.

to something fragrant, harmonious, mature and infinitely subtle. Tracing the evolution of a vintage, of a wine, as it ages is one of the main themes of this chapter in particular.

I am English. My half-century in wine has been dominated by Bordeaux because it has been my major occupation and because it is endlessly fascinating. Not that I taste and drink it exclusively, as my tasting books will testify, but I always 'come home' to Bordeaux. Its top wines set the standards.

While it is easy to be diverted by the rich, red, sweet and easy 'gold medal' award wines from other areas and from other countries, and to be taken in by the glib, specious global taste so prevalent in modern offerings, I would like to point out that red Bordeaux or claret, good claret, is not 'old hat'; it remains the best of all beverages. Its colour is not only entrancing by candlelight but, more usefully, tells us much about content and, very accurately, its maturity: its nose – smell, fragrance, you name it – gives not only sensual pleasure but awakens the salivary glands. It is rarely too heady, too alcoholic; its acidity refreshes, its tannin, obtrusive when the wine is tasted alone, does several jobs. Tannin leaves the mouth clean and dry between one forkful of food and the next. It is an anti-oxidant, helping to preserve the wine and, the medical world agrees, keep our arteries clear. Claret aides the digestion, calms the soul, stimulates civilized conversation. Claret works on so many levels, appealing to both intellect and the senses. What more can one want?

Excerpt taken from *Michael Broadbent's Vintage Wine*, published by Little Brown/Websters (London) 2002, and reprinted here with kind permission of the author's family.

With the owners of the Médoc's first growths firmly established amongst the nobility, they and their châteaux became a prime target for protagonists of the Terror. Jane Anson reveals who survived the guillotine – and who did not.

SURVIVORS OF THE REVOLUTION

Jane Anson (2012)

By the time the French Revolution swept into Bordeaux, the first growth châteaux were well established as serious forces guiding the local wine market, and their owners found much of the 18th century a profitable and enjoyable place to be. Their status as nobles, however, meant that inevitably they were directly in the firing line of what was about to happen. The huge social changes that rocked France would cause three of the five estates to lose their owners by the time the dust had settled.

Bordeaux suffered one of the harshest reprisals of any French city during the Revolution, mainly because of its association with the political faction known as Les Girondins, who had initially been enthusiastic supporters of the 1789 uprising, but who were then seen as enemies of the revolutionary forces by the early 1790s. Even though most of the parliamentarians in the city had no connection to them at all, they were damned by association. Of the 800 families that comprised the Bordeaux nobility, around half were to disappear by the early 19th century. In total, 79 Bordeaux nobles, including 36 members of parliament, were beheaded. A further 408 people chose exile, most heading to Spain, and those who remained behind were stripped of their titles, and taxed so harshly as to threaten all remnants of their former existence.

The last years of the Ancien Régime, in contrast, were both prosperous and successful, and all five first growths reaped the benefits. Over in England, the Pontac's Head remained in business, fully supporting Haut-Brion until 1780, by which time François-Auguste de Pontac had long since passed away (nearly 90 years earlier, in 1694, with his job title in the *National Dictionary of Biography* listed as 'tavern keeper'). His reputation as a generous and flamboyant host held true to the end, perhaps indicating why he died with no shortage of debts but a distinct shortage of children. The renown of his château, however, was firmly established, and it continued to grow under the joint ownership of his niece, Therèse de Pontac (and so the Lestonnac family at Margaux), and his nephew Louis-Arnaud le Comte.

Le Dernier Banquet des Girondins by Henri Philippoteaux (1850): the Girondins opposed the monarchy but resisted revolution. Their defeat in 1793 marked the start of 'the Terror'.

Meanwhile, at Lafite and Latour things were going from strength to strength. The only son of Alexandre and Marie-Thérèse, Nicolas-Alexandre de Ségur was born in Bordeaux on October 20th 1697. When his father died in 1716, he inherited at the tender age of 19 not only his father's post as *Président à mortier* of the Bordeaux parliament (it would take the Revolution to stop this handing down of titles through family), but also châteaux Lafite and Latour. Two years later things looked up for Mouton also, as the young marquis Nicolas-Alexandre bought the Seigneurie de Mouton from the Foix-Candale family. Although he sold it two years later to Baron Joseph de Branne, it was at this point that Mouton's future as a wine estate began in earnest, and its wines started to be taken seriously by the merchants of the Place de Bordeaux. Prices began to climb, and although still lagging behind the other 'firsts', quickly equalled the best 'second category' wines such as Pichon de Longueville.

A PLANTING FRENZY

Right from the start, Joseph de Branne – son of Bertrand de Branne, an adviser to the king – clearly had ambitions for his new acquisition, promptly changing its name to Brane-Mouton and constructing winemaking facilities. It seems certain that vines were already present (records attest to vines at the time of the rebellious Duke Jean-Louis de Nogaret's marriage to Marguerite de Foix-Candale in 1587), but he began greatly to expand the plantings. In fact this period saw a frenzy of vine planting across Pauillac, suggesting that there was good money to be made from it, as the Bordélais have never been shy of earning a living.

Baron Joseph busied himself by buying up as much land as he could in the Baronnie de Mouton. His day job, as with so many of the leadings lights of the time, was as a councillor in the Bordeaux parliament, but he sank his wealth into the vineyard. By his death in 1769, the estate was making enough wine to be using barrels as payment for hunting rights and other arrangements that existed with neighbouring *seigneurs*. But there were also wranglings going on over non-payment of rents, which reached a head after his death when his widow, Elisabeth Duval, found to her dismay that the majority of tenants refused to pay rents in the absence of her husband. That same year, 1769, she paid a *notaire* called Moutardier for his assistance with the terroir of the Seigneurie de Mouton, and made an appeal directly to the king for her rights as the Seigneuse de Mouton to be confirmed. This the king did on June 17th 1769, in a document headed 'Louis par la Grace de Dieu, Roi de France et de Navarre', today tucked neatly away in the city's archives.

A rash of receipts from notaries during the following years attests to the fact that Elizabeth Duval and her son, Hector, were not only receiving rents, but also paying their own, in full, to various other *seigneuries* and to Moutardier's widow. Almost invariably the payments included barrels of wine (in both old and new barrels), as well as cash, most usually paid in silver coins.

PRINCE OF VINES

Back at Lafite and Latour, having sold off Mouton, the Marquis de Ségur (*pictured left*) was determined to have his remaining estates celebrated not just in the taverns of London, but in his home country.

France was late to the Bordeaux party. Not only because of the perceived 'Englishness' of the wine, but also because, in a country that was really a patchwork of often-warring mini-kingdoms, geographically, it was a long way from Paris. In the early 18th century, Burgundy (in a constant jostling for position with Champagne) was known as the favoured wine region of the kings of France, due in large part to its close proximity to the French capital, and the links that many Paris merchants had with the region.

Undeterred by this, Nicolas-Alexandre found a way to put both wines before King Louis XV in the early 1720s, where they became favourites of Madame de Pompadour in the same way that Haut-Brion had become a favourite of Charles II of England 60 years earlier. By all accounts this personal charm offensive won't have been too difficult.

The Marquis de Ségur was right at home in the extravagant court of Louis XV, as he was known to be the wealthiest man in Bordeaux, and was more than happy to show off his riches. He had a mansion house in Paris, was frequently present at the court of Versailles (often enough to have been crowned 'Prince of the Vines' by King Louis), and began to invest heavily in his vineyards back in the Médoc.

The first growth owners would have enjoyed extravagant lives during these times. All titled nobility – the marquis at Lafite and Latour, the baron at Mouton and the count at Haut-Brion and Margaux – drew serious wealth from their lands: it is estimated that 86 percent of de Ségur's capital came from his two wine properties. So it is hardly surprising that they would have spent lavishly on decorating their homes and entertaining within them. It is again a Bordelais historian, this time Michel Figeac, who has uncovered some of the most fascinating information about their daily lives. Simply looking at the numbers of beds in their houses proves enormously revealing, as these were among the most expensive household items before the Revolution – a master's bed cost around 300 *livres* (around 20 percent more than the yearly average salary for a priest at the time), and a simple bed for the servants would have cost around 50.

With fireplaces being the only source of heating in houses (or wood burners for the truly wealthy), beds were of enormous importance, and the owners of the first growths would have enjoyed the most extravagantly carved wooden four-posters with taffeta and satin decorations, covered with two mattresses, feather pillows, woollen sheets and blankets, and extra thick foot-covers. The Count de Fumel had 300 sheets and blankets at Haut-Brion, but although pillows were recent inventions in the 18th century, no mention is made of them at the estate.

Up in Pauillac, de Ségur was known for his lavish feasts, and the inventories of kitchen equipment are just as revealing as those of the bedroom. Owners of these estates would have had huge kitchens full of several hundred cooking pots and pans, ranging from soup cauldrons to fish kettles to meat spits. Poultry were a particular favourite, as were ortolan, the tiny songbirds that were captured alive, force-fed, drowned in armagnac, plucked, then stripped of their feet. The remainder was roasted and eaten whole, bones and all. Ortolan would be netted in huge numbers, fed with oats and millet in darkened rooms till their livers became engorged, when they were considered ready for the 18th-century table. This delicacy was at its height before the Revolution, but even today it is not illegal to eat ortolan, just to kill them. (President Mitterand caused a minor posthumous scandal by enjoying a plate of them for his last meal in 1996.)

SPLITTING LAFITE AND LATOUR

Despite de Ségur's clear enjoyment of the two properties, his joint ownership of Lafite and Latour was not quite to last until the Revolution. Nicolas-Alexandre had four daughters, and when he died in 1755, the ownership of the two was split between different parts of the family. His grandson, Nicolas de Ségur, became sole owner of Lafite (thus also looking after the interests of his mother, Marie-Thérèse, the eldest daughter) while the other three daughters retained their ownership of Château Latour.

The split gave rise to changes not only in the way the properties were run, but also their commercial strategy. Both had previously been looked after by a local notary, Maître Suisse, and sold to Bordeaux merchants at the same price. A look into the archives of the Lawton brokerage family will quickly confirm this, with Abraham Lawton's ledger of December 16th 1757 noting purchases of Suisse-Latour and Suisse-Lafite both for 1,300 *livres* per *tonneaux*. Decades pass before both are sold for the exact same price again.

Maître Suisse continued to run business at Latour until 1774, while a Mr Domanger took over at Lafite – to the great benefit of Latour, because the Ségur family, before the split, put most of their energies into developing Lafite, producing around one-third more wine there (in the 1750s, the average was 107 *tonneaux* at Lafite compared to 70 *tonneaux* at Latour). All this was to change, and Latour's vineyards grew from 38 hectares in 1759 to 47 hectares in 1794.

The split was to prove beneficial for Latour in other ways, as only one of its many owners, the Comte de Ségur-Cabanac, was directly affected by wider political events. The others – essentially the Comte de la Pallu and the Marquis de Beaumont – avoided the guillotine. Ségur-Cabanac's part (27.06 percent) was sold to Jean Courregeolles-Toulon, the widow of a noted Bordeaux doctor, but the running of the estate remained in the hands of the manager, and out of the hands of the state, as it was never declared a *bien nationaux*.

Latour didn't, however, escape hardship entirely, and the new manager, Poitevin, who took on his role in 1797, wrote widely about the difficulties he was facing in restoring the vines to their former health, as well as his – largely successful – battles to keep the prices of the wine as high as he believed it deserved to be.

By 1842, the number of inheritors was once again creeping upward, and the decision was taken to form a Société Civile du Vignoble de Château Latour (a non-trading company, and the first such vineyard entity in France), which remained in place, with only family members, until 1962, nearly 250 years after Alexandre de Ségur married Marie-Thérèse de Clausel in 1695.

Mouton joined Latour in escaping the worst traumas of the Revolution mainly because there was no majestic house for the state to take over. Owner Hector de Branne was spared his life but was financially ruined by the punishingly high taxes that fell to all remaining nobles. Records of the Revolutionary Year XI (1802) show that of 170 of the 600 most highly-taxed people in the Gironde *département* were 'nobles' (the others being mainly négociants, property owners, doctors or other professionals). Hector de Branne is listed as the second most highly taxed, receiving land taxes of 8,792 francs (the currency of livres having been jettisoned in 1795).

Lafite, meanwhile, managed to lose two owners in the space of eight years. First was Nicolas de Ségur, who proved to have a gambling habit that forced him to sell the estate in 1786, three years before the Revolution; it was sold for 880,000 livres to his cousin, Nicolas Pierre de Pichard.

Pichard was a magistrate and a lawyer and had been president of the Bordeaux parliament since 1760. He had clearly put his legal brain to good use, as his purchase was the result of overturning another, in 1784, using complicated laws surrounding lineage. He was also one of the richest men in the region. Besides his wine properties in Pauillac and Sauternes, he owned a polyculture farm in Les Landes, where he had 143 sheep, 24 cows and eight pairs of oxen, plus one of the largest and most luxurious houses in the city of Bordeaux, on Rue de Marail. If we look back at the inventories of kitchens, bedrooms and general household goods, it is clear to see that he was an ostentatious and generous host. His Bordeaux town house, for example, had 13 serving platters and 314 plates, and his wine cellar contained – besides Bordeaux – bottles of champagne, Muscat, port, sherry and Marsala.

END GAME

None of this helped Pichard much when the Revolution came. Even before this, a series of disastrous harvests (causing resentment that would fuel the start of the unsettlement) had shaken Lafite to its core. Before he knew it, Pichard was arrested by revolutionary forces, his lands and goods confiscated (their estimated worth more than one million *livres*), and he was marched to the guillotine. Pichard died in Paris, along with his wife, on June 30th 1794, at the height of the Terror. Lafite became the property of France.

Equally unlucky were the Fumels at Haut-Brion and Margaux. Joseph de Fumel had owned both estates since 1749. He was a descendant of the Lestonnacs and a military commander who was ennobled as a result of his successful career. In 1773, Fumel became governor of Château Trompette, a fortress that had been built on the site of today's Place des Quinconces in central Bordeaux after the Hundred Years War. Its initial purpose was to display the might of the French, who had newly regained ownership of Bordeaux, and to ensure the English didn't try their luck again. By the 18th century, it was still an important military site, intended to protect the increasingly busy and wealthy port – although it, too, didn't survive long after the Revolution, being torn down definitively in 1818.

In 1781, Fumel was awarded the Grand Croix of the Royal and Military Order of Saint Louis, and it was during his period of ownership that Thomas Jefferson (*pictured left*) undertook his celebrated visits to Bordeaux and Château Haut-Brion. The first of these took place on May 25th 1787, just two years before the Revolution, after which Jefferson famously sent a few bottles of the 1784 vintage of 'the very best Bourdeaux wine…of the vineyard of Obrion' to his brother-in-law, Francis Eppes (it is worth noting that all original first growths attracted his attention, with him both writing favourably about their wines, and sending examples back to the fortunate Eppes).

Fumel also displayed a passion for both estates that led to him writing one of the leading 18th-century tracts about viticulture. Putting his strategic background to good use, he formalized the state of affairs with the Le Comte side of the family, assigning the 'Chai Neuf' part of Haut-Brion to them, which included a building and vines. He promptly set about making his part even more impressive with the addition of several new wings to the château, and re-landscaping the parks and gardens.

His loyalty to King Louis XV, however, was a store for trouble, not only for him but also for his daughter. As the king's health failed, his mistress Madame de Barry began looking for protection after he died, and she alighted on the idea of marrying her youngest brother, Jean-Baptiste-Guillaume-Nicolas, to Marie-Louise-Elizabeth Fumel. The future father-in-law dutifully played ball to a certain extent, by making Jean-Baptiste governor of Château Trompette, but he was less than keen to give his daughter's hand, until Louis himself intervened and forced the marriage through. The Fumels still refused to let Jean-Baptiste take their family name, even after the king died from smallpox in 1774, so he resorted to taking his mother-in-law's family name – Hargicourt.

Château Lafite Rothschild: its revolutionary bottles rest peacefully, but its aristocratic owner, Nicolas Pierre de Pichard, fared less well. He was lost to the guillotine in 1794.

Despite this link with royalty, at the start of the Revolution Fumel remained popular with the people of Bordeaux. At the fall of the Bastille, he sided with the commoners, relinquishing control of Château Trompette and melting down all his gold to give to those in need. In recognition of this, he was elected mayor of the city on February 19th 1790, but he retired from the role in 1791 as the mood against the nobility turned darker.

He retired to Haut-Brion until 1793, when the Terror swept down from Paris. The revolutionary committee, headed by the bloodthirsty Jean-François de Lacombe, arrested and imprisoned him and confiscated Haut-Brion (only for Lacombe to install his mistress in it immediately afterward).

Fumel was officially arrested for harbouring refractory priests – members of the clergy who had refused to take the Revolutionary Oath. But he had also been denounced by 82 of his peasant tenants, not in Pessac but from his lands farther south, near today's town of Agen. On July 27th 1794, Fumel was guillotined in front of large and enthusiastic crowds in Place Gambetta in Bordeaux (then called Place Dauphine, or briefly Place de la Revolution). Three days later, his daughter Marie-Louise suffered the same fate. He left behind a poignant set of instructions to the bailiff of the Haut-Brion estate, Sieur Giraud, on how to look after his vines, what dates to harvest, how many workers to employ, what rates to pay them, when to prune and how to look after the château and its outbuildings 'during my absence'.

Meanwhile Mary-Louise Fumel's husband, Jean-Baptiste – by now Monsieur le Comte d'Hargicourt – had shown a distinct lack of gratitude for his skin-saving marriage. He emigrated early on in the troubles, leaving the château to be sequestered by the revolutionary forces, and his wife and father-in-law to meet their fate. The day after Fumel's death, Robespierre was overthrown in Paris, and four days later members of Bordeaux' revolutionary council were themselves arrested and guillotined – but just too late for the Count of Haut-Brion.

First published as chapter three, 'Revolution', of *Bordeaux Legends* by Jane Anson, published by Stewart, Tabori & Chang (New York) 2013.

Bordeaux' complex distribution network – its 'market-place', peopled by négociants, courtiers, brokers and châteaux owners – is the main route to its finest wines. Buying direct from the property is almost unheard of. Margaret Rand explains how it works.

SUR LA PLACE DE BORDEAUX

Margaret Rand (2007)

There is a collection of wine labels in Bordeaux's Musée des Chartrons that takes one right back to the glory days of the *négoce*. These were the days when they called the shots, and when they printed their names on the labels larger than the names of the châteaux. 'C Lehmann & Co, Cos d'Estournel', the labels say, or 'Château Larose, B Rouleneau Aîné, Bordeaux'. These were wines that they had blended in their own cellars, with whatever additions they deemed necessary to bring them into line with the tastes of their customers. Then, as now, the châteaux sold their wine to the *négoce*, and the *négoce* disposed of it as they could. But that is about the only similarity that remains. The workings of La Place, as Bordeaux's internal market is called, have changed and are changing again; and whether we're seeing another evolution, or a gradual fraying at the edges, is very difficult to tell.

Its name, La Place, is the only concrete thing about it. In no sense is it a place. Instead it is a market conducted in offices, in cars, on telephones, on emails and on iPhones and BlackBerries; it's nebulous, 'individually weak but collectively strong', as Jean-François Mau of Yvon Mau puts it. Its players are châteaux, brokers, négociants and the people who buy from them. Négociants like Sichel, CVBG, Yvon Mau and Mahler-Besse are on La Place; they buy from the châteaux via courtiers (brokers) and sell to the likes of Lay & Wheeler or Berry Bros, who are not on La Place, and who in turn sell to you and me.

That's the classic model at its simplest. A few weeks ago the wine trade gathered in Bordeaux for the En Primeur tastings, and flocks of wine merchants – Corney & Barrow, Justerini & Brooks, Farr Vintners – raced from tasting to tasting, assessing the vintage, trying to get a feel of what prices might be. But they cannot buy direct from the châteaux, not even for ready money. Instead they must deal with négociants. Each négociant has an allocation of the grandest wines, and if it wants to buy more it will either have to wheedle the château or buy from another négociant – undoubtedly at a higher price.

It's easy to portray La Place as self-serving, existing only to create margins for a group of people who could easily be dispensed with. 'Why do the châteaux do it?' we cry. 'Why do they allow all these middlemen to take huge profits, when they could be selling direct and getting the profit themselves?' Well, they do it partly because it spreads the risks, and partly because it's an extremely cheap way of getting a lot of wine on the market very fast.

Let's look at the second reason first. Pichon-Baron, to take an example of a good-sized Médoc château, makes about 400,000 bottles of wine a year. If it were selling direct it would have to have a sales force, and agents in every country in the world where fine wine is drunk. Instead, it sells to around 100 négociants, with about 80 percent going to the top 25 of those. Once Pichon-Baron announces its ex-château price, the wine will be sold, probably within days if it's a vintage in strong demand. It remains at the château for the *élevage* and bottling – the days when the négociants handled those are long gone – but it has been sold. And if those négociants sell it on at a profit, even an enormous profit, if the market is rising fast, the château has no reasonable grounds to object. It has got the price it asked for. If, sometimes, a château misjudges the market and sells cheaply, only to see vast profits going to the *négoce*, one might detect a certain irritation; but it works the other way, too. There have been vintages, like 1997, which the châteaux sold expensively,

Awarded *deuxième cru* status in the 1855 Classification, Château Pichon-Baron, is one of the unofficial 'Super Seconds', its wines comparable in quality and price to those of the premiers crus.

and the *négoce* found hard to sell on – though it sold in the end. The *négoce* can always, of course, refuse to buy – but if they do they may well find that their allocation in the following year is very much less. And, says Jean-François Mau: 'There are two prices from the château: one is the price to the négociant, and the other is the minimum price the négociant must sell at. You must respect the second price if you want to keep your allocation. There's normally about 10 percent difference between the two, En Primeur.' Otherwise the négociant's margins vary between about 10 and 18 percent, depending on the market and the price of the wine.

When négociants trade between themselves – ideally, always at a profit – this ups the market price of the wine. This is important to the châteaux. A healthily rising price on La

(*Left to right*) Christian Seely of Château Pichon-Baron, Mathieu Chadronnier of CVBG and Jean-Christophe Mau of négociant Yvon Mau.

Place indicates strong demand – which in turn means that future ex-château prices can rise. Cos d'Estournel, for example, used to be a lot less expensive. Former owner, Bruno Prats, explained to me that by not charging too much ex-château, he could watch the price rise nicely on La Place – and, in time, charge more ex-château and get it. Well, it worked.

These are curious times in Bordeaux. On the one hand prices and demand for the top wines seem to have no limits. But the rest of Bordeaux is struggling. The *négoce* queue to buy the top wines En Primeur every year; lesser châteaux would be delighted to sell En Primeur but the *négoce* doesn't want them. Only in a year like 2000 or 2005 is there sufficient demand across the board for some of these châteaux – those at *cru bourgeois* level, probably – to get a taste of the En Primeur market. They may well sell some of their wine through négociants in the end, but the sales will be later and slower – and may only happen at all because a courtier has a supermarket on the line wanting x thousand cases of a *cru bourgeois* at €y per bottle. And no, that won't be many euros. 'At the very lowest end,' says Jean-François Mau, 'a négociant might take just €0.04 per bottle. There are no profits there except for good retailers.'

La Place only works, in fact, for a few wines. 'The better and sharper négociants have identified a shortlist of 50 to 60 *grands crus* that are seriously high quality, with strong and strengthening demand around the world. They concentrate on those. They always want more of those wines.' Thus says Christian Seely of Pichon-Baron. Given that there are thousands of châteaux in Bordeaux, that's a very small slice of the market. But in terms of profitability, it's the biggest slice. And Seely reckons that the process of concentration applies to the *négoce* as well. 'There's a large number of négociants – about 440 – and some are very small. There's more and more of a tendency for châteaux to work with a smaller number of highly professional négociants who can offer real service in terms of world-wide distribution networks. The châteaux that can pick and choose are the top *grands crus*. Some still use 80 négociants because they always have; if you're dealing with about 100 – which we are – a lot are getting five cases a year. It's not sensible. But if you look at them individually and cross them off, they come back saying they've been selling your wine for years and they're very strong in restaurants in Clermont-Ferrand or whatever. It's much more difficult than it sounds.'

In 2000 about 400 châteaux sold their wines En Primeur on the Place, says Mathieu Chadronnier of CVBG – 'and that could be considered a maximum number'. Even in 2005 only about 250 took part. In many years it's as few as 150: it depends on the demand for the vintage. 'A château may produce a tremendous wine in a lesser year, but it will still be difficult to find a market for it En Primeur.'

But even with fewer châteaux and fewer négociants (perhaps) concentrating on each other, life on La Place is still not simple. Seely is unusual among top *grands crus* in not putting all his other wines on La Place: AXA Millésimes, as well as owning Pichon-Baron, has Petit Village, Suduiraut – and Pibran, a *cru bourgeois*. 'It's seriously high quality, but it's not one of the magic *grands crus*, and the Place isn't particularly interested. We now distribute it on an exclusive direct basis.'

Many of his colleagues use different tactics. 'If you want to buy the top wines, you have to buy the second wine and the third wine as well,' says Jean-Christophe Mau, Jean-François' son. 'If we want to buy Angélus, we have to buy Carillon d'Angélus and Fleur de Boüard. And Fleur de Boüard is complicated to sell, because it's expensive. We bought the 2004 and the 2005, and we have sold none.' Yes, again, he could decline to buy the other wines – but what his allocation of the top wine would be the following year I leave to you to guess. 'It's like going to buy an Audi, and having to buy a Volkswagen and a Skoda as well.' He adds that nearly all the second growths are difficult to sell because they're expensive – exceptions include Léoville-Barton and Rauzan-Gassies, which are not expensive. Pavie, too, has something of a reputation for sticking on the market – again because of its price. And that's in spite of whacking great Parker points.

La Place is not a place of strict divisions. Many négociants own châteaux, some négociants have exclusive distribution rights to certain châteaux, Millésima (itself on La Place) sells direct via mail order, and some proprietors form négociant companies. Gonzague Lurton and his nine siblings, all of whom inherited châteaux from their father, André, did exactly this in 1993. But even when proprietors do this, they generally continue to sell the bulk of their wine through other négociants: Gonzague sells about 20 percent of his wine, Durfort-Vivens, through his company, with the rest going to about 50 other négociants. It's a way of getting a better seat on the merry-go-round, not bypassing it.

What then of the courtiers? They are the Mr Two-Per-Cents who know everybody, know who needs cash and who is flush with it, and maintain utter discretion to both sides. If you want to do a slightly ticklish deal with a friend, a courtier will act as a go-between, loyal to both of you, so that neither side is left feeling embarrassed or unhappy. (And remember that Bordeaux is a close and complex network of marriages and friendships. Every deal is likely to be with somebody you know socially – or, perhaps worse, with somebody you don't know at all.) 'Honesty. Confidentiality,' says courtier Timothée Bouffard if you ask him the most important qualities of a broker. 'If a broker breaks confidentiality once, he's dead,' echoes Jean-François Mau.

Bouffard deals with perhaps 1,000 châteaux, 150 to 200 of them on a regular basis, and with perhaps 50 négociants, at all levels of the market. Brokers like him are, if you like, the glue that holds La Place together. And La Place has so far shown itself to be infinitely adaptable. Each generation predicts its collapse, and each generation watches it simply change. Foreign wines with Bordelais owners try it from time to time, if their owners are high-profile enough to attract interest, but the jury still seems to be out on how well it works for them. Says Chadronnier: 'La Place works well for a limited number of foreign wines, like Opus One, but for each of them it works quite well.' The latest straw in the wind is that the first growths, according to one source, are demanding that the *négoce* give them the details of their customers. Is this because they simply want to know where their wine is going? It was a common complaint in the past that the négociants were secretive about such matters, though now they are acknowledged to be far more transparent. Or is it because one day the top wines might try life off La Place? La Place would survive without them. Amoeba-like, it would simply change its shape.

First published as 'La Place' in *Decanter* magazine 2007, and reproduced here with kind permission of the author and publisher.

Through famine, war, plague and pestilence, Bordeaux has survived and still survives. John Umberto Salvi shows how this region, led by the research departments of its university and its major châteaux, is using the latest technological developments to adapt, change and meet its future.

THE FIRST GROWTHS SHOW THE WAY FORWARD

Count John Umberto Salvi MW (2020)

Bordeaux has always had its accusers, but 'stagnation' has never been one of its greater crimes. The last 20 years in particular have seen so much progress that it's hard to encompass it all. Science teaches us more and more each day, and research from Bordeaux University's Department of Oenology and the analytical centres of numerous individual châteaux (first growth châteaux Cheval Blanc and Margaux among them), have led to new winemaking skills the like of which we older oenologists could never have imagined. (I come from the days of the great professors Emile Peynaud and Jean Ribereau-Gayon in the late 1950s, a time when we did not yet know what malolactic fermentation was!)

To my mind, it has been the first growths, together with châteaux Cheval Blanc, Ausone and Petrus on the Right Bank, that have led the way in wine quality and in progress, for two good reasons.

Firstly, they are very old winemaking properties and were able to secure the finest soils, the finest slopes and the finest expositions long before anybody else came along. Paul Pontallier, late of Château Margaux, often stated that it was the great soils that enabled him to make fine wine under even the most adverse weather conditions. Château Petrus has its own personal jewel – its blue clay soil – which retains water under even severe drought conditions and is ideally suited to its Merlot grape. These days, new allocations of such prime land can no longer be found in any of the prized appellations of Bordeaux. Secondly, thanks to their renown and therefore their great fortune – not to mention their observation and dedication – they are able to test out and (if found satisfactory) to integrate the most recent technology as soon as it becomes available.

Sometimes a great château can take much convincing that a new project is worthwhile. And some new techniques have simply not passed muster. When the new optical sorting machine from Bucher, Vaslin & Pellenc was first put on the market in 2008 for checking grapes as they arrived in from the harvest, Château Haut-Brion rented it for two years before making the purchase. Jean-Philippe Delmas confided that if there was rot and the grapes had begun to stick together, then the machine was 'absolutely useless'. But its merits eventually overcame this disadvantage. The machine detects chlorophyll in the berries and removes green and unripe ones; it also extracts leaves and grass. Using high-speed cameras and image-processing software, an infrared light detects foreign bodies such as small animals, twigs, wood and plastic, and removes these too. A third vision system will select berries by degree of ripeness and can detect and remove any pink ones.

The optical sorting machine was a great invention, and has now been superseded by an even more modern version that sorts the grapes by density. On the market since 2017, this machine bathes the grapes in an infinity pool of sugar water that the winemaker adjusts by concentrating or de-concentrating to the preferred Brix level. Thus, it can be set so that overripe berries, stalks and other lighter 'MOG'[1] rise to the surface and are removed, while heavier whole berries proceed to the sorting tables and the hopper. All of which ensures that the final must quality is exactly as desired.

In the vineyard, new technology abounds. Making biofuel from waste material – the pressed-out 'pomace' of seeds and stems that was once used as low-grade fertilizer – is one that impresses me most. Also, drones are now used for aerial crop analysis; automatic irrigation techniques can detect when a vine's search for water causes it too much stress; grape-harvesting machines can measure acidity and sugar levels on a computer mounted on the dashboard, and frost can be combatted by using helicopters.

But for the future of Bordeaux' vineyards, it is climate change that holds the attention more than any other subject. It is held responsible for the worrying rise in alcoholic content of the wines of Bordeaux. We only need to go back to 1975 to find a vintage when the must weight of Château Margaux' grape juice did not even reach the legal minimum. Just a few years ago, in 2010, it made a wine with an alcohol level exceeding 15%. Château Haut-Brion has seen a similarly steep increase.

In fact, there are many other reasons why alcohol levels are increasing, and moderation of these factors has today become a very important subject. Bordeaux will never win a weight-lifting competition with California or Australia. Its wines should all be about delicacy, finesse, purity and elegance, rather than extraction and power. The questions raised then are: 'What are the other factors that increase the alcohol content?' and 'How can we bring it back down to the level we would like – around 12–13%?'

Philippe Dhalluin, winemaker and managing director at Château Mouton Rothschild, told me that 'rising alcohols are largely caused by the increasing efficiency of the vineyards', adding with a wry laugh: 'In the winery, the solution is easy: just add water!' But his humour hides his concern. Dilution is never an option in a wine cellar, certainly not one of Mouton's calibre. There are technical ways of removing alcohol and

[1] MOG, 'matter other than grapes'.

At the forefront of research into the way vines express their terroir, viticulturist Professor Kees Van Leeuwen has achieved great results in matching grapes to specific Bordeaux soils.

one that is used in many countries is the 'spinning cone', which separates alcohol by rotation under vacuum. But the French authorities are resolutely against use of this technique as it obtains alcohol that has not been taxed – nor would any quality cellar adopt such an aggressive procedure with its wines.

All agree that a problem that starts with the vines should be solved with them too, and there is one measure that would legally reduce alcohols without loss of quality, but that this is such a long-term and expensive option that it would be reckless to undertake it. This is to uproot the existing vines and replant on less vigorous American rootstock with less vigorous French grafts. The drastic production and profit losses that would be incurred here – essentially the same recourse as that taken to save the region from phylloxera 150 years ago – are almost unthinkable, especially as the juice from new vines is almost always excluded from the top wines for a minimum of five years.

No businessman in his right mind would pursue such a route, and yet François Pinault of Château Latour is doing so. With the support of Cornelis ('Kees') van Leeuwen – professor of viticulture at Bordeaux Sciences Agro (part of Bordeaux University's Institut des Sciences de la Vigne et du Vin) whose specialist fields are terroir and the effect of water on grape quality potential, phenology modelling and the impact of vine nitrogen status on aroma expression – Latour is analyzing its ground structure through bore-hole trials, and rearranging its vineyards so that its grape varieties are planted on best matched soils to reduce vigour and increase quality. Kees is a brilliant scientist, and the time and money spent on this project will certainly be rewarded with top quality production. He has already seen good results from his time working at Château Cheval Blanc, where he persuaded Pierre Lurton to plant his Cabernet Franc and Merlot on the best matching soils.

There are other factors that contribute to higher alcohol content and these, too, are being deeply researched. Accurate 'canopy management' – achieving the optimum quantity of leaves on the vine to generate the level of photosynthesis that produces the right balance of sugar in the grapes – is a key concern. There are now formulae available to get this right. Another is yield. A great deal of study has gone into (and is still going into) the optimal weight of grapes – or number of bunches – that will enable a vine to give of its very best. Over-cropping will produce weak flavours, while too few bunches will cause the grapes to be over-tannic. Hang-time is also a factor: winemakers have learned not to make wine with over-ripe grapes (a process that has been actively encouraged in the past). Philippe Dhalluin's comment: 'When the grapes are ripe, we pick; we don't wait. We do not have hang-time here as they do in California, as rot comes very quickly in our humid climate.'

There are arguments (and no small amount of scaremongering), about the introduction of hitherto forbidden grape varieties – four red and three white, including Portugal's Touriga Nacional and Alvarinho – as a means of maintaining balance and refreshing acidities in the face of hotter climate conditions. At this stage, the request applies only to a 10 percent content of Bordeaux' generic Bordeaux and Bordeaux Supérieur wines and it is unthinkable that such varieties would be introduced to the classed growths of the Médoc, Graves or Saint-Emilion. But perhaps they will eventually have to submit to such measures. For the foreseeable future, all that may be needed is an adjustment of the present permitted varieties. A little more Malbec and Carmenère and an increased percentage of Petit Verdot, which ripens perfectly in a warmer climate, will help bring down the alcoholic strength bumped up by Merlot, which does not respond well to hot weather. Rest assured, Bordeaux will not make port or even burgundy...

All these improvements help to improve alcohol content, as does the method of pruning and lastly (but far from least), collection of virus-free rootstock and French varietals. Huge work has been done on producing healthy, virus-free clones, and each of the first growths has its own nursery of virus-free plants collected by massal selection. These are the vines selected from the château's best older vinestock and propagated to produce healthy, not-too-vigorous, virus-free new plants. This development of vine reserves is on-going and regarded as of supreme importance by all the best châteaux.

One other element of wine, also of vital importance and about which our knowledge is far from complete, is tannin. Tannin is the major contributor to longevity in a red wine, and an integral part of great Bordeaux. It is known that there are a number of different tannins in a wine and that they all have different sized molecules. We know that these molecules tend to combine and grow in size until they are too big to remain in suspension. They then precipitate as sediment. However, we still have no accurate way of measuring tannin potential, and the late Denis Dubourdieu (who was the world expert on the precursors of aromas in Sauvignon Blanc), believed that once this subject was fully understood, wine would be even more precise and balanced than at present. Tannin is the subject of much research that will provide a pathway for further improvement in the years to come.

In addition, Alain Vautier at Château Ausone has chosen his own path of research: an in-depth study of ergonomics. He has made considerable alterations to his cellars and *chais* and talks very persuasively about the way these have added vigour and energy to his wine. His is another line of questioning that opens the way to future improvements, and one, certainly, that few other winemakers have yet considered.

So, are the great wines of today any better than those of the past? Do recent vintages taste better than the 1961, 1953, or even the great 1875 and 1870?

As Paul Pontallier put it: 'In recent years, our greatest advances have been in suppleness and precision. And we must continue to work towards these two factors without fail.'

Suppleness in a wine is its ability to be fruity, fresh, easy to drink and thoroughly enjoyable while relatively young, but at the same time to mature with grace and beauty. Precision is the perfect harmony between all elements – acids, tannins and alcohol – to

The 'winery under the hill' – wine production at Château Cheval Blanc anticipates the future.

make a clear, clean, complete, perfectly balanced wine with no rough edges or elements out of proportion. To achieve this requires consummate skill.

So the great Bordeaux wines of the future will be more supple and more precise; they will have perfect balance and length; they will have crystal purity of fruit, and they will be unblemished. But will they taste better or give more pleasure than those of the past? At my age, I am in a position to arbitrate, and no wine has given me more pleasure than the magnum of 1870 Château Lafite that I drank twice – once with Michael Broadbent and once with Peter Sichel – or the 1806 Château Lafite that I drank with Martin Bamford and John Davies, and which gave me six minutes of bliss before it disintegrated. But perhaps because I am old and sentimental, I should reserve judgement.

Bill Blatch's work as a Bordeaux négociant has given him the inside track on its most unique and interesting wines for half a century. He has not missed an En Primeur campaign since 1970. Sauternes has long been one of Bill's great loves; here, he charts the journey of this fabulous sweet wine from 19th-century Russian court to the kitchens of Ken Hom, and assesses its chances of success in the future.

LIQUID GOLD LEGEND

Bill Blatch (2020)

What makes Sauternes special is noble rot – *Botrytis cinerea*. Without it, this would be just another sweet wine. With it, comes a multiplication of aromas and flavours, a total transformation into a unique product that amateurs of good Sauternes now know so well. Yet for centuries its potential was not realized.

The area of Sauternes had a reputation for producing good but basic white wines, which were often late-harvested but only ever 'botrytized' by accident. The Dutch merchants who had settled in Bordeaux in the 15th century (largely taking over the void left by the departing English, after Castillon) satisfied the enormous demand for white wines from the peoples of northern Europe by sourcing the best of these '*vins de Langon*' – not yet called Sauternes. Happily they had mastered the art of stabilizing the wines with sulphur and could therefore ship in barrel directly from the port of Barsac. The proprietors quickly cottoned on to this trend, switching away from producing red 'claret' for the English market, and taking up the production of sweet white, much better suited to their terroir, thus paving the way for the glorious sweet white wines that were to come.

So the more white vines were planted, the more Sauternes' special botrytis spore population began to build up, growing in the area's unique microclimate over the years and the centuries. Yet still it was unexploited.

Stories abound about how this changed and how nobly-rotten grapes began to be used deliberately. Most are apocryphal and are posterior to the real start of the trend in the 1700s: viz, pickers were not allowed to harvest until the boss came back from the war (Yquem) or until it stopped raining (La Tour Blanche) and they 'discovered' the marvellous result. Some legends are probably borrowed from the Rheingau, where at Schloss Johannisberg in 1716, the harvest was allegedly not allowed to start until the delayed messenger from the proprietor, the Prince Bishop of Fulda, had arrived with instruction. Or from Tokaji, where harvesting of botrytized grapes probably first began

Records only hint at it; full admission of the initially unpalatable truth had to wait until the late 1700s. But it is a fact now universally acknowledged that the finest wines of Sauternes are made with fruit affected by *Botrytis cinerea*, 'noble rot'.

as early as the 1600s. (It was Henri de Vaucelles, during one of his wonderful lengthy discourses at Château Filhot, who told me that it was the Hungarians who lifted the taboo on botrytized grapes in Sauternes.) Such stories became something of a fashion in the 1800s, used by the châteaux to promote themselves; they then stuck. However, it was likely not any single event that revealed the beauty of botrytis but, instead, a very gradual evolution – estate records attest to it as early as 1740 at Château Filhot and hint at it in offical manuscripts as far back as the 1600s.

USHERING IN THE GOLDEN AGE

Whatever its origins, it is clear that harvesting nobly-rotten grapes in several passes really only got going in the late 1700s. At this stage, the vineyards were no longer concentrated on the flat land by the river but around the newly developed châteaux on the misty higher ground – on land more capable of attaining the purest form of botrytis. But it was still a matter of selecting only the affected berries. The person who seems to have been instrumental in starting this was Françoise-Joséphine de Lur Saluces at the old estate of Yquem. When her clients demanded more of her botrytis *cuvée*, she asked her manager, Garros, to research the matter. He set about studying and then implementing the '*trie*' system of harvesting, and achieved resounding success. Clients were prepared to pay handsomely for the vastly superior wines that resulted, and other estates followed suit. Modern Sauternes was born. (A classic case of demand coming up from the consumer to the producer.)

However, it wasn't enough just to make it; Françoise-Joséphine had to promote it too. In those days, for a product to be fashionable it had to be accepted at the royal court. Then occurred a remarkable coincidence: she received a visit from Thomas Jefferson on his famous tour of Bordeaux' wine regions. He fell in love with the wine and had some shipped to America, preaching his discovery to the political shakers and movers of the time, including George Washington, who also had some shipped. It wasn't long before Sauternes caught on elsewhere, at Versailles and in all the European courts.

The first golden period for Sauternes came in the 1800s, between the Restoration and the extravagant yet ultra-refined time of the Second Empire. Just as the Parisian aristocrats and *nouveaux riches* came to love the finesse and elegance of a fine Sauternes, they also came to appreciate the image of prosperity and luxuriousness that it imparted. Its alluring and special sweetness was totally in line with what they were used to in other wines: champagne was sweet then, as was white Rhône and even Montrachet, we are told. It became widely served in the Paris salons, at fashionable dinners in London, and at all the great European tables, especially the Habsburg court in Vienna and that of the tsar in Saint Petersburg, either as a reception wine alongside champagne or during the formidable banquets that followed. Menus of the time list literally dozens of dishes with each course, and the wines would invariably follow the same pattern: Madeira or sherry with the consommés, Sauternes for the '*relevés*' (spicy appetizers), Chambertin with the *entrées*, Médocs for the roasts and champagne with the dessert. Nobody seemed to worry about drinking sweet wine before going on to the reds. The banquets lasted six hours or more so everyone had time to acclimatize. Sauternes became so desirable that in 1859, Grand Duke Constantin, brother of the tsar of Russia, paid 20,000 francs for a *tonneau* of Yquem – supposedly its weight in gold coins. Even the Emperor Meiji of Japan served it and encouraged his admirals to do likewise.

BRING ON THE FINEST VINTAGES...

As if to order, this golden age of Sauternes drinking corresponded to two golden series of Sauternes production: first, from 1828 to 1851, after which there was a pause during the oidium years; then second from 1858 to 1878. Bordeaux négociants vied with each other to secure allocations of the best wines; in 1847 Cruse even bought all the Yquem, and again in 1869 it bottled a specially engraved carafe for Russia (of which Alexandre de Lur Saluces still owns replicas).

Phylloxera from 1878 and mildew from 1882 took heavy tolls on the vineyards; even the sturdy Sauvignon, still the predominant grape, sufferred terribly. The vines had to be grafted onto new rootstock, a process that took up to 25 years. During the resulting quality interval, Sauternes was plagued by the double whammy of tiny crops and low prices. Then unexpectedly, the young vines produced the amazing 1893, 1899 and 1900, still considered landmark vintages today. Their reputation kept enthusiasm for Sauternes alive during the 'Belle Epoque', even maintaining it when prices plummeted with yet another run of disastrous years during the 1900s and 1910s, and then with all the restrictions of the Great War.

The 1920s ushered in a third golden age of Sauternes production: 1921, 1924, 1927 and 1929 were all great years and the ones in between were almost as good. Sauternes was still popular during these '*années folles*' and prices rose at a staggering rate.

The 1930s, as for the red wines, saw yet another ghastly series of vintages. Only the 1934 and 1937 made anything decent. It was probably just as well; after the Great Depression, nobody had any money to buy the wines anyway. Most estates scraped a few pennies together by expanding red wine production. Virtually all of them were put up for sale: Suduiraut was bought in 1940 by Léopold Fonquernie, who thought nothing of signing the purchase *sur plan* without even visiting the property before rushing off to the war.

The generally very poor quality of the wartime vintages is often accounted for by the lack of sprays and personnel. Daniel Lawton's diary reports that this was certainly the case in 1942, when only a third of the crop could be saved from mildew, but for the rest it was rather the very wet and cold autumns that, war or not, sealed their fate. Only the 1943 lives on today as a faint testament to the torrid summer of that year. One consolation: the Third Reich appropriated less Sauternes than red wines.

The post-war 1940s saw a sorely needed run of excellent vintages: 1945, 1947, 1948 and above all 1949 – all of which have still tasted fabulous on the few occasions I have been lucky enough to try them. But yet again it was not to last; the 1950s, 1960s and 1970s brought another series of generally poor wines, alleviated only by the occasional successes of 1959, 1967, 1975 and 1976. Luckily these three decades coincided with the 1945–1974 '*trente glorieuses*', a period of economic boom with newfound prosperity and spending power, and so, notwithstanding the very low prices, at least there was a market for the wines.

The French could at last revive their parents' indulgence of '*les années folles*'; the Japanese, new to the joys of wine and typical of a nascent market, fell in love with the sweetness and cachet of great Sauternes and used them lavishly in the department stores' biannual offers of gift packs of one red, one white (I was involved with shipping a full container of Yquem in 1978 to partner Margaux in Mitsukoshi's and Daimaru's most expensive gift pack); America and Britain, already not averse to drinking sweet wines, sherries and ports, also drank large quantities of Sauternes. In 1975 Sherry-Lehmann in New York ran a promotion on the albeit rather mediocre Yquem 1968 and easily sold through thousands of bottles in a week, while in Britain, alongside the traditional consumption of great Sauternes in London clubs, boardrooms and from private cellars, there was an enormous market (by today's standards) for generic Sauternes. It was more of a Sunday lunch thing in the industrial Midlands and North. As an Allied trainee in 1971, one of my tasks was to come in at 5am, help sterilize the bottling line, then check in the road tankers of Sauternes and sweet German wines. Yes, road tankers of Sauternes!

Back to the *crus classés*: during the speculative bubble of the late 1960s-early 1970s fine wine boom, the prices of Sauternes pretty much kept up with the spiralling reds but, when the bubble broke, they also followed them downwards into the ensuing 1974–76 crash. At Allied's fire sale at Christie's in March 1976, the most depressing experience of my vinous life, Haut-Brion '66 slumped to £66 per case, but so did Sauternes' Château

Guiraud '70 to £18. And it was in that same year of total depression that de Pontac gave up and uprooted all his vines at Myrat. To add insult to injury, the three vintages 1972 to 1974 got rained out: Yquem declared no wine in 1972 or 1974. The quality of 1975–76 brought brief respite but the prices remained low, again tracking the reds, then Sauternes had a variety of problems of its own: in 1977 (frost), 1978 (too late ripening), 1979 (autumn rains), 1980 (again too late ripening), 1981 (autumn rains) and 1982 (heavy October rains, after the reds had finished).

1983–91 saw another brief period of prosperity for Sauternes. It was a breath of fresh air for the weary but uncomplaining Sauternais, but started one year later than for the reds, which had turned the corner with a great 1982 vintage. Sauternes got revenge with the 1983, which was infinitely better for whites than reds. Like most négociants at the time – and even today – I had been regarding Sauternes as something of an afterthought, but it now seemed to present an opportunity. So I started visiting and tasting, and finally buying as much as the bank would allow me of this great vintage. Subsequently, 1984 produced light but good enough wines from rather swollen grapes but we sold them quite well for immediate consumption; 1985 was adequate but too dry for any real botrytis. It was the early harvest of the flattering 1986 that sparked off the next little Sauternes boom, crescendoing into the magnificent trio of 1988-1989-1990.

In Paris, fine Sauternes was once again served as an apéritif. I remember well an evening at the Closerie des Lilas in Montparnasse in 1992: first growth Sauternes was flowing at the bar by the glass just as it would have been at the Café Anglais in the 1860s or *chez* Escoffier at The Savoy in the 1890s. The word spread abroad and, just as for haute couture, the home market set the trend for the rest of the world, which quickly, especially Stateside, espoused the cause and created a mini Sauternes boom. We sold the fine-styled 1988s and the stronger 1989s very well, but yet again the market was not to last. The 1990s, richer wines still, had trouble finding a market in the recessionary years that followed the Gulf War. They would sell later but it took time and I had no cash left.

Meanwhile, 1992–94 saw yet another series of poor harvests. The reds produced huge volumes and sold low while Sauternais refused to put their name to such dilute wines and declared virtually nothing.

In 1995, it was too dry for much botrytis, but the following year, 1996, ushered in the most incredible run of vintages that Sauternes has ever known. Of the ensuing 24 vintages, 1996–2019, only two were poor, six were good and 17 superb. Such a rally of quality had never happened before and all the famous names and vintages became readily and permanently available, disinclining people to stock them. It was an *embarras de richesse* rather than any disaffection for the wines themselves that caused the market's stagnation. At the turn of the millennium, Sauternes, which in the 1800s had traditionally sold for 15–20 percent more than the top Médocs and, for the 1900s, had kept more or less apace with them, suddenly lagged far behind, and to this day has still never caught up.

EMBRACING THE RICHESSE...

Sauternes was never associated with the French Paradox that helped propel the red wines. It completely missed the speculative boom of the last 25 years. La Tour Blanche 1989 opened at the same price as Lynch-Bages (18 euros); 28 years later, the same châteaux' 2016s were released respectively at 27 euros and 96 euros. And we sometimes still hear people say they don't drink Sauternes because it's too expensive. Expensive? No, it's a steal! Especially when all the extra costs, risks and threefold lower yields are factored in.

I always find it magnificent that the more they suffer financially the more uncompromising is the Sauternes growers' quest for quality. Any other vineyard area in the same situation would have compensated by shortcuts such as overproduction and artificial concentration. Not the Sauternais: chaptalization, which had given Sauternes a reputation of heaviness post World War II, has been banned for a long time, as has reverse osmosis, while cryo-extractors[1] have not been used since the 1990s except – as one château once put it – to keep the beers cool for the pickers.

Huge efforts have been made in the vineyard over the past 20 years towards greater precision, to ensure the wines are no longer heavy but fresh and attractive. Canopy management is used to lower the pH of the fruit; there is more precise measurement of the grapes' evolution as harvest approaches, and, perhaps most importantly, production of the *grand vin* is now limited to only the best parcels. The first thing Silvio Denz did when he bought Lafaurie-Peyraguey in 2014 was to restrict production of his *grand vin* to the heart of his vineyard, as it had been in the 1920s; the wine immediately took on new-found finesse and complexity. At every property, only *rôti* grapes are now used (the final concentrated stage of botrytis), *pourri plein* grapes (the intermediary phase) henceforth being assigned to dry or second wines. Finally, most estates are now largely organic, with Guiraud and Climens fully biodynamic, which creates added purity in the flavours.

SAUTERNES AND THE FUTURE

Dry white wine has developed recently as a good way of using up the produce of vines that are either too young or showing too little propensity for botrytis. Since Yquem shocked the world in 1959 with Ygrec, many châteaux have followed, similarly using the first letter of their name for their dry wine: R de Rieussec, S de Suduiraut, etc. Following Olivier Bernard's landmark creation of the dry wine Clos des Lunes in 2011, from his newly acquired Sauternes vineyards, an estimated 500 of the 2,200 hectares of the appellation have handed over to dry wine production. There was even a concerted attempt to apply for an appellation 'Sauternes Sec', but this got shot down by the traditionalists. (Dry

[1] Chaptalization is the addition of sugar to unfermented must to increase its potential alcohol content; reverse osmosis filters a wine to reduce its alcohol, and cryo-extraction can be used to extract more flavour from the grape skins.

Sauternes must currently, unimaginatively, be called just 'Bordeaux'.) Another interesting newcomer to the dry wine scene is Château Climens which, with Sancerre's Pascal Jolivet as consultant, released the excellent Asphodèle in 2018. The development of second wines has had a similar effect in encouraging younger drinkers to get on board with a lighter, more fruit-driven wine. The Symphonie cuvée of Clos Haut-Peyraguey, advertized as *le nouveau Sauternes qui étonne par sa légèreté*, does indeed surprise with its lightness.

The last 40 years have also seen enormous progress in the cellar. Until the late 1970s, most of the *crus classés* were fermented in tanks, then aged in barrel. This had the advantage of enabling better technical control but did not allow for separation of the different, often very small 'lots' as had traditionally been the case at Yquem, Fargues and Climens. From the late 1980s onwards, there has been a reversion to total barrel fermentation, providing an enormous extra dimension of complexity to the wines.

The problem of generic Sauternes has been addressed too. In the past, there have been too many small growers providing wines of insufficient quality, prolonging the old image of Sauternes as a heavy, sulphurous wine that stops you sleeping. Now a cooperative has been founded, Sauternes Vignerons, in conjunction with the quality-focussed Vignerons Tutiac group (part of Uni-Médoc), to provide tighter controls and improvements.

No review of positive developments would be complete without mentioning the rise of the recent trend of mixology. Many châteaux now strongly encourage Sauternes cocktails, usually including various fruit juices, and barmen are taking up the challenge to create Sauternes-based bar drinks that are more interesting to their younger clients.

The barrel *chai* of Château d'Yquem, where wines mature for 30 months in new French oak.

Over the last two decades of financial hardship, the Sauternais have put the few resources they had to incredibly good use to prepare for the rebirth of popularity that they are sure will finally come. All the boxes are ticked for this to happen: availability of the greatest quality vintages of all time; prices that have remained low; vastly improved exposure at home and abroad; the generics now cleaned up. Even stocks at the châteaux and négociants have at last started to drop. The only unticked box remains the small rise in consumption. This is an enormous box to change but I don't buy the argument that people no longer want to drink sweet: they have no problem in ingurgitating vast quantities of 115g/l Classic Coke with their hamburgers. What they are really saying is that they don't want to be seen drinking an outdated product.

ON SALT, SWEET, SZECHUAN AND SCALLOPS

It is unrealistic to imagine Sauternes returning to its 18th-century statutory place in the middle of an all-day banquet, but modern shorter menus accompanied only by Sauternes are perfectly possible and regularly practised at the châteaux. In his recently renovated early 14th-century fortress at Château de Fargues, le Comte de Lur Saluces likes to serve it with quail dishes that are as delicate as they are succulent; Philippe and Aline Baly at Coutet invariably pair their wine with a simple roast chicken. Other recent trends have involved successfully matching Sauternes with Chinese food (with French chefs fully supportive of the idea): Ken Hom cooked a fantastic Szechuan dinner at Suduiraut in 2003 that spurred some of us to open Sauternes even with takeaway.

Traditionally, we were always told Sauternes is a dessert wine to be served at the end of a meal. But it has often been swamped when the desserts became too sweet. Today, most chefs are recommending much more delicate combinations of fresh fruit – peaches, pears, mangoes – with lighter, zestier coulis than before. In January 1997 Ben Howkins of Royal Tokaji and I organized a taste-off at De Echoput restaurant in the Netherlands between 5-puttonyos Tokajis and 1989 Sauternes, with the chef serving eight sample dishes with each. Ben's wines, with their higher acidity and lower alcohol, scored unanimously with the very sweet desserts, while the softer style of Sauternes was more at home with the saltier, more savoury dishes.

I think that salt rather than sweetness is starting to become recognized as the key to accompanying Sauternes. It doesn't necessarily require a complicated dish devised by a great chef; the same pleasure can come from something savoury yet very simple: crisps (potato chips) are perfect and open the door to enjoying Sauternes outside the meal.

The other traditional accompaniment is, of course, foie gras, especially for the French at Christmas. It is strangely the most perfect combination. Other very soft-tasting foods such as scallops and lobster provide the same association. Yquem has always served lobster with Sauternes but I only discovered this magical combination for myself in 2007, when I took a delegation of *premier cru* owners to Anthony's Pier 4 in Boston. I will never forget their enthralled faces as, adorned with the restaurant's bibs, we cracked the shells, munched the broiled morsels dipped in melted butter – also a very soft taste – and sipped Climens and La Tour Blanche 1998.

The greatest vintages of the past were all produced in exceptionally hot conditions: 1869, 1893, 1921, 1949. They were all very close to today's levels of sweetness but they were few and far between. Today, we get hot conditions almost every year, especially in July and August. So the grapes accumulate more sugar before the botrytis hits. Additionally, drier Septembers, the other phenomenon of recent climate change in southwest France, retard its onset, providing even more concentration. The result is a gradual increase in sweetness from roughly 70–90g/l residual sugar in the 1970s to 80–120g/l in the 1980s and 1990s, and to 120–140g/L since then. Yet the wines of today seem lighter than those of yesterday: they have style and freshness that ages them gracefully.

Surrender is not an option for the Sauternais. After overcoming all the obstacles of the past, they will keep up their search for excellence come what may. They have to; unlike their competitors at home and abroad, they all depend, in the final account, on sweet wine, and will continue to be proud of being the ambassadors to the world of the magic they wring out of their nobly rotten fruit – that ineffable '*apothéose du goût*' of Frédéric Dard, which will finally bring, in some form or other, as it has done so many times in the past, the recognition that they all deserve.

The best it can be: 1921 Château d'Yquem. Michael Broadbent called it 'one of life's sublime experiences – perhaps the most staggeringly rich Yquem of all time,' and (uncharacteristically) refused to spit it out.

CHAPTER SEVEN

CADS, BOUNDERS, SCRAPES AND SCANDALS

Not everyone plays a straight game. And nature doesn't always deal an honourable hand. But the critters, fakes and fraudsters will always lose in the end...

Nicholas Faith (1981)
The Phylloxera Predicament

Cyrus Redding (1833)
Bolstering with Beni Carlos

Joseph-François Audibert (1896)
A Recipe for Fake Lafite

Nicholas Faith (1999)
Desperate Times,
Desperate Measures

How long did it really take before the first growth châteaux realized that tearing up their beloved vineyards and replanting them in their entirety was the only appropriate solution to the root-gnawing destruction of *Phylloxera vastatrix*? Nicholas Faith peers beneath the accepted version of events and finds that what really happened in the Médoc presents a more complex story.

THE PHYLLOXERA PREDICAMENT

Nicholas Faith (1981)

The traditional account of the ravages of phylloxera in the Médoc is simplicity itself. The dreaded louse arrived in 1878 or 1879 and the result was that the owners of even the most renowned growths replanted their entire vineyards with vines grafted onto resistant American stock within a few years – soon enough, indeed, for the great vintages of 1899 and 1900 to confirm what had already become apparent with the wondrous 1893s: that the new vines could produce wines worthy of their pure French predecessors.

The most amazing aspect of this simple explanation is its obvious inherent implausibility: owners of major châteaux do not habitually tear up their vineyards within a few years of the arrival of even the most dreaded disease (and phylloxera was probably less appalling a problem in the 1880s than mildew). And yet the replanting would have been completed within a very few years, for wines as great as those of the immortal years of the 1890s could not have been made from vines planted in that same decade.

Even more amazingly, the truth was known to generations of *régisseurs* and *maîtres de chai*, and, presumably, to their employers as well, yet, until very recently, the tradition persisted, and even now sales catalogues describe wine made in the late 1870s as being the last of the 'pre-phylloxera' era. In the most literal sense they are, in that they were the last made before the louse had started its work in the Médoc. But in the more common sense meaning of the term – that the wine was made from ungrafted French stock – wines were 'pre-phylloxera' for much longer.

The true story is by no means inaccessible. It survives, not only in folk memory at the estates, but in written sources like the Gilbey diaries, so piously preserved at Château Loudenne, and the minutes of the anti-phylloxera committees, now available in the Archives Départementales de la Gironde. The reality, it transpires, was, as so often, much less simple, much less clear-cut than the generally received mythical account. But it is enormously important; it demonstrates very clearly the gulf in thinking and thus policy

'The Phylloxera, a true gourmet, finds out the best vineyards and attaches itself to the best wines.' In fact phylloxera was less discriminating than this cartoon (*Punch* 1890) allows – it devastated every vine it came into contact with.

between the ordinary peasant wine grower and the better estates – and the equally deep chasm between the generality of estates and the few major *crus* at the summit of the Médocain hierarchy. The true story also calls into question two of the most generally recognized truisms about the great wines of the Médoc: the need not to manure the vines lest they produce too abundant a crop, and the supposedly vital role played by old vines in the making of great wine.

Despite the inherent improbability of the legendary sequence of events, it has been challenged only in the last decade by two of the two leading figures in the study of the wines of Bordeaux, the geographer and historian, Professor René Pijassou in France and Edmund Penning-Rowsell in Britain. In the latest edition of his classic *Wines of Bordeaux*, the latter states boldly that 'the first completely post-phylloxera vintage was 1918' – an apparently iconoclastic statement that may, in fact, have understated the length of time taken for the transformation caused by the little louse.

Professor Pijassou has attacked the subject twice: first in his contributions to the two-volume *History of Château Latour*, published in 1974, and then in his thesis on the Médoc, of which an abridged version was published by Jules Tallandier in 1980. Nevertheless it is worth taking his ideas a stage further for two reasons: first, the professor was not concerned so much with the wines themselves, and the reputations of individual vintages; second, as an historian thinking of the Médoc through the ages, he quite rightly treated the phylloxera as merely one of the three plagues (the other two being mildew and the worldwide slump which cut demand for Bordeaux's products) that nearly ruined Bordeaux during the last quarter of the 19th century. And because the other two disasters loomed at least as large on the Médocain scene at the time, phylloxera, though treated with the professor's customary thoroughness, is not considered in isolation. It is only if the spotlight concentrates on the louse and its consequences that its full implications emerge.

The only point on which myth and reality agree is the date at which the louse arrived in the Médoc. It was one of the last major French wine-growing areas to be attacked by *Phylloxera vastatrix*. Indeed, although it had reached the department of the Gironde in 1869, it was not until a decade later that it crossed the estuary of the River Gironde. By that time the owners of the châteaux of the Médoc could take advantage of the results of the intensive search for remedies conducted by French scientists over the previous decade. By 1880 (out of hundreds proposed in attempts to win the government prizes offered for solutions) they had come up with two that had helped other stricken regions. One, flooding the whole vineyard, was clearly impracticable in a wine growing region whose best wines were, by definition, grown on gravel slopes. But the other solution – injecting carbon sulphide into the roots of the afflicted vine – was clearly practicable, if expensive. Moreover, in the first years of the 1880s, the technicians perfected a new machine named *salvator vitis* by the grateful viticulturalists. This enabled the chemical to be applied in the course of normal agricultural work, while the vineyard was undergoing one of its annual ploughings. This not only reduced the labour costs of the treatment, but it also minimized its major disadvantage: the damage and disturbance it caused to the vine's roots. In some cases the remedy had proved worse than the disease, with vines unaffected by the louse dying because their roots had been too badly cut about by the treatment. And, wherever the chemical was used, heavy applications of manure were required to counteract the damage it caused – a clear breach of the tradition whereby too heavy doses of manure militated against the quality of the wine by inducing the vine to produce grapes too freely.

Carbon sulphide was cheap enough to be used by any grower with a sizeable holding – especially after the development of *salvator vitis*. But another – and even more effective – chemical treatment was developed in the 1880s. This involved applying potassium sulpho-carbonate, and was both expensive and involved enormous quantities of water. Transporting 30 litres – over seven gallons – of water to every single vine was a major task not lightly to be undertaken except by the more conscientious *grands crus*. And, given the general state of despair that gripped the Médoc in the 1880s, it is not surprising that not even the easier remedies were universally applied. In 1888 the Gilbeys at Loudenne, the northern outpost of the gravel banks of the Médoc, noted how much of the peninsula had been devastated. Two years later the anti-phylloxera committee of the sub-prefecture of Lesparre (which included the Bas-Médoc and the northern part of the Haut-Médoc down to, and including, Pauillac) note that: 'In the space of five years we have seen vines disappear from those communes where the soil is clay or chalky. The only vines which have resisted are those on sandy or gravelly soil.' Fortunately these covered 'by far the greatest proportion of our *arrondissement*'.

By that time the final, and most radical, solution to the problem had been found. Between 1885 and 1890 the great French scientist Millardet had developed a number of vines based on American stocks, suitable for grafting with the varieties used in the Médoc. In 1887 the French government had allowed growers who replanted with American-based vines a tax exemption until the new plants had come into leaf a fourth time. Even before these developments 'every grower had a nursery of American plants', according to official minutes of a meeting in 1884. Even so, it was the combination of Millardet's work and the generous tax concession that galvanized the growers into action. But even then the process was by no means sudden: the chemical remedies had succeeded in checking the ravages of the louse, and complete replanting with totally new plants was a hazardous leap into the unknown for a community as conservative as the viticulturalists of the Médoc.

It took yet another incursion of the plague to convince them that mass replanting was inevitable. The minutes of the anti-phylloxera committees for 1890 record that the vintages of 1888 and 1889 had been free enough from trouble to produce a false sense of euphoria: 'At that moment we could believe that the invasion by the phylloxera had lost its intensity. The majority of the growers shared this idea and some of them replanted parcels of their holding with French stock. But in June this year we witnessed a renewed incursion of phylloxera. Vines three or four years old were badly affected, and in many plots which had hitherto resisted the plague we can now see numerous cases where the meagre vegetation (or examination of the root system) indicate the presence of the phylloxera louse.'

The members of the committee – and the thousands of growers they represented – could no longer delude themselves: the phylloxera, they finally admitted, was an endemic problem requiring literally root-and-branch treatment. It was not – as they had clearly hoped until that moment – merely one of the many epidemic plagues, like oidium, mildew, aracthnose or *coulure*, to which their precious vines were traditionally subject and which they had learned to combat, or merely endure. But even then replanting was by no means rushed. In 1894 the Gilbeys noted only that phylloxera had reappeared and that they were satisfied 'that all replanting should be with American stocks'. The next year they reported in their diary that their *régisseur* was 'anxious to continue on with American stocks as has been done on most parts of the estate during late years'. It was only in 1901, at the ceremony during which Sir Walter Gilbey was presented with the gold medal of the agricultural society of the Gironde, that he could talk of the plague in the past tense, and mention the methods that 'were employed' to a 'successful issue' of the problem.

The Gilbeys' can safely be taken as typical of the best practices employed by owners of vineyards other than classed growths; lesser growers clearly planted in a rush, encouraged first by the tax relief and then spurred on by the renewed onslaught of 1890. The

Gilbeys, and others like them, simply replanted their estate, rather faster than they would otherwise have done, in the 1890s. Even then the bulk of their 1899 and 1900 vintages would have been made from pre-phylloxera, purely French vines. The vast majority of their American-based vines would simply not have been sufficiently mature for their grapes to be worthy of their *grand vin*, made only from vines at least five years old.

The picture was very different for the handful of classed growths (representing, after all, only 61 growths in the Médoc – not counting Haut-Brion – a tiny proportion of the thousands of owners in the peninsula). They were under enormous pressure not to replant, and were, in any case, far less susceptible to the blandishments of the authorities than their lesser brethren. Their reputations counted far more in cash terms than a few years of tax relief, for one thing, and they were far better able to support the costs of the new chemical treatments than most estates. But the crucial element in their balance was the unyielding insistence of the all-powerful merchants of the Quai des Chartrons in Bordeaux that they would simply not buy wine made from American-based stock. At Latour, which was probably typical, in the 1890s when everyone else in the Gironde had become resigned to the need for complete renewal with American stock, four-fifths of the new plantings were with ungrafted stock. In the words of Professor Pijassou: 'It was, indeed, only from 1901–02 that the American grafts finally gained full acceptance on the major estates…even in 1924 there were still several thousand pure French vines on the estate, even though all new plantings had for years been made with grafted plants.'

This is not surprising. As late as 1907 the contract for a five-year *abonnement* (subscription) made by Latour with three Chartronnais shippers stipulated that during the five-year period no new plantings should be made with American grafted stock – the fact that the *régisseur* managed to evade this, by then, ridiculous restriction does not alter its significance. For the shippers were clearly terrified of any further damage which could be caused to the already battered image of their products by the suspect quality of wine produced from American grafts. In the 1880s enormous long-term damage had been caused to their exports to their major market in Great Britain by the sale of half a dozen vintages that had suffered from mildew. These had the nasty habit of turning unpredictably sour in the bottle, and the experience had accelerated a major shift in the drinking habits of the English upper classes, who had largely deserted claret in favour of heavily promoted brands of champagne and Scotch whisky. So the Chartronnais could well do without any other element of uncertainty in their wines.

Obviously every major estate had its own rhythm of replanting. But there is no reason to suppose that Latour was singled out for special treatment by the merchants who in that same year, 1907, arranged *abonnements* with most of the classed growths. Indeed, the production figures for the *grands crus* confirm the general picture painted by the *régisseur* of Latour: a slow start to replanting in the 1890s, and a sharp acceleration (both in the speed of replanting and in the proportion of American vine stocks) after the turn of the century. At the moment when lesser growers like the Gilbeys had virtually completed their accelerated replanting programme, the major growths had barely embarked on theirs.

In the 1880s the classed growths, stricken by mildew (and by the first onslaught of the phylloxera), produced a third less wine every year on average than they had in the late 1870s. After the mildew had been mastered, production leapt in 1886–87 and remained well above the levels recorded in the late 1870s – which themselves were high by historical standards, since they came at the end of two decades of prosperity when enormous profits had been reaped from rapidly increasing harvests. Professor Pijassou's figures show that production in the 1890s was two-fifths above the average for the 40 years from 1879 to 1921, and 14 per cent above that for the 1870s. Significantly, it dropped sharply after 1900 and more especially after 1907. The averages for the following 15 years were obviously affected by the problems created by World War I, but the drop had been very marked even before 1914. Professor Pijassou attributed this decline vaguely to the general *sagesse* of the growers, their wariness in the face of a market which simply could not absorb the quantities of wine produced in the 1890s.

Nevertheless there is a more persuasive explanation of the fall than that provided by Professor Pijassou: that yields dropped because of the accelerated replanting programme undertaken after 1900. And this idea is also supported by the otherwise inexplicable fact that, in the words of Michael Broadbent (in his *Great Vintage Wine Book*): '1920 was the first unqualified *grande année* after 1900.' Although there have been other prolonged gaps between great vintage years, most notably between 1929 and 1945, these can usually be explained by climatic conditions. What stands out from a careful reading of Broadbent's notes is that a number of vintages of the first two decades of the 20th century, which either enjoyed good weather (like 1911), or (like the 1918 vintage) which were thought highly promising when they were young, turned out to be 'disappointing' or 'light' when they matured. Both the inability to make wine worthy of the weather in good years and the lack of staying power among these vintages can most logically be explained by the presence in the vineyards of an overwhelming proportion of young vines, planted as a result of the accelerated replanting programmes undertaken after 1900.

If these suppositions are correct – and they have the great merit of fitting in with the known qualities (and quantities) of the wines and the facts of life in the Médoc – then a number of conclusions flow from them. First, that it was manifestly not that great pair of twins, the vintages of 1899 and 1900, that proved triumphantly that grafted vines could produce wines as magnificent – and as long-lasting – as their pure French predecessors; that honour belongs rather to the series of fine vintages from 1920 to 1929, 10 years with a proportion of great years unsurpassed in the history of the Gironde. (Michael Broadbent rates four out of the 10 as either 'very good' or 'outstanding', as good a record as that of the 1890s and better than any other before or since.)

But these points are, really, academic. Others call into question some of the fundamental beliefs regarding the conditions required to make great wine. First that, contrary to received opinion (and to the regulations surrounding the production of fine wines in France) the lavish use of natural, or even chemical, fertilizer does not necessarily dilute the quality of the wine produced. During the 1890s – a decade of great wines – the vines were force fed, not only by the enormous quantities of natural manure distributed round the base of the vines, but also by chemical fertilizers. The most effective chemical treatment against phylloxera contained a high proportion of potassium, and, for the first time in the history of the Médoc, other chemical fertilizers were used to offset the debilitating effects of the mildew, or of phylloxera (and of the remedies used to combat them). Yet the great vintages of 1899 and 1900 bear triumphant witness to the lack of ill effects on the wine.

A further shadow of doubt is cast over Médocain lore by the ability of the wines made in the 1920s to stand the test of time. The wines of that wonderful decade clearly contained an unusually high percentage of grapes from what might be called 'young adult vines', planted since 1900. They also included less than their fair share of grapes from older vines, those aged over 25 which are commonly supposed to provide the wine with its depth and long-lasting qualities.

The figures, and the tasting notes, are persuasive, but because they related to only a few estates, they are not conclusive. Indeed, it is highly regrettable that the English visitors to the Gironde in the first three-quarters of the 20th century never got round to making any of the elementary enquiries that would have enabled the history of the phylloxera in the Médoc to have been written with the benefit of contemporary wisdom. For now [at the time of writing] there are only a few survivors who, like Marcel Grangerou, the retired *mâitre de chai* at Château Margaux, can remember vines 'being grafted on the spot' after World War I, and who, before that war, saw the persistent efforts still being made with the cumbersome implements used to spread the chemicals which fought the dreaded louse. All we can say with any certainty is that the received version of events is rubbish.

First published as 'Phylloxera – What Really Happened in the Médoc' by Nicholas Faith, in *Christie's Wine Companion* (London) 1981, reprinted here by kind permission of the Faith family.

Cyrus Redding was a Cornish-born journalist and free-market thinker vociferous in his condemnation of wine tariffs and any form of 'adjustment' to a natural product. In his *A History and Description of Modern Wines* (1833), his praise of Lafite and Montrachet is as glowing as it would be from today's wine writers, but his views on the way claret was presented for market are far more controversial.

BOLSTERING WITH BENI CARLOS

Cyrus Redding (1833)

The first growths of Médoc are never sent to England in a perfect state, but are, when destined for that market, mingled with other wines and with spirit of wine. Their taste of the pure wine is not spirituous enough for the English palate, and more body is given these wines by the mixture of Hermitage, of Beni Carlos from Spain, and alcohol, ordinarily to the extent of three or four-twentieths percent. By this means all the delicate flavour, the delicious and salutary quality of the wine is destroyed to give it a warmer and more intoxicating effect, without which in England these wines would not find a market. Mixing Hermitage or Beni Carlos alone with the wines of Médoc would not perhaps be prejudicial, though it must alter the quality, and Beni Carlos is often mixed with Médoc wines when they are nearly worn out, to restore their body. Natural and healthful wines, the genuine offspring of simple fermentation, are not the fashion in England; hence artificial means must be used to please an artificial taste.

White wines are often mixed with very high-coloured red, such as *palus* wines, or those from certain cantons of the Dordogne, the Lot et Garonne, and Languedoc. These practices have increased in France of late years, and though occasionally useful, are too frequently prompted by lucre. To such an extent is the practice carried, that serious fears are entertained by many Frenchmen it will do an injury to the credit of the wines of Bordeaux, and by that means to the commerce of the city. False stamps are sometimes put upon the bottles. The best mode for the stranger is to deal with old and respectable merchants alone…

Bordeaux wines in England and in Bordeaux scarcely resemble each other. The merchants are obliged to 'work' the wines before they are shipped, or, in other words, to mingle stronger wines with them, such as Hermitage, or Cahors, which is destructive almost wholly of the bouquet, colour and aroma of the original wine. So much are the merchants sensible of this, that they are obliged to give perfume to the wine, thus mixed, by artificial means, such as orris root and similar things. Raspberry brandy is sometimes employed, in minute quantities, for the same purpose, and does very well as a substitute in England, though any Frenchman conversant with these wines would instantly discover the deception. The perfume is sensibly different from that given by nature. These operations cause the clarets of England to be wines justly denominated impure, though not injurious to the constitution. It is only encouraging a coarseness of taste, which, after all, is but matter of fancy, while wholesomer wines cannot be drank. When old, claret is apt to turn of brick-red colour; this arises solely from mingling it with more potent wine.

Thus far belongs to the wine while in the hands of the foreigner, or when it is transmitted to the hands of respectable merchants in England, of whom alone wine should be purchased. But there are large quantities of what is miscalled claret, manufactured in this country, for making which, as well as improved claret of prime character, many receipts are extant. A very inferior French wine, sold to the adulterators at a few *sous* per bottle, is now frequently mingled with rough cider, and coloured to resemble claret, with cochineal, turnsole, and similar matters. This is pronounced of fine quality, and sold as such in this country. Certain drugs are added as they appear to be wanted, and the medley, to which a large profit is attached from the imposition, is frequently drunk without hesitation, and without any discovery of the cheat.

New claret is made to imitate old by uncorking and pouring a glassful out of each bottle, then corking the bottles, and placing them for a short time in an oven to cool gradually, they are then filled up again and finally corked, and passed for nine-year old wine. Port is put into warm water, which is urged to the boiling point, and then, as already stated, the wine is put into the cellar, and deposits a crust that looks the growth of years. Madeira is thus, as before remarked, artificially treated. The fumarium seems to have had the same object of forcing a premature mellowness.

A vast deal might be written upon the methods adopted and ingredients used in carrying on these deceptions; the present object is only to touch upon the subject in order to illustrate certain principles recorded in this volume, but more especially to show the reader how necessary it is to form a just judgement, and obtain a perfect acquaintance with genuine wine of every species, that he may thereby be better enabled to escape imposition…

In the better Bordeaux wines, even 'when prepared' for the English market, the fine qualities of the pure wine still exist, though they are to be less strongly traced. In the wines of Portugal they cannot be traced at all.

Excerpt from Cyrus Redding's *A History and Description of Modern Wines*, Whittaker, Treacher & Arnot (London) 1833.

A RECIPE FOR FAKE LAFITE
LES VINS D'IMITATION

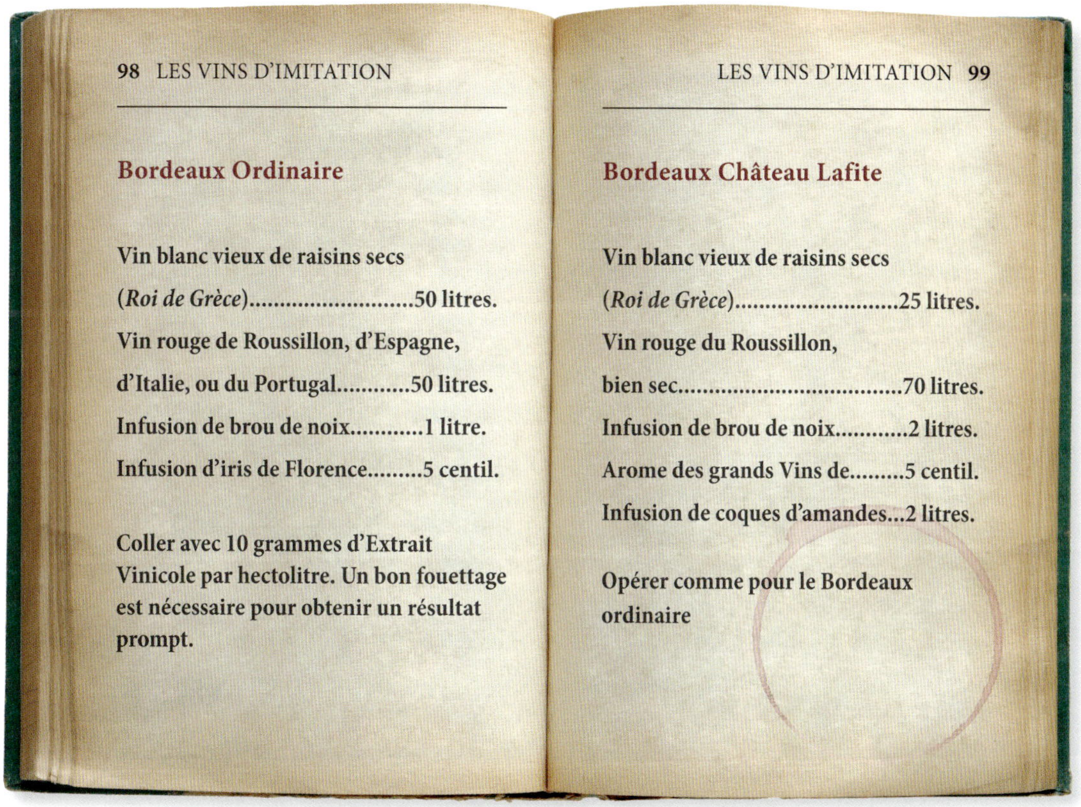
98 LES VINS D'IMITATION

Bordeaux Ordinaire

Vin blanc vieux de raisins secs
(*Roi de Grèce*)............................50 litres.
Vin rouge de Roussillon, d'Espagne,
d'Italie, ou du Portugal............50 litres.
Infusion de brou de noix............1 litre.
Infusion d'iris de Florence.........5 centil.

Coller avec 10 grammes d'Extrait Vinicole par hectolitre. Un bon fouettage est nécessaire pour obtenir un résultat prompt.

LES VINS D'IMITATION 99

Bordeaux Château Lafite

Vin blanc vieux de raisins secs
(*Roi de Grèce*)............................25 litres.
Vin rouge du Roussillon,
bien sec....................................70 litres.
Infusion de brou de noix............2 litres.
Arome des grands Vins de.........5 centil.
Infusion de coques d'amandes...2 litres.

Opérer comme pour le Bordeaux ordinaire

In *L'Art de faire les Vins d'Imitation* (1896) Joseph-François Audibert lists an infusion of almond shells as the critical ingredient in elevating fake *Bordeaux Ordinaire* to the heights of Château Lafite. This kind of subterfuge was not unusual. Wine has been manipulated and counterfeited, with varying degrees of gustatory success, since Roman times.

Nicholas Faith charts the beginnings of the 1970s 'Cruse Scandal' through the antics of a swaggering fraudster so ingenious and compelling that he brought down one of Bordeaux' noblest merchant families.

DESPERATE TIMES, DESPERATE MEASURES

Nicholas Faith (1999)

The 'greed' of the growers, combined with the sheer physical shortage of wine bearing the precious AOC label, had reduced many shippers to desperation. For a year they had happily been selling, at inflated prices, wine they did not possess, confident of being able to buy the necessary quantities in time to meet the delivery dates. Nevertheless, by the spring of 1973 they were seemingly faced with only two, equally unappetizing, alternatives: failing to deliver the wine, or buying it at prices so far above the level at which they had previously sold it that their fragile finances could not stand the strain.

Relief for half a dozen of the less scrupulous was sudden, if unexpected. It came in the person of old Louis Bert's notoriously disreputable grandson, Pierre, accompanied by an apparently unlimited supply of *acquits verts* [wine accreditation documents]. Pierre Bert had learned all the tricks of the trade from his grandfather. He had learned to love wine but to despise the rules that surrounded its sale – an attitude highly convenient for anyone whose livelihood depended on turning the law's restrictions to his own ends. For Pierre Bert possessed all the attributes required in someone destined to expose the essential hypocrisy of French wine laws – and the tricks of those who had to comply with them. He was a compulsive exhibitionist, a trait that invariably led him to expose many of his schemes to discovery by the police, the Ministry of Agriculture's fraud squad, or the tax authorities. (He displayed this compulsion early in life: he was clever enough to be considered for the *prix d'honneur* at the Jesuit school he attended, but ruined his chances by being caught singing the *Internationale* in the street just before the prize-giving.)

For he was the brightest and most engaging of souls, small and perky, witty and literate[1], able to clothe his cynicism and his misdeeds in a style entirely suitable for an age that cherishes anti-heroes of the requisite quality and panache.

His career, however, had already been rhythmically punctuated by brushes with the law. Like Jean Cordier, he had inherited his business from his grandfather; his father had died after a short spell of imprisonment on charges of collaborating with the Germans. So when Louis Bert died at the age of 90 – after a heroic attempt to ward off the effects of a severe winter by sliding barefoot on the ice – he bequeathed a business in very poor financial shape. Pierre found that he owed 15 million old francs to the authorities to compensate for the excess profits made during the war: a fine he could meet only by selling Château Rolland, the lovely house in Barsac his father had given him as a wedding present. So he cheated in the simplest possible way: he started to fill in his record books indistinctly, hoping to ensure that the authorities could not follow the pattern of his trading practices. But, true to form, he felt impelled to boast of his misdeeds: an informer told the Fraud Squad, another fine was imposed, this time 300 million old francs – the equivalent of four months' sales. So he had to sell a 75-percent controlling interest to a well-known but equally well-detested local character, Monsieur Grenouilleau, who, in theory, took over the responsibility of paying the fine. But, through an unforeseen legal oversight, this had been levied on Bert in person, not in his capacity as managing director of Louis Bert & Cie. Grenouilleau promptly refused to pay and an interminable lawsuit ensued.

So Bert became a broker, welcomed by the many shippers who disliked Grenouilleau – and especially by the wholesale merchants on the Quai de Paludate. In 1969 he finally won his case against Grenouilleau and was able to set up again as a merchant after a dramatic reconciliation with his cousin, Bertrand de Pinos, who had originally helped Grenouilleau oust Bert from the family firm. By this time Bert was an expert on every type of wine fraud, and he was soon 'cooking' wine on a large scale, melting sugar in a jam-making cauldron to produce a syrup which, in its turn, would boost the alcoholic content of a 'Barsac' or a 'Sauternes' and thus increase the price. Unfortunately his partner bought all his sugar, 90 tons of it, from a single grocer and this alone was quite enough to arouse suspicions. After a slapstick episode when Bert, fleeing from the fraud squad, hid a crucial *acquit vert* under the cloth covering the high altar of a village church before handing it over to his customer, his ingenuity was again rewarded only with a massive fine.

Nothing daunted he soldiered on, only to be caught, like so many of his colleagues, short of suitably accredited wine. Then in the offices of an old friend and good customer, a self-made shipper called Lucien Castaing, he noticed a secretary using a small machine to frank *acquits verts* with an official stamp. For, in an effort to simplify the administration of the wine laws, the authorities had allowed suitably approved shippers to stamp their own *acquits verts* to avoid a visit to the local tax office every time they wanted to move a load of wine. The controls were still stiff enough: the master certificate, green for AOC wines, white or straw-coloured for the cheaper *vins de consommation courante* (table

[1] *In Vino Veritas*, his account of his life and his part in 'Winegate', is a delight, beautifully written, witty and – as far as I can judge – largely accurate. Although Florence Mothe, of the local paper, *Sud-Ouest*, helped to ghost the book, much of its quality is due to its nominal author.

wines), travelled with the wine itself; when it reached its destination a detachable coupon was torn off and returned to the tax office nearest to the seller's place of business, which also received the seller's copy of the certificate.

Bert noted that the detachable coupon did not indicate the colour of the wine involved, or, indeed, its appellation. So the tax office had no means of telling if the colour of the wine received by the purchaser was the same as that sold by the vendor. Only a comparison of the certificate itself (held by a completely different office) with the copy sent to the vendor's own tax office would reveal any discrepancy.

The difference of colour which could thus be concealed was absolutely crucial, for although *red* Bordeaux with the precious AOC label was worth over three times as much as a run-of-the mill red wine, the difference was only 10 percent in the case of white wine. So if Bert could buy ordinary red wine and AOC white, and then switch the certificates so that he was selling ordinary white but AOC red, he would lose only 10 percent by demoting the white wine while gaining 300 percent by promoting the red. The possession of a franking machine would enable him to do just that; the original *acquit* would travel with the red wine, the detachable coupon would then be returned to his own tax office which would already have received an *acquit* relating to a similar quantity of *white* wine. Bert had only to remove the carbon paper separating the original from the copy before filling in the different colours on each one. Moreover, if he sold only to other merchants, the size and price of any transaction would not have to be officially reported to the CIVB – as were all sales to a retail or foreign customer.

For Bert, facing losses of 300,000 francs (£25,000) he could not hope to cover, the idea was a lifesaver. But to carry it out he needed a supplier of good red wine that could pass as claret, he needed cellars and, above all, a frontman without a criminal record, for not even the most gullible tax office would entrust a franking machine to him personally. The supplier was easy to arrange; even in early 1973 there was plenty of wine available in the Midi at a reasonable price and of the right quality. And after a frantic search lasting several weeks he also found a broken-down warehouse 64km from Bordeaux at Saint-Germain-en-Graves, a hamlet so small that it did not even have a café, and leased the place (which would hold only about a thousand hectolitres of wine) from its accommodating owner, Monsieur Ballarin. For his frontman Bert selected his driver, a simple soul called Serge Balan, who, crucially, had no convictions against his name. Balan entered into the spirit of his new role so thoroughly that he even suggested painting a sign on the warehouse proclaiming it as the headquarters of 'Serge Balan et Cie'. Finally, his friend Castaing recommended one Barnabé as a driver who knew how to keep his mouth shut.

It remained only to convince the local tax office at Langon that S Balan et Cie was a solid enough enterprise to allow the issue of a franking machine, and then to deposit the necessary 10,000 francs as evidence of financial solidity (since the alternative, a banker's reference, was clearly not a practicable proposition). The taxman at Langon proved

Pierre Bert (*left*), the compulsive exhibitionist always with a plausible story; Lionel Cruse (*right*), with less swagger and a lot more to lose.

amenable. According to Bert he even complimented Balan on his choice of instructor in the technicalities of wine trading. This seems unlikely, but Balan fulfilled the necessary conditions. For once, French official machinery worked speedily and the franking machine was issued on February 20th, only a month after permission had been granted.

So, S Balan et Cie was in business and on a grand scale: though it was only four months before the law caught up with the conspirators, the profits in that time amounted to 4.7 million francs, an annual rate of over £1 million. For the quantities were, relatively, enormous. Eventually, the judge concluded, S Balan et Cie sold 29,712.67 hectolitres of wine – enough to fill four million bottles. Of this staggering amount 90 percent was sold accompanied by the faked *acquits*, the other 10 percent was merely not of the quality appropriate to the appellation under which it was being marketed.

The fraud itself looks larger when compared with other irregularities discovered by the fraud squad and the tax authorities. In 1972 they had carried out 6,000 inspections throughout France, had uncovered 177 offences serious enough to warrant prosecution, but, in all, these had involved only 25,000 hectolitres of wine.

In Bert's book he compares the four of them – Balan, Ballarin, Barnabé the driver and himself – to the four Musketeers, but with one crucial difference: that the latter-day d'Artagnan and his companions were destined actually to be caught by the lackeys of the Cardinal Richelieu – in the improbable disguise of the inspectors from the tax and fraud squads. Yet, despite the squalor of the setting, the leaky warehouse in the muddy hamlet, he makes the whole affair sound grand, innocent fun – the comings and goings of innumerable impatient tanker drivers, placated by the urbane Bertrand de Pinos, the discovery that Ballarin enjoyed acting as housekeeper (though Bert himself saw to the supply of wines), the wonderment of the locals, their attempts to sell him wine and to pump Madame Ballarin, the local school-teacher, for information.

Bert's heart, so he said, was innocence itself: his attitude that of a smuggler using a false passport to transport goods on which duty had in fact been paid. For, he claimed, he was selling only wines of decent quality, thus shielding the public from less scrupulous suppliers.

Whatever the attitude, his discovery of a magic source of AOC claret made him welcome to half-a-dozen merchants, and, through them, some of France's biggest retail outlets became indirectly involved. But none of the names of Bert's own customers was well known and certainly none could remotely be described as Chartronnais.

In the third week of April, however, there was a dramatic development. Bert chanced his arm and invited himself to the august – if dilapidated – offices of Cruse et Fils Frères. Bert (who may merely have been hoping for a good story rather than a sale) found in the event that the Cruses, like many of their lesser brethren, were desperately short of AOC claret. But Emmanuel Cruse had retired in 1964 at the age of 80 and since then the business had largely been in the hands of his 'cousin' Yvan, who did the purchasing, and of Emmanuel's son, Lionel – who had the misfortune to be born a hunchback in a family noted for the swagger and physical distinction of its style. Moreover Lionel had lived for so long under the shadow of his formidable father that neither he, nor his family, could conceive of him (thought of as a 'mere boy' even though he was in his 40s) taking over the family business.

Emmanuel was a difficult act to follow. He was a brilliant businessman who had managed to keep the company afloat, even prosperous, during the slump of the 1930s. To make it worse, the family had in the past managed to balance commercial ruthlessness with gentlemanly charm. Emmanuel had (amply) provided the toughness, while his brother Christian had brought complementary qualities: he was a great gentleman, much loved by the English merchants whom he visited for nearly half a century, and a sure guide to the intricacies of Bordeaux. (His influence extended even to Australia. It was a visit to Christian, and the superb wines he offered, that inspired a young Australian winemaker, Max Schubert, to create Grange, then, as now, the country's greatest wine.)

Lionel, Yvan and their uncle Hermann, who together effectively ran the business, knew of course of Bert's reputation; they had been at daggers drawn with the Bert family for generations. So they hesitated before buying from him. Five times in one week Bert visited their offices, thoroughly enjoying his transformation from a mere supplicant broker into a supplier of a status sufficient to allow him to see Lionel, Yvan or their manager, Monsieur Jaubert. Even when the Cruses agreed to buy from him they insisted that the 'AOC' wine they purchased would be exchanged for a similar quantity of *consommation courante* (*cc*)[2] wine. Moreover they would not buy from so transparently artificial a company as S Balan et Cie. Old habits die hard: the Cruses, normally accustomed to satisfying their requirements through only one broker, their 'cousin' Lawton, would unbend enough to admit as suppliers only Bertrand de Pinos and Pierre Servant, another of Bert's inner ring.

It seems absurd that the Cruses should have expected to delude anyone. The alleged need to dispose of *cc* red wine contrasted with the fact that they were buying large quantities at the same time as they were, supposedly, offloading their unwanted surplus onto Bert's associates (and, what is more, at a price well above the going rate). And the refusal to deal with S Balan et Cie – except as a buyer of *cc* wine – looked equally hollow, for all the 'AOC' wine came direct from Balan's warehouse and all the dealings were done with Bert himself, ignoring not only Balan but the nominal suppliers, Servant and de Pinos.

The margins were so good that there was money in it for everyone. The Cruses were 'buying' AOC red wine – mostly, in theory, basic Bordeaux, but also some of 'superior' appellations like Saint-Emilion and Margaux – at about 15 percent below the market price (when everyone else in Bordeaux was clamouring for the same wine at any price) and selling *cc* wine at above the market value; de Pinos and Servant were getting a two percent brokerage fee and also a turn on the 'wines' they were 'buying' from Balan and 'selling' to Cruse.

However, once the system had got going in late May, no wine needed to change hands (or tanker lorries for that matter). Even before they had started to buy wine from Bert, a number of tankers which had arrived at the Cruses' warehouses carrying wine from the Midi bearing an *acquit blanc*, had been equipped with an *acquit vert* and directed to another Cruse warehouse at Ambarès. The Bert-Cruse system took this idea to its logical conclusion: Barnabé would drive to their warehouse, hand in his *acquit vert*, wait a little and then depart with the *acquit blanc*. In the first fortnight of June the Cruses – not counting Bert's other customers – received over 4,000 hectolitres of wine, although Balan's cellars would hold only a fifth of that amount, and themselves received only token amounts from outside. Indeed, once the paper really started flying, the only wines that changed hands were the little bottles of samples, scrupulously supplied to cover each transaction.

Eighteen months later, the judge summed-up how Barnabé spent a typical day, in this case June 7th. Work started at 7am when he left the Balan warehouse driving a tanker containing 15,000 litres of red wine bearing an *acquit vert*. By 8.30am he was parked in the street in front of the Cruses' cellars. He took the *acquit* to the reception, where they told him to wait. This he duly did (except for 10 minutes during which he left his vehicle to buy breakfast, but the period was, the court eventually concluded, too short for even a part of the wine to have been unloaded). He was then given an *acquit blanc*, which he checked to see that the quantities corresponded with the *acquit vert* he had handed in. Then he drove back to Saint-Germain-en-Graves, arriving there at 11.20am, and parked his lorry

[2] *Consommation courante* was then the official term for *vin ordinaire* or, today, *vin de table*.

in front of the warehouse (which was full of white wine). At 12.30 pm he drove off again with another *acquit vert*, arriving at the Cruses about 2pm. After an hour's wait (not even a snack this time) he returned to Saint-Germain, unloaded and was off-duty by 4pm.

In the mythology that soon came to surround the whole operation the alarm was originally sounded by the locals at Saint-Germain. They, so the story went, suspected that something unusual was happening at the warehouse because there were so many comings and goings – like Barnabé's on June 7th – between midday and 2pm when all self-respecting inhabitants of the Gironde stopped work. In reality the operation was so blatant, involved so many people, who as time went on drank a little too much and found local girlfriends, that discovery was inevitably only a matter of time. The prosaic fact is that the Bert-Cruse prosecution resulted from a tip-off, probably by someone on the fringes of the business, since the authorities did not immediately grasp the nature of the fraud.

For it was only three weeks after Bert/Balan/de Pinos/Servant started to deliver to the Cruses that two squads from the Tax Office descended on Bert's office in Bordeaux and on the warehouse. At the office they rummaged through all the papers and address books.

At the warehouse there was a typical piece of Bert slapstick: the inspectors naturally asked his secretary for the register containing the details of wine transported to and from the cellars. But, immediately they had arrived, Bert had kicked it under a cupboard in the kitchen, and it was finally unearthed only that afternoon. The inspectors then departed bearing with them documents and samples of all the wine they found. (According to Bert's account they were only jolted by de Pinos, who breezed in and thoroughly disconcerted them with his aristocratic disdain for their activities.)

Bert did not warn the Cruses – a piece of forgetfulness that suggests he had always had the idea either of revenging himself by dragging them down with him, or of sheltering behind the protective screen that everyone assumed surrounded a house so important.

Five days later, on the 27th, the Cruses finally unbent enough to agree to buy – a little Saint-Emilion directly from S Balan, without going through Servant or de Pinos. But the next morning, sharp at 9am, 10 inspectors from the tax squad turned up at 124 Quai des Chartrons, demanding an immediate inspection. They were received by Monsieur Jaubert, the *maître de chai*, who kept them waiting half an hour while the Cruses pondered what to do. (Jaubert also telephoned Bert, who rushed over, saw the inspectors and promptly strolled past on the improbable pretence that he was merely a passer-by.)

Excerpt taken from Nicholas Faith's *The Winemasters of Bordeaux – The Inside Story of the World's Greatest Wines*, Prion (1999), and reproduced here by kind permission of the Faith family.

CHAPTER EIGHT

BORDEAUX ENTERS THE MODERN WORLD

The way it presents itself on the international stage is intentional and effective, displaying its might through both the grandeur of its buildings and the stature of its wines, but Bordeaux may face difficulties ahead.

Hugh Johnson (1989)
Le Grand Théâtre

James Lawther MW (2017)
A Toast to the Finest

Stephen Brook (2020)
The Culture of Hype

Mathieu Chadronnier (2020)
Bordeaux Goes International

Andrew Caillard MW (2020)
Red Obsession: When Bordeaux Met China

Peter Vinding-Diers (2020)
Bordeaux – Beware the Portuguese...

Bordeaux' 18th-century change in fortune had everything to do with the vineyards surrounding it and the wine it successfully traded from its port. Hugh Johnson charts its transformation from provincial town to burgeoning new city.

LE GRAND THEATRE

Hugh Johnson (1989)

Bordeaux began the 18th century as a town still surrounded by its medieval walls. By the time of the Revolution in 1789, it was the most handsome modern city in France and the country's greatest port. It had added to its ancient wine trade in quantity and had revolutionized it in quality. More dramatically, perhaps, it had become the country's principal point of contact with its colonies: half of all colonial trade, above all West Indian trade, passed through Bordeaux's famous crescent-moon-shaped harbour. To celebrate its worldly success, in the 1780s its citizens built Le Grand Théâtre, symbolically upstaging the Gothic cathedral, the heart of the old town, with something more in keeping with the spirit of the times; it was the most magnificent theatre built in Europe since the Romans.

The theatre, crowning the hill rising from the port, with its spectacular peristyle of Corinthian columns and arcades down each side, was the climax of half a century of perpetual building activity that had caused the town to resemble one great mason's yard. When the royal architect Jacques Gabriel arrived in 1729, summoned by the intendant, the king's deputy in the province, he wrote: 'I will swear, Monseigneur, that I have never seen such a fine prospect and such a grand spectacle as this port; it demands some great work, which posterity will find worthy of commendation. I shall stay here for as long as it takes to draw up the plans.'

It took much longer than he ever expected. He found the citizens extremely loath to do away with the walls that gave them their identity and privileges (and at whose gates they gained a very useful income from taxes). His first great project was to open the town to the river in a magnificent three-sided square, the Place Royale, richer than the Place Vendôme in Paris, its buildings sumptuous with sculpture by the master-sculptors of Versailles, Verbeckt and Van der Woort. Gabriel died before it was even started, a dozen years later, with his son in charge.

Veuë et Perspective de la Place Royalle de Bordeaux.

The frontage of Bordeaux' Place de la Bourse (constructed 1730–1775), today recognized by UNESCO World Heritage as an 'outstanding urban and architectural ensemble'.

The succeeding intendant, Louis-Urban Aubert, Marquis de Tourny, arriving in 1743, was shocked to find Bordeaux still 'a muddle of ugly houses without symmetry or convenience, among which wander narrow streets with never a right angle'. He immediately banned all new buildings until he had personally approved the plans.

Under Tourny the pace quickened. The town was seriously inconvenienced, to say the least, by the massive fortress, the Château Trompette, built by Charles VII against its northern wall in the 15th century to encourage loyalty to France after the defeat of the English. Louis XIV had modernized and enlarged this great excrescence (today its size can be judged by the vast emptiness of the Place des Quinconces that stands on its site). All the merchants who were not citizens of Bordeaux, which included almost all the growing class of wine traders, coming from Holland, England, Germany, Ireland and Scandinavia had to make their base on the far side of the fortress, downstream from the city and completely removed from it; almost as a separate town. This was *palus* land, partly covered in vines and named after an old Carthusian monastery in its midst, the Chartrons.

Tourny commissioned Gabriel Junior to link the two with boulevards around the Château, and had the wonderfully dreamy idea of a public garden of extraordinary elegance to be the meeting place between them, 'where merchants, often having occasion to meet, would strike many more bargains; it is a sort of second stock exchange, an evening one'. Guards were to be kept at the gates so that the '*petit peuple*' would not venture in. There were only second-rate vineyards on the site when Gabriel moved in in 1746, to play with ideas that he afterwards put to use for the Place de la Concorde in Paris and the Petit Trianon at Versailles.

By the 1780s, course upon course of creamy stone had risen along a two-mile stretch of the muddy banks of the Garonne, above the crowded shipping with its chaos of cordage and the bullock sleds with their dead weight of barrels groaning down to the tide. The streets and squares, in a consensus so perfect that one hand might have designed the whole, stretch back half a mile from the river. Perhaps no other city has ever caught the spirit of its own flowering so completely in its architecture, so that even the dwindling houses of the *petit peuple*, moving away from the centre, built of the same stone, share the same sense of proportion, beguiling not by ornament but by harmony.

What had produced this flowering? Civic pride, diligence and a strong itch for gold. The *parlement* where de Pontac had presided continued to produce a race of lawyers, the *noblesse de robe*, whose wits and ambitions made short work of the old *noblesse d'épée*, families whose inheritance ran back to deeds of knightly valour, but liked to hunt their land, rather than farm it. Their property was fractioned by feudal custom. Some was share-cropped on the various intricate systems of *metayage* or *bourdieux* derived from the 'complant' of the Middle Ages; very little was rationally managed. Alongside and overlapping with the *parlementaires* were the risk-taking merchants, the négociants who freighted ships for the booming West Indies; with luck a much more profitable pastime even than waiting for Dutchmen to come and haggle over the latest vintage.

Excerpt from the new edition of *The Story of Wine, from Noah to Now*, by Hugh Johnson, Académie du Vin Library (London) 2020.

Writing in 2017, James Lawther looks at the critical nurturing stages - or *élevage* - that ease a wine towards its long and graceful maturity. The all-important oak regime (the right forest, cooperage, cask size and toast) or storage in vat, the options around lees-stirring and micro-oxygenation, and the time spent in barrel can make or break a wine if wrongly applied.

A TOAST TO THE FINEST

James Lawther MW (2017)

The embryonic 2016s having been tasted and a futures campaign in full swing, now seems an appropriate time to bring the topic of *élevage* to the fore. With or without glowing scores, the majority of these young Bordeaux will spend up to 18 months in oak barrels and/or tank and much can happen during that period. Customers have to keep the faith and pray that the finished wine will turn out as expected, for as Louis Mitjavile of Domaine de l'Aurage in Castillon and Château Tertre Roteboeuf in Saint-Emilion declares 'poor *élevage* can destroy a wine'.

Firstly, it is important to understand the concept of *élevage*, a word that translates poorly into English. The essence of the term is that of preparing and improving for the future, as one does a child, so 'ageing' and 'maturation' do not quite get to the heart of the matter. Recently, 'raising' and 'bringing up' have been proffered, but I've finally decided that 'nurture' is about as close as we will get in the English language. Better, probably, just to stay with the French term.

Turning the notion into detail, a number of changes or improvements are solicited by the process of *élevage*: a softening or refinement of tannins by polymerization (so controlled exposure to tiny amounts of oxygen), the addition of oak tannins for structure, the provision of *sucrosité*, or sweetness, for texture, additional aromatic complexity and a natural clarification of the wine. Ultimately what is required is pre-bottling stability so the wine can reveal and express itself in bottle over a period of time.

The oak barrel has long been recognized as an ideal conduit for *élevage*, but the choice of barrel, percentage of new oak, toasting of the barrel and execution of the process are another matter. 'One of the hardest tasks for any producer is to choose the barrel and toast that works with his or her grapes,' says Louis Mitjavile. All agree that a defined approach is necessary. 'The techniques used should apply to the style of wine being produced,' states Fabien Teitgen, technical director of Château Smith Haut Lafitte in Pessac-Léognan. 'Most producers know the parameters of *élevage* but are less adept at piloting around them hence the need for a strategy to be worked out in advance,' cautions François Witasse, the CEO of Tonnellerie Demptos.

The biggest change in winemaking in Bordeaux over the last 10 years has been the steady retreat from over-ripeness and excessive extraction, the emphasis now on fruit and finesse. In the 1990s and early 2000s it was all about power and concentration and to hone the wines a greater percentage of new oak with a heavier toast was used. Today, most coopers will tell you that 90 percent of the demand is for a *moyenne* or medium toast, while at individual châteaux less new oak is being employed.

Among the classed growths in Saint-Emilion *élevage* using all new oak is still practiced at Cheval Blanc and Figeac, but Ausone and Pavie have pulled back to 80 percent and La Mondotte to 70. In the Médoc Cos d'Estournel has announced 60 percent for 2016, the same as Léoville and Langoa-Barton, while Issan is at 50. The 225-litre *barrique bordelaise* remains the principal barrel but 400- and 500-litre casks are also in circulation – witness the ageing regime at Château Quinault l'Enclos in Saint-Emilion – as are concrete eggs and amphorae (Château Pontet-Canet puts about a third of its wine through the latter).

The single most important element for the winemaker is the consistency in style of the barrel. A varying nuance from one cooper to the next is acceptable and even encouraged for aromatic complexity and structure but an off-key note from an individual cooper is a no-no. In a world where every aspect of winemaking is controlled, the cooper and barrel have to fall into line (particularly at the highest level) – hence the regular tastings at châteaux with coopers to check wines and barrels and the occasional change in partners. 'I don't want to dictate to the cooper which forest to use or how to dry the oak as that is his job, but I want him to see and taste what we do and don't want here,' explains Pierre-Olivier Clouet, technical director at Château Cheval Blanc.

The same approach has been taken at Château Figeac since 2012. Wines are regularly tasted in different barrels to ensure they correspond to the Figeac style. In this way some coopers have been brought in and others eliminated and it has been empirically shown that Demptos barrels work particularly well with Figeac's Cabernet Franc, Sylvain barrels with the Merlot, and Bel Air with Cabernet Sauvignon.

Each cooper has a house style and range of barrels dictated by the provenance of the oak, the length of air-drying and the toast. For fine wines we are generally talking fine-grained oak from French forests. The Tronçais forest in the centre of France still has a reputation but there are others like Jupilles, Loches and Fontainebleau, all managed by the proficient Office National des Fôrets (ONF), where quality fine-grained oak can be found. And given the intricacies of sourcing, coopers now tend to class their barrels by grain and toast rather than individual forest. There's more consistency this way as well.

The standard length of time for air-drying the wood tends to be around 24 months, but push it towards 36 months as Tonnellerie Sylvain do for the Grande Réserve barrel and the imprint of the oak is less. Conditions, of course, matter: UV from sunlight is necessary to break down the harsher tannins, as is rain to leach them away. Tonnellerie Bel Air taste samples of the stave wood in water solution to judge when the air-drying has had its full effect and to help blend and assemble the staves. Technology can also be brought into service. Radoux's Oakscan system uses near infrared spectrometry to measure the tannin level in staves, allowing the tannin potential for each barrel to be tailor-made for the customer.

Toasting is usually described as light, medium or heavy but with the vagaries of human interpretation there's room for subtle nuance. The intensity of the heat and flame and length of toasting are the guiding parameters, a light toast providing a milder character compared to the smoky, coffee notes from a heavier toast. All this may seem far-fetched but having had the opportunity at Château Léoville-Poyferré to taste the same lot of wine (a parcel of Cabernet Sauvignon) aged in Orion and Vicard barrels with different air-drying periods, heat and toast, I can promise there is a difference.

Producers have to weigh this up when they make their choice of barrels. François and Louis Mitjavile have stayed faithful to Radoux's fine-grained barrel blend (with a

A cooper 'toasts' barrels in his workshop in Pauillac – the choice of forest, the percentage of new oak used and depth of toast can heavily influence the flavour of a wine. France's towering oak woodlands, first cultivated for Louix XIV's warships, today provide the vital raw material.

medium+ toast) since it was developed in the early 1990s. It suits their predominantly Merlot fruit, which is pushed to the bounds of *surmaturité* so is the only barrel used for Tertre Roteboeuf, Roc de Cambes and l'Aurage. Château Léoville-Barton used to work with just one cooper (it was a sign of integrity for Anthony Barton) but has added another couple for a little more versatility. At the other extreme neighbouring Château Léoville-Poyferré uses 14 different coopers. 'We aim to get something distinct from each, with the final blend of everything bringing more complexity,' says cellar master, Didier Thomann.

Pushing for further control, a rare number of châteaux guarantee their own production of barrels. Fabien Teitgen of Château Smith Haut Lafitte explains: 'Back in the early 1990s when the Cathiards bought the property it was harder to guarantee the provenance of good, fine-grained oak, so working through the *merrandiers* (stave producers) Daniel Cathiard started buying directly from the Tronçais forest. The next step was to create a cooperage which opened in 1995 and now produces 550 barrels a year: 90 percent of our needs.' There's more of a mix of forests now, and over the years the toasting has been toned down, but the absence of intermediaries means there is a bigger budget for quality oak.

The cooperage owned by Château Lafite Rothschild, La Tonnellerie des Domaines, takes on another dimension altogether. Based in Pauillac, it assures the total production of barrels for the Bordeaux châteaux owned by Domaines Baron de Rothschild (Duhart-Milon, l'Evangile, Lafite, Rieussec) as well as a percentage for the overseas estates – some

Alain Nunes at work in the cooperage of Château Margaux – owning its own *tonnellerie* will mean greater control over the way oak influences the wine.

2,000–2,500 barrels in all a year, all made individually from start to finish by five coopers. A longstanding relationship with two *merrandiers* guarantees the supply of oak, and the Rothschild research and development service monitor quality. There used to be the same toast for all the barrels, but now it varies for each property. 'We maintain a short and discreet toast for Lafite that preserves the purity of the wine but are happy to add a little more volume and structure to the other wines through a longer toast with the temperature moderated,' explains Eric Kohler, the technical director for the Bordeaux châteaux.

MATTERS OTHER THAN OAK

The classic mode of *élevage* in Bordeaux is over a period of 18 months, give or take a couple of months either side, the wine racked from barrel to barrel every three months to eliminate the lees and clean and sulphur the interior of the barrel. Racking, or *soutirage* as it is known in French, is executed '*à l'esquive*', by gravity, or by using compressed air, the wine syphoned from a hole in the bottom of the barrel until the lees deposit appears, identified by a glass held to a candle flame, and the decanting ceases.

Other cellar practices are also employed. Regular topping-up or *ouillage* helps avoid microbiological spoilage (volatile acidity, *Brettanomyces*), the bung left at the top for sampling and verification. In some cases, the barrel is rolled with the bung to the side in April (following the harvest) providing a more hermetic seal but making access to the wine difficult. Traditionally, the blending of different grape varieties would already have been carried out in January but some now leave it to June or later still prior to bottling (hence the guesstimate of some En Primeur/futures samples).

During this period the wine is gradually clarified and prepared for bottling by steady decantation. This for practitioners is an important element. There is an uptake of aromatics from the toasted oak (vanilla, spice, coffee, etc) as well as oak tannin, and through restricted amounts of oxygen (via the bung-hole and staves) the tannins are softened by polymerization. A number of reputable names like Lafite, Léoville-Barton and Léoville-Poyferré still favour the process of regular racking and have yet to be convinced they should change the system, although they may be a little less systematic than in the past. Their knowledge is mainly empirical. Clearly, there is greater exposure to oxygen but to what degree has yet to be calculated, although at certain châteaux an optical fibre captor is now being used to measure oxygen dissolved in the wine in barrel for the 2016 vintage.

There is, however, another way to analyse and practise *élevage*. Fabien Teitgen again elucidates: 'In the past the grapes were less ripe and the tannins consequently rustic, so repeated racking helped soften them and make the wine more presentable for bottling. Today, the story is different. The grapes are riper and the tannins qualitative so there is less need to rack; the emphasis now on gentle refinement and the preservation of the fruit.' So at Château Smith Haut Lafitte, as at a growing number of châteaux, he only racks once (usually around May) during the 18 months while maintaining careful control of hygiene through regular topping-up, tasting analysis and by maintaining the cellar temperature at 12°C. 'The less intervention, the more the wine is preserved,' he concludes.

Christophe Coupez, an oenologist with OenoCentres Pauillac, concurs. 'Since 2003 when winemakers worked in a traditional fashion but the wines tired and dried rapidly, there has been a definite decrease in regular racking. Another benefit has been the improvement in the problem of microbiological spoilage as the wines are moved less and so the SO_2 coverage stays more constant.' He estimates that of OenoCentres' 250 clients in the Médoc, only 10 percent still work in a traditional way.

Consultant Stéphane Derenoncourt was one of the first in the 1990s to reduce racking and to keep the wine on lees. He offers both a cultural and technical point of view. 'With today's global consumption wines are drunk earlier and earlier so there is less need for a high percentage of new oak and heavy toast and more for the preservation of fruit, which is riper but more fragile. The advantage of the lees is that they are reductive and absorb oxygen, are comprised of dead yeast cells which, broken down, contribute polysaccharides or *gras* to the wine, and they act as a buffer between the wine and barrel, permitting a finer uptake of the oak.' Of the 70-odd Bordeaux clients of Derenoncourt Consultants, all work with minimal racking.

Haut-Médoc fifth growth Château Belgrave provides a glowing example of these modern trends. The wine, which has a majority Cabernet Sauvignon in the blend, is matured for 12 months in barrel, one-third of which are new, and then for another six months in stainless steel tanks. Racking is not systematic and only carried out if necessary. 'I'm more than ever convinced that red wine, like white, should be protected from oxygen to preserve the fruit,' says estate manager François Laura. In a recent tasting of assimilated classed growth 2002s, Belgrave was one of the fresher wines with the fruit still intact.

BATONNAGE AND CLIQUAGE

Elevage on lees with limited or no racking is a more reductive method, and alongside there are two other procedures that can be used if required. *Bâtonnage*, or lees stirring, is one and the other is *cliquage* or micro-oxygenation. Lees stirring appears to be a restricted practice in red winemaking in Bordeaux, occasionally used at the beginning of *élevage* to add volume and mouthfeel if a wine appears thin. It is more a procedure associated with white wine where stylistically volume, mouthfeel and added aromatic complexity are desired.

Cliquage, whereby a measured amount of oxygen is injected into the wine, has its advocates but again seems to be generally in decline. 'Some producers are still equipped for micro-oxygenation but improvements in methods of vinification mean there is less of a problem with reduction, which is what *cliquage* was used for, and regarding polymerization the barrels themselves provide sufficient oxygen,' states oenologist Christophe Coupez.

Continuing exponents include Louis and François Mitjavile, as it works for their style of wine. 'We work in an oxidative manner to stabilize the wine but apply a precision as to when and how much oxygen to use. Racking is limited but we've worked with the same oenologist for the last 15 years and her sole job is to calculate and administer the dose of oxygen required,' explains Louis Mitjavile.

FINING AND FILTERING

There are two other procedures for consideration prior to bottling: fining, or *collage*, and filtration. Fining further clarifies the wine by precipitating the particles in it with the help of egg white (traditional in Bordeaux) or another fining agent. By and large the process is generally deemed beneficial to the wine by most oenologists and winemakers in Bordeaux. It helps stabilize colour and removes any particles that might eventually appear in the bottle.

Recent changes include the choice of execution in barrel or tank and a reduction in the volume of fining agent used. In most cases the fining agent (or number of eggs) is adapted to the year. Real eggs are still used at some châteaux like Lafite and Léoville-Barton, with liquid albumin an alternative. Christophe Coupez recounts that one year a trainee carried out trials at the OenoCentres lab that proved that gelatin was more efficient than albumin but the *grands crus* still went on cracking eggs. Old methods die hard for some.

The take on filtering prior to bottling appears to be pragmatic. For most châteaux contacted, the answer was that it was not a systematic practice but depended on the analysis of the wine and its turbidity or microbiological population. Only then was the decision taken as to whether or not to filter (often using membrane filters) and if so to what degree. 'You don't want to allow anything into the bottle that might eventually degrade the wine,' was the oenologist's view from Christophe Coupez. Only Fabien Teitgen admitted to not filtering at Château Smith Haut Lafitte. 'We filter the second wines, but if everything has gone according to plan, we neither fine nor filter the *grand vin* as the wine is generally clear and we don't want to lose anything from it.'

When it comes to *élevage* there is much to consider. A successful vintage is more than half the battle but this can be put in jeopardy if the nature of 'nurturing' is misplaced. The savvy châteaux have recognized that they need to adapt the type of procedure to the style of wine they produce and have added controls and greater rigour to the process. But looking at the areas where a château can come unstuck, the correct choice of barrels and toast (at minimum €700 a barrel), hygiene, the racking regime, fining and filtration – it does send a shiver down the spine when one thinks of the draft going out for that futures order.

First published in Issue 56 of *The World of Fine Wine* (2017) and reprinted here with kind permission of the author, James Lawther MW, and editor, Neil Beckett.

Stephen Brook takes a look at the unique way Bordeaux handles its brand image and asks whether wooing the world's press is enough to keep this region in the pole position it has occupied for so many generations.

THE CULTURE OF HYPE

Stephen Brook (2020)

It's often noted that Burgundians know nothing about Bordeaux and its wines – and vice versa. This is an exaggeration, though it retains a nugget of truth. These two great French wine regions are poles apart culturally. This is not a novel observation. Indeed, Jean-Robert Pitte, a professor at the Sorbonne, wrote an entire book, *Bordeaux Bourgogne: Histoire d'une rivalité* (2016), on this very theme.

Just a couple of examples. In Bordeaux you will encounter people with names such as Basile, Vanessa, Diana or Jennifer – that would be inconceivable in Burgundy. This may be to do with the fact that Aquitaine was English-owned for centuries, or it may be that some Bordelais believe that an English name confers a certain cachet.

At celebrations organized by the Chevaliers du Tastevin at Clos de Vougeot, and just about anywhere where Burgundy's wines are praised and consumed, the *ban bourguignon* is an unavoidable part of the proceedings. It entails raising both arms in the air and twisting them in time to a raucous ditty with the words '*Lala, lala, lalalala layla, lala, lala, la, la, la*'. Can you imagine such a thing at Haut-Brion?

Another striking difference is that Burgundy excludes, while Bordeaux includes, at least in terms of embracing those it considers helpful to its promotion, such as merchants, auctioneers and journalists. I have visited Burgundy and its growers every year for over three decades, and can count on the fingers of two hands the number of times I have been invited to stay for lunch, let alone dinner. Without fail, a 10.30am appointment will come to an end at noon, and the visitor will be politely shown the door. Hungry after a morning of tastings? That's your problem, monsieur.

I used to find this irksome, but soon came to understand that for the Burgundian, noon is the time when family members return to the homestead from pruning or tractoring or delivering bottles. It's the sacred lunch hour, and outsiders have no place. You can taste from every barrel in the cellar, but that hospitality doesn't extend to the dining room.

Bordeaux celebrates in style: fireworks are launched above the cellars at Château Mouton Rothschild as it hosts the biennial Conseil des Grands Crus Classés of 1855 dinner to celebrate the start of Bordeaux' international Vinexpo exhibition in 2013.

It's the exact opposite in Bordeaux, where it's assumed that a visitor with a late-morning appointment will stay for lunch. Indeed, when researching one of my books in Saint-Emilion, I was amazed to find that my programme, organized with enthusiasm by the local *syndicat*, included lunch and dinner every day, weekends included. The Bordeaux proprietor will usually use the occasion not just to offer a fine meal, but to open some older vintages for the delectation of the visitor.

The Burgundian really couldn't care less. On one occasion, a grower with whom I spent a morning in order to research a profile for a magazine, had suggested, when I made the appointment, that I might like to stay for lunch. With pleasure, I responded, hoping that a mature Richebourg might be brought up from the cellar for my appreciation. But *sur place*, when I had completed my interview, it was clear that the owner had completely forgotten his offer. (However, after an embarrassing few minutes all around, his wife did rustle up a rather good meal.)

BORN TO BE HOSPITABLE

Burgundy's wine culture is about the nuances of *terroir*; Bordeaux' is about selling wine that's produced in far larger quantities than from patchwork Burgundy, and all those who can serve that purpose are coralled into a network of hospitality. A lunch will always take the same form. Coats and bags are deposited in the hallway of the château and one is led into a salon, where a small table supports a bottle of champagne (often Pol Roger, sometimes Bollinger) and some glasses. In comes the butler or maid (often on hire from the local *traiteur*, or caterer) with a plate of goujons or roundels of toast with foie gras to stimulate the appetite. Then the host rises to his (and occasionally her) feet and leads the way into the dining room. Lunch is invariably a butler-service event, so guests must calculate how much meat or veg to convey onto one's plate without either appearing greedy or depriving others of their fair share. The dishes are always replenished, however, so seconds are in order. No need to panic.

If the aim is to impress, it usually succeeds. In contrast, the Burgundians *en fête* are after a good time. Other than the rather forced jollity of the Chevaliers du Tastevin dinners, usually accompanied by indifferent wines, the highlight of the Burgundian wine calendar is the Paulée de Meursault (other *paulées* are available, but all agree that Meursault does it best). This is in effect a giant bottle party. Each producer, who may be accompanied by family or guests, will bring a basket stacked with a few bottles or magnums of a venerable or prized vintage. These will be poured and later circulated in the course of a five-hour lunch. Those lucky enough to attend can often taste spectacular rarities.

This is not the Bordeaux way. At a formal dinner, for example during the En Primeur tastings or Vinexpo, invited merchants or journalists will find themselves at a large round table in the company of two or three château owners or winemakers. They will have brought bottles – often very fine bottles – that will, in due course, be delivered to your table. There's a certain amount of swapping with other tables to provide more variety, and certain journalists, towards the end of the evening, will be seen roving the room in search of wines to try on distant tables. (I plead guilty.)

Here again the aim is to impress. Brigades of waiters and waitresses, quite often students from a local catering college, will swoop in from the kitchen with such efficiency that a few hundred guests can be served almost simultaneously. Moreover, the food will usually be excellent, provided by one of the many highly professional *traiteurs* who flourish in Bordeaux.

Access is the name of the game. The privileged guest, sipping champagne or Sauternes during the prolonged apéritif hour before a grand Bordeaux dinner, will be in the company of dozens of château owners. Reach out a hand, even to someone you've never seen before but vaguely recognize, and it will instantly be shaken: '*Bonsoir, monsieur*.' Everyone present is within the magic circle. You have been appointed, like it or not, as an ambassador for Bordeaux.

Over 20 years ago I was present, along with 400 other guests, at the Fête des Vendanges, a great feast organized each year before the harvest by a leading château. I could see from the menu that 1985 Haut-Brion was to be the final wine of the evening, but what I hadn't anticipated was that it was to be served in magnums only. Moreover, on a very warm evening each magnum had been lightly chilled before serving to ensure that it would retain its freshness and digestibility in the glass. Other blandishments include guests of honour who are often prima donnas or celebrated actresses. Who wouldn't want to be around when, as once happened, Gina Lollobrigida was escorted between the tables by the château owner? These feats of generosity, glamour and service are to be observed at all such events in Bordeaux. If you're lucky enough to be present, it's hard not to experience a wave of self-satisfaction.

This warm embrace of the wine trade is not extended to mere consumers, of course. Although châteaux are more open to visitors than they were in the past, most wine tourists making their way up the roads that connect Margaux to Saint-Julien and Pauillac are confronted by closed gates or notices that read 'by appointment only'. Some 25 years ago a delegation of Bordeaux worthies came to London to ask friendly journalists (over a good lunch, of course) what they could do improve the image of their region. 'Try opening your gates,' was my suggestion, and it did not go down particularly well.

FEES, FACTOTUMS AND FIXERS

Oeno-tourism has been slow to come to Bordeaux. Showcase châteaux such as Pavie, Smith Haut Lafitte or Lynch-Bages have become adept at offering tours and tastings, though at a price. A fee is understandable, as the cost of staffing the tours and the wines to be poured needs to be recouped. Napa does it differently. Visitors are courted, and the customary tasting fee will be refunded if you buy a bottle or two. In Australia, too, the 'cellar door' is always open for visitors to enjoy the wines and other merchandizing. However, in Bordeaux, most prestigious châteaux make little effort to welcome visitors.

In Burgundy, top growers sell to a band of importers and perhaps a few private customers and restaurants. In Bordeaux, châteaux sell to négociants, who distribute their wines worldwide. Châteaux have no direct influence over who sells or buys their wines. That's why it's important to have influential writers and critics on their side. A high score from a wine guru may just persuade a group of merchants or consumers to buy Château X in preference to Château Y. And the other way around the following year. No wonder top châteaux treat the media with affection and respect.

Consultants, too, form part of the hype machine. They are rarely present in Burgundy, where savoir faire is passed down (not always successfully) from one generation to the next. But in regions such as Tuscany or Bordeaux, where estate owners are often rich and enthusiastic but short on expertise, the consultant is an essential member of the team. Nothing wrong with hiring good advice, of course. But choosing the right consultant also adds lustre to the estate. In Italy, take on Carlo Ferrini or Riccardo Cotarella and you can be certain, at the very least, of media attention.

In Bordeaux, the consultant is more than an adviser on viticulture or vinification, suggesting how high your canopy should be or which coopers are best suited to your style of wine. They have influence too. Michel Rolland, notoriously, had the ear of Robert Parker for many years. This was perfectly understandable because, broadly speaking, they liked the same style of wine. I once asked a château owner with a group of properties why he had chosen a particular consultant rather than another of similar renown. 'He's good at what he does,' was the reply, 'but he also has a track record of getting his clients' wines onto airline lists.'

Many of the older generation of consultants were invisible. In decades of visits to Bordeaux I never encountered Jacques Boissenot, who advised most of the top estates of the Médoc, or Gilles Pauquet in Saint-Emilion. Others, such as Stéphane Derenoncourt, court importers and the press assiduously, with regular tastings that provide a showcase for all their clients. Wine writers like, for sound reasons, to be on close terms with consultants such as Derenoncourt, as they can be invaluable sources of information.

SAVE TIME AND SCORE IT?

Admission to the magic circle of Bordeaux carries its own risks. I doubt there is much corruption as such – no wine writer of any importance would, I assume, be foolish enough to accept backhanders in exchange for favourable ratings – but what has happened is that independent assessment has been almost abandoned. And there are stories of bribes, often in the form of a few cases of wine, being offered. Newly minted bloggers would be particularly susceptible to a helping hand.

Back in the 1980s or even 1990s revered critics such as Robert Parker would not hesitate to give a poor score to a wine he considered below standard. These days a poor score has become close to inconceivable. A score below 90 has become the equivalent of a smack in the face. In an article some years ago I predicted the scores that the major critics would give the 2014 vintage when, a few months later, the wines became available for tasting En Primeur. My educated guesses, made without tasting a single wine, were alarmingly accurate. That, simply put, is because critics now score the brand and not the wine. No one is going to rate a first growth or scarce Pomerol at below 96; likewise, no obscure fifth growth or Côte de Bordeaux red, however fine, will ever be scored at 93 or higher.

Bordeaux has succeeded in imposing its own self-valuations on its critics. Price has become equated with quality, as has been the case since the 18th century. This is why new owners of certain properties relentlessly push up their prices, because this is the best way to confer prestige on the wines. For Bordeaux as a whole, it may be a costly business organizing lavish dinners with superlative vintages, but it has paid off in establishing a group of wines as safely within the band of the world's most appreciated and sought after.

For the wine critic it's a tricky balance. Without access, an article or vintage assessment becomes impossible. I am not immune. In order to research my own publications on Bordeaux, I have accepted offers to stay at comfortable châteaux for extended periods. I do my best not to let my own judgements be swayed by this quid pro quo (which I disclose), but one can never be certain.

SCHMOOZE OR YOU LOSE?

It's not only the wine press that is courted and pampered. Top châteaux will lay on lavish feasts for négociants and brokers too. Corinne Mentzelopoulos of Château Margaux once described such events as a way of thanking the Bordeaux wine trade for their success in selling her wines (not an arduous task, I would have thought). She intimated that it was also a way of keeping the trade on her side. Selling top claret in a great vintage is a doddle (except when grotesquely overpriced); selling the same label in a mediocre year such as 2013 is another matter.

Maintaining brand loyalty – both to Brand Bordeaux and individual châteaux – is crucial. By 2020 the region was having to face the threat of USA tariffs, the cold shoulder from China, the uncertainties of Brexit for the important British market, not to mention the growing climatic vagaries bringing drought, frost and hail in their wake. There are other challenges that are stylistic rather than economic. A colleague who is involved in assessing the wine lists of top restaurants worldwide notes that there are a growing number of such lists that ostentatiously scorn Bordeaux in favour of, usually, 'natural' or other styles considered trendy. This is sommelier-driven, and Bordeaux producers and merchants are not always aware of how old-fashioned and stuffy their offerings appear to sommeliers (and their clients) in search of novelty rather than reliability.

It's hard for individual châteaux to promote their wines worldwide since they don't know precisely who is buying their superb wines. In contrast, their Napa Valley equivalents stage auctions and other events targeted very precisely at super-rich clients and social media. Australia has its highly regarded agricultural shows, awarding medals that confer more prestige than most medals from wine competitions. Bordeaux doesn't have such marketing opportunities at its disposal, which is why generic marketing campaigns, prestigious tasting events, and the assiduous wooing of the media are such necessary tools. Whether they will continue to be effective as they have been in the past is undoubtedly open to question.

First published in *Bordeaux, People, Power and Politics*, Mitchell Beazley (London) 2001, and here revised and updated by the author, Stephen Brook.

Bordeaux' marketplace – 'La Place de Bordeaux' – has always maintained its position of strength by adapting to changing times. Now, the market is ripe for Bordeaux to use its trade links for fine wines made outside the region. Mathieu Chadronnier, president of super-négociant CVBG, explains that embracing the international fine wine circuit will bring even greater success.

BORDEAUX GOES INTERNATIONAL

Mathieu Chadronnier (2020)

In more recent years, one of the most visible evolutions of Bordeaux as a marketplace has been its gradual opening to fine wines from outside the region. Many have questioned whether this new trend was an illustration of weakness, showing a need for the *négoce* to look to other wine regions for development of their sales and profit margin. But this perspective is largely missing the point.

First of all, this is not a new trend. Instead, it reflects a new reality: the advent of fine wines as a cross-regional category. That 'La Place de Bordeaux' (Bordeaux' much-respected marketing network) has embraced this new international structure so successfully is a testament to its age-old ability to adapt and change as the fine wine markets develop. It also illustrates the role Bordeaux can play in a globalized fine wine world.

A (NOT SO) NEW TREND

The fine wine trade calendar is well organized. It has its seasons. The latest burgundy vintage is launched at the beginning of the year; Bordeaux' En Primeurs are released in the spring. And now, in September, our focus is on the 'Beyond Bordeaux' campaign, which has steadily gained momentum and depth of offer to the extent that it is now a key moment of the year for the wine trade.

The first time Bordeaux took on the distribution of a great wine from outside the region was in 1998. The wine was a new creation – a joint venture that crossed two hemispheres – and the vintage released by La Place was its first. Almaviva was the brainchild of the late Baroness Philippine de Rothschild. In what seemed a radical move at the time, she partnered with the Chilean powerhouse Concha y Toro to create a top-quality Cabernet Sauvignon-dominated blend that would become a first growth equivalent in Chile. From the onset, she used Mouton Rothschild's best négociants to handle its distribution, which proved to be a stroke of genius, paving the way to international success.

Opus One in California's Napa Valley, the winery joint-venture of Baron Philippe de Rothschild and Robert Mondavi, conceived after they met in Hawaii in 1970.

A few years later, encouraged by the positive outcome of her Andean endeavour, Baroness Philippine got together with her partners in California's Napa Valley, the Mondavi family, to decide on the next step for Opus One – their joint-venture wine forged in 1978. At the time, Opus One was exporting around 17 percent of its production, which certainly made it one of Napa's more international fine wine brands, both in terms of percentage and case sales. Yet, its founding partners felt the potential was even greater, but that to realize it a new route to market was necessary. La Place de Bordeaux seemed to be the obvious choice. In July 2004, the Rothschild and Mondavi families hosted the négociants at the winery for an in-depth discovery tour of Opus One, followed, in typically French fashion, by a festive dinner hosted by Baroness Philippine and Robert Mondavi. Two months later, in September, La Place de Bordeaux took on the international distribution of Opus One, launching the 2001 vintage.

Exports of Opus One rose from 17 percent before the initial release through Bordeaux to more than 50 percent in just 10 years, and the wine became a textbook illustration of how to succeed with La Place – a real-life example that is set to become a business school case study.

Opus One was a turning point. It provided Bordeaux with a resounding demonstration of the value of its open market distribution system. If La Place de Bordeaux did not *create* the reputation of Opus One, it clearly *accelerated* it in a way that a traditional network could not achieve. It also provided Bordeaux with something very precious: a new horizon. It would, however, take another five years before this new horizon would become a tangible point of focus.

In 2007, another immensely successful winery approached the Bordeaux' marketplace seeking a change in momentum. But this time, the winery had no link at all with Bordeaux. Masseto was to introduce another turning point.

A legendary 'Super Tuscan' Merlot, Masseto is uniquely Italian. As the wine had no ties with Bordeaux, the process of introducing it to the Bordeaux marketplace took longer. The team at Masseto needed to understand the culture and distribution methods of the négociants. Equally, the négociants needed to truly understand the terroir, background, identity and aspiration of Masseto. It took almost two years from the initial conversation with five négociants to the actual launch of Masseto's 2006 vintage – almost two years, many meetings in Bordeaux, an extensive visit to Masseto, comprehensive tastings and a press conference in Milan. It took a great deal of vision and no small amount of courage to overcome some of the obstacles – the financial crisis of 2008 being not the least of them. Eventually, on September 1st 2009, it happened: the launch was success beyond expections. Another moment of epiphany.

From then on, things accelerated. Another Italian monolith joined the following year: 'Solaia' from Antinori in Tuscany. Then came Hommage à Jacques Perrin from Château de Beaucastel in Châteauneuf-du-Pape, Seña (a collaborative wine from Chile's Viña Errázuriz and Robert Mondavi), l'Aventure (a California blend of Bordeaux and Rhône varieties), Verité (Sonoma), Clos Apalta (Chile), Maya, Promontory, Joseph Phelps and Inglenook (each from Napa), Nicolás Catena Zapata and Cheval des Andes (Argentina), Vin de Constance (South Africa), to name a few. All these wines have benefited from making the switch to La Place. And more producers show interest every year.

A CROSS REGIONAL CATEGORY

There is of course nothing new in the fact that fine wines are produced in every major wine country. What is new is that the demand for these wines has become global. Buyers

The new Errázuriz winery in Chile's Aconcagua Valley – home of Seña, Chile's first 'icon' wine (launched 1995), the joint venture of California's Mondavi family and Viña Errázuriz.

have embraced the fact that more regions than ever before produce world-class wines, which in turn has led La Place to broaden its offering from both historical wine regions and new. Gathering together some of the most iconic wines from so many different countries and regions may seem counter-intuitive. But as a group they offer easier access for the consumers – and easier access to the trade, which previously could only source these wines through exclusive sales channels.

And nor does it mean that the old Bordeaux wine hierarchies are being *challenged*; instead they are being enriched. Historical wine icons (from Tuscany and the Rhône Valley) are enjoying new global renown, their success inspiring many others, while younger stellar-quality wines from new terroirs in Chile, Argentina and South Africa are being discovered from pioneers who aspire to create enduring brands that will stand with the best in the world.

Fine wine may be very diverse in its geographical origins, but it appeals to the same consumers in every market. This is especially true as the next generation of fine wine buyers grows to appreciate the latest diversity of this offering. Some of these relatively new wines were created the same decade these contemporary wine lovers were born.

The success achieved in selling fine wine across a global spectrum clearly demonstrates the new reality: that fine wine is a cross regional category. This is precisely where the value lies, and the reason La Place's recent venture has been so successful.

For Bordeaux, this whole development is not defensive. Quite the contrary; it is about acknowledging today's reality, and embracing the future.

THE POWER OF THE OPEN MARKET

A great fine wine brand is a blend of many components: great terroir, history, skilful and inspired winemaking, sheer quality, identity of style, status, critical acclaim, distribution and visibility. Of these, 'visibility' is probably the hardest to gain, as it can only come once the others have been achieved. And it is of critical importance. A great brand must be present in the right places and it should also be at the centre of the attention of the international fine wine trade. No fine wine brand, even those produced in very small quantities, can be called 'great' unless it has a true international presence.

Here lies the value of the open market. It offers the ability to address a larger spectrum of distribution – and to move a product (a wine) swiftly. Thus an international presence can be more easily achieved.

Instead of having one single importer per market, an open market allows for multiple importers for each market. The number of trade players who become a stakeholder in the distribution of the brand is increased by at least one order of magnitude. So is the number of individuals who become involved in telling the story of the wine and enhancing its reputation. An open market makes it possible to address a much larger audience compared to exclusive channels.

Some tend to see the open market as speculative. To me it is rather an acceleration platform. Of course, it means relinquishing some control over distribution, but to the benefit of engaging with a much wider spectrum of the trade, and addressing a much larger group of potential consumers. For a brand that has already established itself to a certain level, an open market distribution is a natural next step. This is a key point. An open market does not work for every brand. It requires a rock-solid foundation on which to build. Being certain of engaging with the right brands, and those interested in Bordeaux for the right reasons, is key to success. However, an open market does not mean an unstructured market. It requires connections and a 'hub'.

THE ROLE OF BORDEAUX

Bordeaux is the leading region within the broader fine wine category. The role of a leader is to consolidate and stimulate, not to exclude. So it is only natural that Bordeaux becomes the hub that embraces the distribution of the best wines from around the globe. It already has an open market culture, established networks, critical mass and a unique distribution system. While this may have raised eyebrows in the early days, Bordeaux' new openness is now a fully accepted reality, presenting a clear way forward. The benefits of concentrating the best fine wines in one hub are evident in terms of developing the category at large, but in the resulting understanding of market dynamics, it works for individual wines too.

As a result, Bordeaux has emerged, more than ever before, as the epicentre of the fine wine world. Every economic or cultural field has its epicentre. Silicon Valley is the epicentre of tech. London is the epicentre of finance. Switzerland, of watch manufacturing. Chamonix for mountaineering. For fine wines, the epicentre, the hub, is Bordeaux.

Is this all a move *away* from Bordeaux as we know it? Far from it. Bordeaux remains the most important fine wine region of the world. The depth of its fine wine offering is unrivalled. The emulation among its producers leads to a pace of refinement of viticulture and winemaking that has accelerated well beyond that experienced through its centuries of history. But the fine wine world is moving fast. Where it was once owner of the sole truly internationally traded fine wine, Bordeaux is now the leader in a much broader category of global wine. And it is only fitting that Bordeaux should take the lead and contribute a centralized distribution system.

The Place de Bordeaux has always demonstrated an ability to see where the opportunities lie. Here, what is at stake is an understanding of what the future of fine wine holds, and fully accepting that Bordeaux' position is to take lead. In the end, the future of fine wine is all about evolution.

Following a modern-day silk road through the prism of Bordeaux' *grands crus classés*, the Australian film documentary, *Red Obsession* (2013) observes the risks and opportunities people take in pursuit of their love of wine. It is a study of the human spirit set against the Bordeaux and Chinese landscapes as the European debt crisis and global uncertainty take hold. Andrew Caillard was associate producer.

RED OBSESSION: WHEN BORDEAUX MET CHINA

Andrew Caillard MW (2020)

Wine and film rarely mix well, although the lead times and collaborative nature of making wine and films are very similar. It's usually the stories around wine, rather than about wine itself, that are the most successful or memorable. *The Secret of Santa Vitoria*, a story about a hilltop town hiding its million bottles of wine from the Germans during World War II, starring Anthony Quinn, captures the triumph of good over evil rather than whether the wine tasted any good. *Sideways*, where wine and wine country are accessories to the fact, is a story about human fallibility, infidelity and conceit. Nonetheless it unwittingly hurt the reputation of Merlot and propelled the cause of Pinot Noir. *A Walk in the Clouds*, Anthony Quinn again among the stars, is a silly romantic chocolate-box melodrama set against the backdrop of a post-war Napa Valley. *Bottle Shock* was a half-witted production about American economic power and smart-arse savoir faire through the prism of Steven Spurrier's Judgement of Paris. The critically acclaimed *Mondo Vino* is a cult documentary film about globalization and uses the wine business as a case study. It goes close to the essence of wine, but polarized critics and audiences alike. Bordeaux did not really come off well, with the greed factor being an underlying theme. The beautiful *Tu Seras Mon Fils* (*You Will Be My Son*) filmed at Château Clos Fourtet, was about inheritance and succession. *Somm 1, 2 & 3*, *Sour Grapes* and a myriad of other films portray human ambition, failure and success in varying proportions. But rarely does film ever capture the sensory or emotional impact of wine. A glass of Château Lafite Rothschild is not any different from two-buck chuck from a camera's perspective.

Since the early 2000s I have visited Bordeaux every April (well, almost!) to taste and provide Australian collectors with analysis and advice about the quality of the latest vintage. The En Primeur week is a fixture on the international calendar and attracts a who's who of the most powerful and distinguished wine journalists in the world. The Bordeaux wine trade, particularly the *Union des Grands Crus* and other leading châteaux, puts on an extraordinary charm offensive that takes the cause of fine wine and the business of selling it to a near-religious experience.

The Bordelaise are the doyens of luxury marketing. They invented selling wine as real-estate-in-a-bottle by activating history and provenance, particularly the 1855 Bordeaux Classification and the hierarchies of a post-Napoleonic French aristocracy. Nothing is more aspirational than filling up a cellar of first growth real estate, especially if it is pointed up and validated by the most influential palates in the world. The very mention of a Robert Parker score of 100 points, in 2010 anyway, could trigger an avalanche of orders from the international fine wine buying fraternity. Parker-points, as they were called, of 95+ also enabled château owners to push their prices up and optimize profit. Meanwhile the négociants, the longstanding piggies in the middle, were being played off handsomely through preferential allocations of vintages. While wine business was on a high, the entire Bordeaux system seemed to be either pivoting to a new reality or surging towards a crisis. No matter. It seemed like a good subject for a film.

THE BUBBLE BUILDS

The rise of China and the creation of new wealth in those parts saw demand for fine red wine increase dramatically. The châteaux kept pushing up their prices and the Chinese didn't seem to care. Bordeaux négociants and château owners travelled extensively to China pushing their wares, as did other French and European luxury brands. The Chinese walked or drove around Shanghai and Beijing like billboards, wearing bling of every ilk, and taking luxury to a new level of consumption. Château Lafite Rothschild became a household name, the apogee of sophistication and success. Smuggling and counterfeiting of older vintages became commonplace. Lafite became a currency for currying favour with Chinese government officials. 'Mules', with bottles strapped to their bodies or hidden in suitcases, travelled through the Hong Kong Shenzhen border to avoid taxes. In Bordeaux, the négociants and château owners began to believe that this strange, exciting and lucrative market would continue forever more.

In April 2010 at the annual Primeurs tastings in Bordeaux, the mood among *grand cru* châteaux and négociants was euphoric to say the least. The 2009 was hailed as an exceptional vintage. Chinese wine trade and media types were omnipresent and guests of honour were everywhere. Chinese flags fluttered atop the towers and crenulations of all the major châteaux. Ex-cellars prices were also rising as château owners jockeyed for a position of exclusivity and prestige. The more expensive the wine became, seemingly the more the Chinese market lapped it up. And of course, château owners were able to justify it all with the escalating scores from prominent wine writers and the massive investments in new wine cellars and vineyard management. Building cranes could be seen across the Saint-Emilion and Médoc skyline. Astonishing works had been completed at châteaux Cos d'Estournel and Cheval Blanc. And there was more to come.

'Conspicuous consumption': model Kathy Chow wears a $15 million jade necklace and admires an $80,000 bottle of 1961 Château Petrus at a Christie's auction press preview; her backdrop is a Chinese oil painting by Chen Yifei worth an estimated $3.5 million.

Many observers, including myself, thought the heart of the Bordeaux wine market was beating far too quickly. Usually négociants spread their risks by building relationships and distribution networks with clients across many countries. But the market power of China, Hong Kong and the emerging super-airline Emirates was drawing their focus away from traditional markets. Countries like Australia, even with the strongest dollar in 50 years, were now a sideshow. It was difficult to secure allocations of the best wines and to attract serious attention. Few of the protagonists even bothered to come to Sydney or Melbourne, preferring the excitement, riches and low-hanging fruit of China. I was not alone in believing that Bordeaux had entered a classic market bubble, in the same way tulips and spices had become speculated commodities in the 17th century.

LET FILMING COMMENCE

Not long after the 2010 April Primeurs tastings I was flying back to Europe on a new Qantas A380 via Singapore. By coincidence, I bumped into filmmaker Warwick Ross and quickly found myself talking about Bordeaux and China. By another coincidence, about six months later in November, I was flying up to Hong Kong for the Hong Kong International Wine & Spirits Fair and found myself on the same plane as Warwick and his wife Margot. We agreed to have lunch and talk about the idea of a film together. By this time the 2010 Bordeaux harvest had taken place and reports were suggesting that it would be another vintage of the century. If this was the case, 2009 and 2010 would be the first double-great years since 1899 and 1900.

In late February 2011, a meeting took place at 'the table of knowledge' in Woollahra (Sydney), a favourite haunt of Warwick Ross and long-term collaborator David Roach. They had both worked together on the famously successful Australian comedies *Young Einstein* (a phenomenal hit in France) and *Reckless Kelly* with the mercurial actor-comedian Yahoo Serious. Although they were excited about this wine story's potential, they pointed out that financing usually takes at least six months to a year. Nonetheless, Warwick was persuaded to throw caution to the wind and seize this 'once-in-a-lifetime opportunity'. In hindsight this was an enormous personal undertaking.

Apparently, it takes months or years rather than weeks to plan a film, but I jumped into the process of making a filming schedule, without actually knowing how it was all done. Nor had I fully appreciated the resentment left by the award-winning, but polarizing cult wine documentary *Mondovino*. The Bordelaise will forever be distrustful of filmmakers. Château Latour, for instance, used the experience of Jonathon Nossiter's *grand opus* as an excuse not to be filmed initially, although the estate's director, Frédéric Engerer, graciously agreed to be interviewed when we came back later in the year.

A visit to the first growth Château Lafite Rothschild was the number-one priority. Because of its positioning on the original 1855 Classification, as 'the first among equals', it had quickly won China-wide acclaim and deference as the best of the best. Gifting a bottle of Lafite could open doors or expedite red tape like an engine lubricant. In October 2010, Château Lafite announced it would release its 2008 Vintage with the Chinese symbol '8' on the bottles. It declared: 'The shape of the symbol seems to offer a perfect representation of the slopes of the vineyard and commemorates the launch of our Chinese wine project.' It had also partnered with CITIC, China's largest state-owned company, to develop 25 hectares of vineyard at Penglai in Shandong Province.

After an unbearable two weeks of cajoling, Château Lafite's administration permitted us to interview its technical director, Charles Chevalier. If Château Margaux had not agreed to be interviewed, I don't think we would have got our foot in the door. Corinne Mentzelopoulos and Paul Pontallier activated the first domino and then everything else started to fall in place. As more people agreed to be involved, appointments came thick and fast, but I was so anxious about locking in the Lafite interview that we found ourselves committed to driving all the way from Château d'Yquem to keep our appointment – a journey involving about the furthest extremities of the Bordeaux wine map.

We all assembled in Bordeaux on a cold spring day, March 28th 2011. The working title of the project was 'The Fine Wine Game'. Our team comprised collaborators Warwick Ross and David Roach (Lion Rock Films), Kiwi sound recordist Grant Lawson, Emmy-winning London-based Australian cameraman Lee Pulbrook and executive producer Robert Coe. A few days before we had been shooting live auction footage in Hong Kong with John Kapon of Acker Merrall & Condit. We also interviewed a few wine collectors, notably the flamboyant and personable businesswoman Kelly Cheng. She boasted paying 1.5 million HK dollars for a bottle of Lafite, driving the point of a market out of control. A year later, she ended up being convicted of commercial fraud from her business dealings, much to our astonishment and regret.

During the first week of filming in Bordeaux we stayed at Martin Krajewski's beautifully restored Château de Sours in Entre-Deux-Mers, not too far away from Saint-Emilion. Martin is one of the most generous people in the wine trade. When I told him about the project, and knowing we were working on a shoestring, he offered to put us all up. Within a week he had converted our small film crew into wine lovers for life.

The first morning of filming was at the ancient Château d'Yquem. While we waited for director Pierre Lurton to turn up, we captured cold, early-spring images in the vineyard. By the next week summer conditions prevailed: the following Friday it was 32°C without any clouds in the sky. Over a two-week period we watched the whole Bordeaux landscape come to verdant and beautiful life. The unseasonably warm weather certainly contributed to the buoyancy and positive feeling about the 2010 vintage. However, early bud-burst exposes the vines to spring frosts and storms. Localized hail in the Bordeaux region later that May hit a number of vineyards.

We criss-crossed the Bordeaux wine region covering around 2,000 kilometres over that fortnight and interviewed a remarkable cast of winemakers, wine writers, négociants and collectors. We interviewed at least 40 people but the most memorable were the late Paul Pontallier, Corinne Mentzelopoulos (Château Margaux), Christian Moueix (Château Lafleur-Pétrus) and Thomas Duroux (Château Palmer). Paul could talk about wine in the most beautiful way. He possessed a natural authority, and his superb grasp of the English language made tasting wine with him a magical, informative and captivating experience. Corinne's generosity of spirit and empathy for the land, so easily captured on camera, gives an extra resonance to Château Margaux. Together Paul and Corinne made a great working team. They balanced authority and grandeur with a warm, down-to-earth realness, like farmers playing dress-up. And whenever I think of Margaux I think of Ernest Hemingway, who famously loved Château Margaux and Marques de Riscal, and Paul Pontallier had worked with both. Such is the way the bell tolls in the world of wine.

That Christian Moueix accepted to be interviewed surprised everyone around him. He is a self-described farmer, and when we caught up with him at Château Lafleur-Pétrus, he was in a very cheerful mood, having enjoyed a few magnums with friends at lunch. His delightful enthusiasm infectiously draws the audience into the film. This ability to communicate is further exemplified when he talks about the future of Bordeaux. Who else could think up a story about a boy and a girl on their first date in Seattle where the enjoyment of a bottle of claret would decide the outcome of the evening? 'What a drama,' he says.

Thomas Duroux at Château Palmer, half Italian-half French and gifted with a sensibility for nature and nurture, is able to distil complex ideas into simple concepts. His gentle optimistic voice, even after a hailstorm had damaged his vineyard when we caught up with him again in June, underpins a resilience that is an essential part of a wine producer's armoury. The weather in Bordeaux can explode violently without much warning, as has happened here in New South Wales, Victoria and South Australia this summer, 2020, with a particularly bad bushfire season.

Most surprising of all the participants in Bordeaux was oenologist Michel Rolland, who was poorly treated in *Mondovino* and potentially had much to lose. He is one of the most engaging, entertaining and delightful people you could ever meet. In the end he landed mostly on the cutting-room floor, which I think is probably what he had hoped for. He has polarized the international wine trade for so long, but he is a hero to many, too. He makes wines that have a generous swagger and universal appeal. Penfolds winemaker Max Schubert would have loved him, but these two generations never crossed.

HOTFOOT TO CHINA

Over a period of 16 months we filmed through the four seasons of Bordeaux, visited Hong Kong three times and travelled through China on several occasions, including visits to the wine regions of Ningxia, Shandong Province and Xinjiang Uyghur Autonomous Region in the far northwest. This scheduling was not easy. Professor Demei Li, who was consulting for Jaibelan in Ningxia, and Fongyee Walker, who passed her MW a few years ago, played a crucial role in bringing our itinerary to life. Marcus Ford (who now works for Wines of South Africa) at Summergate proved to be an invaluable help. Australian cinematographer Steve Arnold came along with us a few times as well. Lee and Steve are both real cameramen who get stuck into a story with great gusto, empathy and courage. When we interviewed Château Latour collector Francis Ford Coppola (of *The Godfather* and Inglenook winery fame) in Hong Kong, he was more interested in talking about the legendary Arri Alexa, 'a true cinema' digital camera, with the film crew than about Bordeaux.

China's bewildering vastness and potential as a wine producing country completely took me by surprise. The contradictions are so extraordinary. The rapid building of infrastructure threatens to destroy the beauty of the landscape and profoundly toxify the air. Yet the pace of change, the will to learn and desire for modernit may well result in new rapid ways of empowering and developing the Chinese economy. The rate of pollution cannot continue and the government knows it. Nonetheless, we filmed new vine plantings on the bleak gravelly plains of Ningxia, where Genghis Kahn subjugated the Western Xia, remnants of the Great Wall, herds of camels grazing through wine farms, and a vineyard adjacent to a cemetery in Turfan – a predominantly Muslim region that boasts over 30,000 hectares of 'Thompson Seedless' vines and an emerging wine industry (despite its history of making wine 2,500 years ago). The ambition behind China's economic growth is astonishing.

Our encounter with Bordeaux Collector Peter Tseng in Shenzhen was probably the most bizarre yet funny of all our interviews and location filming. Only directors with a sense of timing and comedy could pull off and integrate the musings of one of the largest sex-toy manufacturers in the world into a serious narrative about the shift of economic power from the West to the East.

Perhaps the most exhilarating experience was interviewing the greatest interviewer of all time, Michael Parkinson, a Bordeaux lover, to some degree a history maker and an extraordinary observer of our modern times. For me he exemplifies those rare charismatic powers of empathy, trust and persuasiveness. Not once did he proffer advice but rather showed his warm and skilful art of bonding with the subject. Wine writer and former Shakespearean actor Oz Clarke, who was also interviewed, is a great storyteller and shares a similar optimism and interest in others.

The nitty gritty of trade with China, however, was told through the likes of wine experts Jancis Robinson MW, Simon Staples, Jeannie Cho Lee MW, Debra Meiburg MW, Simon Tam, Ch'ng Poh Tiong, Demei Li, Fongyee Walker MW, Chris Myers, Paulo Pong and other contributors, including the fashion icon Yue-Sai Kan. Literally hours of footage had to be binned and dissected to find the story's thread. Many interviews and sequences, some very good, were left on the cutting-room floor.

TIMES OF SHAPE-SHIFTING

The editing was frustrating because the unfolding narrative was not always obvious. The film could never be about the aesthetic of Bordeaux wines or the landscape. The arc of the story had to go deeper and into the realms of politics and conflict. Tension is a word that wine writers often use to describe an exciting wine. Without tension and gear-change, a film can be very dull. While this post-production work was happening, the inevitable occurred in April 2013. President Xi Jinping announced austerity measures and forbade government officials from accepting gifts or consuming luxury goods with state funds. Suddenly Bordeaux' market access looked very shaky. News began leaking of Chinese buyers not honouring their En Primeur purchases. Sales and prices fell dramatically causing sudden inertia. It was like watching someone climbing to the top of Mount Everest and then jumping off. The story that we had been following was now becoming a cautionary tale about modern-day business between the West and the East.

Film editor Paul Murphy painstakingly went through every shot with co-directors Warwick Ross and David Roach. Even when the story sequence had been locked and the documentary narrative completed, there was still the question about who would do the voice-over. Although actor Russell Crowe had intimated he might do it, everyone was uncertain because of his very heavy schedule at the time. So, a back-up voice-over was completed and dropped in with some degree of disappointment. Although done well, the potential Hollywood lustre was not there. At the eleventh hour, executive producer Rob Coe received a call from the US East Coast where Russell Crowe was filming *Noah*. The filming had been stopped because of Hurricane Sandy; a massive flood had drastically damaged the set. While this was happening, Russell stepped out of his schedule and hurried to a studio in New York where he narrated the film in one session with his superb rich, authoritative voice. The film *Red Obsession* was completed.

By the time the film was released, the Chinese Juggernaut had well and truly jack-knifed. Nonetheless *Red Obsession* was selected and screened at Berlin, Tribeca, Seattle, Sydney and other film festivals, winning several plaudits. In Australia it won two Australian AACTA Awards for Best Feature Documentary Film and Best Direction of a Feature Documentary film. Elsewhere, *Red Obsession* became a cautionary tale and case study used by business schools and universities. It did well in Australia and enjoyed moderate success internationally. Actor Robert de Niro, who selected *Red Obsession* for Tribeca, described the film as 'wonderful'.

THE FINAL ACT

Seven years later there have been many changes in Bordeaux. Martin Krajewski sold Château de Sours to Chinese billionaire Jack Ma and now makes wine at his Lilliputian property, Château Séraphine in Pomerol. Paul Pontallier at Château Margaux died, aged 59, in 2016; négociant Mahler-Besse changed hands; many of the protagonists have retired or are nearing retirement. New building works have been completed, notably Sir Norman Foster's Château Margaux winery pavilion, the new stables at Château Pontet-Canet and new cellars at Château Montrose. In China, the anti-corruption austerity measures led to massive challenges in fine wine distribution. Wine production in China also fell. But new Chinese fine wine brands like Ao Yun (an LVMH project), Silver Heights and Grace Vineyards have started to win international praise.

China still promises to be an important market for Bordeaux, but bizarre behaviours and excitement have given way to more realistic and transparent demand. The stories of Coca-Cola being added to Château Lafite are true, but rarely does this type of thing happen in the primary first-tier cities at least. China now has a small but influential fine wine network of wine experts and sommeliers who have done much to establish an informed market through education, wine shows and media. Nonetheless, conspicuous consumption of luxury brands is still a Chinese thing. Correspondingly, fake goods, including counterfeit wines, are aplenty. While Bordeaux is still greatly respected, burgundy has now become the fashionable wine for Chinese collectors, Domaine de la Romanée-Conti and Armand Rousseau being the leading brands. No one but the very rich can afford them.

Warwick Ross and Rob Coe, with editor Paul Murphy, have just completed a ripping new feature documentary film called *Blind Ambition*, which is about four Zimbabwean sommeliers competing in the World Blind Wine Championships in France in 2017 and 2018 (it will be released in late 2020). This story was brought to us by Jancis Robinson MW and South African wine writer Erica Platter. I never really thought I would ever be involved in making films, yet both these stories found me. The people behind wine are really more fascinating and memorable than wine itself. A tasting note is a transient and inconsequential thing, yet activates and propels fine wine trade. A documentary film is a lasting fragment that can unearth consequential truths of far-reaching impact. For me, it is the personal connections, whether fleeting or long term, that have been the reward. I feel lucky to have met so many great people in and around wine. Because of my work and *Red Obsession*, Bordeaux will always be close to my heart.

Red Obsession from Lion Rock Films was released in 2013.

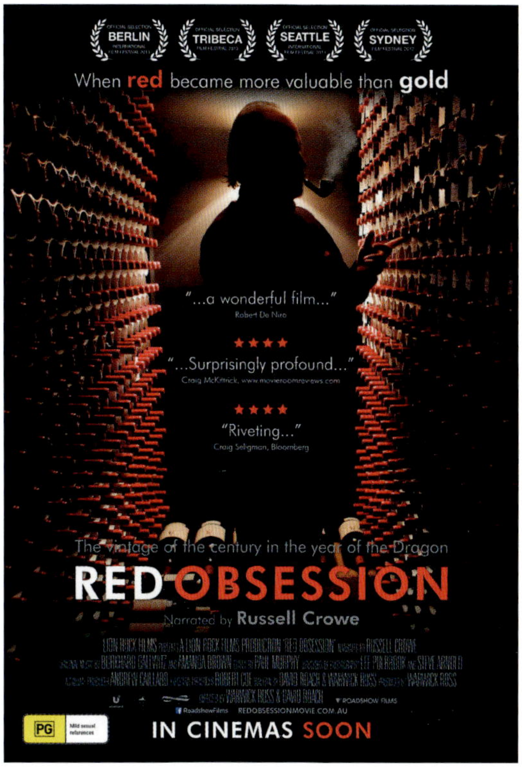

Peter Vinding-Diers looks back at his quarter-century in Bordeaux – a time of discovery and oenological revelation, from which his findings at Château Rahoul still influence the world of winemaking today – and wonders if his favourite wine region is about to take a turn in the wrong direction.

BORDEAUX – BEWARE THE PORTUGUESE...

Peter Vinding-Diers (2020)

My wife, Susie, and I left Bordeaux 20 years ago, having spent a quarter of a century there. They were happy years, and for me, as a vigneron, they were perhaps the summit of my life – they gave me all I could hope for.

I had three major successes during that time. I managed to get the château I directed in the 1980s, Château Rahoul, at Portets in the Graves, accepted as a member of the celebrated Union des Grands Crus – a process that was like getting the camel through the eye of a needle. Through an experiment I carried out in 1985, I managed to prove my theory that every vineyard has its own signature yeast. And I managed to prove that we can get rid of hydrogen sulphide in a wine (the smell of rotten eggs) simply by using dry ice.

I remember organizing the first tasting in London for the Union des Grands Crus members and their wines. It took them out into the world – we then visited Australia, Singapore, South Africa and Chile, among other places, showing the flag of Bordeaux everywhere. Then later, building up forgotten vineyards to renewed fame became an obsession with me. This led in 1990 to the renaissance of the famous wines of Tokaji – but that is another story.

THE WILDER THE BETTER

But back to those yeasts. When I was a young vigneron at the experimental research institute in Stellenbosch, I had been seriously worried that something was vitally wrong in the way we made wines, keeping them cold, using yeasts from a can, and centrifuging them to 'clean their character'. I found the wines boring. It just could not be right that a wine made in cool Constantia would be identical to one made in hot Tulbagh. But I was firmly put down as being ignorant. In 1985, years later, I began working at Château Rahoul, in the Graves.

His decade as winemaker at Château Rahoul gave Peter Vinding-Diers insight into the experimental side of Bordeaux' oenology and viticulture.

By this time I had become convinced that the wines we made all tasted the same way because of the yeast we used. I was the very willing pupil of Brian Croser when he came to Rahoul to help make the wine (the château briefly had Australian owners), but when he suggested using commercial yeast, I put my foot down. We went in to Bordeaux and bought Agar petri dishes, Pasteur loups and so on, and my old brass microscope was taken out of its box ready for use.

We were then able to isolate the different yeasts out of a natural yeast ferment of Rahoul's white wine. We found three volatile and two first-class yeasts which dominated the fermentation. Of the two good ones, we now had to choose. We fermented some of each in tiny 5ml glass jars, and after a week we put them to the sniffing test. As we stood in the kitchen, our noses in those tiny ferments, Susie pointed to Number R2. We all agreed.

From that point on, it became my absolute conviction that wherever I was, the local yeast, for better or worse, would be the one I used. Generations of winemakers have been filled with nonsense about the 'danger' of wild yeasts, but I was going to prove this wrong.

I broadened the experiment by fermenting with three different yeasts. I used batches of must from the same parcel of white vines at Rahoul. To one, I added the yeast of Château Lynch-Bages (my friend Jean-Michel Cazes had given me his natural yeast); to another I added yeast from Château Angludet (where Peter Sichel had done the same), and in the third, I used our own from Rahoul.

We made two barrels of each batch, which eventually became 300 bottles. The wines not only turned out to be totally different, but were each true to the taste of their own château. Finally I had cracked the mystery, my theories confirmed. Natural yeasts gave their own specific fingerprint to a wine.

I then invited the members of the Académie des Vins and the Union des Grands Crus, plus Professor Ribereau Gayon from the University of Bordeaux (who'd previously doubted me) to a tasting held at Rahoul in spring 1986 after the wines had settled down and were bottled. Needless to say, it caused quite a stir. And a few days later, I got a letter from the *académie* informing me that they had elected me a member. A great honour indeed.

Denis Dubourdieu came over to the château one evening and tasted the three wines. He was so impressed that he said: 'You'd have to be an idiot not to believe in this!' and went on to create a dedicated yeast laboratory at the University of Bordeaux. There, he proved scientifically what I had discovered organoleptically.

THE POWER OF CO_2

I will never tire of challenges, and the moment you get on top of a problem is a good one. One year I had moved all our barrels of young white wine into the orangerie at Rahoul. I felt that it was too cold in the cellar, and wanted the wines to go through a malolactic fermentation, for which I needed more heat. The orangerie was south-facing and nice and warm.

When the malo was over, I racked the wines carefully and sulphured them. So far so good. But when I tasted them, the entire production was full of hydrogen sulphide (H_2S), which gave the wine a taste of rotten eggs. All our famous whites!

How could I ever solve this problem? In the textbooks they will tell you of copper as the only way to cure this fault in a wine, but then you run the risk of a copper casse, where the wine suddenly will be full of brown specs floating around in the bottle. Not recommendable.

Then I thought that perhaps a spot of dry ice would do the trick. Dry ice is carbon dioxide in its solid form, and the bubbles it caused as it evaporated into the wine would 'lift' the fruit, and maybe mask some of the H_2S. I drove into Bordeaux and got some granulated dry ice, and rushed home to put it the wine. I threw a few of the small smoking sticks into each barrel, and had hardly finished before the whole room gave off a terrible stink of rotten eggs.

'This is the end,' I thought. 'Now you have ruined everything, you bloody fool!' I just stood there, sobbing at the very idea. But then I took a sample out of a barrel and tasted it. Crystal clear! Absolutely no trace of H_2S whatsoever. A miracle, nothing less. The other barrels were identically clean and the wine was superb.

When I had recovered from the shock, the first thing I did was to call Murray Tyrrell in Australia. He was the only person I could think of who would understand what had happened. Silence at the other end, when I told him. Then he grunted: 'Let me try it. I will call you back in an hour's time.'

And he did, jubilant. 'You have just saved 500 hectolitres of wine!' he shouted into the phone. 'What a trick! Thank you, mate.'

When I think about it, this was almost as important as the yeast discovery.

THE CHANGING FACE OF BORDEAUX

Being a member of the Académie des Vins was a delight for me. Members gathered every now and then for lunch and all brought their wines to taste. It was an occasion to meet and discuss, and great friendships took hold. There was absolutely no snobbery. The wines were enjoyed by all – and were a great inspiration for me, as a young vigneron.

Back then, Bordeaux wines were relatively affordable too. I remember a lunch at the Lucas Carton in Paris, when this famous restaurant was in the hands of Monsieur Alain Senderens. Hugh Johnson and a few other friends were there. I ordered a bottle of the legendary Yquem 1967 up from their cellars. It was a good moment to drink it, and if my memory does not fail me, it cost something like 70 francs (approximately £10)... Back then, the *crus classés* were not exactly overvalued. (Hugh remembers this lunch with a smile: the sommelier sampled too much and was carried out.)

I remember, too, that Château Branaire-Ducru came up for sale at some five million francs (£562,000). And in 1976, my old friend Raimond 'Papa' Dupin encouraged me to buy his château, Grand-Puy-Lacoste, for 12 million (£1.3 million), payable in several installments). I have always regretted that I was not able to do this – nor had I enough knowledge of financial affairs back then to take him up on his offer. But I am happy that it fell to a good friend, Xavier Borie, who still makes wonderful wines there.

Little by little Bordeaux began to change. New faces, new ideas, and most of all, new money rolled in. It became fashionable to own a château of some renown and many of the best were sold at outrageous prices to people who had little or nothing to do with the wine trade – but who, it seemed, were after the glory of having their own *grand cru*.

This had all started, as if out of nowhere, in 1977, when the Greek supermarket tycoon André Mentzelopoulos bought Château Margaux for 72 million francs. What money! Everyone raised their eyes to heaven. The courtiers of Bordeaux were convinced his ownership of this great Bordeaux château would be short-lived, but in fact – even though he at first knew very little about wine – he turned the whole property around and it once again began to make the really lovely wines of which it is uniquely capable. His daughter, Corinne, has steered it back to the pinnacle of quality. Gradually, more and more Bordeaux châteaux began to sell at higher prices.

For a while, the system of En Primeur sales was a lifesaver. It gave château owners a chance to realize some money from their wines before they were ready to bottle. They were wise enough to understand that the négociants and their customers, who would have to wait until they were in bottle, should also have a chance to sell and make some money. The system worked very well and all were happy, until an influx of high-powered journalists began to award points to these new wines, which sent prices soaring to dizzy heights.

Now there was a race on to please the palates of these journalists (who regarded themselves as demigods), and, naturally, some of the wines lost their way and began to look more like their brothers and sisters from the Côtes du Rhône, than their elegant former selves. Some, but not all…

But let us leave the point-pushing journalists and my summary of Bordeaux' woes alone, because in its return to elegance (which it is now most assuredly pursuing) Bordeaux faces a much bigger problem: climate change.

WHAT'S TO BE DONE ABOUT CLIMATE CHANGE?

Whatever is happening, the extreme summer heat we are experiencing, combined with huge storms and excessive rainfall, certainly points to a catastrophic new turn of events. Whether they are naturally occurring or induced by human error, they raise big questions for our agriculture, and of course our viticulture.

For a start, what can we do now to avoid high alcohols that have risen in our wines due to climate change?

For the growers and château owners, the immediate answer will of course be to go into their vineyards and select the vines that thrive during times of heat stress. But this has been made very difficult due to the recent flawed policy of using only single clones for new plantations – as if one virus-free vine strain would be enough to defeat all future problems.

It all began in the 1950s, when French vignerons worried that their massal selections (the process by which they took cuttings from their very best vines to propagate new vineyards) were getting out of hand. So they asked The Institut National de l'Origine et de la Qualité (INAO) to intervene and help them in keeping their varieties clean of mutations. This in itself was very commendable, and the INAO of the day did a great job. But soon the mantle was taken up by the professors at the University of California at Davis, who banned field selection and instead advocated heat treatment. It became all about indexing and re-indexing sick plants, treating them with heat and naively believing that the resulting 'new' material would suit all future plantings.

The few who stood up and complained were not heard, and the fad for laboratory clones spread like wildfire. Now everybody was planting the same material, which meant that from hectare to hectare there was no variation. The difficulty of having 10,000 plants all the same now presented itself. What would happen if that plant did not turn out to be resistant to the problem you were fighting – whether it be a virus, high winds, or high temperatures – after all?

Now, in the face of extreme heat, we run the risk of whole vineyards dying before our eyes, thanks to flawed intelligence, minimal clonal variation, and not enough people standing up and objecting.

Thinking viticulturists in Bordeaux who had the courage to stick to their gut feelings, like my old friend Jean-Michel Cazes at Château Lynch-Bages, who kept on selecting the best vines among the very old plants in his own vineyard, were to be proved right. It turns out that Jean-Michel's course of action is the only reasonable way forward – the only way we can hope to sustain the vineyards with stronger material.

But not everyone has had his foresight. General panic seems to have set in at the INAO, causing it to adopt new ideas that are both unrealistic and dangerous to the future of Bordeaux. These desperate measures include the planting of new grape varieties in an attempt to combat warm climates of the future. While not in itself a bad idea, the varieties chosen seem to be entirely inappropriate to the region.

Indeed, a new Portuguese tradition seems already to be taking hold. The INAO has recommended introducing plantings of the old Oporto variety, Touriga Nacional. The first plants have already been established in the vineyards of the former Toulouse-Lautrec property, Château Malromé, by its Chinese owners, the Huynh family.

And to further add to the chaos, they have also declared the Alvarinho variety suitable for future Bordeaux white wines. Alvarinho (or Alvariño in Spain) sells for about 2.50 euros a bottle, so why propose this grape in Bordeaux, where it is unlikely to add any quality?

Another possibility is the age-old Bordeaux variety Castets, which declined to near extinction only to be rediscovered in a corner of Pyrenean France. Loïc Pasquet, of Liber Pater in the Landiras region of Graves, claims it to be the 'original' Bordeaux grape, but who can judge if his wines cost 3,000–5,000 euros a bottle? Certainly not I. In principle, however, as a native of Bordeaux, this is a good idea. Perhaps it should be trialled.

Other proposed white grapes are an old brainchild of the Institut National de la Récherche Agronomique (INRA): Liliorila, a crossing of Baroque and Chardonnay, and Petit Manseng from the Jurançon. But what do these plants have to do with Bordeaux? They might be heat-tolerant, but why not research them more deeply?

To be fair, these suggested varieties are at this stage only to be used on an experimental basis – authorized at a maximum of 10 percent of a Bordeaux or Bordeaux Supérieur blend. But as temperatures become hotter, and they make stronger wines, they will almost certainly undermine the status of the vines that have given Bordeaux so much glory. Surely this would be a mistake?

Of Bordeaux's own varieties, we already know that Cabernet Sauvignon will grow happily in much warmer parts of the world (it is happy in the 40°C heat of Australia's Coonawarra and Yarra, and basks in Chile's Aconcagua Valley, for example), so why replace it in Bordeaux? Merlot, too, thrives in the hottest wine regions – and if anything, it improves with an early ripeness. So surely there will be no problem for this grape in a warmer Bordeaux? Petit Verdot, which formerly struggled to gain ripeness in its Left Bank home, looks as though it will now produce wines that are infinitely more lovely under warmer conditions. So I would see no problem here, either.

It should not be forgotten, also, that local Sauvignon Blanc and Sauvignon Gris have also proven themselves particularly well adapted to warm weather conditions. And think how Sémillon flourishes in Australia.

At this point, I return to my new country, the old Norman kingdom of Sicily and the Research Institute of Marsala, where many of the very oldest vines known on the Island have been researched, DNA-tested and replanted. All of them originally came from Greece, and before that they may have originated in Georgia, where stood the cradle of all viticulture. Their history in Sicily dates back around 3,000 years.

Here, to my amazement, we find not a single variety that will produce more than 10% – or at the most 12% – alcohol. They produce wines with the perfect pH, nice acidities and a flurry of intriguing flavours. The results of trial micro-vinifications have for the most part been stunning, and it is here – if not in Bordeaux's own vineyards – that I suggest we will find the answer to the future of warm weather vines.

Why, one wonders, doesn't the INAO correspond with its Mediterranean colleagues? It seems this institute has gone astray with the reclassification of Saint-Emilion and the premier classed growths too. (Don't get me started…!) What has gone wrong, I wonder?

As a result of all this I can only cry, Bordeaux is dead, *vive* Bordeaux!

CHAPTER NINE

A POTTED BORDEAUX HISTORY

Bordeaux has had its influencers over the years – not least Eleanor of Aquitaine in 1152, the Irish 'Wild Geese' traders and the crusaders of Queen Anne's English court – but few have had more far-reaching effects than Napoleon with his 1855 Classification of the Médoc.

Edmund Penning-Rowsell (1979)
British for 300 Years

Charles Ludington (2013)
The Paradoxical Rise of Claret

Giles MacDonogh (2020)
The Wild Geese

Cyril Ray (1974)
The Classification of 1855

Bordeaux' famous link with England began with the marriage of Eleanor of Aquitaine to Henry II in 1152 and continued for 300 years, but the trading of wine between the two only really started in the 13th century – and from then on, never looked back. Edmund Penning-Rowsell (one of Bordeaux' longest-serving commentators) charts Britain's route to becoming a nation of wine drinkers.

BRITISH FOR 300 YEARS

Edmund Penning-Rowsell (1979)

The beginnings of the Bordeaux wine trade with England can be firmly dated as not being substantial until the 13th century. In an edict of King John of 1199, the regions from which came the wines chiefly drunk in England were enumerated, and Gascony was not even mentioned; the leading supplies came from further north in the Poitou. It was in the 13th century that the Bordeaux vineyards really began to be extended, and then expanded rapidly in the 14th century – a period of great prosperity for medieval Bordeaux – and further still in the 15th century. All other forms of agriculture became of minor importance. In the 13th century the most prolific area was the Graves, pressing in on Bordeaux itself, where several of the parishes contained vineyards. There was even one in the garden of the archbishop, who was one of the largest vineyard owners, a prominence he shared with the dean and chapter of the cathedral of Saint-André. The former owned vineyards in Pessac and Mérignac; the latter possessed vineyard properties in the main Graves communes, including Pessac, Léognan and Villenave d'Ornon, as well as others in Listrac, Moulis, Avensan, Blanquefort and Le Taillan in the Médoc. But neither archbishop nor chapter seem to have spread their vine properties so far afield as those communes in the Médoc most famous today, such as Pauillac, Saint-Julien or Margaux.

The reason for this expansion of wine growing must have been based on the trade with England, and later to some extent with the Low Countries. There was no great market for Bordeaux wines in Paris or in other French centres of population. For one reason, overland transport was too arduous and for another, regions as far north as Normandy produced their own wine, while Paris relied on the wine from districts relatively easy of access, including Burgundy, whose produce came down the Seine, and Champagne, whence still wine was transported down the Marne. The Bordeaux trade was sea borne and its natural outlets were maritime, non-wine-producing countries, including England, Scotland, Ireland, the Low Countries and the Baltic States. Of these, England was the most accessible, with its convenient ports at Bristol and Southampton, the chief English landing places for wine imports from Bordeaux in the Middle Ages.

Wine was indeed the leading French export of this period, and Bordeaux was almost certainly the chief exporter. It remained so for many hundreds of years, for until internal transport improved in the 18th and 19th centuries, Bordeaux could not depend on a substantial domestic demand outside the region. For much the same reason the English had to rely on Bordeaux for their table wines until the struggles with France that began at the end of the 17th century and continued intermittently until the defeat of Napoleon. This may explain the comparative rarity of burgundy in England right up to the end of the 19th century; it was difficult and expensive to transport to England and a ready market could be found nearer at hand.

Throughout the English connection, the Bordelais, well aware on which side their bread was buttered, set out particularly to win the support of the English kings in the 13th century. They had three possible competitors: La Rochelle; the wine growers of the Haut-Pays, and, as the Bordeaux vineyards began to be developed, the more distant part of the Médoc, with its ease of access to the sea.

La Rochelle was a thriving rival wine port long before Bordeaux became important for wine, and had the advantage of being right on the sea, whereas to reach the Girondin port, ships had to make the difficult 60-mile (97km) passage up the estuary – a disadvantage with which the Bordelais have to reckon even today. Fortunately for Bordeaux, its rival was much more open to attack and capture by the French king. When in 1224 the latter's troops struck south and captured several Atlantic ports, the Bordelais were quick to write to Hubert de Burgh, the king's *justiciar*, or head of the royal administration, reaffirming their loyalty to the English Crown and contrasting this with the infidelity and frailty of those towns further north which had surrendered. Therefore, as the French gradually encroached over the years on to the English king's possessions, the commercial standing of Bordeaux was improved.

Although demand from the Low Countries and others beyond the English Channel could take up the greater part of Bordeaux's wine exports, these markets could only be reached with the approval of the English king and his fleet. Accordingly the Bordelais were enthusiastic for the English connection for 200 years after the rest of the English territories in France had largely been taken over by the French kings. From the fall of La Rochelle in 1224 can be dated the supremacy of Bordeaux as a wine trading centre and port.

Meanwhile, it appears as if the Bordelais decided that to have the English king on their side was not only a matter of politics and business, but it was also good for what now would be called publicity. We all know these days that for some curious reason if a well-known personality, be it king, queen, president or film star, is known to be partial to a particular wine or brand of drink, this is a valuable commendation for other consumers.

As the expertise of such personalities lies in other fields, this might seem a doubtful recommendation, but in view of the successful association of cognac with Napoleon and a Scotch whisky with a British commander-in-chief in World War I, there is no doubt this works even in the 20th century. Certainly it did with Bordeaux in the 13th century.

There was in England then a taste for the wines of Anjou and of the Rhine, but were it known that the king drank the red wines of Bordeaux, this should assure their success. So it did. Whereas in 1199, the Gascon wines were not even mentioned among the leading wines consumed in England, from 1206 onwards they appear among those bought for the royal table or offered as presents by the king. In 1214 John was thanking the governor of Bristol for apprising him of the arrival there of a consignment of Bordeaux wines; and in 1215 he had bought 120 *tonneaux* of Gascon wines for his personal use.

Such was the royal interest in Bordeaux wine that by 1219, Henry III was writing to the mayor of Bordeaux, complaining that a check had shown a shortfall in the amount of wine gauged in the *tonneaux*, and denouncing this fraud. By 1224 three-quarters of the wine drunk in the royal palaces came from Bordeaux, and by the middle of the century it was the customary wine to celebrate any solemn or festive occasion, as champagne is today. Sixty years later so much gold was being sent out of England to pay for the royal wines that Parliament protested (Simon, *History of the Wine Trade in England*, 1906–09).

The Bordelais did not confine their attentions to the king. They made suitable presents to the English notabilities and entertained the British merchants who made their annual trip to Bordeaux to buy the young wine. In the accounts of the archbishops of Bordeaux for 1382 and 1386, there are entries relating to the entertainment of 'the merchants of England and Britain'. The English wine fleet left the English shores late in September, arriving in the Gironde in the first half of October, when the young wine was just about made. They spent eight to 10 weeks in Bordeaux, tasting and bargaining, and then returned to England in time for Christmas. The voyage from Bordeaux to the English Channel ports took about 10 days. The royal butler had first choice of their purchases. The wine, of course, was drunk at once – *le vin de l'année*, as this would now be called. It had to be drunk young, as before the development of the wine bottle and the cork, no wine could be kept sound for any length of time.

First published in the fourth edition of *The Wines of Bordeaux* by Edmund Penning-Rowsell, Penguin Books Ltd (London) 1979, and reprinted here with kind permission of the author's son, also Edmund Penning-Rowsell.

Despite being at war with France, the wine of choice at Queen Anne's court (1702–14) was undoubtedly Bordeaux. Charles Ludington, specialist in the history of Britain's wine industry and Teaching Associate Professor at North Carolina State University, traces the emergence of the wine connoisseur via Charles Spencer, Robert Walpole, 'The New French Claret' and Britain's quest for 'Politeness'.

THE PARADOXICAL RISE OF CLARET

Charles Ludington (2013)

Clearly, queens and kings, Stuart and Hanoverian, saw nothing wrong with drinking French wines even if France was the avowed enemy. And just as clearly, luxury claret was their favourite French wine. Individual exceptions aside, luxury claret was the preferred wine of most English political leaders during the early 18th century, a preference that can be seen in John Gay's first published poem, 'Wine' (1708). The poem is set in the Devil Tavern in Temple Bar, London, where the narrator has gathered with his friends:

> The stair's ascent now gain'd, our guide unbars
> The door of spacious room, and creaking chairs
> (To ear offensive) round the table sets.
> We sit; when thus his florid speech begins:
> 'Name, Sirs! the wine that most invites your taste;
> Champaign, or Burgundy, or Florence pure,
> Or Hock antique, or Lisbon new or old,
> Bourdeaux, or neat French white, or Alicant.'
> For Bourdeaux we with voice unanimous
> Declare, (such sympathy's in boon compeers.)

So claret it was, and unanimously so. From here, the 'sanguine frothy juice' is brought in to the table and the toasts proceed from 'glorious Anna' and the 'Royal Dane' (Queen Anne and her husband, Prince George of Denmark), to the dukes of Marlborough, Devonshire, Godolphin, Sunderland, Halifax and 'all the worthies of the British realm'. It is no coincidence that everyone mentioned as a 'worthy' was pro-war, and either avowedly Whig or, like Marlborough and Godolphin, becoming increasingly Whig in his politics.

Literary critics argue over whether Gay was being ironic or genuine in his praise of Whigs, but in either case these critics have overlooked the meanings of claret. If Gay's praise was ironic, he was using claret to highlight the hypocrisy of preferring French wine in a time of war with France (and when French wines were officially being embargoed). If he was being genuine in his approbation, he was using the most fashionable wine to praise Whig worthies and thereby seek a patron for his poetic efforts. Whatever the case, Whig leaders seem to have outdone their Tory rivals in the consumption of luxury claret and other French wines. After all, with a few notable exceptions, Whigs were the most fashionable people in early 18th-century England, and luxury claret was undoubtedly the most fashionable wine.

John Hervey, First Earl of Bristol

As we have seen, John Hervey, Whig MP for Bury St Edmunds, purchased slightly more than one hogshead (over 252 quart bottles) of luxury claret per year during the War of the Spanish Succession. That trend continued long after the war ended and Hervey was made 1st Earl of Bristol by the new king. In fact, during the 40-year period from 1702 to 1742, Hervey made – or at least entered into his expense book – 125 purchases of wine, of which French wine accounted for at least 57 percent of the his expenditures. Haut-Brion, Pontac, Lafite, Latour and most of all Margaux, or what he sometimes modishly called 'Chateau Margaux'[1], accounted for half of his outlay on French wines, or 28 percent of his total wine expenditures[2]. As for his other French wine purchases, they were sometimes as expensive as luxury claret (champagne was even more expensive), but in no instance were they so popular[3].

[1] In John Hervey's expense book, Margaux is variously spelled Margoose, Margous, Margoo, and sometimes referred to as Chateau Margou, Margou-Claret and Chasteau Margoux. His use of 'Chateau' to denominate a Bordeaux winery is only used for Margaux, and was first written on September 29th 1716. This is the first use of which I am aware of the term 'château' to designate a winery.

[2] Hervey purchased his wine from a number of different merchants and often already in bottles. His bottle purchases were part of a trend that began in England with Charles II, but which for most of the 18th century affected only a tiny percentage of wines. Significantly, it was wealthy English consumers who were the first to bottle-age luxury claret.

[3] Among the estate-grown clarets purchased by Hervey after 1702 the prices varied between roughly £40 and £50 per hogshead, while generic clarets purchased by Hervey cost between £25 and £40 per hogshead. Given that English import tariffs on all wines stayed the same from 1705 until 1745, price fluctuations in this instance can be attributed to the varied results of each vintage and changing transport costs. [On average, burgundy and Hermitage cost the same as luxury claret; however, champagne was consistently the most expensive wine of all. This is no surprise, for champagne, along with burgundy, had high transport costs to England.]

Charles Spencer, 3rd Earl of Sunderland

Hervey's wine purchases represent one of the most complete early modern English records of individual taste over time, but other, less complete records indicate that his penchant for luxury claret was typical of his political and social milieu. For example, when Charles Spencer, 3rd Earl of Sunderland – son-in-law to the 1st Duke of Marlborough, First Lord of the Treasury and passionate Whig – died suddenly in 1722 in the wake of the South Sea Bubble collapse for which he was blamed, he left behind an impressively diverse and well-stocked wine cellar. French wines were his favourite, comprising 11 out of 28 entries (including bottled and casked wines). Among bottled wines, and therefore probably his finest wines, the most numerous was Lafite, with Latour following slightly behind. Interestingly, there was only one listing for Portuguese wine: a hogshead of white port.

Sir Robert Walpole

British monarchs and leading Whig aristocrats loved luxury claret, but perhaps no one was as devoted to it as the man who succeeded Sunderland as First Lord of the Treasury, Sir Robert Walpole (1676–1745, *pictured right*). Walpole was the son of a prosperous country gentleman, Colonel Robert Walpole, whose modest political and financial success had enabled his son to go to Eton and then Cambridge. At these institutions, young Robert saw that there was a larger, more powerful and elegant world outside of the family home in rural Norfolk, and it was this world upon which he set his sights.

In the end, he exceeded even his own lofty expectations, becoming the most powerful Whig leader of the 18th century, the first de facto prime minister of Great Britain, and a man of considerable fashion. According to Walpole's biographer, Sir John Plumb, 'in the brilliance of his taste and the grandeur of his opulence, he outshone the aristocratic world in which his talents had won for him and his family a distinguished and enduring place'. So, while Walpole's father the country squire drank mostly red port, such a wine would not do for the son who razed his family's modest ancestral home and built a palatial pile, the humbly named Houghton Hall. With political power and a palace of his own, the younger Walpole needed a wine to match his elevated station in life. That wine was luxury claret.

At the height of his power in 1733, Walpole spent over £1,150 on wine, a sum that amounted to more than the annual income of a prosperous country gentleman like his father. Of this amount, luxury claret accounted for 35 percent of the volume and 44 percent by value. Specifically, Walpole purchased seven hogsheads of Margaux, three of Lafite, one of Haut-Brion and 36 bottles of unnamed 'New French Claret'. Taken together, Walpole's purchases of claret in 1733 amounted to approximately 234 bottles per month, or nearly eight bottles per day, more in volume and far more in value than any other type of wine in his cellar[4]. To be sure, Walpole also bought large amounts of fashionable burgundy and champagne, which were slightly more expensive owing to their high transport costs. More noticeably, he purchased vast quantities of inexpensive white Lisbon and red port. These wines seem to have been his workaday wines, or the wines for his 'public tables', where he entertained dozens, sometimes hundreds of City merchants and professionals, and prosperous country squires, who formed the core of the Whig party.

However, when Walpole meant to impress the elite among whom he had placed himself, his wine of choice was luxury claret. In a letter to Frederick, Prince of Wales, written in July 1731, John, Baron Hervey (second son of the 1st Earl of Bristol), described one of Walpole's semi-annual 'Norfolk Congresses', which were gatherings of Walpole's cronies at Houghton, as being 'a little snug party of 30 odd, up to chin in beef, venison, geese, turkeys, etc; and generally over the chin in claret, strong beer and punch. We had Lords spiritual and temporal, besides commoners, parsons and freeholders innumerable.' The claret in question was Haut-Brion, and since Walpole's 'Norfolk Congresses' were meant to pay thanks, intimidate and impress with their material surroundings, so, too, was the wine he served there.

POLITENESS AND THE TASTE FOR LUXURY CLARET

But what, other than the apparent quality of the wine, made luxury claret such a compelling indicator of Walpole's status as one of the most powerful and fashionable men in England? Indeed, what does luxury claret's success on the English market in the early 18th century tell us about the society for which it was created? The answer, in short, is politeness. 'Politeness' as a model of behaviour was a major aspect of early 18th-century English urban culture, especially in London. From its origins in the courts of Renaissance Italy, politeness spread to the court of Louis XIV in France, and then to England, where it moved beyond the court and into the town. There, in its new urban setting, it was transformed into a broad concept used to describe and prescribe the conduct and manners of the social elite, and an aesthetic standard for numerous types of human behaviours and artifacts. Of course, politeness was always contested by allegedly impolite forms of behaviour, and rarely did the English elite as a whole achieve the lofty standards of politeness that were proposed; the calls for polite behaviour would not have been so strident and numerous were the model more consistently upheld. Nevertheless, politeness was the hegemonic ideal of elite male behaviour from roughly 1690 to 1760, precisely the period in which luxury claret arrived on the English market to stay.

[4] Each of these wines cost £45 per hogshead. The approximately 25 dozen (300) glass bottles that were eventually needed for each hogshead were included in the price of the wine, but added to the cost were charges for racking and bottling, corks for sealing the bottles, hampers for transporting them.

Not surprisingly, given the deep divisions within England in 1689, politeness was a contested ground between Tories and Whigs, and it was the latter who claimed the prize. Post-1689, or 'modern', Whigs embraced the newly combined aristocratic-mercantile elite and the commercial economy for which it stood. They explicitly rejected the backward-looking aristocratic culture of the Tories, and also the civic humanism of the Old Whigs, who were suspicious of trade and condemned luxury on the grounds that it softened and corrupted the ruling elite. The triumphant Whig vision of politeness was anti-court and anti-French, gentlemanly not aristocratic, discursive not codified, and urban not rural – although a neoclassical pile in manicured parkland was certainly polite. Broadly speaking, politeness was 'situated wherever gentlemanly (and ladylike) society existed (the club, the drawing room, the coffee house, among others)', and 'its characteristic activity was conversation, the substance of which was worldly, urbane things'.

Indeed, 'things' were very important for polite behaviour, and all of these things came at a price. Clothing, furniture, cutlery, chinaware, lacquered snuff boxes, silver candlesticks, lead crystal vessels of all sorts, paintings, music and literature, were all important to the performance of politeness. And men were just as involved as women in thinking about and purchasing items that helped to fashion their identities. So politeness was judged by one's behaviour, but also by whether one owned the right items, whether they were sufficiently genteel in design, and whether one was capable of appreciating their beauty, and using them in the 'correct' way. After all, the successful display of politeness was proof of one's good taste, and taste was a sign of virtue. This virtue was what gave the post-1689 elite the right to rule and simultaneously denied that right to those who had money but poor taste, or more often, those who did not have the means to purchase the objects that would signal whatever taste they had. This idea of taste was not entirely new in the 1690s, but it acquired prominence in England in the late 17th century, and quickly became a justification for political power.

Indeed, according to the leading historian of politeness, this behavioural ideal reached maturity in England between 1700 and 1715. It is no coincidence that this was precisely the period in which luxury claret became firmly established as a symbol of allegedly superior taste of those who consumed it. Certainly other wines had the potential to be polite; wine was a key motif in classical civilization, which was itself a model for polite culture. Furthermore, because wine in England was imported, consuming wine, like going on the Grand Tour, was an inherently cosmopolitan act and therefore a sign of one's politeness. Lastly, all wines could be part of polite display – chilled in a large silver wine cooler, served from a crystal decanter, poured into crystal glasses and consumed while sitting around a mahogany table. But inasmuch as luxury claret was the preferred wine among England's most polite people, it was the most polite of all wines.

The politeness of luxury claret may also be measured by its importance in promoting conversation, and while this is difficult to measure, it is telling that wine features

Benjamin Ferrers' c1720 painting *Sir Thomas Sebright, Sir John Bland and Two Friends* shows gentlemen in 'polite' company, almost certainly discussing claret.

prominently in a number of so-called Conversation Pieces, a genre of painting that was immensely popular in early and mid-18th-century England. Conversation Pieces typically depicted gentlemen or ladies, and sometimes both together, engaged in decorous conversation inside their well-appointed homes, or in manicured parks outside their homes. These paintings emphasized the social nature of polite society, and provide visual evidence of specific polite behaviours, such as appreciating wine. For instance, a painting by Benjamin Ferrers painted c1720 depicts *Sir Thomas Sebright, Sir John Bland and Two Friends* sitting around a cloth-covered table smoking pipes and drinking. The men are clearly relaxed – three of them have removed their wigs – and a servant arrives through a door with a ceramic pitcher, probably wine directly from the cask, to join the pitcher already on the table. The central figure, Bland, holds a crystal decanter full of wine in his right hand, while pointing to the wine with his left hand, as if about to comment upon it…

Thinking [and talking about] wine is precisely what William Hogarth depicts in his painting of *Mr Woodbridge and Captain Holland*, which was also completed around 1730. This conversation piece shows two men, a successful lawyer and a naval officer respectively, sitting around an ornately carved wooden table in the middle of what must be Woodbridge's office. In the background are a marble-mantled fireplace, shelves lined with law books and a panelled wall upon which hangs a landscape painting. A servant or clerk walks through the door with a note in his hand. On the table are a book, a scroll and a bottle of wine in a wicker covering. Both men wear perukes, jackets, silk stockings and buckled shoes. They are not aristocrats, but they are both wealthy. Holland holds an empty glass in his right hand and casually points to Woodbridge with his left. Woodbridge, meanwhile, holds a walking stick in his left hand, while his right hand is raised, eye-height, and in it he holds a full glass. He is looking intently at the glass and its contents. By painting the gesture of contemplation, Hogarth's painting is the most successful of all in capturing the connection between politeness and wine appreciation.

Of course, we can never know if the wine depicted in any of these paintings was luxury claret, but that is beside the point. What matters is what the sitters wanted to convey, and what the viewers believed. The point of each painting was to use wine to convey the sitters' politeness, and the types of men in these conversation pieces were precisely the type who formed the market for luxury claret – aristocrats, wealthy gentry and successful professionals. These men not only had the money for polite performance, they also enough money to record that performance on canvas, which in turn helped to reinforce and publicize their polite taste. Wine was a prop in their polite performance, and because luxury claret was the most popular wine among polite men, a knowing 18th-century viewer might guess that luxury claret was the wine in the glass. More certainly, the men in the paintings were all engaged in thinking about or discussing their wines. What could be more polite than thinking and talking about an imported product that was both expensive and distinct, that differed subtly from year to year and from vineyard to vineyard, and that changed over time (and often for the better) while simply resting in one's cellar? And what polite person would not want to talk about that?

THE EMERGENCE OF THE WINE CONNOISSEUR

In fact, it is possible to trace the increasing sophistication in the language used to talk about luxury claret during the early 18th century, as well as a desire to think about and discuss the particularities of wine in general in the early 18th century. As we have seen, the advertisements for claret in *The London Gazette* began by using only price to distinguish between the different qualities of generically named claret. But soon the most expensive claret became 'New French Claret', and this was quickly followed by specific estate names such as Haut-Brion, Margaux, Lafite and Latour. By 1711, even these names began to be elaborated upon, so that the top wines were now referred to as coming from 'the best growths', and being 'deep, bright, fresh, neat' in taste and colour. These descriptions of wine pale in comparison to the purple prose of 21st-century wine writing; however, they mark the beginning of a trend towards more florid description. The price of claret was no longer sufficient to distinguish luxury claret from the traditional sort; the new consumer, a self-fashioned connoisseur, wanted more information, more to talk about. And increasingly those selling the wine were providing it.

Excerpt from *The Politics of Wine in Britain, A New Cultural History* by Charles Ludington, Palgrave Macmillan (UK/USA) 2013, and reprinted here with kind permission of the author. (Please note, the author's footnotes have been significantly abbreviated for this volume, with his permission.)

Lynch, Boyd, Kirwan and MacCarthy were the names of soldiers-turned merchants, 'Wild Geese', who fled persecution in Ireland to seek their fortune in Bordeaux – their names still resonate in the quality wines made at their châteaux: Lynch-Bages, Lynch-Moussas, Boyd-Cantenac, Kirwan and MacCarthy-Moula. Historian Giles MacDonogh explains how Jean-Baptiste Lynch and his allies became major players in the region.

THE WILD GEESE

Giles MacDonogh (2020)

Europe returned to peace in 1713 after a quarter of a century of strife[1]. For the Catholic Irish who had pinned their hopes on King James II and the Old Pretender[2], the game was up. A German George ascended the throne of Great Britain, and Ireland was handed over to a Protestant Ascendancy. The wary had already seen disaster coming. Following the Treaty of Limerick in 1691, about 19,000 Irish soldiers and their families – the 'Wild Geese' – were allowed to flee to France, where they continued to fight for the Catholic cause. Later, some of these turned their swords into ploughshares, or rather trading counters, and went into business, forming the core of a mercantile community that lasted until the Revolution or in some cases later.

In Jerez in Spain, and on the west coast of France, Irish-Catholic businessmen settled and began to trade in food, wine and spirits. Bordeaux and Nantes despatched provisions to the French West Indies, which lacked all basic necessities. Bordeaux's hinterland was largely planted with vines, which meant that the vital foodstuffs needed to be sourced elsewhere and delivered to the port. Ireland had the answer to the problem with its superabundance of cheese, butter, pickled salmon and salt beef, as well as hides and tallow. Ships were loaded with Irish provisions and brought to Bordeaux to be forwarded to French planters in the Indies – or simply to feed the Bordelais themselves, who had grown used to bringing in their food from elsewhere. The vessels then returned to Ireland laden with Bordeaux wine. The traders didn't even need to visit the old country, as the business in the Irish ports could be performed by members of the extended families they had left behind.

1 The Nine Years War (1689–97) and The War of Spanish Succession (1701–14): peace was restored by the Treaty of Utrecht of 1713–15.

2 The 'Old Pretender' was James Francis Edward Stuart, son of James II by Mary of Modena. His attempts to secure the English, Irish and Scottish thrones all met with failure.

In peacetime at least, business boomed in Bordeaux. There was land to be purchased and quick returns on trade for people wanting to share in the lading of a vessel. For the richer merchants there was the added incentive of acquiring nobility, which not only increased their status, but absolved them of paying most taxes.

HOME AWAY FROM HOME

Protestant traders from the British Isles had already discovered the potential of the port some time after the restoration of the English monarchy. The oldest dynasty in the city was that of the Boyds, who arrived in 1670 – Protestants who bequeathed their name to Château Boyd-Cantenac in Margaux, a property they owned until shortly before the French Revolution. Other Protestant families that were part of the same clan were the Dicksons, Skinners, Woodwards and Blacks. The Boyds had been caught red-handed smuggling wool into France – prohibited by the English, but not the French – so found themselves in Bordeaux in disgrace. The Boyds were linked to the Bartons too, who were also accused of illegally trading in wool. The Bartons were Irish Ascendancy Protestants and remain the owners Château de Langoa and producers of the classed growth wines of châteaux Léoville-Barton and Langoa-Barton to this day.

Among the Catholics, the most successful was probably the Lynch family: Catholic soldiers from Galway, where they enjoyed a quasi-hereditary control of the town hall until they were dispossessed by Cromwell. The first of the Bordeaux Lynches was John, an officer in King James's army who chose to leave Ireland because of his 'attachment to that prince and to preserve the free exercise of his religion'. He maintained some contacts with shippers in Galway, set up shop as a tallow merchant and was naturalized French in 1710. Lynch was allied to another Galway sept, the Kirwans, and quite possibly to the Clarkes (former owners of Château Clarke in Listrac) as well. Mark Kirwan was naturalized in the same year as Lynch, but it was to be another 30 before France became his exclusive home. Possibly Kirwan was originally in charge of assuring shipments from Ireland.

It is unlikely that any of the Irish merchants dealt exclusively in wine before the mid-18th century. Bordeaux re-exported the products of the French colonies, chiefly sugar, coffee and spices, undercutting the produce of the British islands. Some families were also involved in the slave trade, like the Coppingers of Cork and Martells of Jersey. Other products that made their way from France to Ireland were brocaded silks, dried fruits, Gascon brandy, chestnuts and pepper. Some of these products were also being taken to French India. Wine certainly made up a good deal of the cargo charged for Ireland. A French traveller noted the availability of 'Bordeaux claret' in every little inn, when such things were hard to obtain in England. The massive drunkenness the trade occasioned elicited particularly pious comments from the Lord Lieutenant, Lord Chesterfield, who in 1746 wrote: '5,000 tuns of wine [4,500,000 litres] imported *communibus annis* into Ireland is a sure but indecent proof of the excessive drinking of the gentry there.' The following year he expressed his disgust once again: 'Drinking is the most beastly vice in any country, but it is a really ruinous one in Ireland – nine gentlemen in 10 in Ireland are impoverished by the great quantity of claret which, from mistaken notions of hospitality and dignity, they think it necessary should be drunk in their houses.'

THE BENEFITES OF THE 'LANDED'

To be truly upwardly mobile in 18th-century Bordeaux you needed to own land. We don't know what he had to offer exactly, but in 1743, John Lynch's son Thomas-Michel managed to win the hand of a very rich heiress: Elisabeth Pétronille Drouillard. Perhaps Irish tallow was highly prized in the West Indies? Her father, the shipowner and banker Pierre Drouillard, had bought the former Carmelite property at Château Dauzac in Labarde, south of Margaux, and created a wine estate – now significantly smaller than it was in Pétronille's day. She appears to have been her father's sole heir when he died in 1740 and by 1750 she was wealthy enough to add to the family holdings by purchasing the Bages lands in Pauillac for 84,000 *livres*. The Lynches possessed land in Cantenac too. The Lynch name still remains at châteaux Lynch-Bages and Lynch-Moussas in Pauillac as well as at Pontac-Lynch, the estate contiguous to Château Margaux to the south.

Thomas-Michel now lived the life of a lord, and as the local squire he applied to the archbishop of Bordeaux to use the vacant de Giscours pew in Labarde parish church. He gave the other immigrant clans a wide berth, preferring to 'integrate his family with the good families of local origin'. The Lynches didn't like the imputation that they were foreign; Thomas-Michel's son, Jean-Baptiste, was to declare in an impassioned speech 'They tell you that I am Irish, that I am ready to leave; that a ship is at hand to take me back to the bosom of my family! How absurd. My family has resided in France for three generations, my father was born among you and I have never left France. I have no more relatives in Ireland; I have no friends there; all my relatives are in France, all my friends are in Bordeaux.'

When Pétronille died, Thomas-Michel made a second good match to Rosalie de Nort, which brought him the Ile du Nord in the Gironde estuary. This would also have been planted with vines before phylloxera eliminated many uneconomic estates. Possibly more important still was the fact that his second marriage provided Lynch with the connection whereby his sons could enter the local court, or *parlement*, as counsellors, a position only eligible for members of the *noblesse de robe* or *robins*[3] such as the de Norts. Thomas-Michel also acquired the manor at Formingley in the Entre-Deux-Mers across the River Garonne from Bordeaux. He bequeathed the land to his sons, the future mayor of Bordeaux, Jean-Baptiste, who was born in Bordeaux on June 3rd 1749, and his younger

[3] Nobles of the robe, *noblesse de robe* or *robins*, were the hereditary nobles who acquired their rank through holding a high state office.

Bordeaux mayor Jean-Baptiste Lynch, and his legacy, the Pauillac fifth growth Ch Lynch-Bages.

brother, Thomas-Michel. Jean-Baptiste became a peer of France while Thomas-Michel represented the city as a deputy during the *Directoire* and became mayor of Pauillac. Within two generations the Lynches had climbed the social ladder to enter the French nobility, amassing rents from their properties in Bordeaux's new town while they divided their time between their counting houses in the city and their vineyards in the Médoc.

ALTERNATIVE ROUTES TO THE TOP

Many of the Irishmen who landed in Bordeaux in 1691 were perceived as coming from gentry families back home, and as a result, found it relatively easy to acquire letters patent of nobility. Being a noble was highly advantageous, as it exempted the bearer from most taxes as well as export duties. There were two ways in which an Irishman might assume nobility: either by suing for recognition of letters patent, or by purchasing an office under the Crown that entailed nobility of the first or second degree. In the first instance the Athlone Herald could assist: James Terry (1669–1725) had been appointed by the Stuart King James II in 1689 when he set up his court in exile at Saint-Germain-en-Laye near Paris. Terry spent a quarter of a century compiling pedigrees for the expatriate Irish families. At Terry's death, the papers passed to the d'Hoziers, the hereditary armorialists of the French court. Achieving recognition of nobility was a long, drawn-out and expensive process but it was generally worthwhile because of the money you saved and the dowries you could expect for your sons. A lengthy petition needed to be sent to Versailles with an attestation provided by the relevant heraldic authorities that the petitioner had enjoyed armigerous status for three generations. These petitions could take years to be answered and one assumes that bribes were in order as well.

The four most important Irish-Catholic families in Bordeaux were the Lynches, the Mitchells, the Dillons and the MacCarthys. The Lynches had their letters patent as first degree nobles recognized by the Cour des Aides in Bordeaux in 1755 after presenting a family tree proving 15 generations of armigers and a quasi-hereditary tenure of the town hall in Galway City. The mayors of important French towns were generally accorded nobility of the first degree – that is to say they could pass on their status to their children. In terms of aspiration and success, the achievements of the Lynch family beg comparison to the MacCarthys, who have also left their name attached to a château – the rather less distinguished Château MacCarthy-Moula in Saint-Estèphe. It should be remembered, however, that it used to include the entire neighbouring Marbuzet estate. Dennis MacCarthy's father arrived at the same time as John Lynch. MacCarthy might have been the richest of the Irish merchants in the port. Having no heirs he imported two nephews – Daniel and Jean – from Ireland, sending them to the Collège de Vendôme where Balzac was later an unhappy pupil. MacCarthy was keen to acquire nobility and bought the *seigneuries*, or manors, of Marlière, Beaujé and Fondival. This was, however, insufficient and MacCarthy had to prove his descent from both the MacCarthy Reagh, or king, and his kinship to James II's earl of Clancarty before his letters patent could be granted.

The Mitchells were from Dublin, industrialists doubly related by marriage to the Lynches: Thomas-Michel's daughter Peggy Elise married François-Patrice Mitchell in Dublin in 1774. Pierre Mitchell created the Verrerie Royale in 1723. Glassblowing had been considered a respectable activity for nobles since the 15th century, so they were not liable to 'derogation' under the strict laws regarding what they might or might not do. Patrice Mitchell petitioned for recognition in 1738, adding that he possessed a fortune 'well sufficient to keep me in a state of nobility'. He had developed the Château du Tertre in Arsac, close to Labarde, and the bottles he produced became important for luxury wines. By 1789 he was paying one of the highest 'capitations' (income taxes) in the port. His sisters married into the *parlementaire* nobility, including members of the family of the fabulously rich mayor François-Armand de Saige, who was decapitated during the Terror.

The Dillons were bankers. Robert Dillon of Terrefort set up Bordeaux's first established bank having previously worked in Dublin and Rotterdam. He had a large estate at Blanquefort to the north of the city and was distantly related to the aristocratic Irish Dillons of Paris, who produced the last pre-Revolutionary archbishop of Narbonne as well as the memorialist Madame de la Tour du Pin Gouvernet. Robert Dillon's great-uncle had been James II's duke of Tyrconnell, so proof of nobility would not have been difficult to produce. Dillon's Dublin business had been closed down by a measure aimed directly at clearing Catholics out of the banking sector and Robert Dillon had moved to Bordeaux to lick his wounds. His naturalization came at the fairly steep price of 1,080 *livres*.

The alternative to acquiring letters patent of nobility was to purchase an office under the Crown. One method was to find an 'office' in municipal government. Bordeaux was administered by a mayor and nine *jurats* who served in the *jurade* for nine years, a third of their number being renewed every three. The job came with nobility, and a ship-owner like O'Quin could therefore pass it on to his son on his retirement. François-Patrice Mitchell was a *jurat*, but already noble. The courts – the *parlement* and the *cour des aides* – offered only 'gradual' nobility, requiring two to three generations before it stuck. Many of the new men who bought offices at the courts were 'unfinished' when the nobility was abolished during the French Revolution.

A more secure bet was the office of *secrétaire du roi*. There were 20 on offer in Bordeaux. The job was a sinecure but carried not only plenty of privileges but also transferable nobility. For that reason it was not only highly sought after but extremely expensive. To qualify as a noble you simply had to hold the office for 20 years. Not for nothing was it the costliest office under the Crown, but the good news was that it could be resold for a profit. Royal secretaries were exempt from most taxes and onerous civil duties and if you were a merchant you were also excused toll charges (the notorious *octroi*) and export duties. There was a joke in the Ancien Régime that had Adam had any sense he would have obtained an office as *secréraire du roi* then all men would have become noble. This *savonette à villain* (a bar of soap that washed away the 'common' man) attracted many members of Bordeaux's foreign colony, from Christopher Smith to Lynches' cousin, Mark Kirwan. George Boyd may have bought one too, as he called himself 'de' Boyd, although he does not appear on the list of local nobles.

The commercial value of nobility was such that if you could afford it, it made no sense to forgo it. When that other Lynch kinsman Jacques Clarke was arraigned before the revolutionary tribunal during the Terror he found an ingenious way of denying his nobility: 'I am not noble,' he proclaimed. 'I have always paid duty on shipment.'

JOINING THE RIGHT CLUB

Jean-Baptiste Lynch may have professed an undivided loyalty to Bordeaux and France, but the city could boast a bit of British style. One thing admired all over Europe was freemasonry. In Bordeaux freemasonry seems to have kicked off when a trio of British sailors founded a lodge there in 1732. The Catholic Church took a dim view and most of the members were Protestant at the Loge de l'Amitié, founded after the Seven Years War. In 1775, the Loge Française was created, haunted by members of the *robe* like the President Le Berthon and his son-in-law, Jean-Baptiste Lynch. It is likely that marriages were also arranged at its meetings.

If freemasonry was divided on religious lines, Le Musée was not. Founded in 1783, it was based on a progressive Parisian organization that had enjoyed the patronage of Marie-Antoinette and organized lectures on improving subjects. There was a library where foreign journals could be read. The commercial oligarchy of the city was enthusiastic, not just Protestants like Hugh Barton and William Johnston, but also Catholics like

Jean-Martin Clarke, numerous MacCarthys and Patrice Mitchell. Barthélémy MacCarthy was responsible for proposing the schoolmaster Jean-Baptiste Lacombe, who was to become notorious as the president of the military tribunal that organized the Terror in Bordeaux from 1793. His candidacy was rejected.

When the Seven Years War broke out in 1756, the regional governor Louis-Urbain-Aubert, Marquis de Tourny, was faced with a large foreign community in Bordeaux and had the business of choosing who to expel as enemy aliens. His attitude was that the few English people in the port were natural suspects, unless proven otherwise, while the Irish were generally allies (unless he knew something that made that unlikely). The Scots fell somewhere between the two. Behind his usually benevolent attitude was the knowledge that the shippers were responsible for a lot of trade, and trade brought prosperity to Bordeaux. Besides, without the merchants from the British Isles, there would be no one to buy those expensive wines that were produced on the estates of the *robins*; nor would Bordeaux or the French colonies be a better place deprived of the staples they brought in from Ireland. There is no question they were spoiled; Tourny's biographer L'Heritier throws some light on their exasperating practices: 'Shippers demanded to be able to import and export at will, buy and sell when they wished, defraud their taxes and bend the rules yet while seeking the protection of the king in ridding themselves of troublesome rivalries or in winning back their fortunes in the wake of ruin. It was a hotchpotch of rights, wishes and abuses which they threw willy-nilly behind the screen of liberty.'

The Irish were still huge consumers, but of the second quality of Bordeaux wines, as the first growths went increasingly to London. In the 1770s, the Irish imported 50,000 tuns (45 million litres) of wine, of which about half came from Bordeaux – twice the English and Scottish totals put together. Even in 1788, two years after the signature of the Eden-Vergennes Commercial Treaty that should have liberated the wine trade, the English imported a paltry 505 tuns (454,500 litres) between July and December, while the Irish took 1,600 tuns (1.4 million) of which 1,000 tuns were consumed in Dublin alone. It could be, however, that the Irish were re-exporting a percentage of the wine to England, or smuggling it across the Irish Sea.

HEADY TIMES

The Lynches do not appear to have been so greatly involved in trade by the time of the Revolution. Their names are not among the groups of merchants who took up options or subscriptions on the first growths. The most probable explanation is that they had been won over to the life of *robins*, looking after their estates and making their money in the courts. The Revolution initially allowed landowners the chance to increase their landholdings when all Church land was put on the market in 1790. The new *département* of the Gironde had a total of 567 Church properties to dispose of, of which 142 were snapped up by chiefly French wholesale merchants. The Swede Luetkens bought the abbey of the

Governors of Bordeaux during the Seven Years War (1756–63) knew that ceasing trade with the British Isles, despite being at war with them, would be a mistake. Merchant ships continued to sail. *Bordeaux Harbour* by Joseph Vernet (1759).

reformed Cistercians or Feuillants in Saint-Estèphe for 485,000 *livres* and the abbey in Vertheuil further north was bought initially by one Coiffard, who sold it on to Robert Skinner in 1797, whose name it still bears today.

The other big property sale accounted for the estates of the *émigrés*: chiefly noblemen and women who had fled France when the Revolution turned against the royal family. This new attack on the elite was a bit close for comfort, particularly for those who had opted to become nobles in the course of the century. All sorts of shenanigans were used to ensure that the property stayed in the family. The Boyds had gone bankrupt at the end of the Ancien Régime, and their land in Cantenac was bought by the Danish-born shipowner John Lewis Brown. The Kirwans retained their property nearby, although the present 'château' was constructed during the *Directoire*. It was no mean feat to hang on to it, seeing as 11 Kirwan boys had fled to England, possibly to fight in the army. There is a rumour that Mark de Kirwan was executed, but this is wrong: he was still alive during the *Directoire* when the family got into trouble again for publishing monarchist newspapers.

Jean-Baptiste Lynch who had become a councillor of the *parlement* in 1770 and was received at court by Louis XVI in 1781, had risen to become one of the *parlement*'s presidents and was therefore in the firing line once the Revolution shifted to the left and went for the nobles. He appeared on the list of *émigrés*, although we have his own testimony that he did not leave France. He is supposed to have accompanied his father-in-law to Versailles when the latter was elected deputy for the nobility in 1789 and been imprisoned during the Terror. His land at Ludon in the Central Médoc was put up for sale as well as his town palace in the Chartrons. But for some reason his estates in Margaux (Château Dauzac) and Pauillac were not included in the sale. It is likely they had been transferred to someone else's – probably his wife's – name.

The Revolution became steadily more extreme, and the defence of being a vital cog in the machinery that brought in provisions and prevented famine no longer pulled as much weight. With the suppression of the Girondin party in Paris (many of whom were merchants advocating a limited revolution), the noble traders of Bordeaux lost their last protective covering. There had been a half-hearted uprising against Robespierre's Jacobins, so now *négociantisme* or 'wholesale trade' became a crime in itself. When the People's Representatives arrived in Bordeaux with the Terror, it was the moment to take cover. A *comité de surveillance* was created, modelled on the Committee of Public Safety in Paris, and a military tribunal was set up under the presidency of Jean-Baptiste Lacombe, the same schoolmaster who had been rejected by the Musée. The court was composed of seven judges, known as the 'Seven Deadly Sins'.

Bordeaux and the department of the Gironde had sinned. The department's name was changed to 'Bec d'Ambès' and the guillotine trundled out onto the place Dauphine to receive its first victims, among them the former mayor, Saige, and the Marquis de Lur-Saluces, whose family had recently acquired Château d'Yquem. The only member of the Irish colony to lose his life was Father Martin Glynn, rector of the Irish seminary in the rue du Hâ, although his underling, Dr Everard, was only saved from lynching by his ragged soutane. Another who came close was Theodore Martell of the brandy-shipping dynasty originally from the Channel Islands. It was possibly the case that the Terror was shut down by events in Paris just a bit too soon to get round to dealing with them. Robespierre's representative Marc-Antoine Jullien had certainly sized them up: 'Merchants and lawyers only supported the Revolution at the beginning in the secret hope of exchanging the domination of the nobility by that of their own class, envying their titles and privileges. It is against this new aristocracy we should be fighting, it is thus the first duty of the Terror.' Hard reality also put paid to social theory: these were the men who provisioned not only the port, but also an entire region that produced only one notable crop: grapes to be turned into wine; and a wine often too expensive for local customers.

As the Revolution turned into the Empire, Bordeaux stagnated. There were no fortunes to be made in a time of British blockade, and war with Britain and its powerful navy continued almost unabated. It was a period of idleness for the merchants when young men were sucked into the army, and there was little in the way of manpower to work on the land. The American writer Washington Irving arrived in Bordeaux in 1804, at the end of the short-lived Peace of Amiens. He was able to see at first hand what had happened:

'The merchants appear to be the chief sufferers, as I see their vessels laid up in the river totally dismantled of their rigging. And they universally complain of want of business.'

TALES OF BRANDY AND SUBTERFUGE

The only flourishing trade was with America. France had lost its islands, and with them access to coffee, cane sugar, cocoa and spices. Cut off from Ireland, Bordeaux no longer benefitted from preserved meat, fish and dairy products. Permission to ship wines to the British Isles was on one day and off the next, and a lot of wine was distilled to make brandy because it was more likely to keep that way. As Madame de la Tour du Pin writes in her memoirs, on the family estate at Bouilh on the Dordogne River: 'The war with England reduced the price of wine to nothing, above all the whites, which have never been worth much in our part of the country. They sold for around four or five francs a hogshead. My husband installed a brandy still and spent a good deal of money getting it to work properly.'

Brandy made up a good proportion of the alcoholic liquor that managed to thwart the blockade. It could be taken to the Channel Islands (hence the interest shown in brandy by Channel Island natives like Martell). After that no one bothered too much about how it made its way to the other side of the Channel. Wine might be shipped to Spanish or Portuguese ports to be forwarded in neutral ships or vessels that could simply allow themselves to be captured as 'prizes' (but the cargo was naturally paid for). The emperor had to be aware, however, that punishing Britain meant punishing his own people too, and up until 1807 this sort of commerce was tolerated. This was, however, brought to an end by an order in council that year, which was the last nail in the coffin of Bordeaux's formerly flourishing port. As the American consul reported '...from the Baltic to the Archipelago [the Azores] one sees only despair and poverty... grass is growing in the streets of this great town, its splendid port is deserted.'

THE RISE OF LYNCH AND FALL OF BONAPARTE

If Jean-Baptiste Lynch had indeed been in prison in Paris until the Ninth Thermidor brought the Terror to an end, he was now free to return to public life. He remained a 'personality' in Bordeaux and in 1809 he was elected president of the *conseil général* of the Gironde and mayor. The final selection was made by Napoleon, who was presented with a list of three candidates. Lynch appeared to be Napoleon's man. In 1810 Lynch went up to Paris to celebrate the marriage of Napoleon to Marie-Louise of Austria and receive the title of 'count'. Lynch used the opportunity to lavish praise on his master: 'Italy and Germany twice brought to heel, Great Britain banished to the middle of the seas; they follow the flight of your eagles from the banks of the Baltic to the Mediterranean.'

Expressions of devotion, together with round-ups of young men for his master's armies, sustained him in office in 1813 and earned Lynch the Grand Cross of the Légion d'Honneur the following year; but if his published correspondence is anything to go by, he was already a convinced 'Legitimist' committed to restoring the Bourbon monarchy and plotting 'in petto' to bring Napoleon down when he travelled to Paris to collect his medal. Lynch had gushed about Napoleon until the Russian campaign, when he apparently changed his mind and branded him a 'mad despot'. But the emperor continued to festoon him with honours right up to the moment Lynch betrayed him.

In his letters, Lynch made out that his loyalty had never been called into question, but there does seem to have been a strong streak of opportunism in his character. Writing during the Hundred Days, Lynch claimed that he had only held office in order to have the chance to unseat the usurper and to find an occupation that would take his mind off the death of his only daughter. There were other mitigating factors: he hoped the 'foreigner' (Napoleon) would recall the Bourbons and that by accepting to become mayor he would be in a position to bring this about.

According to his apologia, Lynch's faith in Napoleon had been shaken by two things: the killing of the last member of the royal house of Condé, the duc d'Enghein in 1804, and the deposing of the king of Spain in favour of his brother, Joseph Bonaparte in 1810. The toppling of the Spanish king led to Lynch's decision to oppose his emperor. He skirts lightly over the years of victory to dwell on the disasters of Moscow, Leipzig, Dresden and the approach of the enemies of France; and then there is trade: '...the utter ruin of the treasury, the annihilation of trade, the wrecking of private fortunes, the crushing weight of taxes. The horrifying rapidity of depopulation by conscription and extraordinary levies, and everything pointing to a general catastrophe...' The letter highlights a Bordelais sense of trading privilege. The local revolutionary leaders had had the sense to spare the city for the sake of subsistence. Napoleon had failed to succour the commercial oligarchy and those who depended on foreign trade.

Lynch was summoned up to Paris to receive his cross. In his letters he makes great play of his unhappiness on leaving Bordeaux and the efforts of his faithful secretary de Mandenard to dissuade him: 'Don't you believe the time is right to rescue our country and to seek the return of our legitimate sovereign? Must we wait to act, so that France falls apart and every one of our regions falls prey to a foreign power or general who will fight over them for a century? Must we wait for this lovely country to return to government by the family to which it rightfully belongs?'

It was not until he reached Paris that Lynch began to change his mind. Napoleon asked him for a greater contribution from the region and after meeting some Legitimist members of the Polignac family his thoughts turned to revolt. He received his Grand Cross on January 8th 1814, feeling '...one of the greatest sufferings he had ever experienced'. As he travelled back to Bordeaux he observed a particularly bright star from an inn in Maintenon. The plot got underway once he reached the city. Among his fellow conspirators was the Marquis de Lur-Saluces, the son of the owner of Yquem, the Swedish merchant Luetkens (owner of the vast Abbaye des Feuillants) and Colonel Bontemps Dubarry, proprietor of Château Saint-Pierre in Saint-Julien – all four important wine producers and three out of four from the Médoc. Indeed, Lynch had envisaged the Médoc as the best place to stage a British landing and it was de Lur-Saluces who hung a white Bourbon flag from the town hall on the day the British Field Marshal Beresford entered the city. The plan was to bring a small force directly into the Médoc while Bordeaux would be liberated by just a thousand troops. That way the population would not react to the idea that the Bourbons had been restored by France's enemies and the British army would only need to appear if proper muscle were required.

'Carried away by the glory [Bordeaux] would acquire and the prosperity that would follow,' Lynch and his caucus of growers despatched messengers to the advancing armies which had by now taken Toulouse. A family member of Henri de La Rochejacquelein, the illustrious chouan[4] who had fought valiantly against the Revolution in the Vendée, was considered an apt emissary for Louis XVI's nephew, the Duc d'Angoûleme, who had been fighting with Wellington in Spain, while Bontemps-Dubarry was sent to talk to the Iron Duke himself. Wellington awarded the job of securing Bordeaux to Beresford, his second-in-command and commander of the Portuguese army. When Beresford's men rounded on the city on March 12th, Napoleon's soldiers began to dismantle the military installations. Meanwhile, Lynches' men rode out to meet the nephew of the new king, Louis XVIII, who he was later to call 'the image of divinity on earth'.

There was still no indication that the city was going to give in without a fight. The mayor was even accompanied by his Bonapartist assistant, who nearly died of apoplexy when Lynch gave his outriders the signal to don white cockades and welcome the prince: 'Despite my efforts to stem the eruption of an all too justified sentimentality,' wrote Lynch that same year, 'I was only able to utter a few words to his Royal Highness, of which the last were to perish on the hand which he so affectionately offered me and which I bathed with my tears. That this adorable prince should deign to lean towards me; that I held in my arms the representative of those I had for so long borne in my heart.'

Back in the city the signal was given to hoist the white flag from the spire of Saint-Michel and a Te Deum was sung in the cathedral to welcome the prince. According to report, the Duc d'Angoûleme was received with great enthusiasm in the beleaguered city, with '...mothers, whose children were not yet dead, blessing the return of the prince...' In the duke's cavalcade were the Médocain Duluc from Château Branaire and the Comte Marcellus, a man of letters whose family owned Château Loudenne. When the news of

[4] The 'Chouan' brothers were counter-revolutionaries who instigated uprisings against the French Republic from 1794 to 1800 in western France, and subsequently any fighter rising up against the Revolution became dignified as a chouan. Henri de La Rochejacquelein, a young general renowned for his bravery during the Vendéan insurrections of 1793, who was killed in 1794 aged 22, was one of the most famous. ('Chouan' was a nickname, thought to derive from '*chat-huant*' or screaming cat.)

Bordeaux' treachery reached Napoleon in Paris, he ordered an army of 6,000 men to advance on Bordeaux and retake the city, however, on April 11th, he agreed to abdicate and a new Te Deum was sung in the cathedral.

THE FINAL ACT

A new mood of optimism gripped the city in much the same way as it had in 1713 and 1763. By a curious twist of fate the vintage turned out to be one of the largest in recent memory, evoking visions of British fleets carrying off the wine in quantities unseen since the Middle Ages. The honeymoon was brief. On March 9th 1815, Napoleon returned from exile in Elba, landing at Golfe Juan. One of his first recorded utterances was: 'I will forgive all of them, except Lynch and Lainé (the prefect of the Gironde).' The mayor, who by now had added another Grand Cross to his collection of Légion d'Honneurs – this time awarded by Louis XVIII – thought it prudent to leave. As luck would have it, he had been entertaining the Duchesse d'Angoûleme on the first anniversary of the liberation of Bordeaux, a meeting that enabled him to facilitate his one and only trip abroad.

Given a little time to prepare their departure by Napoleon's envoy Clausel, Lynch and the royal princess made their way to Pauillac, where they boarded a ship for England. Once in London, the royalist mayor was treated as a celebrity and travelled up to Scotland, even planning a trip to Ireland. The crowning glory of his stay was his presentation at court where the Prince Regent told the grandson of a Wild Goose: 'Count, you have shown great proof of your loyalty, you have rendered your name illustrious.'

Lynch was still touring the British Isles when the news of the Battle of Waterloo reached him. He returned to Bordeaux, where his title of count was confirmed by letters patent and he was named Peer of France and Honorary Mayor of Bordeaux for the rest of his life. His speeches before the House of Peers betray a weakness for a British-style constitutional monarchy, but then again, Louis XVIII also claimed to admire Westminster. After the July Revolution of 1830, he retired to Château Dauzac, where he died five years later. He was 86. His brother died in 1840 and the male line of the Bordeaux Lynches expired with him. The Pauillac and Labarde estates were sold off in three lots: Bages, Moussas and Dauzac, thereby ending a century of Lynch involvement in Bordeaux wine.

The Revolution and the Napoleonic Wars had ended the cosy existence of many of the Irish-Catholic families in Bordeaux and the Jacobite cause that had brought the Lynches to France had gasped its last. By the middle of the 19th century such families as remained had been assimilated into the local nobility or *haute bourgeoisie* and the Irish Catholic colony that had been such a feature in Bordeaux was no more than a memory.

Admired, respected, frequently questioned but never superseded, the commercial importance of the Médoc's only ranking system has never been in doubt – its authority still reverberates down the years. Cyril Ray tells the story of its creation, and explains how one château refused to accept the justice of its decision.

THE CLASSIFICATION OF 1855

Cyril Ray (1974)

On Christmas Eve 1853, Napoleon III set up an Imperial Commission, under the chairmanship of his cousin and heir-apparent, Prince Napoleon, to plan and put on an Exposition Universelle de Paris in 18 months' time.

Napoleon III's reign as emperor was merely a year old; his marriage to the lovely Eugénie already contracted, but not to be embarked upon until the following month.

The Exposition of 1855 was to be, in Philip Guedalla's words, 'a shade more modish, a thought less improving', than the Great Exhibition of 1851 which Napoleon had visited in Hyde Park with his then hosts, Queen Victoria and her Prince Consort. Victoria and Albert were to pay a return visit in the summer of 1855 – to the court and to a universal exhibition.

'Modish' though the Exposition Universelle was meant to be, and although good claret and Sauternes have always been *à la mode*, nevertheless its display of the red and white wines of the Gironde must have been one of its least important attractions.

Yet the selection that was made is still of enormous commercial importance, the manner of its making still a matter of controversy, when so much else about the Exposition Universelle de Paris of 1855 has ceased to matter, or has been forgotten.

There are hundreds and thousands of Englishmen and Americans, Germans and Japanese, who can trot out the names of Lafite and Latour, Mouton and Margaux, who have never known, and could not care less, that Napoleon III, Emperor of the French, had a cousin (and, until the birth of his son, an heir), whose name was also Napoleon.

Yet it was Prince Napoleon himself, as president of the Imperial Commission, who set the ball of controversy rolling down the years to our own time, when the reverberations are still in our ears.

First, the commissioners invited the Bordeaux Chamber of Commerce to set up a *complète et satisfaisante* representation of the wines of the *département* of the Gironde, and to display them according to the *communes* they came from, except for those which were to be displayed by name, according to merit.

(It is worth noting, at this point, that the representation was to be of the *département* of the Gironde – the whole Bordeaux region, that is, which includes Saint-Emilion and Pomerol; Fronsac, Bourg and Blaye; the Graves and the Sauternais, along with other, lesser, districts, as well as the Médoc.)

The first reaction of the Bordeaux Chamber of Commerce was that they wanted no part in picking out the best wines of the region. They proposed that they should put the wines of the region on show without any indication of owners or relative status, arguing that one exhibition could not, in any case, alter an order of merit that was already (as will be shown in the course of this chapter) established and well-known but might more likely disturb a classification based on long experience.

Prince Napoleon insisted not only that the names of growths and proprietors should be indicated, but that an up-to-date table of merit should be drawn up, and the Chamber of Commerce got rid of the awkward problem by calling upon the *courtiers* – the Bordeaux brokers who, as middlemen between growers and merchants or shippers, were then, as they are now, the men who know most about the relative prestige and prices of Bordeaux wines.

It was the obvious thing to do and, indeed, in those days, a sort of officially obvious thing to do, for there was a Chamber of Brokers, attached to the Bourse de Bordeaux, that was a more formally constituted body than the Brokers' Syndicate of our own time, for its members were nominated by a governmental decree.

On April 18th 1855 (with the Exposition Universelle due to open on May 1st, though eventually the opening was postponed for a fortnight) the joint committee set up by the Chamber of Commerce and the Chamber of Brokers presented to Prince Napoleon their classification of the red and white wines of the *département* of the Gironde, 'the elements of which' – of the classification, that is – 'have been drawn from the best sources'.

All the wines of the Gironde were called but, with the exception of Château Haut-Brion, a red Graves, none but the red wines of the Médoc and the white wines of the Sauternes region was chosen.

Apart from Haut-Brion, the red wines of the Graves, which throughout the Middle Ages and up to the second or third decade of the 18th century had been far more highly regarded, both in France and in England, than those of the Médoc, had by now fallen far behind in the care with which they were made and, therefore, in the esteem in which they were held and the prices they could command.

This is the point: the prices. When the committee talked of drawing 'from the best sources', what it meant was the records of the relative prices for the leading Bordeaux wines – records that had been carefully tabulated for more than a century past.

As Edmund Penning-Rowsell has put it: 'Too often the 1855 classification has by inference been presented either as the beginning of things, rather like the Creation; or, to use another Biblical simile, like the Tablets of the Law, handed down by the brokers of Bordeaux to the Médocain proprietors...with Haut-Brion's owner smuggled in on the old-boy network. As will have been seen already, the 1855 Classification was no more produced suddenly out of thin air than Man was created in Seven Days. It was little more than a codification of previous practice and classification.'

The same scholarly writer quotes Professor Pijassou[1] as dating the beginning of classification by price on the Bordeaux market from between 1725 and 1735: it was a convenience for the trade, because grouping the vineyards into classes (originally there were four, by 1855 there were five) made it easy to establish a price structure for the 50 or 60 best wines of the region – which by now were almost exclusively from the Médoc.

As early as 1730, a report (quoted in André Simon's *Bottlescrew Days*) refers to first-class growths, of which there were three, Haut-Brion, Lafite and Château Margaux – I have modernized names and spellings – selling at 1,200 to 1,500 *livres* a tun; second-class growths at 300 to 500; and third-class growths at 100 to 200.

Already it is a matter of a number of classes, each separated from the others by differences in price.

In 1785, François-de-Paule Latapie, Inspector of Manufactures, in a report to the royal Council of Commerce on conditions in the Generalité of Bordeaux, singled out one red Graves, Château Haut-Brion, as being, 'sold at the same price as those of the other *grands crus* of the Bordelais, Lafite, Latour and Château Margaux'.

A couple of years later, Thomas Jefferson, United States Commissioner and Minister in France, reported that there were four leading red Bordeaux wines (and he already used in English the literal translation of *crus*, 'growths') – Margaux, Latour, Haut-Brion and Lafite – grouping them by vintage and by price; five second growths at from half to two-thirds the price; and seven third growths, among them Mouton, cheaper still.

That was almost on the eve of Revolution and of the birth of the new Republic which, when it put up for auction the Domaine de Lafite, the previous owner of which had lost his head on the guillotine three years earlier, was able to describe it as, '*premier cru du Médoc*'.

In 1824 two writers, Wilhelm Franck and Alexander Henderson, both give Lafite, Château Margaux, Latour and Haut-Brion as 'first growths', placed thus by price. Franck made Château Brane-Mouton (as it then was: the owner of Château Mouton was Baron Brane or Branne – the name is variously spelled) the top of the 'second growths', as it is in a list of 1827 in the possession of Ronald Barton of Léoville and Langoa, but Henderson makes it sixth of the second growths, after Rauzan, Durfort, Lascombes, Léoville and Larose.[2]

1 R Pijassou, *Bordeaux au XVIIIe Siècle* (1968).

2 Rauzan has become Rausan-Ségla and Rauzan-Gassies (note the difference in spelling); Durfort is now Durfort-Vivens, and Larose is Gruaud-Larose; Léoville is split into Léoville-Barton, Léoville-Lascases and Léoville-Poyferré.

Henderson gave the prices fetched by the first and second growths in 1815 as 3,100 francs and 2,300 francs a tun, respectively, and in 1818 3,300 and 2,500 francs.

A list published by N T Thierry, the Bordeaux shipper, gave the prices for 1821 as 3,200 francs a tun for the same first growths and 2,300 francs a tun for five second growths, of which Mouton came fourth after Rauzan, Léoville and Larose.

And, only nine years before the classification of 1855, Cocks refers to his 'denomination of growths' as 'being established by custom, according to an estimate determined by trade... price having appeared to me the best test of the quality supposed to exist in each wine'.

He then went on to list the first growths as being Lafite, Château Margaux, Latour and Haut-Brion, in that order, which is the one in which they were to appear nine years later, and it is significant that he heads the list of his second growths with Mouton, again foreshadowing the controversial classification of 1855.

For, sure enough, though only after months of hesitation and wrangling, when the committee set up by the Chamber of Commerce and the Chamber of Brokers produced their list, the first growths were Lafite, Château Margaux, Latour and Haut-Brion, in that order, and at the head of the second growths was Mouton.

Mouton had done well to reach this position.

True, it had belonged at one time to Baron Hector de Brane (or Branne) a great innovator and improver, styled 'The Napoleon of the Vines', and said to have been responsible, with his neighbour d'Armailhacq, for the introduction into the Médoc of its most important vine, the Cabernet Sauvignon.

But Brane sold Mouton in 1830 in order to concentrate on what is Château Brane-Cantenac, which he had bought (as Château Gorce) in 1820, and had come to believe was the better growth.

A Monsieur Thuret bought it for 1,200,000 francs, and so let it run down (to be fair to him, this was the period when the Médoc was ravaged by oidium) that he sold it to Baron Nathaniel in 1853 for 1,125,000.

To reach, as we shall see later, the same price-level as Lafite and Latour by December 1854, and top place of the second growths by the following spring, was clearly more than Baron Hector de Brane could have expected: his Brane-Cantenac, for which he had sacrificed Mouton, lay nine places lower.

There are now, and there must have been in 1855, some 400 named growths in the Haut-Médoc alone, not including what was then known as the Bas-Médoc (now Médoc Maritime) where there are now almost as many, or any of the other great regions that lie around Bordeaux. In the *département* of the Gironde as a whole, which was the region the classification committee had been bidden to concern itself with, there may well be, and may well have been then, a couple of thousand named wines. [In 2020 there are around 6,000.] What the classification of 1855 did was to select from these a mere 62 peers of the realm, as it were – and I use the analogy deliberately, for there are five ranks of the

'I was commissioned by the Syndicat des Grands Crus Classés to do a complete version of the 61 châteaux of the 1855 Classification and had a wonderful time visiting each chateau.' Carl Laubin's 1987 collage of the Médoc's classed growths arranges the buildings in five tiers, top to bottom, according to each property's place in the rankings.

crus classés, precisely as there are of the British peerage: Lafite, Château Margaux, Latour and Haut-Brion are dukes; Mouton the senior marquess; and if Palmer, for example, is an earl, then Beychevelle is a viscount, Cantemerle a baron.

After these come nowadays the *crus exceptionnels* (an unofficial but widely recognized category), then the formally accepted *crus bourgeois* and *crus artisans*, as we might refer to baronets, knights and esquires – to say nothing of many a nature's gentleman and rough diamond that we have all met in our time in this or that French restaurant or knowledgeable British wine merchant's list.

Let us not, though, pursue the analogy too far: the important thing is that any claret listed in the 1855 Classification is a nobleman – one of a mere 62 picked from a

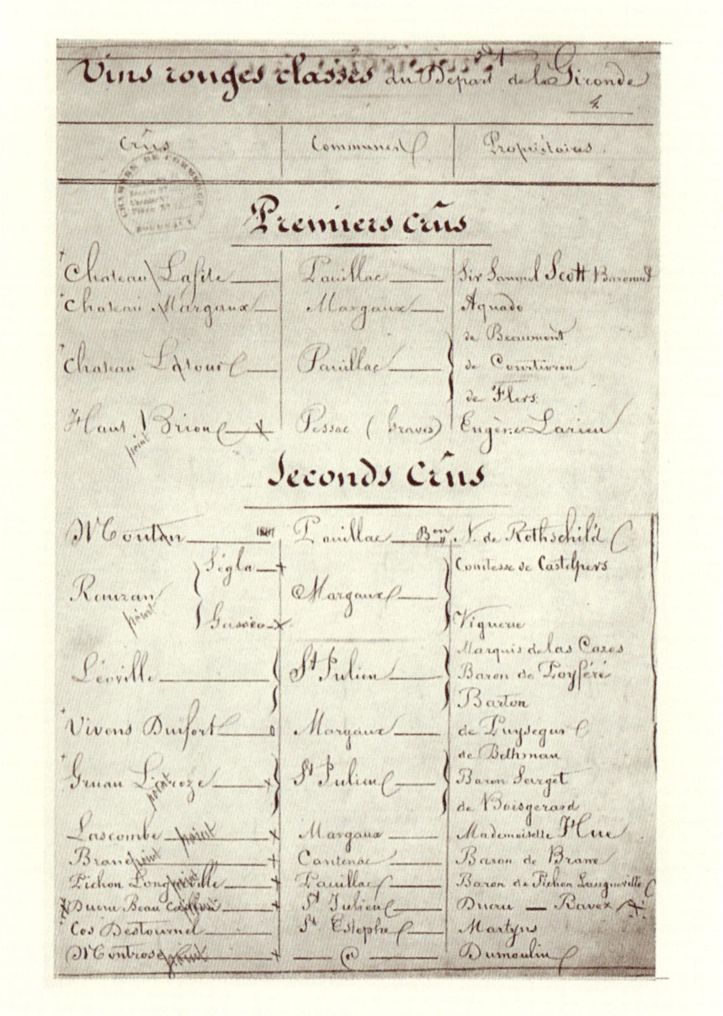

Vins rouges classés du Département de la Gironde

Crus	Communes	Propriétaires
Premiers Crus		
Château Lafite	Pauillac	Sir Samuel Scott Baronnet
Château Margaux	Margaux	Aguado
Château Latour	Pauillac	de Beaumont de Courtivron de Flers
Haut Brion	Pessac (Graves)	Eugène Larrieu
Seconds Crus		
Mouton	Pauillac	Bon N. de Rothschild
Rauzan Ségla Gassies	Margaux	Comtesse de Castelpers Viguerie
Léoville	St Julien	Marquis de las Cases Baron de Poyféré Barton
Vivens Durfort	Margaux	de Puységur
Gruau Larose	St Julien	de Bethmann Baron Sarget de Boisgérard
Lascombe	Margaux	Mademoiselle Hue
Brane	Cantenac	Baron de Brane
Pichon Longueville	Pauillac	Baron de Pichon Longueville
Ducru Beaucaillou	St Julien	Ducru — Ravez
Cos Destournel	St Estèphe	Martyns
Montrose	—	Dumoulin

The courtiers who eventually finalized Napoleon III's 1855 Classification knew to expect controversy: 'You know as well as we do, Sirs, that this classification is a delicate task and bound to raise questions.' This is the original classification document, showing Mouton Rothschild at the head of the second growths.

couple of thousand or so to appear in the Debrett or *Almanach de Gotha* of clarets. This is much more to the point than to think of a fifth growth as being in some sense *fifth-rate* as compared to a first. And just as it is the custom in Britain to refer to any peer other than a duke as 'Lord', simply, whether he is the latest of a long line of marquesses or a newly created life baron, so each of the classified clarets other than a first growth refers to itself on its label not as a second or a third, a fourth or a fifth, but as a *grand cru classé du Médoc* – a lord.

Although, as we have seen, classifications of clarets, based on price, had been in existence for a century before 1855, this was the first to have been commissioned by a governmentally appointed body, and officially drawn up; it was realized at the time that it was the most important ever made, and that its effects must necessarily be commercially far reaching. The committee went to great pains, therefore, to give it as permanent a validity as they could, and took into account not only the prices prevailing at the time, but those of many years past, and also the soil and the subsoil of each vineyard.

How sound their judgement was in general was confirmed by Ronald Barton in an article[3] written in 1963, after 40 years' experience of owning and administering Léoville-Barton, a second growth, and Langoa-Barton, a third: 'Basically, the classification remains sound, for it is based on the soil and the subsoil, and this has not changed. Given equal conditions a second can still, and will normally, produce a better wine than a third, a third than a fourth, and so on...

'The perfect proof of this is to be found in the vineyards of Léoville-Barton and Langoa. The two vineyards are run as one property and equal care is bestowed on both. And yet it can be said that always, whether the wine be good, bad or indifferent, the Léoville turns out to be the superior of the two.'

All the same, changes do happen. Again to quote Mr Barton: 'Some wines [after the classification of 1855] lost their popularity through lack of attention to the vines and to vinification, while others increased in popularity through improved methods of cultivation.'

And this latter is precisely what happened at Mouton – just too late, though, to affect the classification of 1855.

It has been argued that Mouton failed to be classed as a first growth in 1855 only because there was not then a proper château, as such, on the property – only a group of farm buildings. But I have seen all sorts of explanations put forward. Baron Philippe has a dry sense of humour, and sometimes pulls the legs of his interlocutors: at a press conference at Château Mouton after its elevation to the company of the first growths in 1973, an English voice asked why it had not happened in 1855. Baron Philippe smiled

[3] 'How the Clarets were Classified': *The Compleat Imbiber*, No 6.

and said that his great-grandfather, who had bought the property only in 1853, lived in London: 'Do you think a French jury at that time would have given a *premier cru* to a British neophyte?'

But France was madly anglophile at the time: queen and emperor were exchanging princely gifts and cousinly visits, and their troops were shoulder to shoulder outside Sebastopol. Great-grandfather Nathaniel was of the English branch, certainly, but after a crippling fall in the hunting field he had settled in Paris in 1851, and married his cousin Charlotte, daughter of the French Baron James, who was to buy Château Lafite in 1868.

All that could be said against Baron Nathaniel was that he was a newcomer among the wine growers of the Médoc. But so were many other owners of classed growths, among them the Pereires at Palmer. This period, from 1830 to 1880, was the great expansionist age in the Médoc – as is evident from the architectural style of many of its most important châteaux. No, it was nothing to do with the existence or not of a château, or the nationality of an owner[4].

As Mr Penning-Rowsell has pointed out, the classification of the wines of the region, from its earliest days, was based on price: 'It was not the reputation of estate or owner, the size or style of the château which counted but the hard commercial facts as they existed on the Bordeaux market.'

4 In 1973, after a long campaign by Baron Philippe de Rothschild, Château Mouton Rothschild was at last awarded first growth status. Cyril Ray continues further in his book: 'To have passionately desired, and campaigned for, agitated for, and intrigued for a reclassification – ah yes, that is very much another matter, for now and again, *after* his great-grandfather bought the property, in 1853, Mouton fetched as much as one or other of the 1855 first growths, sometimes as much as any of them...Now, with the decree of June 1973, Mouton has taken the rightful place that Baron Philippe has earned for it, and it may be that the sense of injustice will burn less fiercely in his breast...For the past half-century, at least, more has been said and written about Mouton than about all the other first growths put together, and all because of the question: should it not be reclassified as a first growth? Nine-hundred and ninety-nine times out of a thousand, the answer has been yes...But I wonder whether, now that it is a first growth, it will ever again enjoy quite the same, sort of publicity that it won by being a second...

Excerpt first published as chapter IV of *Mouton Rothschild, the Wine, the Family, the Museum* by Cyril Ray, Christie's Wine Publications (London) 1974, reprinted here by kind permission of Cyril's son, Jonathan Ray.

CHAPTER TEN

DINING OUT ON BORDEAUX

How best to serve it, with what and who with? Creating the right setting for claret – at lunch, dinner or even breakfast – is of fundamental importance to our enjoyment of this finest of wines.

Michael Schuster (2014)
All Pleasures Fancies Be

Fiona Beckett (2020)
Bordeaux for Lunch

George Saintsbury (1920)
Baron Elie de Rothschild (1968)
and Christian Seely (2020)
The Climate for Claret

Hugh Johnson (2020)
The Bordeaux Club

Michael Schuster shares the lessons and the thrills from a very special Bordeaux first growth tasting and dinner, which showed that despite the inevitable pleasurable tension, it is not always the case that the food or the wine has to take priority – occasionally, if rarely, the best of both go supremely well together.

ALL PLEASURES FANCIES BE

Michael Schuster (2014)

Younger Bordeaux first growths (mostly Parker 100-pointers) to taste; mature bottles of the same at table with six dishes from Michel Roux Jr; Gerard Basset MS MW OBE as master of ceremonies throughout – funds permitting, who wouldn't be tempted? And among the 18 tasters were people who had flown in from Sweden, Finland, Monaco, Turkey…specially for this Antique Wine Company (AWC) extravaganza in London on November 28th 2013.

We tasted the five younger wines at AWC's purpose-built wine academy, followed by dinner at Roux at The Landau close by. AWC's managing director, Stephen Williams, sees this sort of event as a 'catalyst, bringing people together in an entertaining way for both sensual and intellectual pleasure', and he also made the point, of which we do need reminding in today's tasting and score-oriented wine market, that: 'We so often taste and judge in a sterile environment; we also need to drink and enjoy these wines with food, too.'

AWC Wine Academy, opened in 2011, is an exceptional teaching/wine tasting room, with air-conditioning, unobtrusive sound amplification and an excellent PowerPoint facility. Here, after a glass of Krug Grande Cuvée and canapés, Gerard Basset led us through the tasting of the five Left Bank first growths. There was plenty of useful background information, on Bordeaux and on each wine, and given the wines in question, it wasn't long before price was under discussion. Gerard suggested that Robert Parker had 'made' the recent price of fine wine, and noted that two consequences of the substantial price increases had been the emergence of wine as a significant investment vehicle, followed by a concomitant rise in the making of, and market for, fakes.

Discussing style and quality he mentioned an interesting common thread between the four Médoc properties (Latour, Lafite, Margaux and Mouton) – that of father Jacques and son Eric Boissenot as consultants, who look primarily for freshness, elegance and overall harmony, rather than super-ripeness, power and concentration. Another common

The late Gerard Basset MS MW OBE (*left*) as master of ceremonies and, in Roux at The Landau's private dining room, chefs Michel Roux Jr (*far right*) and Chris King.

thread, he noted, was that, on asking the individual château directors what he should emphasize in his introductory remarks, all of them replied that the most important aspect of their success was their terroir. About which he could talk all night…except that we still had to taste and to drink, and to dine!

The relatively new (November 2010) Roux at The Landau had us in a private room round a long table. And after the tasting of five relatively young top clarets, from 2010 back to 1996, we enjoyed drinking more mature bottles from 1996 back to 1986. Introducing the meal and his approach to cooking, Michel Roux said: 'I am looking for enough flavour, but not too much.' In so saying he could have been the culinary arm of the Boissenot consultancy! And the six dishes were each a triumph of the culinary art, a delight to the eye (something he is particularly keen on), and beautifully managed in terms of portion size (modest, we were after all having six courses), subtlety and balance of flavours and textures.

I have described the wine and food pairing in my notes below. One's reactions to these are, of course, a very personal matter, and I felt that three of the combinations were particularly successful and rewarding. But these were with wines that were splendid even on their own, without food, so it was essentially a question of not marring that splendour. And I wonder whether the two trickiest marriages, with the 1986s, were really because a 1986 Pauillac first growth would be a difficult partner in almost any marriage? It was not a year in which it was easy to ripen fully the small, thick-skinned grapes, and I'm not sure they will ever mellow sufficiently to give unalloyed pleasure. Which perhaps begs the question as to what we are to understand by 100-point wines, these being the particular focus of the evening. In the case of the 1986 Lafite and Mouton, 'drinking pleasure' would no longer seem to be the primary point – which it surely should be? Am I just being impatient? I think not. It is, I suppose, an imponderable. And in any case for a different article.

This was a wonderful tasting, and a magnificently paced, organized and orchestrated dinner. Even for the wealthiest among us it is a privilege to drink such fine wines, and an even rarer occasion to enjoy them with such beautifully and specifically conceived dishes. My notes on the wines and the food give you my own view. Gerard's conclusion was that 'both wines and dishes were truly exquisite, some absolutely sensational. Of course we all have our own preferences, and that is what makes it exciting'. Which it most certainly was.

TASTING

2010 Château Haut-Brion

A dense, ripe nose still with a marked youthful oak character; rich, concentrated, finely but very firmly tannic and with the vintage's fresh acidity; a noticeably powerful wine, firm and muscular and with plenty of sinew alongside the abundance of ripe fruit; mouth-coating, long to taste and with fine minerally length, but also a clear alcohol warmth on the aftertaste from its 15% ABV. Ample, abundant and very complete to taste, if still with a Mediterranean rather than an Atlantic accent! Despite its size, however, it has the polish characteristic of Haut-Brion, and one cannot but be impressed by its overall presence. It will need at least a decade more. Drink 2025–50+. (18.5 points)

2009 Château Mouton Rothschild

Still noticeably oak-vanillary, but with a gentle minerality behind the wood and fruit; beautifully balanced, finely tannic wine, the year's acidity clear but in no way intrusive; a splendid Cabernet blackcurrant-cassis fruit core framed by a great finesse of texture; long, graceful and elegant across the palate, wonderfully tenacious in flavour, followed by a superb aftertaste. Harmony, class, persistence, a wine of great beauty and finesse, and a remarkable expression of Cabernet Sauvignon. A 10-year wait at least. Drink 2025–45. (19+ points)

2003 Château Latour

A narrow mahogany-mature rim; a warm, ripe, sweet, faintly gamey bouquet, warm, welcoming and very seductive already; just delicious in balance, a rich, fleshy, very supple wine with an ample but gorgeously textured tannin; abundantly juicy but with a marked minerality behind the ripe fruit, long, complex, mouth-coating, and with great length of aftertaste. A most complete and splendidly balanced wine for the year, with nothing to suggest an excessively hot vintage, just a hint of warmth, but already a wonderfully gratifying glass, remarkably flattering to taste for a 10-year old Latour. Drink now to 2030+ (19 points)

2000 Château Margaux

Dark red, narrow brick-rimmed; an early bouquet that is warm, minerally and with a hint of cassis; medium-full wine with a lovely balance of fruit to tannin and acid; concentrated in the way of the best Margaux, remaining delicate, that is, long and cassissy to taste – like the nose – with the year's crispness and its firm tannin texture, too. So there is still a touch of austerity here, especially after the particularly seductive nature of the first three wines, but this is long, close-grained, complex and very persistent. If the firm tannins soften this should blossom into a lovely wine in a decade or so. Drink 2023–40+. (18+ points)

1996 Château Lafite Rothschild

Youthfully dark, narrow bricking rim; just a touch of Cabernet herbaceousness in the nicest way, and really only by comparison with the previous wines. Beautifully balanced with fine, firm tannins, freshness and considerable fruit concentration; a vital, complete, racy and fragrant wine, with a lovely sweetness of fruit, if also a hint of austerity from the slightly cooler year, but tannins of great class and polish, and a great tenacity and complexity; intense and delicate at once, effortlessly long to taste and also to finish. A great Lafite in the classical style, exciting but still youthful. Needs at least 10 years more before it really flourishes. Drink 2024–50+. (19.5 points)

DINNER

1989 Château Haut-Brion

Dark, mature mahogany; initially warm and truffle-scented to smell, with forest-floor, undergrowth maturity and the characteristic Haut-Brion 'brick-dust' aroma also very clear – a bouquet of great presence and complexity; on the palate this had wonderful overall richness, sweetness of fruit, velvety suppleness and great length of flavour and aftertaste. A warm, gently spicy, most gratifying claret, almost burgundian in texture and sweetness. Real glossiness still to come, since there is still a very fine tannin, but this was an absolutely gorgeous glass of wine in glorious early maturity, and for the majority of guests the wine of the evening. Drink now to 2040+. (19.5 points)

Petit tartare de chevreuil, with juniper, celeriac and apple The wine perfectly combined with a lightly spicy venison tartare, whose particular succulence was rendered wonderfully fresh and gently crunchy by the juniper berries, celeriac and apple. Beautifully conceived.

1990 Château Margaux

Mature mahogany red; a seductive, warm-year, 'caramel-and-fruitcake,' Merlot-dominated bouquet; a gently rich, sweet-cored, just-about-silken Margaux, beautifully proportioned, long, graceful and flowing, still very delicately dry in texture (you notice the Cabernet Sauvignon next to the 1989 Haut-Brion) and with superb length; a ripe, warm, subtly mineral, enveloping joy to drink, the very image of Margaux delicacy and finesse. Great wine, fully mature but with decades in hand. This was my wine of the night, though one of the initially poured bottles was less than perfect. Drink now to 2040+. (20 points)

Boudin noire de lièvre façon Campagnarde, with braised savoy, Alsace bacon, and chestnuts The hare black pudding was so delicate in both flavour and texture that it married perfectly with the Margaux; it was most distinctive to taste but not too strong, with a delicious sweetness from the savoy cabbage and a subtle granulation from the bacon and the chestnuts. Another wonderfully conceived dish and pairing.

1996 Château Latour

Dark, brick-rimmed red; on the nose, Latour's hallmark 'gravel' very clear behind the ripe fruit; an elegant, concentrated midweight, still fresh in acidity, still finely tannic; this is a wine with a splendid core of sweet red fruit, markedly mineral in aromas (echoing the character of the nose), prolonged and imposing to taste, a wine of great poise, tenacity of flavour, complexity and length. Delicious in early maturity, but with a real bouquet, harmony and polish still to come. Next to, and following, the 1989 Haut-Brion and the 1990 Margaux, you notice the more vital, cooler vintage 'edge' of 1996 in contrast to the hot-season suppleness of those two earlier years. Drink now to 2040. (19+ points)

Fricasée d'homard et ris de veau aux cèpes with penny bun cream and red onion petals This combination was trickier, not quite the totally happy marriage of the first two pairings. The dish itself was a delight to look at, and quite delicious – the wine on its own, equally so. But the particularly sweet flavour profiles of the lobster and veal sweetbreads did slightly 'dry' the cooler vintage Latour tastes. An imaginative partnership, and it's great to try it, but an unlikely long-term relationship, I would think.

1986 Château Lafite Rothschild

A dark, immature red, by some way the most youthful in appearance of the first four wines; also the tightest and least open on the nose, with no fruit sweetness yet, just fresh, cool, mineral aromas; these impressions are mirrored on the palate, an elegant, medium-full wine with a lively acidity and a very fine-textured, but still very firmly dry, tannin. The core is red-fruit ripe, dense and complex, and there is considerable length on the finish (the acidity ensures that), but the unyielding frame of tannin and acid make this a likely tough prospect for many years to come. The 1996 Latour gives a great deal more pleasure at 10 years younger. I last tasted this in 2002, when I noted 'leave 10 years'. And 12 years on I see no reason to change that figure. A wine that impresses but doesn't, as yet, flatter to taste. Will the sinews yield before the fruit retreats? Try in another 10 years…or after 24 hours in a decanter? Drink 2024 to who-knows-when. (18.5 points?)

Jarret de veau glacé, with well-buttered potatoes and truffled Cornish sea salt The truffled sea salt was a lovely idea, and the glazed veal shank absorbed some of the wine's chewy tannin, but the fruit thus revealed still seemed obdurate. Guests voted with their glasses; the Lafite glasses remained with the most wine in them and got no 'favourite' votes.

1986 Château Mouton Rothschild

Like the 1986 Lafite, inky and youthful in appearance; a marked gravel and mineral impression on the nose, with a hint of blackcurrant sweetness as it sat in the glass; a rich, concentrated, sweet-fruited wine, but with a still forbiddingly grippy tannic structure at nearly 30 years of age; plenty of savour, but with the emphasis on the cooler mineral aspects of the terroir rather than flesh and ripe fruit; long and complex to taste and long to finish, too, but remaining overall austere at its heart. For its first two decades this was a hugely impressive wine, with the fruit-oriented character and finesse of the best Moutons, but tasted/drunk on a number of occasions over the past six years it has gone increasingly into its shell, and has also become increasingly variable. On this occasion it was very much a pair with the 1986 Lafite, revealing them both (and the vintage?) as rather difficult, noticeably lacking in drinking charm and appeal by comparison with the 1989, 1990 and 1996. Here, too, probably another decade required, or maybe a day in a decanter? Impressive rather than pleasurable. Drink from 2025 on? (18.5 points)

Cheeses: Vacherin Mont d'Or, St Nectaire, Comté The cheeses, the Comté in particular, naturally absorbed much of the tannin, but the fruit still tasted rather charmless, with little to seduce; there was also plenty of 1986 Mouton Rothschild left in many glasses.

1990 Château d'Yquem

Amber gold; honey and burned caramel to smell; a rich, intensely sweet, unctuously textured wine, long, luscious yet fresh, subtly spicy, silken, succulent and classy, and with great length. Lovely mature d'Yquem. A slightly 'burned' maturity, perhaps, but that is a character of many older Sauternes. Doubtless decades of ageing in prospect. (18.5 points)

Tarte au potiron épicée, with maple-pecan ice cream, orange caramel This was another superb food and wine combination, never that easy with sweet wines. The pumpkin tart was a supple, lightly ginger-spiced dessert, with a crisp-yet-melting pastry, the maple-pecan ice cream was soft and delicately textured, with a crunchy pecan-flavoured biscuit as a foil. The weight, sweetness and textures of both dessert and wine matched and flattered each other perfectly. A greatly satisfying pairing to finish the meal.

First published in Issue 44, of *The World of Fine Wine* (2014) and reprinted here with kind permission of the author, Michael Schuster, and editor, Neil Beckett.

Expert wine and food matcher Fiona Beckett asks how Bordeaux sits with the world of the modern-day lunch, and finds that – if the right bottle is chosen – it is adaptable enough to take on burgers, Berkswell cheese and even oysters from the Bassin d'Arcachon.

BORDEAUX FOR LUNCH

Fiona Beckett (2020)

A lunchtime claret. I can't think of another wine that is associated with a meal in quite the same way. It says something both about the wine, the meal and the diner, who is almost certainly of a certain age and lifestyle – a habitué of gentlemen's clubs, most probably.

It refers to a modest red Bordeaux rather than a classified growth, although ironically the ideal food for both may not be that different. I remember having a 1970 Château Latour at The Connaught Hotel with a magnificent game pie, but took equal pleasure from a meal at Rules where I drank a then three-year old 2010 claret with a venison cottage pie, served with an appropriately retro pie frill. Maybe the Brits like Bordeaux so much because it goes with gravy and pastry?

Does Bordeaux have any place in restaurants and with the type of food we eat now, though? The old-school dining establishments I've mentioned are hardly typical. Most restaurants today serve lighter, more plant-based food with which white Bordeaux, or even rosé might be said to pair better than red. Asian food is popular but the Chinese fondness for Bordeaux almost certainly doesn't translate into a desire to drink it with roast beef and Yorkshire pudding. They're more likely to pair it with Sichuan beef – the combination of tannin and spice being regarded as a bonus to ramp up the intensity of the taste experience rather than a problem.

The wines themselves have also changed, in becoming fleshier, higher in alcohol and more fruit forward. Merlot, a more forgiving grape variety than Cabernet – or young Cabernet at least – predominates on the Right Bank, and these days shows more prominently on the Left. Unlike Cabernet it can handle tomato, which makes it suitable for drinking with Italian food, though I still hold to the theory – tested out for a feature I once wrote for *Decanter* – that Bordeaux goes better with butter-based dishes than those cooked in olive oil. And because of that tomato tolerance – and even tomato ketchup-tolerance – modern, young Bordeaux is as good with a high-class burger as a steak.

But the natural register for the wines – as in so many other wine-producing areas – is the food of the region, which is basically that of southwest France and, contrary to it's high-flying image, is quite rustic. Or as Marc and Kim Millon so nicely put it in their 1982 book, *The Wine and Food of Europe*: 'Bordeaux does its job of satisfying the appetites of hungry men and women without unnecessary embellishment.'

Epitomized by the iconic La Tupina (on the riverbank in Bordeaux' vibrant Capucins district, specializing in authentically traditional Bordelais cooking), it's a robustly carnivorous cuisine of roast and grilled meats and game birds, fine lamb from Pauillac, the humbler cuts braised with beans, everything copiously spiked with wine-friendly garlic.

The southwest of course is the land of duck and duck fat – foie gras at the top end, humble salads of *gesiers* (gizzards) at the bottom. There are game birds in season, served bloodily rare; snails (more garlic) and *saucisson* (more fat). It's the perfect cuisine to tame tannic wines – not, as I say, that Bordeaux is so tannic these days.

Bordeaux is used to cook with too – well, why wouldn't you when it's so plentiful? The description 'Bordelaise' indicates a rich sauce made with shallots, bone marrow and red wine, or there is the *marchand du vin* (wine merchant's) sauce which includes demi-glace: both are fabulous with steak.

Fish, too, gets the red wine treatment. The famous *lamproie a la Bordelaise*, which is made from the ugly fish found in the Gironde, is traditionally cooked in claret, while zander is served at La Tupina with red-wine-friendly shallots, which join garlic and onions

Bordeaux' La Tupina restaurant specializes in authentic regional fare: here, *agneau et haricots Tarbais* (*left*) and its counter of local meats.

as the key ingredients in so many Bordelais dishes. And even oysters work with red wine if you serve them with crépinettes – the little sausage patties covered in caul fat that are traditionally served by the oyster beds of the Bassin d'Arcachon.

Less controversially, on the face of it, there is also – and always on a French table – cheese, but that can be a bit of a minefield, not least because in France, as elsewhere, the most prestigious wines are saved for the cheese course. I remember a dinner in the private dining room at Berry Bros & Rudd when an exemplary cheeseboard of beautifully kept British cheeses was served with a fragile 1945 Clos Fourtet Saint-Emilion and a 1990 Château Margaux to the detriment of both.

Sheep cheeses such as Ossau-Iraty and Berkswell, and harder British territorial cheeses such as Cheddar and Red Leicester, are more forgiving of a fine red than pokey (strong, sharply-flavoured) blues or the 'stinky' washed-rind cheeses that are popular on the eastern side of France, though the northern French cheese Mimolette goes particularly well with Bordeaux. As does Roquefort, of course, but with Sauternes rather than a highly rated red.

Ah, the sweet wines of Bordeaux: always the adventurous frontier of food and wine pairing. That other classic, Sauternes and foie gras, may be old school but it does work (along with duck or chicken parfait for those who feel uncomfortable eating foie gras). More daringly you can pair it with savoury dishes with a touch of sweetness such as lacquered pork, quail or duck or chilli-spiked Thai food.

Such pairings belong more in the world of Michelin-starred fine dining admittedly, as do the more cutting edge pairings for the underestimated Bordeaux rosé. The sommelier at Hélène Darroze once memorably paired lobster with morels and *vin jaune* for me, not with a sweet Bordeaux as I'd expected but with Château Le Puy's Rose-Marie rosé, but that's the exception rather than the rule. The problem remains that somms would rather serve something edgier.

Maybe the answer, going forward, is to think of Bordeaux as it always has been: a wine to drink at home – the case for this being stronger than ever given the prices it fetches in most restaurants these days. And the time to drink it? Well, how about for breakfast like a media mogul my husband once worked with who habitually drank Château Palmer with his bacon and eggs?

Beats a lunchtime claret hands down.

Perhaps it was a particularly British thing to worry about the correct temperature at which claret should be served, but, while others held firm views, the Victorians and Edwardians could not make up their minds on the subject…

THE CLIMATE FOR CLARET

Three Grandees of Bordeaux

The celebrated wine commentator George Saintsbury (1845–1933) had some alarming experiences, while Baron Elie de Rothschild of Château Lafite (1917–2007) took a more relaxed attitude. Christian Seely, proprietor of Left Bank châteaux Pichon-Baron, Pibran and Suduiraut and Right Bank Petit-Village is well placed to advise us for today.

GEORGE SAINTSBURY'S CONCERN

I have endeavoured to keep clear of the most commonplace of topics in these notes. Perhaps, however, something should be said on two such. I have lived through two or three different phases of attitude to the temperature at which claret should be drunk. There was the Ice Age – certainly a barbarous time. It is well that Browning's 'Bishop Blougram' was not an Anglican prelate, for his directions to my sometime colleague in journalism, Mr Gigadibs,

> *Try the cooler jug,*
> *Put back the other, but don't jog the ice,*

are very harrowing. Icing good claret at all is, as has been said, barbarous; but the idea of subjecting it to processes of alternate freezing, thawing and freezing again is simply Bolshevist. Some readers may remember 'marsupial' claret jugs with a pouch for ice. Then came the warming period, determined by not always well understood imitation of French ways. (It is in one of Sandeau's books, I think, that an uninvited guest complains of the claret jug being unwarmed and the champagne un-iced.) Unfortunately, people used to put it close to the fire and parboil it. Now, and for some time, the books have recommended nothing more than the bringing it up in time to let it get the temperature of the dining room, which is sound enough…' (1920)

BARON ELIE DE ROTHSCHILD'S SUGGESTION

There is a great deal of snobbish talk about the best way to treat and drink claret, but it is all great nonsense. The best way to treat and drink claret is to pull out the cork and lap it up. Claret is a pleasure, not a puzzling and dreadful duty. Do not put it in the refrigerator, do not shake it as it if were a cocktail – these are the only don'ts. Room temperature is best for red wines – a little cooler does not matter, a good deal warmer is a mistake. Should you be obliged to get a bottle out of a very cold cellar at the last minute you can take off the chill by swilling out a decanter with hot water and pouring the wine into it. (1985)

CHRISTIAN SEELY'S ADVICE FOR TODAY

I actually think there is little to be added to Baron Elie's advice. Pull the cork and drink, and do not worry too much. Obviously, the temperature matters, and makes a difference to how you will enjoy the wine, though hopefully not as to *whether* you will enjoy the wine. Old sayings about room temperature were almost certainly based on a time when they were lower than they usually are today, at least in France and the UK. On the other hand, in Asia, air-conditioned room temperatures today can be very cold, so the concept of room temperature ceases to make much sense.

I remember arriving for dinner at friends' houses in the England of my youth and seeing decanters of claret gently warming by the open fire. In the case of very grand friends, with big houses and no central heating, this could actually be quite a good idea, as the room was more or less freezing, but generally speaking it's not doing the wine any favours.

I was once served a decanted bottle of Colares in a big hotel in Cascais, Portugal, which actually had steam rising from it; it had been heated to the temperature of warm tea. When I protested, the sommelier told me this was how it should be done. He was wrong.

Generally speaking, it seems obvious that if the wine is cold, you can warm it in the glass in your hand, but if it is too warm there is nothing you can do. So if obliged to choose between imperfect temperatures I would go for too cold. In fact, cellar temperature seems to me to be perfectly OK as a starting point, provided you bring the wine up for decanting an hour or so before serving. The wine will warm a little in the decanter, and if it is still cool, then swill it with your hand around the glass until it is where you want it to be. I have never used a thermometer to test the temperature of a wine: it just seems common sense that you can feel when it is at more or less at the right temperature to drink. (2020)

Excerpts from George Saintsbury's *Notes on a Cellar Book*, Macmillan (1978; first edition 1920) and *The Story of Château Lafite* by Cyril Ray, Christie's Wine Publications (London) 1985.

There have been many tributes to Michael Broadbent (1927–2020) a man who fully justified the cliché 'a legend in his lifetime'. He was an essential presence at gatherings where fine wines, young or old, were to be assessed. Hugh Johnson was privileged to dine with him many times in the perfect circumstances for discussing wine: a small circle of like-minded friends who reserved their best bottles for these occasions.

THE BORDEAUX CLUB

Hugh Johnson (2020)

The members of the Bordeaux Club were there for the long haul, and so were their wines. The members, over a period of more than 60 years, were two history professors, a farmer, three wine merchants, a doctor, an author and an artist/pianist/auctioneer. No prizes for guessing the name of the latter.

The club was started by two very different claret lovers: the gentle Harry Waugh and Sir John (known as 'Jack' by all) Plumb, a celebrated history don and, by his own estimation, the rudest man in Cambridge. No one argued. There were six members at any one time. When they invited me to join in 1993 they were, besides Harry and Jack, John Jenkins, a farmer with an historic estate near Cambridge, Neil McKendrick, the other history professor and Master of Gonville and Caius College. And of course, Michael.

We took turns to host dinners. Three dinners a year meant that your turn came up every two years. Jack and Neil could entertain in their rather splendid college rooms, John's manor was the house where King Charles I was lodged on his way south to eventual execution, Michael had the boardroom at Christie's, I had our country house in Essex and its garden for summer dinners. When Harry died, aged 97, he was succeeded by Louis Hughes, a Harley Street practitioner whose speciality, infertility, produced some highly improper stories, which Michael could usually cap with worse ones of his own. Louis gave his dinners at the Savile Club in Mayfair. John Avery was to join us in due course, with the extraordinary resource of Avery's, his family firm's cellars in Bristol.

Almost as much thought went into the food at our dinners as into the choice of wine. The rule (occasionally broken) was that the wine was Bordeaux. Except, of course, for champagne. After a while I started to be called the Champagne Man, on the basis that I had bought a case of Perrier-Jouët 1911 at the Christie's auction of Peter Palumbo's cellar. Why he sold it I could never make out. On the first occasion that we drank it, on a summer evening in the shade of an apple tree at Saling Hall, we agreed, no one dissenting, that it was the best bottle of champagne we had ever drunk. Having set a standard like that I had some difficulty maintaining my reputation.

Michael fell naturally into his inevitable role: the member who kept the score – not in any Parker sense, but meticulously recording each wine we drank in a little red notebook, his wrist watch beside his plate to time the evolution of each wine from decanting until the last glass, which not infrequently revealed qualities we had missed, or failed to appreciate at first. (He was also club secretary, in the sense that he told us who would host next.)

I remember a tasting of Château Lafite given by another doctor, Martin Overton, in Fort Worth, Texas, in 1979. When the houseguests, Michael and I, came down to breakfast next day, Michael headed straight for the sideboard and the almost-empty decanters. There was enough of the 1814 left for us each to have a little breakfast glass. It had been subdued in the evening; overnight it had blossomed into a true beauty. Michael held the view (which I shared with him) that the longer you stay with a wine the better you understand it, and of course the longer it stays with you, the better.

When Michael set up the Christie's Wine office in Bury Street, St James's, it rapidly became a focal point for the then relatively few people interested in fine, and especially old, wines. He sometimes let friends borrow it to open exceptional bottles. When I returned from my first trip to Australia with a mixed case of wines that excited me, Michael let me invite a dozen friends and colleagues to taste them at Christie's. That may have been where London first met Grange Hermitage – as it was then called.

Anyone who tasted or drank with Michael will remember how meticulous, focussed and methodical he was. He applied the tasting protocol he set out in *Wine Tasting*, his first book, published in 1968, to every glass he lifted. Even in a pub or Indian restaurant he would instinctively tip his glass to look at the colour, give it one swirl and one sniff, usually make one remark (rarely as rude as most wines deserved), then settle down to enjoy, or at least drink, it. When we were both on the British Airways wine committee in the 1980s there were two words he used that always amused me: 'plausible' and 'specious'. One learned that plausible meant possible (in selecting from a range of samples); specious meant no.

There was always a hint of Sir Galahad Threepwood about Michael: debonair and roguish. Punctilious as he was, I always felt he welcomed a spot of trouble – especially in the company of our mutual friend, Len Evans. The two competed together hilariously in practical jokes and dirty stories. His three-quarters-serious feud with Serena Sutcliffe, Christie's vs Sotheby's, kept him amused for years. Sir Galahad was always threatening to write his memoirs; sadly Michael limited himself to tasting notes.

He never, to my memory, talked about wine in a general conversation unless a companion expressed interest, or an opinion. He was never, for one moment, a wine bore, but let it have its natural place, either as pleasure or business – and often as history. Yes, he did reminisce, about such extraordinary experiences that one was all ears. The discovery of magnums of Château Lafite that had been gathering dust for over a century in a Scottish castle. Perhaps that was the moment when he realized that wine, however fine, is nothing without interested drinkers – who evidently are rare in the Scottish Highlands. The earl didn't have the buddies to get through a double magnum, so it was never opened. And what is true of earls in the Highlands is true to some degree of every enthusiast who buys great wine, lays it down – then looks around for the occasion to drink it. Once Michael had made a market, the supplies, better than he had ever imagined, came flowing in.

There were, of course, auctions of wine already. The City firm of Restells sent out catalogues that were eagerly scanned by bargain-hunters. Although they had something of a of fire-sale look about them, I and many others happily bought mature bottles of fine wine; there was the odd disappointment, low fill or scruffy label, but it was worth a bet. Christie's soon swallowed the family firm; Michael was glad to gain Alan Taylor-Restell as an experienced gavel-hand.

It certainly helped that he and Daphne were such an attractive couple: handsome, disarming, funny and down to earth; ready to get their hands dirty, tell appropriate stories and make realistic appraisals. Daphne was beside him all the way, packing bottles and taking notes. Sadly I've never seen a photo of the two of them among the cobwebs. Few wives would be waiting at the wheel of the car to drive their husbands home after almost nightly dinners. Sometimes Michael would do the driving, taking off his black tie and wearing a chauffeur's cap, with Daphne sitting in the back.

We were once crossing St James's Street when I happened to ask Michael where he changed for dinner. 'Just up there,' he said, pointing to the building next to the Carlton Club. A friend told us of another flat there that was on the market. My wife and I bought the lease and it became our pied à terre for the next 30 years. At one point I had a glassware shop in the building below and hosted a Bordeaux Club dinner starting with champagne in the shop window, watching the street watching us, then repaired to the flat upstairs; it was the only meeting, as far as I know, when we had a female guest: Jancis Robinson MW.

The first meeting of the Bordeaux Club was held at 14 Duke Street, St James's on February 25th 1949. The menu was short: fish, woodcock, Brie and apricot flambé. The wines were Château Couhins 1945 ('very dry'), Gruaud-Larose-Faure 1920 ('a little bit corked'), Mouton Rothschild 1928 ('rather on the light side'), Rausan-Ségla 1929 (a lovely example of this beautiful vintage') and Yquem 1937 ('should last for a long time'), followed by Hennessy 1906. The club really got into its stride at the second meeting the next July at Jack Plumb's college, Christ's. Jack served foie gras, sole Bagration, tournedos Rossini, *foies de volailles au jambon*, cheese, then a fruit salad of peaches and nectarines. The seven wines included Lafite 1926 ('a very good wine indeed') and a magnum of Mouton Rothschild 1920 ('dry and rather uncharitable'). This is Jack Plumb criticizing his own wine.

Michael was invited to join in the early 1980s. The first mention of the club in his *Great Vintage Wine Book* is in 1988. Naturally he kept records of every wine at every club dinner; the routine was that each member wrote to thank the host, and Neil, one of nature's editors and compilers, stitched them together into comprehensive minutes, often read out at the next meeting. They read, years later, like any wine lover's wet dream.

It is worth recounting a characteristic dinner with Michael as host, in one of Christie's boardrooms in King Street, St James's. Whatever other meetings took place there, on these evenings 'board' had its old meaning, as in 'groaning'. Young ladies honed their recipes on us, certain of appreciative and discriminating comments.

On July 30th 2002, though, Michael varied the pattern by inviting us home, for a summer meeting in the two flats he had at the top of a block overlooking the Thames in Fulham. One flat was for work, one for play. Far below the river winds past the Barnes Wetlands Reserve to the west, lakes lively with ducks, banks of willows: almost a rural

Michael Broadbent filled over 150 little red notebooks with his meticulous tasting notes, which were then carefully transcribed to fill the pages of his *Great Vintage Wine Book*.

scene. He had invited the novelist Julian Barnes as his guest. Michael gave us champagne in the flat with the better view in the brilliance of the setting sun, then led us across to flat 87 for dinner.

This is a portrait of Michael, so it must include our surroundings. Two walls are bookcases. It is hard to stop reading the titles of such a catholic library; many leather bindings, one long shelf full of his famous little red tasting books, 150 or so of them covering his whole wine-trade life. The other walls are thronged with his collection of drawings, many of his own displaying his architect's training in fine lines, composition and precision. For many years he was chairman of the Wine Trade's own art club, which held annual exhibitions at Christie's. His own were always some of the most tempting. An equal amount of space is dedicated to the artist Michael most admired and eagerly collected: Charles Keane, one of the principal cartoonists and illustrators of the great Victorian days of *Punch*.

Example: An irate boss is berating a clerk who has been obliged to 'take the pledge' but has clearly failed to keep it. (Irish jokes were still admissible in the 1880s.) '*I'll not stand it, surr! Wid yer plidges! Instid o' takin' plidges ye're always breakin', ye'd better make no promises at-all-at-all – and kape 'em!!*' The point, though, is not the caption but the hilariously expressive pen and ink drawing. Michael adored them.

The dinner was a family affair; Daphne supervising and two grandchildren, very tall Alexander and very pretty Katherine Arbuthnot, butling. We ate foie gras, fillet of beef, creamy cheeses, and poached pears with cinnamon. Michael warned us that one or two of the wines would be 'high risk' – in other words, more instructive than ideal.

We started with two 1989 champagnes, Veuve Clicquot Grande Dame and Roederer Cristal. 1989 was not considered the greatest success in Champagne. (Indeed the only '89 Pol Roger ever drunk in England was shipped especially for my 60th birthday.) We noted that the Cristal had 'a steely centre and waves of lively flavour' while the Clicquot was 'all ready to enjoy'; code, perhaps, for 'going nowhere'. Château Suduiraut 1967 with the foie gras lived up to the high reputation of both château and vintage. Michael's trick at this dinner was to serve Suduiraut again, of a different vintage, at the end of the meal (when of course discussion began about whether he had got them in the right order). Another quibble was that the richness of the '67 – which Michael once described as 'celestial marmalade' – made life difficult for the clarets that followed.

They began with three 1985s: Grand-Puy-Lacoste, Mouton and Lafite. Michael once wrote that the vintage 'seems to encapsulate everything that is good about Bordeaux'. It is certainly my favourite vintage of this splendid decade'. Strangely, we were less than enthralled and ended with very different orders of preference – an unavoidable discussion with such a group of wines. I suggested they were all more or less put out of joint by the super-sweet Suduiraut. Michael called the Mouton 'chunky and uncharming', adding that it is 'an exciting wine that will…continue on its reckless way for another 10 years or more'. 'Reckless'; only Michael would choose that word. I believe in the end Lafite was the favourite. Julian Barnes wrote afterwards: 'The Grand-Puy-Lacoste admirably held its own in more exalted company. I expect the Mouton was better, but actually I got more pleasure from the GPL.' It depends, I suppose, on what pleasure you are looking for. I came down on the side of Lafite. Michael, for once, did not commit.

He can never have thought the next wine would be 'high risk'. Pontet-Canet 1953 is the best year of that château I have ever tasted. Julian called it 'best in show'. Simon Berry described it as 'a monument to the British bottlers' long-lost art' (it can be argued he had an axe to grind, being the scion of a family famous for their skill as bottlers of the best clarets). Perhaps it left the freshest memory of the whole evening. Then came the gambles: La Mission '31 and Château Margaux '27. 1927 was the year Michael was born. 'Rather like me,' he told us, 'despite being conceived at the time of the excellent 1926 harvest and born in a pleasant and balmy May it was downhill from then on, wet and windy weather led to an atrocious harvest. At least I survived.'

'Surviving' was the most you could say of the Margaux. Of the '31, the best Michael could say was that it was 'fractionally better than '30'. He had described the '30 as 'execrable'. It was, said Louis, a salutary exercise for people as privileged as we were to realize that all wines from great estates don't inevitably mature into awe-inspiring survivors.

Moreover, Michael was occasionally obliged to try and sell such things. (Unworthy thought: easier to give them to your friends, in the cause of instruction.)

Michael was the only person I know who would slip a sweet and fruity little Italian wine in as a sort of sorbet at this point in a dinner. It used to infuriate Jack Plumb. This time it was Briccho Quaglia La Spinetta, a Moscato d'Asti with abounding sugar and almost zero alcohol, at 4.5%. In its favour you could say that it cleared the palate from residual tastes of over-aged clarets. It also came at a moment when we expected a variant on the old cheese-versus-sweet debate. Michael set his face against serving Sauternes with sweet dishes of any sort. He drank it with the cheese. 1982 is not nearly as famous for white wines as for reds. Château Suduiraut picked early, before the rains that ended the glorious '82 harvest. The result was 'an intense but elegant wine with fine barley-sugar sweetness and very long'. We were divided about whether it might have been better with the foie gras, keeping the lushness of the '67 for the end.

It is never easy to remember the conversation at such a dinner. Simon Berry is best at making little notes. Louis Hughes told us about a pub-crawl with Dylan Thomas – an appropriately literary note for our guest. Julian, in turn, known for his interest in Anglo-French relations, told us about the Frenchman who gave up trying to learn English when he read the headline 'O Calcutta Pronounced Success'. We ended the meeting with a 1914 Hennessy. If I have painted a picture of a mellow evening I have not misled you.

A quicker sketch, perhaps, of Michael entertaining at Christie's. The keynote was always simple food, if you can so describe brill or turbot at its best, fillet of beef, cheeses perfectly *affinés* and well-chosen fruit. The room sparkled with silver and crystal, the walls covered with relevant paintings, many of them by a mutual friend, John Ward. On the night in question the champagne was Veuve Clicquot 1923. Michael opened a bottle of Clicquot non-vintage to provide for those who think champagne must have bubbles, which were scarce in the '23. We agreed, though, that it was a lovely example of vitality in tranquillity, with a touch of gingerbread and a long, long clean finish.

Starting dinner with foie gras and sweet Bordeaux was a habit of Michael's. There was no assumption, though, that it had to be Sauternes. This evening was the chance for its neighbours across the river in Sainte-Croix-du-Mont and Loupiac. Nobody in England, you can be sure, had tasted the Château des Tastes 1934, at least not for half a century or so. Michael once gave me a copy of *Les Vins de France* by Paul de Cassagnac, a 1927 round-up of the best. Sure enough, Château de Tastes was the one wine from the fringes of Sauternes country that de Cassagnac recommended. You learned from Michael that quality could be inherent (call it terroir if you like) and that an old witness could be as valid as a new one. The 65-year old was in near-perfect shape. If sweet wine of any sort ever comes back into fashion there will be a happy hunting ground on the banks of the Garonne. Curiosity like this defined Michael's love of wine. He was as proud of being the first to recognize the stature of Chateau Musar as he was in discovering ancient clarets.

That night there was also the Loupiac ('Where can I buy a case?' was one reaction) and then, with the fish, one of the club's most highly regarded wines: the rare white Graves of Laville Haut-Brion. We had drunk the '89 before with near-rapture – 'the best Laville ever'. This bottle seemed stuck in a coffin of oak. Mysterious.

Michael served four clarets with the beef, the oldest first. We often discussed whether to go up or down in age, coming increasingly to the view that the strong flavours and tannins of young wines can easily mask the more complex pleasures of mature ones. Our first in this case was Léoville-Las Cases 1949, a bottle that would have been an anti-climax if it had come last. Acetic acid was taking hold. Grand-Puy-Lacoste 1985 (Michael's favourite vintage) was all you would expect. One of us said it 'was still in short trousers'. It was rather passed over, though, in the excited discussion of Cheval Blanc 1985 and La Conseillante 1982. The '82s have their committed fans. John and Neil were blown away. For what it's worth I wrote to Michael: 'The Cheval Blanc completely seduced me. Time (in the glass) only showed how much time it has to go.' Michael rated them both as good examples of their châteaux and their vintages – cool appraisal if ever there was one. By the time we had argued about whether the creamy cheeses, however good, were the perfect match for a perfect Barsac, Château Climens 1985, we probably didn't pay enough attention to the 1914 Petite Champagne cognac. I admit I 'was quite worn out by the end with so many wines to worry about, while not wanting to miss a hint of St James's very best food'.

I have gone into great detail about two dinners, but this was the essence of the Bordeaux Club, and the essence of Michael's appreciation – and his skill. Fine wines must be given time. They must be discussed, compared, reminisced about. It is simply what they are for. It was Michael, with his precise mind, his focus, his enthusiasm and his memory, who sold this truth to the world. To the immense pleasure of his friends and followers.

'The Bordeaux Club' sip champagne one summer under the apple tree at Saling Hall: (*left to right*) Simon Berry, John Jenkins, Michael Broadbent, Neil McKendrick, Hugh Johnson and Louis Hughes.

THE 1855 CLASSIFICATION OF THE MEDOC

First Growths / Premières Crus

Ch Lafite Rothschild (Pauillac)
Ch Latour (Pauillac)
Ch Margaux (Margaux)
Ch Haut-Brion (Pessac-Léognan)
Ch Mouton Rothschild (elevated to first growth in 1973) (Pauillac)

Second Growths / Deuxièmes Crus

Ch Rauzan-Ségla (Margaux)
Ch Rauzan-Gassies (Margaux)
Ch Léoville Las Cases (St-Julien)
Ch Léoville Poyferré (St-Julien)
Ch Léoville Barton (St-Julien)
Ch Durfort-Vivens (Margaux)
Ch Gruaud-Larose (St-Julien)
Ch Lascombes (Margaux)
Ch Brane-Cantenac (Margaux)
Ch Pichon-Baron (Pauillac)
Ch Pichon-Longueville Comtesse de Lalande (Pichon-Lalande) (Pauillac)
Ch Ducru-Beaucaillou (St-Julien)
Ch Cos d'Estournel St-Estèphe
Ch Montrose (St-Estèphe)

Third Growths / Troisièmes Crus

Ch Kirwan (Cantenac, Margaux)
Ch d'Issan (Cantenac, Margaux)
Ch Lagrange (St-Julien)
Ch Langoa Barton (St-Julien)
Ch Giscours (Labarde, Margaux)
Ch Malescot St Exupéry (Margaux)
Ch Cantenac-Brown (Margaux)
Ch Boyd-Cantenac (Margaux)
Ch Palmer (Margaux)
Ch La Lagune (Haut-Médoc)
Ch Desmirail (Margaux)
Ch Calon Ségur (St-Estèphe)
Ch Ferrière (Margaux)
Ch Marquis-d'Alesme (Margaux)

Fourth Growths / Quatrièmes Crus

Ch St-Pierre (St-Julien)
Ch Talbot (St-Julien)
Ch Branaire-Ducru (St-Julien)
Ch Duhart-Milon Rothschild (Pauillac)
Ch Pouget (Margaux)
Ch La Tour Carnet (Haut-Médoc)
Ch Lafon-Rochet (St-Estèphe)
Ch Beychevelle (St-Julien)
Ch Prieuré-Lichine (Margaux)
Ch Marquis de Terme (Margaux)

Fifth Growths / Cinquièmes Crus

Ch Pontet-Canet (Pauillac)
Ch Batailley (Pauillac)
Ch Haut-Batailley (Pauillac)
Ch Grand-Puy-Lacoste (Pauillac)
Ch Grand-Puy-Ducasse (Pauillac)
Ch Lynch-Bages (Pauillac)
Ch Lynch-Moussas (Pauillac)
Ch Dauzac (Labarde, Margaux)
Ch Mouton-Baronne-Philippe (Ch d'Armailhac after 1989) (Pauillac)
Ch du Tertre (Margaux)
Ch Haut-Bages Libéral (Pauillac)
Ch Pédesclaux (Pauillac)
Ch Belgrave (Haut-Médoc)
Ch Camensac (Ch de Camensac) (Haut-Médoc)
Ch Cos Labory (St-Estèphe)
Ch Clerc Milon (Pauillac)
Ch Croizet-Bages (Pauillac)
Ch Cantemerle (Haut-Médoc)

THE 1855 CLASSIFICATION OF SAUTERNES AND BARSAC

Great First Growth / Grand Premier Cru

Château d'Yquem (Sauternes)

First Growths / Premières Crus

Ch La Tour Blanche (Sauternes)
Ch Lafaurie-Peyraguey (Sauternes)
Clos Haut-Peyraguey (Sauternes)
Ch de Rayne Vigneau (Sauternes)
Ch Suduiraut (Sauternes)
Ch Coutet (Barsac)
Ch Climens (Barsac)
Ch Guiraud (Sauternes)
Ch Rieussec (Sauternes)
Ch Rabaud-Promis (Sauternes)
Ch Sigalas Rabaud (Sauternes)

Second Growths / Deuxièmes Crus

Ch de Myrat (Barsac)
Ch Doisy-Daëne (Barsac)
Ch Doisy-Dubroca (Barsac)
Ch Doisy-Védrines (Barsac)
Ch d'Arche (Sauternes)
Ch Filhot (Sauternes)
Ch Broustet (Barsac)
Ch Nairac (Barsac)
Ch Caillou (Barsac)
Ch Suau (Barsac)
Ch de Malle (Sauternes)
Ch Romer du Hayot (Sauternes)
Ch Lamothe (Sauternes)

THE 1959 CLASSIFICATION OF GRAVES

The appellation Pessac-Léognan was added in 1987 to distinguish top reds and whites from basic Graves.

Classified Red Wines of Graves

Ch Haut-Brion (Pessac-Léognan)
Ch Haut-Bailly (Pessac-Léognan)
Ch Carbonnieux (Pessac-Léognan)
Domaine de Chevalier (Pessac-Léognan)
Ch de Fieuzal (Pessac-Léognan)
Ch Olivier (Pessac-Léognan)
Ch Malartic-Lagravière (Pessac-Léognan)
Ch Latour-Martillac
Ch Smith Haute Lafitte
Ch La Mission Haut-Brion
Ch Pape-Clément (Pessac-Léognan)
Ch La Tour Haut-Brion

Classified White Wines of Graves

Ch Haut-Brion (Pessac-Léognan)
Ch Bouscaut
Ch Carbonnieux (Pessac-Léognan)
Domaine de Chevalier (Pessac-Léognan)
Ch Olivier, (Pessac-Léognan)
Ch Malartic-Lagravière (Pessac-Léognan)
Ch La Tour-Martillac
Ch Laville Haut-Brion
Ch Couhins-Lurton
Ch Couhins

THE 2012 CLASSIFICATION OF SAINT-EMILION

Updated every 10 years.
* = 2012 promotions

Premières Grands Crus Classés (A)
Ch Ausone
Ch Cheval Blanc
Ch Angélus
Ch Pavie

Premières Grands Crus Classés (B)
Ch Beauséjour
Ch Beau-Séjour-Bécot
Ch Bélair-Monange
Ch Canon
Ch Canon la Gaffelière*
Ch Figeac
Clos Fourtet
Ch la Gaffelière
Ch Larcis Ducasse*
La Mondotte*
Ch Pavie Macquin
Ch Troplong Mondot
Ch Trottevieille
Ch Valandraud*

Grands Crus Classés
Ch l'Arrosée
Ch Balestard la Tonnelle
Ch Barde-Haut*
Ch Bellefont-Belcier
Ch Bellevue
Ch Berliquet
Ch Cadet-Bon
Ch Capdemourlin
Ch le Chatelet*
Ch Chauvin
Ch Clos de Sarpe*
Ch la Clotte
Ch la Commanderie*
Ch Corbin
Ch Côte de Baleau*
Ch la Couspaude
Ch Dassault
Ch Destieux
Ch la Dominique
Ch Faugères*
Ch Faurie de Souchard
Ch de Ferrand*
Ch Fleur Cardinale
Ch La Fleur Morange*
Ch Fombrauge
Ch Fonplégade
Ch Fonroque
Ch Franc Mayne
Ch Grand Corbin
Ch Grand Corbin-Despagne
Ch Grand Mayne
Ch les Grandes Murailles
Ch Grand-Pontet
Ch Guadet
Ch Haut-Sarpe
Clos des Jacobins
Couvent des Jacobins
Ch Jean Faure*
Ch Laniote
Ch Larmande
Ch Laroque
Ch Laroze
Clos la Madeleine*
Ch la Marzelle
Ch Monbousquet
Ch Moulin du Cadet
Clos de l'Oratoire
Ch Pavie Decesse
Ch Péby Faugères*
Ch Petit Faurie de Soutard
Ch de Pressac*
Ch le Prieuré
Ch Quinault l'Enclos*
Ch Ripeau
Ch Rochebelle*
Ch Saint Georges Cote Pavie
Clos Saint-Martin
Ch Sansonnet*
Ch la Serre
Ch Soutard
Ch Tertre Daugay (Quintus)
Ch la Tour Figeac
Ch Villemaurine
Ch Yon-Figeac

INDEX

Page numbers in *italic* refer to the illustrations.

67 Pall Mall, London 59

A

Académie des Vins 224, 225
alcohol levels 160–2, 226, 228
Alesme, Marquis d' 119
Allen, H Warner 77–8, 79
Alliance des Crus Bourgeois du Médoc 123
Allied 167
Alvarinho grape 162, 227
Angélus, Château 45
Angludet, Château 42, 44, 82, 224
Anson, Jane 14, 126–32, 146–53
Antique Wine Company (AWC) 262–7
Arnault, Bernard 119
Arnold, Steve 218
Asher, Gerald 83–90
Ausone, Château 45, 96–8, *97*, 115, 117, 128, *145*, 159, 162–3, 196
Avery, John 273, 279
AXA Millésimes 157

B

Bache-Gabrielsen, Vincent 44
Balan, Serge 186–7
Baly, Aline 171
Baly, Philippe 171
Bamford, Martin 71, 106, 107, 108, 163
Barbizet, Patricia 74
Barnes, Julian 276, 277, 278
Barre, Paul 117–18
barrels, oak 195–9, *197–8*
Barsac 164, 281
Barton, Anthony 53–4, 71, 198
Barton, Eva 53, 71
Barton, Ronald 101, 107, 255, 259
Barton family 128, 241
Bascaules, Philippe 42, 44
Basset, Gerard 262–4, *263*
Batailley, Château 58
bâtonnage 200
Baudouin, Raymond 108
Beaucastel, Château 210
Beaumont, Marquis de 150
de Beaumont family 66–8
Beckett, Fiona 14, 268–70
Belair, Château 97
Belgrave, Château 55, 57–8, 200
Belle-Vue, Château 44
Bellevue, Château de 131
Beni Carlos 181
Beresford, Field-Marshal 251
Bernard, Olivier 169
Berrouet, Jean-Claude 93–4
Berry, Charles Walter 78, 87, 88, 90
Berry, Simon 277, 278, *279*
Berry Bros & Rudd 154, 270
Bert, Pierre 184–90, *187*
Bettane, Michel 18
Beychevelle, Château 23, 57, 258
Beyerman 87
biodynamic viticulture 48, 51, 117–18
biofuel 160
Blakenham, Michael 73
Blatch, Bill 164–72
blends 181–2
Blind Ambition 221
blue clay 94, 159
BNP Paribas 27
Boissenot, Eric 262–3
Boissenot, Jacques 18, 206, 262–3
Bolaire, Château 43
Bömers, Heinz 126
Bordeaux (city) 192–4, *193*
Bordeaux Chamber of Commerce 253–4
Bordeaux Club 273–9, *279*
Borie, Jean-Eugène 71
Borie, Monique 71
Borie, Xavier 225
Bortoli, Patrice de 44
Bos, Thierry 43, 45
Botrytis cinerea 164–5, *165*
Botta, Mario 119
Boüard, Christian de 129
Boüard, Jacques de 126
Boüard, Josette de 129
Bouffard, Timothée 158
Bouillerot, Château de 43, 45
Boulud, Daniel 71
Bouteiller 22
Boyd family 241, 247
Branaire-Ducru, Château 44, 225
brands 124
brandy 249
Brane (Branne), Baron Hector de 150, 256
Brane-Cantenac, Château 79, 256
Brane-Mouton, Château 147–8, 255
Branne, Joseph de 147–8
Bristol, John Hervey, 1st Earl of 234–5
Broadbent, Michael 12, 14, 108, 109, 144–5, 163, *172*, 179, 273–9, *276*, *279*
Brook, Stephen 14, 122, 202–7
Browett, Stephen 14, 23–5
Bucher, Vaslin & Pellenc 159–60
Burgundy 106–10, 121–4, 202–5

C

Cabernet Franc 52, 80–1, 116, 120
Cabernet Sauvignon grape 23, 24–5, 42, 52, 80–1, 116, *116*, 119, 228, 256
Caillard, Andrew 14, 213–21
Campbell, Colonel 97
Campbell, Ian Maxwell 12, 14, 33–4, 76, 133–5
Canon, Château 73
canopy management 161–2, 169
Cantemerle, Château 107, 258
Cantenac, Jean 96, 97
carbon footprint 50–1
Carmenère grape 80, 162
Cassagnac, Paul de 278
Castaing, Louis 185, 186
Castets grape 227
Cazes, André 128, 130
Cazes, Jean-Michel 126, 130, 224, 227
Chadronnier, Mathieu 14, 48–52, *156*, 157, 158, 208–12
chaptalization 16, 19, 169
Chartronnais 178
Cheng, Kelly 217
Chesterfield, Lord 241–2
Cheval Blanc, Château 21, 99–101, *100*, 108–10, *109*, 117, 119, 133, *145*, 159, 161, *163*, 196, 214, 279
Chevalier, Château 216
China 30–2, 213–15, 218–21
Christie's 144, 274–6, 278
Churchill, Winston 133, 134–5, 135
Clarke, Oz 219
Classification (1855) 117, 123, 124, 216, 253–60, 257–8, 280–1
Classification (1959) 281
Classification (2012) 282–3
Clausel, Marie-Thérèse de 150
climate change 20, 49, 51–2, 119–20, 160, 172, 226–8
Climens, Château 169, 170, 172, 279
cliquage 200
Clos Fourtet, Château 128, 213
Clouet, Pierre-Olivier 196
Coates, Clive 54
Cocks, Charles 76–7, 79, 256
Coe, Robert 217, 220, 221
Comme, Jean-Michel 118

Coninck, Marjolaine Maurice de 119
connoisseurs 239
Conseil Interprofessionnel du Vin de Bordeaux (CIVB) 41
consultants 205–6
coopers 196–7, *197–8*
Coppola, Francis Ford 218
Cordier, Jean 184–5
Corney & Barrow 154
Cos d'Estournel, Château 59, 156, 196, 214
Cos Labory, Château 59
Coupez, Christophe 200, 201
Courregeolles-Toulon, Jean 150
courtiers 158, 254
Coutet 171
Cowdray, Lord 66
critics 206–7
Croizet-Bages, Château 56
Croser, Brian 223
Crowe, Russell 220
Cruse, Christian 87, 188
Cruse, Emmanuel 54, 188
Cruse, Lionel *187*, 188
Cruse et Fils Frères 166, 188–90
CVBG 154

D
Daladier, Edouard 131
Damécourt, Yves 131
Dauzac, Château 248, 252
Davies, John 163
Davin, Isabelle 44
Decanter 53, 74, 268
Delmas, Jean 87, 89
Delmas, Jean-Philippe 160
Denz, Silvio 117, 119, 169
Derenoncourt, Stéphane 200, 206
Desai, Bipin 97
Dhalluin, Philippe 160–1, 162
Dillon, Clarence 88
Dillon family 244
disease *see* mildew; oidium
drones 160
dry ice 224–5
Dubourdieu, Denis 162, 224
Duclos, Michel 36–40, *37*
Ducru-Beaucaillou, Château 71
Dupin, Raimond 'Papa' 225
Duroux, Thomas 217–18
Duval, Elisabeth 148

E
ecosystem preservation 49–50
Eleanor of Aquitaine 54, 230
élevage 195–201
En Primeur market 17, 23–4, 28–9, 121, 154, 156–7, 199, 213, 214, 219, 226
Engerer, Frédéric 74, 216
English market 181–2, 230–2, 233–9, 246
Enjalbert 96
Entre-Deux-Mers 45, 130
Errázuriz 210, *210*
Eschenauer, Louis 126
Exposition Universelle de Paris (1855) 253–4

F
Faith, Nicholas 75–9, 174–80, 184–90
Fargues, Château de 170
Farr Vintners 23–5, 154
Fattorini, Joe 14, 26–32, 53–60, *55–58* (in Marathon du Médoc)
Faugères, Château 117, 119
Ferrers, Benjamin 238
fertilizers 160, 180
Fête des Vendanges 205
Figeac, Château 71, 101, 118, 128, 131, 196
Figeac, Michel 149
Filhot, Château 165
films 213, 216–21
filtering 201
financial crisis (2008) 26, 29–30
fining 201
Flatt, Lloyd 108
'Les Foires des Vins' 21
Foix-Candale, Marguerite de 148
Foix-Candale family 147
Fonbel, Château de 45
Fonplegade, Château 119
Fonquernie, Léopold 167
food and wine 171–2, 262–7, 268–70, 275
Ford, Marcus 218
Foster, Sir Norman 78, 220
Fourcaud-Laussac, Monsieur 99
Franc Mayne, Château 126
Franck, Wilhelm 255
fraud 181–3, 184–90
freemasonry 245
French Revolution 146, 150, 151–3, 245, 246–8
Fresselirat, Florian 39
Fromkin, David 107–9
Fronsac 116
frost (1956) 91–3, *95*, 96, 101, 116
Fumel, Count de 149
Fumel, Joseph de 151–3

G
Gabriel, Jacques 192
Gaby, Château 38
Gardère, Jean-Paul 70, 72, 126, 129–30, 132
Gay, John 233–4
Germany, World War II 126–32, *127*, 136–42
Gibert, André 87–8
Gibson, Clive 66
Gilbey family 174, 176, 177–9
Ginestet 22
Les Girondins 146, *147*
Gladstone, William Ewart 134–5
Gloria, Château 70
Glories, Yves 18
Gotelee, Simon 121–4
Grahm, Randall 123
Grand-Puy-Ducasse, Château 56, 128
Grand-Puy-Lacoste, Château 58, 225, 277, 279
Le Grand Théâtre, Bordeaux 192, *193*
Grangerou, Marcel 180
grapes, and climate change 227–8
new varieties 162
see also individual varieties
Graves 116, 254, 281
Graves, John 57
Grenouilleau 185
Gros Verdot 80
Gruaud-Larose, Château 57
Guinaudeau, Baptiste 120
Guiraud, Château 167–8, 169

H
Hare, Alan 66–7, 68, 70, 72
harvesting machines 160
Haut-Bages-Liberal, Château 56
Haut-Bailly, Château 42, 45
Haut-Brion, Château 23, 66, 68, 83–90, *85*, *89*, *90*, 116, 122, 123, 128, 133, *145*, 146, 148, 149, 151–3, 159–60, 167, 235–6, 254–8, 264, 265
Haut-Marbuzet, Château 59
Healy, Maurice 87–8, 106
Hemingway, Ernest 217
Henderson, Alexander 255–6
Henry II, King of France 54
Henry III, King of England 232
Hermitage 181
Hogarth, William 238
Horne, Robert 135

hospitality 202–5
Howkins, Ben 171
Hughes, Louis 273, 277, 278, *279*
Huisman, Georges 131
Huynh family 227
hydrogen sulphide 222, 224–5

I
Institut National de l'Origine et de la Qualité (INAO) 80, 226–7, 228
Institut National de la Récherche Agronomique (INRA) 227
Institute of Oenology 18
international wines 208–12
Irish families 240–52
Irving, Washington 248–9
Issan, Château d' *46–7*, 54, 60, 196
ISVV 120

J
Japan 71–2, 166, 167
Jean Faure, Château 40
Jefferson, Thomas 75, 86, 116, 151–2, *151*, 165–6, 255
Jenkins, John 273, *279*
John, King of England 230, 232
Johnson, Hugh 66–74, 79, 90, 124, 192–4, 225, 273–9, *279*
Jolivet, Pascal 170
Joyce, James 53
Jullien, André 87
Justerini & Brooks 154

K
Kahneman, Daniel 29
Kan, Yue-Sai 219
Kapon, John 217
King, Chris *263*
Kirwan family 241, 245, 247
Kladstrup, Don 126
Kladstrup, Petie 126
Kohler, Eric 199
Kolasa, John 73
Krajewski, Martin 217, 220
Kramer, Matt 122

L
La Clémence 39
La Conseillante, Château 118, 279
La Fleur-Pétrus, Château 36–8, 45
La Haye, Château 59
La Mondotte, Château 196
La Rochelle 231
La Tâche 108–10, *109*
La Tour Blanche, Château 164, 169, 172
La Tupina, Bordeaux 269, *269*
Labat, Madame (Soussans) 132
Labegorce, Château 119
labels 154
Lafaurie-Peyraguey, Château 169, 170
Laffitte Carcasset, Château 59
Lafite/Lafite Rothschild, Château 23, *27*, 28–33, 48, 58–9, 62–5, 66, 70, 76, 81, 107–8, 112–14, 117, 128, 133, *145*, 147, 149–51, *152*, 163, *183*, 198–9, 201, 214, 216–17, 220, 235, 255–8, 262–4, 265, 266–7, 271, 274–5, 277
Lafleur, Château 117, 120
Lafleur-Pétrus, Château 218
Lagrange, Château 57
Landouar, Damien 38
Langoa-Barton, Château 54, 55, 71, 106–7, 196, 241, 259
Larose Trintaudon, Château 58
Larrieu, Amedée 87
Larrieu, Eugène 87
Lascombes, Château 79
Latapie, François-de-Paule 255
Latour, Château 34, 48, 66–74, *67*, *69*, 76, 81, *120*, *145*, 147, 149–50, 161, 178, 216, 218, 235, 256–8, 262–3, 264, 266, 268
Latour, Louis 124
Laubin, Carl 257
Laura, François 200
Laville Haut-Brion, Château 107
Lawson, Grant 217
Lawther, James 14, 41–5, 195–201
Lawton, Abraham 150
Lawton, Daniel 126, 167
Lawton, Edouard 132
Lawton, William 76
Lay & Wheeler 154
le Comte, Louis-Arnaud 146
Le Crock, Château 59
Le Pin 21, *21*
Le Sommer, Christian 72–3
Lee, Jeannie Cho 219
Leeuwen, Kees van 120, 161, *161*
Left Bank 115–20
Lencquaisang, May-Eliane de 126, 129
Léoville, Château 196
Léoville-Barton, Ch 53–4, 55, 60, 107, 157, 198, 199, 201, 241, 259
Léoville Las Cases, Château 20, 279
Léoville-Poyferré, Château 42, 44, 197, 198, 199
Les Tourelles de Longueville 122
Lestonnac family 146, 151
Lewin, Benjamin 117
Li, Demei 218, 219
Lichine, Alexis 81
Littlewood, Joan 136–42
Locke, John 83, 86
Loiseau, André 131
London 84–6
Loubat, Madame (Petrus) 93
Loudenne, Château 68, 71, 106, 107, 174, 176
Louis XIV, King of France 236
Louis XV, King of France 148–9, 152
Louis XVIII, King of France 252
Ludington, Charles 14, 233–9
Lur Saluces,
  Alexandre de 102, 166, 171
  Françoise-Joséphine de 165
Lur-Saluces, Marquis de 250–1
Lurton, Andre 157
Lurton, Gonzague 157–8
Lurton, Pierre 161, 217
Lynch, Jean-Baptiste 242–3, *243*, 245, 247–8, 249–52
Lynch-Bages, Château 23, 56, 128, 130, 169, 205, 224, 227, 242, *243*
Lynch family 241–8
Lynch-Moussas, Château 58, 242

M
Ma, Jack 220
MacCarthy family 244, 246
MacCarthy-Moula, Château 244
MacDonogh, Giles 240–52
Macron, Emmanuel *31*
McCoy, Elin 14, 115–20
McKendrick, Neil 273, 275–6, *279*
Mahler-Besse 154, 220
Malbec grape 80, 162
Malpel, Maurice 91–3
Malromé, Château 227
Manoncourt, Thierry 71, 128, 131
Margaux, Château 34, 42, 44, 66, 75–9, *77–9*, 86, 87, 119, 145, 151, 159, 160, 167, 180, *198*, 207, 216, 217, 220, 225–6, 234, 235, 255–8, 262–3, 265–6, 270, 277
Marquis de St-Estèphe, Château 59
Martin, Henri 70
Martin, Neal 14, 23–4, 91–5
Masseto 209–10
Mau, Jean-Christoph *156*, 157
Mau, Jean-François 154, 156, 158
Médoc 25, 116–17
  grapes 80–1
  Marathon du Médoc 53–60
  Petit Verdot 41–2, 44
  phylloxera 174–80

Meiburg, Debra 219
Mentzelopoulos, André 225, 226
Mentzelopoulos, Corinne 207, 216, 217, 226
Merlot grape 24–5, 42, 52, 80–1, 116, *116*, 119–20, 228, 268
Meyney, Château 55, 59
Migeon, Florian 123
mildew 48, 131, 166, 174, 175–6, 178, 179
Millardet, Pierre-Marie-Alexis 177
Mitchell family 244, 245, 246
Mitjavile, François 197–8, 200–1
Mitjavile, Louis 195, 197–8, 200–1
Mondavi family 209
Montrose, Château 51, 59, 68, 220
Morrison, Fiona 12, 16–22
Mouchy, Joan, Duchesse de 72, *72*
Moueix, Christian 45, 71, 93, 94, 117, 217–18
Moueix, Jean-Pierre 93–4, 95, 117
Mouton/Mouton Rothschild, Château *17*, 19–20, 58, 76, 80–2, *82*, 101, 111–12, 117, 128, 133, *145*, 147, 150, 160–1, *203*, 208, 255–6, *258*, 259–60, 262–4, 267, 277
Moutte Blanc, Château 43, 44
Murphy, Paul 220, 221
Le Musée 245–6, 248
Musée des Chartrons, Bordeaux 154
Myers, Chris 219
Myrat, Château 168

N
Napoleon, Prince 253–4
Napoleon I, Emperor 22, 124, 231, 232, 249–52
Napoleon III, Emperor 253
Nazi occupation 126–32, *127*, 136–42
négociants 154–8, 207
Nicaise, Cedric 122–3
Nixon, Richard 75
noble rot 164–5, *165*
Nogaret, Jean-Louis de 148
Nossiter, Jonathon 216
Nunes, Alain *198*

O
oak barrels 195–9, *197–8*
OenoCentres Pauillac 200, 201
oenologists 18–19
oidium 48
open market 211–12
optical sorting machine 159–60
Opus One 209, *209*
organic viticulture 48–9, 117–18
Orr, David 72, *72*, 73
Overton, Marvin 87, 88, 89, 90

P
Pallu, Comte de la 150
Palmer, Château 42, *43*, 44, 48, *51*, 79, 82, 119, 126, 132, 218, 270
Parker, Robert 17, *18*, 20–1, 24, 53, 94, 117, 118, 206, 214, 262
Parker, Thomas 24
Parkinson, Michael 219
Pasquet, Loïc 227
Pauquet, Gilles 18, *18*, 206
Pavie, Château 119, 157, 196, 205
Pearson family 66–8, 70
Peby-Faugères, Château 117
Pédesclaux, Château 44
Pelletier de Chambure, Elisabeth *139*
Penning-Rowsell, Edmund 12, 79, 81, 88, 99–101, 107, 175, 230–2, 254–5, 260
Peppercorn, David 96–8
Pepys, Samuel 12, 83
Pernet, Sabrina 42, 44
Perse, Gerard 119
Pessac-Léognan 45
Peters, Tom 124
Petit, Monsieur *72*
Petit Verdot grape 41–5, *41*, 80, 81, 116, 119, 162, 228
Petrus, Château 12, 21, *21*, 31, 91–5, *95*, 99, 115, 117, *145*, 159, *215*
Peynaud, Emile 18, *18*, 117, 159
Phélan-Ségur, Château 55, 59
phenols 18
Philippoteaux, Henri *147*
phylloxera 34, 161, 166, 174–80, *175*
Pibran, Château 58, 271
Picasso, Pablo 82
Pichard, Nicolas Pierre de 151
Pichon-Lalande, Château 57
Pichon-Baron, Château 57, *120*, 155–6, 157, 271
Pichon-Longueville Comtesse de Lalande, Château 57, *120*, 129
Pijassou, René 84, 175–6, 178, 179, 255
Pinault, François 73–4, 161
Pinos, Bertrand de 185, 188–90
Pitte, Jean-Robert 202
La Place de Bordeaux 154–8, 208–12
Place de la Bourse, Bordeaux *193*
Platter, Erica 221
Plumb, Sir John 273, 275, 278
Poh Tiong, Ch'ng 219
politeness, and claret 236–9, *238*
Pollock, David 66
Pomerol 24, 45, 115, 116, 117
Pompadour, Madame de 148
Pomys, Château 59
Pong, Paulo 219
Pontac, Arnaud de 83–7, 88, 90
Pontac, François-Auguste de 85, 146
Pontac, Jean de 83–4
Pontac, Therèse de 146
Pontac-Lynch, Château 242
Pontallier, Paul 159, 163, 216, 217, 220
Pontet-Canet, Château 48, 58, 117, 118, 119, 196, 220, 277
Portzamparc, Christian 119
Prats, Bruno 22, 156
prices 19–22, 29–31, 86, 156, 206, 254
pruning 36–40, *37*
Pulbrook, Lee 217, 218

Q
Quai des Chartrons, Bordeaux 178
Quinault l'Enclos, Château 196

R
racking 199–200
Rahoul, Château 222–5
Ramsay, Jamie 54–60
Rand, Margaret 14, 36–40, 154–8
Rausan-Ségla, Château 73
Rauzan-Gassies, Château 157
Ray, Cyril 14, 62–5, 80–2, 253–60
Reagan, Ronald 17
Red Obsession 216–21, *220*
Redding, Cyrus 12, 77, 181–2
Rhys, Matthew 55
Ribereau-Gayon, Jean 18, 159, 224
Ribéreau-Gayon, Pascal 18
Right Bank 115–20
Roach, David 216–17, 220
Robinson, Jancis 23–4, 26, 53, 219, 221, 275
Rochebelle, Château 40
Rolland, Château 185
Rolland, Dany 116
Rolland, Michel 18, *18*, 58, 117, 206, 218
Romanée-Conti *145*
rootstocks 161, 166, 174
Ross, Martin 14, 111–14, *113*
Ross, Warwick 216–17, 220, 221
Rothschild, Elie de 62, 64–5, 70, 128, 271, 272

Rothschild, Eric de 62–5, *63*, 72, *72*
Rothschild, Baron Philippe de 124, 128, 136–42, *139*, 259–60
Rothschild, Baroness Philippine de 72, *72*, 208–9
Rothschild family 76, 128
Roux, Michel Jr 262–3, *263*
Roy, Jean-Emmanuel 128
Rudd, Hugh 33, 133

S
Saint-Emilion 22, 24, 45, 115, 116, 117, 118, *118*, 131, 203, 282–3
Saintsbury, George 271
Salvi, John 159–63
Sartorius, Damian 54, 58–9
Sauternes 164–72, 270, 281
Sauvignon Blanc grape 228
Sauvignon Gris grape 228
Sayburn, Ronan 59
Schubert, Max 188, 218
Schuster, Michael 26, 262–7
Seagram Château & Estate Wine Company 17
Seely, Christian 156, 157, 271, 272
Seely, James 102–3
Ségur, Alexandre de 150
Ségur, Nicolas de 150, 151
Ségur, Nicolas-Alexandre de 147, 148–50, *148*
Ségur-Cabanac, Comte de 150
Sémillon grape 228
Séraphine, Château 220
Shand, Morton 78, 79
Shanken, Marvin 72
Sichel, Daisy 44
Sichel, Peter 53, 82, 107, 163, 224
Sichel family 128, 154
Simard, Château 45
Simon, Abdallah 17, 20
Simon, André 33, 88, 255
Smith Haut Lafitte, Château 51, 195–6, 198–201, 205
soil 49–50, 94, 159
Somerville, Edith 14, 111–14, *113*
Sours, Château de 220
Soutard, Château 128
Spurrier, Steven 106–10
Staples, Simon 219
Suckling, James 23
Suduiraut, Château 167, 171, 271, 277, 278
Sunderland, 3rd Earl of 235
sustainability 48–52
Sutcliffe, Serena 109
sweet wines, Sauternes 164–9

T
Talleyrand, Charles Maurice de 86
Tam, Simon 219
tannin 162
Tastes, Château des 278
technology 159–61
Teillet, Roger 130
Teitgen, Fabien 195–6, 198, 199–200, 201
Terry, James 243
Tertre Roteboeuf, Château 195, 198
Thatcher, Margaret 17
Theobon, Château 54
Thierry, N T 256
Thomann, Didier 198
Thunevin, Jean-Luc 118
toasting oak 196–7, *197*
La Tonnellerie des Domaines 198–9
Touriga Nacional grape 162, 227
Tourny, Louis-Urban Aubert, Marquis de 193–4, 246
Tronquoy Lalande, Château 59
Trottevieille, Château 128
Trump, Donald 31
Tsen, Peter 219
Tsutsumi, Seiji 72, *72*
Tversky, Amos 29
Tyrrell, Murray 225

U
Union des Grand Crus 20, 213–14, 222, 224
University of Bordeaux 159, 161, 224
Upjohn, Kenneth 33

V
Valandraud, Château 118
Vaucelles, Henri de 165
Vauthier family 45
Vautier, Alain 162–3
Vernet, Joseph 247
Verrier, Jean 131
Vialard, Gabriel 45
Videau, Jean-Dominique 44
Vieux-Château-Certan 131
Villaine, Aubert de 109
Vinding-Diers, Peter 222–8, *223*
vines *see* viticulture
Vinet, Elie 96
vintages 23–5
  1871 33–4
  1875 33
  1982 16–22
  2008 26–32
  Sauternes 166–8, 172
virus-free vines 162
viticulture
  climate change 20, 49, 51–2, 119–20, 160, 172, 226–8
  clones 226–7
  future of 159–63
  biodynamic viticulture 48, *51*, 117–18
  organic viticulture 48–9, 117–18
  pruning 36–40, *37*
  rootstocks 161, 166, 174
  sustainability 48–52
  technology 159–61
  virus-free vines 162

W
Walker, Alan 82
Walker, Fongyee 218, 219
Walpole, Sir Robert 75, 235–6, *235*
warming wine 272
Washington, George 86, 166
water consumption 50–1
Waugh, Harry 70, 73–4, 273
Wellington, Duke of 251
Wertheimer brothers 73
Whigs 233–7
Williams, Stephen 262
The Wine Advocate 23
wine merchants 154–8, 178
The Wine Spectator 23, 72
winemaking
  élevage 195–201
  sustainability 50–1
Witasse, Francesco 196
World War I 179
World War II 125–42

X
Xi Jinping 31, *31*, 219

Y
yeasts 222–4
Yquem, Château d' 71, 99, 102–3, *103–4*, *145*, 164–72, *170*, *172*, 217, 225, 267
Yvon Mau 154

PICTURE CREDITS

Front cover illustration Paul Wearing; p13 Cosmographics; p15 Paul Wearing; p17 Oli Scarf/Getty Images; p18 (*centre left*) Josep Lago/AFP via Getty Images; p21 Neal Martin; p27 Lucy Pope/AdVL; p31 Ludovic Marin/ AFP via Getty Images; p37 Tania Teschke; p41 Alamy; p51 Tobias Webb; p55,56,57,58 The Wine Show; p63 Jos Schmid; p67 Hervé Lenain/Alamy; p69 Cephas; p72 Hugh Johnson; p77 Cephas; p78 Cephas; p79 Caroline Blumberg/Bloomberg via Getty Images; p82 Reuters/Chip East - stock.adobe.com; p85 Mary Evans Library - stock. adobe.com; p89 Patrick Durand/Getty Images; p91 Cephas; p92 Cephas; p95 Guy Charneau/Gamma-Rapho via Getty Images; p100 Reuters/ Regis Duvignau - stock. adobe.com; p104 Eric Brissaud/Gamma-Rapho via Getty Images; p109 (*left*) Blick/RDB/ullstein bild via Getty Images, (*right*) Cephas; p120 Cephas; p127 Alamy; p135 Chronicle/Alamy; p139 Bettmann/Getty; p145 Philippe Petit/Paris Match via Getty Images; p152 robertharding/ Alamy; p161 Cephas; p163 Nicolas Tucat/AFP via Getty Images; p170 Cephas; p172 Cephas; p187 (*left and right*) Alamy; p193 API/Gamma-Rapho via Getty Images; p197 Jean-Pierre Muller/AFP via Getty Images; p198 Cephas; p203 Bertrand Rindoff Petroff/Getty Images; p210 Cephas; p215 C.Y.Yu/South China Morning Post via Getty Images; p243 (*left*) PWB Images/Alamy, (*right*) Cephas; p257 Carl Lubin; p263 (*left and right*) World of Fine Wine; p276 Simon McMurtrie/AdVL; p279 Hugh Johnson.

(*Endpapers and tombstones*) Proudly adorning the keystones of Bordeaux' arches, window-frames and doorways – occasionally delivering water from a fountain – are to be found somewhere in the region of 3,000 'mascarons', ornamental faces ranging from the divine to the grotesque. Some are fanciful, many recall the city's ancient Roman gods, Neptune and Bacchus, but almost all can be linked to an aspect of Bordeaux' history. Officially, they are a piece of baffoonery; unofficially, they are an essential presence to ward off evil spirits.